Leveraging Artificial Intelligence in Cloud, Edge, Fog and Mobile Computing

In an era defined by rapid technological advancements, the convergence of artificial intelligence (AI) with cloud, edge, fog, and mobile computing is transforming the landscape of computing and data processing. These emerging technologies are not only enhancing computational capabilities but also paving the way for innovative applications across diverse industries, from healthcare and finance to transportation and entertainment.

Leveraging Artificial Intelligence in Cloud, Edge, Fog and Mobile Computing explores the symbiotic relationship between AI and these computing paradigms. As AI continues to evolve, its integration with cloud, edge, fog, and mobile computing platforms is unlocking new potentials and driving efficiencies and enabling real-time, intelligent decision-making processes.

The book begins with an in-depth examination of the foundational principles of cloud, edge, fog, and mobile computing, followed by a detailed analysis of how AI technologies are being embedded within these frameworks. It then delves into the unique advantages and challenges of each paradigm, highlighting their roles in facilitating seamless, decentralized data processing and enhancing user experiences.

The book is structured to provide a comprehensive understanding of the current state and future directions of AI in these computing environments.

The book is intended to serve as a resource and inspiration for those seeking to explore the vast potential of AI in the realms of cloud, edge, fog, and mobile computing. Its goal is to spark new ideas, foster innovation, and contribute to the ongoing dialogue on the future of intelligent computing.

Dr. Shrikaant Kulkarni is a Research Professor at Sanjivani University, Kopargaon, India; Adjunct Professor, Victorian Institute of Technology, Australia, and Adjunct Professor at Lincoln University College, Malaysia.

Dr. P. William is the Dean of Research and Development and an assistant professor in the Department of Information Technology, Sanjivani College of Engineering, Savitribai Phule Pune University, India.

Dr. Vijaya Prakash is a professor in the Department of Computer Science and Engineering, SR University, Warangal, India.

Dr. Jaiprakash Narain Dwivedi is an associate professor in the IT Department, Parul Institute of Engineering and Technology, Faculty of Engineering and Technology, Parul University, India.

Advances in Computational Collective Intelligence
Series Editor

Applications of Machine Learning and Deep Learning on Biological Data
By Faheem Masoodi, Mohammad Quasim, Syed Bukhari, Sarvottam Dixit, Shadab Alam

Technologies for Sustainable Global Higher Education
By Maria José Sousa, Andreia de Bem Machado, Gertrudes Aparecida Dandolini

Artificial Intelligence Techniques in Power Systems Operations and Analysis
By Nagendra Singh, Sitendra Tamrakar, Arvind Mewada, Sanjeev Kumar Gupta

Deep Learning Applications in Operations Research
By Aryan Chaudhary, Biswadip Basu Mallik, Gunjan Mukherjee, Rahul Kar

Computational Intelligence in Industry 4.0 and 5.0 Applications: Trends, Challenges and Applications
By Joseph Bamidele Awotunde, Kamalakanta Muduli, Biswajit Brahma

Explainable Artificial Intelligence in Medical Imaging: Fundamentals and Applications
By Amjad Rehman Khan, Tanzila Saba

Parallel and High-Performance Computing in Artificial Intelligence
By Mukesh Raghuwanshi, Pradnya Borkar, Rutvij H. Jhaveri, Roshani Raut

Emotional Intelligence in the Digital Era: Concepts, Frameworks, and Applications
By Pushan Kumar Dutta, Sachin Gupta, Shafali Kashyap, Anita Gehlot, Rita Karmakar, Pronaya Bhattacharya

Deep Learning and Blockchain Technology for Smart and Sustainable Cities
By Subramaniyaswamy V, G Revathy, Logesh Ravi, N. Thillaiarasu, Naresh Kshetri

Computational Intelligence for Analysis of Trends in Industry 4.0 and 5.0
By Joseph Bamidele Awotunde, Kamalakanta Muduli, Biswajit Brahma

Metaverse and Blockchain Use Cases and Applications
By Dileep Kumar Murala, Sandeep Kumar Panda, Sujata Priyambada Dash

Leveraging Artificial Intelligence in Cloud, Edge, Fog and Mobile Computing
By Shrikaant Kulkarni, P. William, Vijaya Prakash, Jaiprakash Narain Dwivedi

https://www.routledge.com/Advances-in-Computational-Collective-Intelligence/book-series/ACCICRC

Leveraging Artificial Intelligence in Cloud, Edge, Fog and Mobile Computing

Edited by
Shrikaant Kulkarni
P. William
Vijaya Prakash
Jaiprakash Narain Dwivedi

CRC Press
Taylor & Francis Group
Boca Raton London New York

CRC Press is an imprint of the
Taylor & Francis Group, an **informa** business
AN AUERBACH BOOK

Designed cover image: Shutterstock

First edition published 2026
2385 NW Executive Center Drive, Suite 320, Boca Raton FL 33431

and by CRC Press
4 Park Square, Milton Park, Abingdon, Oxon, OX14 4RN

CRC Press is an imprint of Taylor & Francis Group, LLC

ISBN: 978-1-032-69952-3 (hbk)
ISBN: 978-1-032-70372-5 (pbk)
ISBN: 978-1-032-70371-8 (ebk)

DOI: 10.1201/9781032703718

Typeset in Times
by SPi Technologies India Pvt Ltd (Straive)

Contents

Part III Leveraging the Potential of AI In Edge Computing

Part IV Advancing AI in Mobile Computing

Part V Case Studies and Applications of AI in Computing

Contributors

Jyoti Agarwal
Department of Computer Science & Engineering
SRMSCET
Bareilly, India

Mohd Wazih Ahmad
Department of Computer Science & Engineering
SRMSCET
Bareilly, India

Bharati Sanjay Ainapure
Department of Computer Engineering
Vishwakarma University
Pune, India

Mowaffak Othman Ahmed Albaraq
National University
Taiz, Yemen

Motea Alsamawi
Department of Biomedical Engineering
University of Science and Technology
Sana'a, Yamen

Bhargav Appasani
School of Electronics Engineering
Kalinga Institute of Industrial Technology
Bhubaneswar, India

Anjali Arora
Shri Ram Murti Smarak College of Engineering and Technology
Bareilly, India

N S Bohra
Department of Management Studies
Graphic Era Deemed to be University
Dehradun, India

Vishwanath Bijalwan
School of Computer Science & Artificial Intelligence
SR University
Warangal, India

Nishant Chavhan
Department of Chemical Engineering,
Vishwakarma Institute of Technology
Pune, India

D Chitra
Master of Business Administration
Panimalar Engineering College
Chennai, India

Anshu Kumar Dwivedi
School of Computer Science & Artificial Intelligence
SR University
Warangal, India

Hemlata Gangwar
Shri Ram Murti Smarak College of Engineering and Technology
Bareilly, India

S Gnanamurthy
Computer Science and Engineering
Kuppam Engineering College
Andhra Pradesh, India

Zameer Gulzar
MIE-SPPU
Institute of Higher Education
Doha, Qatar

Vijay Bhanudas Gujar
Computer Science and Engineering
Arvind Gavali College of Engineering
Satara, India

M Indrasenareddy
BVRIT Hyderabad College of Engineering For Women
Telangana, India

Vaishali Bhanudas Ingle
Department of Electrical Engineering
Sanjivani College Engineering
Kopargaon, India

Fatima Amer Jid Almahri
Department of Information Technology
College of Computing and Information Sciences
University of Technology and Applied Sciences
Oman

Divya Joshi
Shri Ram Murti Smarak College of Engineering and Technology
Bareilly, India

Abhishek Shankar Ippar
Department of Electrical Engineering
Sanjivani College Engineering
Kopargaon, India

Roshni Kapoor
Department of Computer Science & Engineering
Shri Ram Murti Smarak College of Engineering and Technology
India

Pravin B. Khatkale
Sanjivani University
Kopargaon, India

Shrikaant Kulkarni
Research Professor
Sanjivani University
Kopargaon, India

Adjunct Professor
Victorian Institute of Technology
Australia

D. B. Pardeshi
Department of Electrical Engineering
Sanjivani College Engineering
Kopargaon, India

Mudarakola Lakshmi Prasad
Computer Science and Engineering
Institute of Aeronautical Engineering
Hyderabad, India

Rupesh Kumar Mishra
School of Computer Science & Artificial Intelligence
SR University
Warangal, India

Saptarshi Mukherjee
Maulana Abul Kalam Azad University of Technology
West Bengal, India

P Padmavathi
BSAR Crescent Institute of Science & Technology
Chennai, India

Vrinda Parkhi
Department of Electronics Engineering
Vishwakarma Institute of Technology, Pune, India

Ratnesh Ranjan
School of Computer Science & Artificial Intelligence
SR University
Warangal, India

Pundru Chandra Shaker Reddy
Computer Science and Artificial Intelligence
SR University
Warangal, India

Thirupathi Regula
Department of Information Technology
College of Computing and Information Sciences
University of Technology and Applied Sciences
Muscat, Oman

Dharmendra Kumar Roy
Hyderabad Institute of Technology and Management
Hyderabad, India

Muaadh Abdo Al Sabri
Department of Information Technology
Faculty of Science and Engineering
Aljazeera University
Ibb, Yemen

Ebrahim Mohammed Senan
Department of Artificial Intelligence
Al-Razi University
Sana'a, Yeman

Dnyaneshwar Tulshiram Sangale
Department of Electrical Engineering
Sanjivani College Engineering
Kopargaon, India

Payal Rohidas Solase
Department of Electrical Engineering
Sanjivani College Engineering
Kopargaon, India

K Sharmila
Department of CSE (Data Science)
Vaagdevi Engineering College
Warangal, India

Swati Shivkumar Shriyal
Department of Computer Engineering
Vishwakarma University
Pune, India

Yadala Sucharitha
Computer Science and Engineering
VNR Vignana Jyothi Institute of Engineering and Technology
Hyderabad, India

Shazia Tazeen
Department of CSE
Vaagdevi Engineering College
Warangal, India

Vishal Tidake
Department of MBA
Sanjivani College Engineering
Kopargaon, India

Gouthami Velakanti
Department of CSE
Kakatiya Institute of Technology and Sciences
Warangal, India

G Vijayakumar
Department of Electrical Engineering
Sanjivani College Engineering
Kopargaon, India

P. William
Department of Information Technology
Sanjivani College Engineering
Kopargaon, India
Faculty of Information Technology
Victorian Institute of Technology
Australia

Mannava Yesubabu
Computer Science and Engineering
Vardhaman College of Engineering
Hyderabad, India

N Yogeesh
Department of Mathematics
Government First Grade College
Tumkur, Karnataka, India

Preface

In an era defined by rapid technological advancements, the convergence of artificial intelligence (AI) with cloud, edge, fog, and mobile computing is transforming the landscape of computing and data processing. These emerging technologies are not only enhancing computational capabilities but also paving the way for innovative applications across diverse industries, from healthcare and finance to transportation and entertainment.

This book, *Leveraging Artificial Intelligence in Cloud, Edge, Fog and Mobile Computing*, explores the symbiotic relationship between AI and these computing paradigms. As AI continues to evolve, its integration with cloud, edge, fog, and mobile computing platforms is unlocking new potentials, driving efficiencies, and enabling real-time, intelligent decision-making processes.

Our journey begins with an in-depth examination of the foundational principles of cloud, edge, fog, and mobile computing, followed by a detailed analysis of how AI technologies are being embedded within these frameworks. We delve into the unique advantages and challenges of each paradigm, highlighting their roles in facilitating seamless, decentralized data processing and enhancing user experiences.

The book is structured to provide a comprehensive understanding of the current state and future directions of AI in these computing environments. We cover a wide range of topics, including:

AI in Cloud Computing: Exploring scalable AI solutions, the role of cloud platforms in AI development and deployment, and the benefits of centralized data storage and processing.

AI at the Edge: Examining the significance of edge computing for real-time AI applications, reducing latency, and enhancing data privacy and security.

AI in Fog Computing: Understanding the intermediary role of fog computing, bridging the gap between cloud and edge, and enabling distributed intelligence.

AI in Mobile Computing: Discussing the integration of AI in mobile devices, enhancing user experiences through personalized and context-aware applications, and the future of AI-driven mobile technologies.

Case Studies and Applications: Presenting real-world examples and use cases where AI, combined with cloud, edge, fog, and mobile computing, has led to groundbreaking innovations and practical solutions.

As we navigate through the complexities and opportunities presented by these converging technologies, we aim to equip researchers, practitioners, and enthusiasts with the knowledge and insights needed to harness the power of AI in these dynamic computing environments. By understanding the interplay between AI and cloud, edge, fog, and mobile computing, we can better appreciate the transformative impact these technologies will have on our world.

We hope this book serves as a valuable resource and inspiration for those seeking to explore the vast potential of AI in the realms of cloud, edge, fog, and mobile computing. May it spark new ideas, foster innovation, and contribute to the ongoing dialogue on the future of intelligent computing.

Abbreviations

AC	Air Condition
ACC	Accuracy
AD	Anomaly Detection
AE	Auto Encoder
AI	Artificial Intelligence
AIML	Artificial Intelligence Markup Language
ANN	Artificial Neural Network
API	Application Programming Interface
AV	Autonomous Vehicles
AWS	Amazon Web Services
CaaS	Container as a Service
CAV	Connected Autonomous Vehicles
CDN	Content Delivery Network
CI/CD	Continuous Integration/Continuous Deployment
CM	Condition Monitoring
CMS	Condition Monitoring System
CNN	Convolutional Neural Networks
CV	Cross-Validation
DL	Deep Learning
DNN	Deep Neural Networks
DRL	Deep Reinforcement Learning
DSR	Design Science Research
DT	Decision Tree
EC	Edge Computing
EC2	Elastic Compute Cloud (a virtual computing environment provided by AWS)
ECG	Electrocardiography
EEG	Electroencephalography
EER	Equal Error Rate
EI	Energy Internet
e-learning	Electronic Learning
EMS	Energy Management System
EOG	Electrooculography
FAQ	Frequently Asked Question
FPR	False Positive Rate
GAN	Generative Adversarial Networks
GDPR	General Data Protection Regulation (not exclusive to cloud computing, but relevant due to data privacy concerns)
GHI	Global Hunger Index
GMM	Gaussian Mixture Models
HAR	Human Activity Recognition
Heo	Horizontal Electrooculogram

HMI	Human–machine Interface
HOG	Histogram of Oriented Gradients
HVAC	Heating, Ventilation, and Air Conditioning
IaaS	Infrastructure as a Service
IIOT	Industrial Internet of Things
IoT	Internet of Things
IP	Image processing
IS	Information Systems
IT	Information Technology
KNN	K-Nearest Neighbor
LPWAN	Low Power Wide Area Networks
ML	Machine Learning
MRM	Machine Reaction Mode
MSE	Mean Squared Error
NCRB	National Crime Records Bureau
NLP	Natural Language Processing
NN	Neural Networks
P2P	Point-to-Point
PaaS	Platform as a Service
PCA	Principal Component Analysis
PR	Precision-Recall
PRISMA	Preferred Reporting Items for Systematic Reviews and Meta-Analysis
PSO	Particle Swarm Optimization
QoS	Quality of Service
RBFNN	Radial Basis Function Neural Network
RF	Random Forest
RNNs	Recurrent Neural Networks
ROC	Receiver Operating Characteristic
ROI	Return on Investment
RPI	Raspberry Pi
RUL	Remaining useful life
S3	Simple Storage Service (a storage service provided by AWS)
SaaS	Software as a Service
SDGs	Sustainable Development Goals
SEM	Slow Eye Movement
SFDI	Sensor Fault Detection and Isolation
SIFT	Scale-invariant Feature Transform
SLA	Service Level Agreement
SoC	System on Chip
SQL	Structured Query Language
SR	Systematic Review
SVM	Support Vector Machine
tflite	Tensor Flow-lite
TNR	True Negative Rate
TPR	True Positive Rate
t-SNE	t-distributed Stochastic Neighbor Embedding

UAVs	Unmanned Aerial Vehicles
VC	Visual Cryptography
VEO	Vertical Electrooculogram
VGA	Gross Value Added
VLE	Virtual Learning Environment
VM	Virtual Machine
VNN	Variation Neural Network
WM	Washing Machine

Editorial
An Overview

Shrikaant Kulkarni

0.1 ARTIFICIAL INTELLIGENCE AND CLOUD COMPUTING

0.1.1 Introduction

Artificial Intelligence (AI) and Cloud Computing represent two of the most transformative technologies in the digital era. When combined, they create a powerful synergy that enhances the capabilities of both fields. AI benefits from the vast computational resources and scalability of the cloud, while Cloud Computing leverages AI to provide more intelligent and adaptive services. This detailed account explores the intersection of AI and Cloud Computing, highlighting their integration, benefits, applications, and challenges.

0.1.2 The Intersection of AI and Cloud Computing

Cloud Computing provides on-demand access to computing resources over the internet, offering scalability, flexibility, and cost efficiency. AI involves the development of algorithms and models that enable machines to perform tasks that typically require human intelligence. Integrating AI with Cloud Computing involves deploying AI models and algorithms on cloud infrastructure, utilizing cloud resources for data storage, processing, and analysis.

Scalability: Cloud platforms like AWS, Google Cloud, and Microsoft Azure offer scalable resources that can accommodate the extensive computational demands of AI model training and deployment. This scalability is crucial for handling large datasets and complex algorithms.

Flexibility and Agility: Cloud services provide a flexible environment where AI models can be developed, tested, and deployed quickly. This agility allows businesses to innovate and adapt to changing market conditions.

Cost Efficiency: Cloud Computing operates on a pay-as-you-go model, enabling organizations to manage costs effectively by paying only for the resources they use. This is particularly advantageous for AI projects, which can require varying levels of computational power at different stages.

Collaborative Development: Cloud platforms facilitate collaboration among data scientists, engineers, and developers by providing a centralized platform for development, version control, and deployment. This collaborative environment accelerates the development and refinement of AI models.

0.1.3 Benefits of Integrating AI and Cloud Computing

Enhanced Data Processing: Cloud Computing provides the infrastructure to process large volumes of data, which is essential for training AI models. The cloud's distributed architecture allows for efficient data processing and analysis, leading to faster insights and decision-making.

Accessibility and Democratization of AI: Cloud-based AI services make advanced AI tools and frameworks accessible to a broader audience. Small- and medium-sized enterprises (SMEs) can leverage AI capabilities without investing heavily in on-premises infrastructure.

Advanced Analytics and Insights: AI algorithms deployed on cloud platforms can analyze vast datasets to uncover patterns, trends, and insights. This capability enables businesses to make data-driven decisions, optimize operations, and enhance customer experiences.

Automation and Efficiency: AI-powered cloud services can automate routine tasks, such as data entry, customer service, and predictive maintenance. Automation improves efficiency, reduces errors, and allows employees to focus on higher-value activities.

Global Reach and Scalability: Cloud platforms have a global presence, enabling AI applications to scale and serve users worldwide. This global reach is essential for businesses looking to expand their operations and customer base.

0.1.4 Applications of AI in Cloud Computing

Machine Learning as a Service (MLaaS): Cloud providers offer machine learning platforms that allow users to build, train, and deploy machine learning models without deep technical expertise. Examples include Amazon SageMaker, Google AI Platform, and Azure Machine Learning.

Natural Language Processing (NLP): Cloud-based NLP services enable applications such as sentiment analysis, language translation, and chatbots. These services leverage AI to understand and generate human language, improving communication and user interaction.

Computer Vision: AI-powered image and video analysis services on the cloud can be used for facial recognition, object detection, and image classification. These capabilities are applied in various fields, from security to healthcare and retail.

Predictive Analytics: AI algorithms on cloud platforms analyze historical data to predict future trends and behaviors. Predictive analytics is used in finance, marketing, supply chain management, and healthcare to optimize strategies and outcomes.

Intelligent Automation: AI enhances automation tools available on cloud platforms, enabling the automation of complex business processes. This includes robotic process automation (RPA), which can handle repetitive tasks with high accuracy and efficiency.

Personalization and Recommendation Systems: Cloud-based AI services power recommendation engines that provide personalized content and product recommendations. These systems are widely used in e-commerce, streaming services, and online advertising.

0.1.5 Challenges and Considerations

Data Security and Privacy: Storing and processing sensitive data on the cloud raises concerns about security and privacy. Ensuring compliance with regulations such as the General Data Protection Regulation (GDPR) and implementing robust security measures is critical.

Cost Management: While Cloud Computing is cost-effective, managing costs can be challenging due to the variable nature of resource usage. Organizations need to monitor and optimize their cloud expenditures carefully.

Integration Complexity: Integrating AI models with existing cloud infrastructure and applications can be complex. Organizations must ensure compatibility and seamless integration to maximize the benefits of AI and Cloud Computing.

Skill Requirements: Developing and deploying AI models on the cloud requires specialized skills in both AI and Cloud Computing. Organizations may face challenges in finding and retaining talent with the necessary expertise.

Ethical and Bias Concerns: AI models can inadvertently perpetuate biases present in training data, leading to unfair or unethical outcomes. Addressing these concerns requires careful model development and ongoing monitoring.

The integration of AI and Cloud Computing is driving a new wave of innovation and efficiency across industries. By leveraging the scalability, flexibility, and advanced capabilities of cloud platforms, organizations can harness the power of AI to gain insights, automate processes, and deliver personalized experiences. Despite the challenges, the synergy between AI and Cloud Computing presents vast opportunities for businesses to transform their operations and achieve competitive advantages in the digital age. As both technologies continue to evolve, their combined potential will further revolutionize how we interact with data and technology, shaping the future of digital transformation.

0.2 ARTIFICIAL INTELLIGENCE AND EDGE COMPUTING

0.2.1 Introduction

AI and Edge Computing are two groundbreaking technologies that, when combined, offer powerful solutions for real-time data processing, analysis, and decision-making. Edge Computing brings computational power closer to the data source, reducing latency and bandwidth usage, while AI enables machines to perform complex tasks that mimic human intelligence. This detailed account explores the integration of AI and Edge Computing, highlighting their synergy, benefits, applications, and challenges.

0.2.2 The Intersection of AI and Edge Computing

Edge Computing refers to processing data at or near the source of data generation rather than relying solely on centralized cloud infrastructure. AI involves creating algorithms and models that enable machines to perform tasks such as visual perception, speech recognition, and decision-making. Integrating AI with Edge Computing involves deploying AI models on edge devices, enabling real-time data processing and analysis at the source.

Reduced Latency: By processing data locally on edge devices, the delay between data generation and processing is minimized, which is crucial for applications requiring real-time responses, such as autonomous vehicles and industrial automation.

Bandwidth Optimization: Edge Computing reduces the need to transfer large volumes of data to the cloud for processing, conserving bandwidth and lowering costs. Only relevant data is sent to the cloud, optimizing network resources.

Enhanced Privacy and Security: Processing data locally at the edge minimizes the exposure of sensitive information, enhancing data privacy and security. This approach also helps in complying with data protection regulations.

Operational Efficiency: Edge Computing allows for continuous operation even when connectivity to the cloud is intermittent or unavailable. This ensures critical applications remain functional, improving overall system reliability.

0.2.3 Benefits of Integrating AI and Edge Computing

Real-Time Processing and Decision-Making: AI at the edge enables instant data processing and decision-making, essential for time-sensitive applications such as autonomous systems, healthcare monitoring, and financial trading.

Scalability and Flexibility: Edge Computing provides a scalable framework where AI models can be deployed across numerous edge devices. This decentralized approach allows for flexible deployment and scaling based on specific application needs.

Resource Optimization: AI algorithms can optimize resource utilization on edge devices, improving performance and efficiency. For example, AI can dynamically allocate computing resources based on current demands, ensuring optimal operation.

Localized Insights and Actions: AI at the edge can provide insights and actions based on local data, enabling context-aware processing and personalized experiences. This is particularly useful in scenarios like smart homes, retail, and localized marketing.

Reduced Dependency on Cloud: With AI capabilities on edge devices, the dependency on cloud infrastructure is reduced, resulting in lower operational costs and improved resilience against network failures.

0.2.4 Applications of AI in Edge Computing

Autonomous Vehicles: AI-powered edge devices in autonomous vehicles process data from sensors, cameras, and Light Detection and Ranging (LIDAR) in real time to make driving decisions. This ensures immediate response to road conditions, obstacles, and traffic signals.

Industrial IoT (IIoT): In industrial settings, AI at the edge can monitor equipment, predict maintenance needs, and detect anomalies in real time, improving operational efficiency and reducing downtime.

Healthcare and Remote Monitoring: Wearable devices and remote health monitoring systems leverage AI at the edge to analyze patient data in real time, providing immediate alerts for critical conditions and personalized health insights.

Smart Cities and Infrastructure: AI-enabled edge devices in smart cities manage traffic signals, monitor environmental conditions, and enhance public safety by processing data from various sensors and cameras in real time.

Retail and Customer Engagement: AI at the edge can analyze customer behavior in retail environments, enabling personalized marketing, optimizing store layouts, and improving inventory management.

Agriculture and Environmental Monitoring: AI-powered edge devices in agriculture can monitor soil conditions, weather patterns, and crop health, enabling precision farming and efficient resource utilization.

0.2.5 Challenges and Considerations

Hardware Limitations: Edge devices often have limited computational power and storage compared to cloud infrastructure. Ensuring AI models run efficiently on these devices requires optimization and may limit the complexity of models.

Data Security and Privacy: While Edge Computing enhances data privacy by keeping data local, securing edge devices against cyber threats is critical. Implementing robust security measures is essential to protect sensitive information.

Scalability and Management: Managing and updating AI models across numerous edge devices can be challenging. Organizations need robust management frameworks to ensure consistent performance and maintenance of edge AI deployments.

Interoperability: Ensuring seamless integration and interoperability between edge devices, cloud services, and existing IT infrastructure requires careful planning and standardization.

Cost of Deployment: Initial deployment of edge AI infrastructure can be costly, including the expense of edge devices, software, and integration. Organizations need to balance these costs against the long-term benefits of edge AI.

The integration of AI and Edge Computing is transforming various industries by enabling real-time data processing, enhanced decision-making, and improved operational efficiency. By bringing AI capabilities closer to the data source, Edge Computing reduces latency, optimizes bandwidth usage, and enhances data privacy and security. Despite the challenges, the synergy between AI and Edge Computing presents vast opportunities for innovation and efficiency across applications such as autonomous vehicles, industrial IoT, healthcare, smart cities, and more. As both technologies continue to evolve, their combined potential will further revolutionize how we interact with data and technology, shaping the future of intelligent systems and the Internet of Things (IoT).

0.3 ARTIFICIAL INTELLIGENCE AND FOG COMPUTING

0.3.1 Introduction

AI and Fog Computing represent a dynamic combination of technologies that enhance data processing, analysis, and decision-making at the network's edge and intermediary layers. While AI enables machines to perform complex tasks that typically require human intelligence, Fog Computing extends cloud capabilities to edge devices, providing a decentralized computing infrastructure. This detailed account explores the integration of AI and Fog Computing, highlighting their synergy, benefits, applications, and challenges.

0.3.2 The Intersection of AI and Fog Computing

Fog Computing extends the principles of Cloud Computing to the edge of the network, creating a layer that processes data closer to its source. It acts as an intermediary layer between edge devices and cloud data centers, facilitating distributed computing and data storage. AI involves developing algorithms and models that enable machines to learn, adapt, and perform tasks such as visual perception, speech recognition, and decision-making. Integrating AI with Fog Computing involves deploying AI models on fog nodes, allowing for efficient, real-time data processing and analysis.

Distributed Intelligence: Fog nodes can host AI models, distributing computational tasks across the network. This approach optimizes resource utilization and ensures efficient data processing close to the data source.

Reduced Latency: By processing data on fog nodes near the source, latency is significantly reduced. This is crucial for applications requiring real-time responses, such as autonomous systems and industrial automation.

Bandwidth Optimization: Fog Computing reduces the need to transfer large volumes of data to the cloud, conserving bandwidth and lowering costs. Only essential data is transmitted to the cloud, optimizing network resources.

Enhanced Security and Privacy: Processing data on local fog nodes minimizes the exposure of sensitive information to the cloud, enhancing data privacy and security. This approach helps in complying with data protection regulations.

Contextual Processing: Fog nodes can perform context-aware data processing, understanding local conditions and making decisions based on real-time data. This capability is essential for applications in smart cities, healthcare, and environmental monitoring.

0.3.3 Benefits of Integrating AI and Fog Computing

Real-Time Processing and Decision-Making: AI on fog nodes enables immediate data processing and decision-making, essential for time-sensitive applications such as autonomous vehicles, healthcare monitoring, and financial trading.

Scalability and Flexibility: Fog Computing provides a scalable framework where AI models can be deployed across numerous fog nodes. This decentralized approach allows for flexible deployment and scaling based on specific application needs.

Resource Optimization: AI algorithms can optimize resource utilization on fog nodes, improving performance and efficiency. For example, AI can dynamically allocate computing resources based on current demands, ensuring optimal operation.

Localized Insights and Actions: AI at the fog level can provide insights and actions based on local data, enabling context-aware processing and personalized experiences. This is particularly useful in scenarios like smart homes, retail, and localized marketing.

Enhanced Reliability and Resilience: Fog Computing ensures continuous operation even when connectivity to the cloud is intermittent or unavailable. This improves the reliability and resilience of critical applications.

0.3.4 Applications of AI in Fog Computing

Smart Cities: AI-enabled fog nodes in smart cities manage traffic signals, monitor environmental conditions, and enhance public safety by processing data from various sensors and cameras in real time. This facilitates efficient urban management and improved quality of life.

Healthcare and Remote Monitoring: AI-powered fog nodes in healthcare can analyze patient data in real time, providing immediate alerts for critical conditions and personalized health insights. This improves patient outcomes and reduces the burden on healthcare facilities.

Industrial IoT (IIoT): In industrial settings, AI on fog nodes can monitor equipment, predict maintenance needs, and detect anomalies in real time, improving operational efficiency and reducing downtime.

Agriculture and Environmental Monitoring: AI-powered fog nodes in agriculture can monitor soil conditions, weather patterns, and crop health, enabling precision farming and efficient resource utilization. This enhances crop yields and sustainability.

Retail and Customer Engagement: AI at the fog level can analyze customer behavior in retail environments, enabling personalized marketing, optimizing store layouts, and improving inventory management.

Autonomous Systems: AI on fog nodes supports autonomous systems such as drones, robots, and autonomous vehicles by providing real-time data processing and decision-making capabilities. This ensures immediate responses to dynamic environments.

0.3.5 Challenges and Considerations

Hardware Limitations: Fog nodes often have limited computational power and storage compared to cloud infrastructure. Ensuring AI models run efficiently on these nodes requires optimization and may limit the complexity of models.

Data Security and Privacy: While Fog Computing enhances data privacy by keeping data local, securing fog nodes against cyber threats is critical. Implementing robust security measures is essential to protect sensitive information.

Scalability and Management: Managing and updating AI models across numerous fog nodes can be challenging. Organizations need robust management frameworks to ensure consistent performance and maintenance of fog AI deployments.

Interoperability: Ensuring seamless integration and interoperability between fog nodes, edge devices, cloud services, and existing IT infrastructure requires careful planning and standardization.

Cost of Deployment: Initial deployment of fog AI infrastructure can be costly, including the expense of fog nodes, software, and integration. Organizations need to balance these costs against the long-term benefits of fog AI.

The integration of AI and Fog Computing is driving a new wave of innovation and efficiency across various industries. By bringing AI capabilities closer to the data source, Fog Computing reduces latency, optimizes bandwidth usage, and enhances data privacy and security. Despite the challenges, the synergy between AI and Fog Computing presents vast opportunities for innovation and efficiency across applications such as smart cities, healthcare, industrial IoT, agriculture, retail, and autonomous systems. As both technologies continue to evolve, their combined potential will further revolutionize how we interact with data and technology, shaping the future of intelligent systems and the Internet of Things (IoT).

0.4 ARTIFICIAL INTELLIGENCE AND MOBILE COMPUTING

0.4.1 Introduction

AI and Mobile Computing are at the forefront of technological innovation, transforming how we interact with devices and access information. AI enhances the capabilities of mobile devices by providing intelligent features and personalized experiences, while Mobile Computing brings the power of AI to our fingertips anytime, anywhere.

This detailed account explores the integration of AI and Mobile Computing, highlighting their synergy, benefits, applications, and challenges.

0.4.2 The Intersection of AI and Mobile Computing

Mobile Computing involves the use of portable computing devices such as smartphones, tablets, and wearables that enable users to access and process information on the go. AI involves developing algorithms and models that enable machines to learn, adapt, and perform tasks such as visual perception, speech recognition, and decision-making. Integrating AI with Mobile Computing involves deploying AI models on mobile devices, enabling real-time data processing, analysis, and intelligent decision-making.

Enhanced User Experience: AI enables mobile devices to provide more intuitive and responsive user interfaces. Features such as voice recognition, image processing, and natural language understanding enhance the overall user experience.

Personalization: AI algorithms analyze user behavior and preferences to offer personalized recommendations, content, and services. This personalization improves user satisfaction and engagement.

Real-Time Processing: AI on mobile devices allows for real-time data processing and decision-making, which is crucial for applications such as augmented reality, mobile gaming, and health monitoring.

Resource Efficiency: Advances in AI ensure efficient utilization of mobile device resources, optimizing battery life and improving performance. Techniques such as model compression and on-device inference reduce the computational burden on mobile devices.

Connectivity and Accessibility: Mobile devices with AI capabilities can operate independently of cloud connectivity for certain tasks, enhancing accessibility and reliability in areas with limited internet access.

0.4.3 Benefits of Integrating AI and Mobile Computing

Intelligent User Interfaces: AI powers features such as voice assistants (e.g., Siri, Google Assistant), facial recognition (e.g., Face ID), and gesture recognition, making interactions with mobile devices more natural and efficient.

Advanced Camera Capabilities: AI enhances mobile photography and videography by enabling features like scene recognition, image stabilization, and automatic enhancements. AI algorithms can optimize camera settings in real time for better photo quality.

Health and Fitness Tracking: AI-powered mobile health applications can monitor and analyze user health data in real time, providing personalized health insights, reminders, and early diagnoses based on detected patterns.

Augmented Reality (AR): AI enhances AR applications by enabling real-time object recognition, scene understanding, and interaction with virtual objects. This is used in gaming, retail, education, and more.

Predictive Text and Autocorrect: AI algorithms improve text input on mobile devices by predicting the next word and correcting typos, enhancing typing speed and accuracy.

Personalized Recommendations: AI analyzes user preferences and behavior to provide personalized content recommendations in areas such as entertainment, e-commerce, and news.

0.4.4 Applications of AI in Mobile Computing

Virtual Assistants: AI-powered virtual assistants like Siri, Google Assistant, and Alexa offer voice-activated control, perform tasks, answer questions, and provide information, enhancing user convenience and productivity.

Mobile Health Applications: AI in mobile health apps can track physical activity, monitor vital signs, and analyze health data to provide personalized health advice and early warnings of potential health issues.

Mobile Banking and Finance: AI enhances mobile banking apps with features such as fraud detection, personalized financial advice, and customer support chatbots, improving security and user experience.

E-commerce and Retail: AI in mobile commerce apps provides personalized product recommendations, visual search capabilities, and customer service through chatbots, driving sales and customer satisfaction.

Social Media and Content Platforms: AI algorithms curate content, recommend friends, and filter out harmful content on social media platforms, enhancing user engagement and safety.

Mobile Gaming: AI enhances mobile gaming experiences through intelligent NPC behavior, personalized game recommendations, and real-time analytics to adjust gameplay difficulty.

0.4.5 Challenges and Considerations

Privacy and Security: The use of AI on mobile devices raises concerns about data privacy and security. Ensuring that personal data is securely processed and stored is critical to maintaining user trust.

Resource Constraints: Mobile devices have limited computational power, memory, and battery life compared to desktops and servers. Efficient AI model deployment and optimization are necessary to ensure smooth performance.

Network Dependency: While on-device AI reduces reliance on cloud connectivity, many advanced AI applications still require internet access for data synchronization and additional processing.

User Acceptance and Trust: Users may be wary of AI features that collect and analyze personal data. Transparency about data usage and robust privacy controls are essential for gaining user acceptance and trust.

Model Update and Maintenance: Keeping AI models on mobile devices up to date can be challenging. Regular updates are needed to improve accuracy and add new features, which must be managed without disrupting user experience.

Interoperability: Ensuring that AI applications work seamlessly across different mobile operating systems and devices requires careful development and testing.

The integration of AI and Mobile Computing is revolutionizing how we interact with technology, offering intelligent, personalized, and real-time experiences. By leveraging AI, mobile devices can provide enhanced user interfaces, advanced camera capabilities, personalized health insights, and much more. Despite the challenges, the synergy between AI and Mobile Computing presents vast opportunities for innovation and efficiency across various applications, from virtual assistants and mobile health to e-commerce and gaming. As both technologies continue to evolve, their combined potential will further enhance our everyday lives, making mobile devices smarter, more responsive, and more integral to our daily routines.

Part I

Harnessing the Potential of AI in Cloud Computing

1 Working toward a Comprehensive Approach for Ensuring Security and Privacy in Artificial Intelligence

M Indrasenareddy, N S Bohra, Saptarshi Mukherjee, Yadala Sucharitha, Mannava Yesubabu and Mudarakola Lakshmi Prasad

1.1 INTRODUCTION

Concerns about privacy are among the most common ones when it comes to artificial intelligence (AI) technologies. The fact that there is no universal agreement on what "privacy" actually is in philosophical or legal works is evidence that this idea has proven to be somewhat nebulous. A "concept in disarray" and, more dramatically, like plunging into an "unknown swamp" are terms often used to characterize it in philosophical writings [1]. Indeed, there are philosophers who now hold the view that privacy is not a distinct idea. Consequently, many people's worries about privacy are unfounded and hard to pin down, which makes it tough to address these issues and clarify how AI technologies do or do not endanger people's interests. For anyone worried about the privacy risks posed by AI-related technologies, this essay will highlight some key differences that are often disregarded and explain what these differences mean [2]. The right to prohibit others from acquiring or using one's information without one's consent is a typical way that people think about privacy, but it's also about having control over one's own information [3]. While we will refrain from getting too bogged down in the debate, we will say that it is incorrect to automatically associate a loss of control with an absence of privacy—there are valid arguments against this "control" view of privacy. To grasp the error of this thinking, one must bring to light some frequently overlooked aspects of privacy, such as the crucial role that beings endowed with semantic knowledge play [4].

Directly delving into those debates is outside the scope of this essay. Instead, it will go back to the original question and try to answer why this kind of user control is valuable. It safeguards people's other interests, the conventional wisdom goes, because unauthorized parties could use personally identifiable information to

DOI: 10.1201/9781032703718-2

commit a wide range of crimes (such as denying a loan application or committing identity theft) against an individual. We call these kinds of interests that have a vested interest in protecting "private" information "security interests." On the other hand, we'd want to argue that the security interests aren't the only essential ones at play here; the interest in privacy is the more accurate description [5]. Similarly, we call this additional concern an interest in privacy in and of itself. We contend that this neglected but important concern has long been central to the concept of privacy and holds great significance due to its relationship with individual agency. Unfortunately, this second interest underlying privacy has been mostly overlooked in discussions of the AI-privacy relationship; this essay aims to rectify that oversight by investigating the AI-privacy interaction in this light [6]. Data security in the AI setting is, hence, of paramount importance. Due to the serious consequences that may result from their disclosure or abuse, it is critical to appreciate the significance of taking precautions to safeguard these details [7]. The significance of protecting AI data will be discussed in this part, along with rules and practices that ensure its security. Approaches that maintain data integrity will also be illustrated.

Another crucial component that needs to be considered while building a workable framework is AI security. Attacks, such as those that take advantage of flaws in algorithms or alter input data, are a real possibility for AI systems. The handling of outcomes or the compromise of users' privacy and security are two major outcomes that might result from these attacks [8]. The right to privacy has evolved into an essential guarantee in the era of AI. There are serious concerns about invasions of privacy associated with collecting and processing massive volumes of personal data. Thus, it is of the utmost importance to tackle the privacy concerns related to AI and implement measures to safeguard individual data. The ethical and regulatory framework pertaining to AI must be considered alongside data protection, security, and privacy. Responsible and ethical usage of AI, particularly with regard to privacy and security, can be achieved through the establishment of regulatory and ethical frameworks [9]. An all-encompassing framework to guarantee privacy and security in AI is the goal of this research. This goal is accomplished by conducting an extensive literature research on the topic of AI security and privacy in order to assess its development. Furthermore, a workable strategy is suggested, which addresses important areas including AI data protection, AI system security, personal privacy, and applicable ethical and regulatory frameworks [10]. The outcomes in important domains can be quantitatively measured through the execution of a case study that assesses the efficiency attained. Along with that, there are measures like balanced accurateness, data protection, and retention valuation, as well as facial recognition recall and accuracy.

In order to compare and emphasize the quantitative and qualitative métiers and aids of the proposed model, concrete findings are presented through the examination of data and analysis. We conclude by comparing and discussing the results obtained with previous relevant efforts of the proposed framework. In conclusion, the significance of creating and implementing strong AI models is emphasized, as are the other viewpoints and obstacles that necessitate consideration in this dynamic field. This study reviewed surveys and compiled key findings from relevant research on AI privacy and security, including recent advances, practical uses, future possibilities, and challenges. Here are the six main areas where our study made a significant impact:

(i) The underlying concepts of numerous AI applications were briefly reviewed and summarized in this paper.
(ii) We did a thorough review of older polls that were pertinent. In this work, we address shortcomings in previous surveys about the creation of seemingly safe AI applications, which is how our research adds to the field.
(iii) Machine learning (ML) tasks, including federated learning and deep learning (DL), can be classified using the theoretical framework we provided.
(iv) We introduced a new way to attack AI systems; it shows and assesses complex attacks on different types of applications.
(v) To protect AI systems from hostile attacks, we laid out a new paradigm for privacy and security in the face of AI system assaults, which provides examples of cyber defensive tactics.

In order to accomplish the goals that have been set out, this chapter is structured as follows: Section 1.2 details the materials and method, Section 1.3 describes data protection and privacy of AI, Section 1.4 discusses the model development of which assurances the security and privacy in AI, Section 1.5 presents results and discussions, and Section 1.6 shows the conclusions.

1.2 RELATED WORKS

When crafting this method, we kept in mind a number of important ideas related to AI privacy and security. The first step is to set up a framework that will serve as a guide for protecting AI systems from harm and for keeping sensitive information private. To keep AI systems safe from intrusion and other forms of malicious manipulation, it is necessary to set up controls, audits, and security measures. Contrarily, privacy in AI is concerned with protecting individual data, which includes ensuring appropriate consent and avoiding disclosures that are not authorized [11]. Furthermore, preexisting ethical and legal frameworks are taken into account, which set standards for the prudent application of AI and the safeguarding of personal data. A holistic strategy for guaranteeing privacy, security, and ethical compliance in AI implementation is developed by integrating these ideas. The literature that was considered for this investigation was chosen using content analysis. In order to draw reasonable and objective conclusions from collected data, content analysis is commonly used [12]. The goal is to find the most important parts of earlier research that have already been looked at. It also makes it possible to make qualitative adjustments in addition to quantitative ones. Since content analysis paints a comprehensive picture of AI's uses in privacy and security, we may accept the study's findings [13]. Finding and choosing publications that had already been peer-reviewed was how samples were obtained for this inquiry. The collected articles were sourced from reputable scholarly journals. What follows is an overview of the steps taken to locate appropriate literature for this study: keywords including "artificial intelligence," "artificial intelligence in security and privacy," and "computational intelligence" were utilized throughout the database searches. Since this is the case, we were able to track down academic articles on how AI may help keep private information safe [14]. These papers were chosen because of their relevance to the topic of using natural language processing (NLP), DL, and

ML to protect personal information. A two-step, iterative process that considered the aforementioned criteria at each stage was used to choose the articles. In particular, we checked the titles, abstracts, and keywords of the articles to make sure they met the criteria in the first round. Second, we read and researched each article to make sure they were all relevant to the review's aim [15].

A number of prominent AI security and privacy stances have been examined and compared after reviewing relevant literature. The goal of this exercise has been to catalog all of their shared and unique traits. This sheds light on the ways in which various settings tackle security and privacy issues, while also adding to the body of knowledge in the field. In order to safeguard sensitive information, the work [16] emphasizes privacy-preserving techniques and the significance of privacy in ML. Membership inference attacks are also addressed in [17], which is pertinent to our situation because they have the potential to jeopardize data privacy. One important part of our method is the differential privacy that is described in [18]. Our methodology is in line with the recommendations made in [19]. Design, control, and maintenance are the three separate phases of an AI life cycle that are associated with activities such as optimization, categorization, regression, and investigating data structures. This article discusses four distinct forms of AI and their potential real-world applications: expert systems, fuzzy logic, metaheuristics, and ML. By going over 500 articles, we were able to identify trends, obstacles to practical application, and areas for further study in the area of AI for power electronics [20]. The Excel spreadsheet that goes along with this post contains a bibliography of publications that are suitable for statistical analysis.

AI is useful in many different contexts. This section discusses the potential benefits of AI in engineering settings and provides an overview of some of the many industries that have already begun to apply AI methods. Research into the unique traits and capabilities of intelligent robots is just one area of engineering that is making use of AI approaches [21]. It includes articles penned by professionals and scholars in the fields of business and academia. Building empirical, data-driven models of system dynamics is central to the field of study known as system identification and function approximation [22]. It would be highly beneficial for transportation systems to have an AI-based decision-assistance system. One possible use of clustering is the classification of drivers into distinct groups according to their actions on the road. The utility and efficacy of computer-aided design might be greatly enhanced with the use of this technology.

Increased travel demand, carbon emissions, safety concerns, and environmental damage are some of the problems that the transportation sector is using AI to solve. In this age of abundant data (qualitative and quantitative) and AI, it is more realistic to consider ways to address these challenges. The transportation industry is making use of a wide variety of AI methods, including but not limited to genetic algorithms, simulated annealing, artificial immune systems, ant colony optimizers, bee colony optimizers, and fuzzy logic models. The success of any transportation system depends on people's ability to comprehend the interdependencies between data and AI and the many components and characteristics of that system [23]. The transportation authorities are expected to swiftly reduce congestion, make customers' travel times more predictable, and enhance the economics and efficacy of their vital assets by utilizing these technologies. AI can handle both structured and unstructured medical records. While DL and NLP are popular AI tools for unstructured data, neural networks, and support vector machines are typical AI approaches for structured data. AI methods are currently being used in the fields of cardiology, neurology, and cancer [24].

A variety of methods and solutions used in AI security and privacy are highlighted in the review of related publications. When it comes to building and implementing AI systems, these papers lay a good groundwork for comprehending the difficulties and solutions to guarantee privacy and security [25]. It is feasible to determine the merits and shortcomings of each of the evaluated publications by conducting a comparison analysis [26]. Some shared characteristics include offering fresh perspectives, zeroing in on particular privacy and security concerns, and delivering credible experimental findings. Nevertheless, there are constraints, including context-specific applicability, solution-level scalability and performance, and scenario-or threat-specific absence of consideration [27]. What often gets handled during implementation are the parts of research that are supplied in a specific setting. Thus, a thorough and methodical strategy is required to maximize the numerous possible advantages of AI when it is applied to the public sector [28]. There are still many obstacles for the public sector to overcome in the field of AI, despite the fact that many companies and government organizations across the globe have begun working on AI implementation and applications.

We may expect most AI solutions "will likely stay poor and highly specialized" for the foreseeable future. There are a number of perceived implementation of complexity-related hurdles that prevent the public sector from investing in AI research and development [29]. The four main issues that have been identified as limiting the use of AI technology are AI security, connectivity and quality of systems and data, financial viability, and expertise and specialty. Research has shown that AI safety—defined as the process of guaranteeing that AI systems and their outcomes are secure—is a major concern with AI [30]. Included in this category are both specific to information security and more generalized security concerns. Difficult and perhaps dangerous situations can arise when AI learns bad habits from its surroundings or gets its environment's context wrong [31]. This viewpoint highlights the importance of AI systems that can withstand manipulation by humans. Google has discovered numerous real-world security issues, making it a frontrunner in AI research. The safety of the AI system's learning process is of the utmost importance when using reinforcement learning for AI applications [32]. While carrying out its intended functions, the entity must also avoid unintended consequences, such as disturbing the work environment. As an example, a surgical assistant robot needs to be able to experiment with different cuts and techniques without hurting the patient. Therefore, preventing mishaps and guaranteeing the safe operation of AI applications are closely related to AI implementation and progress in order to protect humanity [33].

Since AI systems can only learn as smart as the data they are fed, and data is considered "[t]he fundamental driver of current AI systems," data quality and integration are of the utmost importance. Particularly problematic for businesses is data that is either of low quality or untrustworthy. In order to successfully deploy AI in the public sector, it is necessary to collect, aggregate, store, and use data that is both unbiased and relevant. Failures can occur due to inaccurate or faulty data [34]. Consequently, a major barrier to implementing AI solutions is the need to create an all-encompassing, high-quality AI system that can manage the interconnections among data, approaches, and processes and integrate data [35]. Security and privacy in AI have come a long way, but there are still many unanswered questions and neglected areas that need more investigation. For instance, it is critical to handle the sensitive nature of the training data and methods for protecting sensitive information during use as the use of pre-trained models grows in popularity.

By taking a more comprehensive view of these methods and answers, our work stands out. We integrate several solutions into a cohesive framework while considering individual privacy and security considerations. The aforementioned literature review summarizes the most important methods and findings in AI privacy and security, drawing attention to the variety of technologies utilized and the outcomes of each study. These results lay the groundwork for further study and technical developments in the field of AI security and privacy.

1.3 DATA PROTECTION AND SECURITY IN AI

Data privacy and security are of the utmost importance when it comes to training AI models. Because they may include personal information, it is critical to keep these records secure. For AI models to be accurate, fair, and dependable, training data must be of high quality and be representative of the population at large. Consequently, establishing confidence in AI systems relies heavily on data protection. Appropriate policies and procedures must be put in place to protect sensitive data utilized in AI. This entails putting safeguards in place to avoid illegal access. Additionally, data anonymization or pseudonymization methods must be in place to safeguard individuals' privacy [36]. These procedures involve removing or masking identities or personally identifiable information. Furthermore, data confidentiality during transmission and storage can be achieved by utilizing encryption techniques. There are a number of ways to make sure that AI data is secure. Methods for validating and cleaning data to remove biases and inaccuracies are one [37].

Because of the potential dangers and weaknesses of AI systems, their security has recently become an important issue. Many security holes and threats could potentially compromise these systems. Attacks on these vulnerabilities might originate from a variety of sources, including insufficiently robust AI algorithms, tampered training data, flawed system architecture, or exploitable implementation flaws. Adversarial attacks, model manipulation, biases, breaches of sensitive information, and unjust and harmful decision-making are all examples of how these risks might develop [38]. Protecting AI systems from various forms of attacks and malevolent manipulations is a challenging task.

Because there are several obstacles associated with using massive volumes of personal data, privacy is of the utmost importance in AI. For instance, in order to train models and draw conclusions, AI makes use of massive amounts of personal data. Some examples of such sensitive data are medical records, personal preferences, and geographic locations. Therefore, it is important to handle personal data securely and ethically by addressing privacy challenges [39]. The management of personal data in AI necessitates the implementation of measures to safeguard the privacy of individuals. This includes doing things like reducing data collection and using data for only pre-agreed reasons, as well as getting people's informed consent before collecting and using their data.

1.4 A FRAMEWORK TO GUARANTEE THE SECURITY AND PRIVACY OF AI

As AI takes center stage in our daily lives, it is imperative that we establish safeguards to protect our personal information and the integrity of our AI systems. Strong and realistic safeguards have to be put in place because implementing AI systems could compromise data security, privacy, and safety. So, to tackle these issues in a methodical way while still protecting data and AI models and adhering to legal and ethical standards, it is necessary to establish a suitable framework [40].

The important steps in developing the framework are shown in Figure 1.1. First, the framework's goals and precise scope are defined in the scoping phase. This is where we learn about the AI security and privacy concerns that will be addressed and the overall goals of the framework. Next, all potential dangers to the safety and

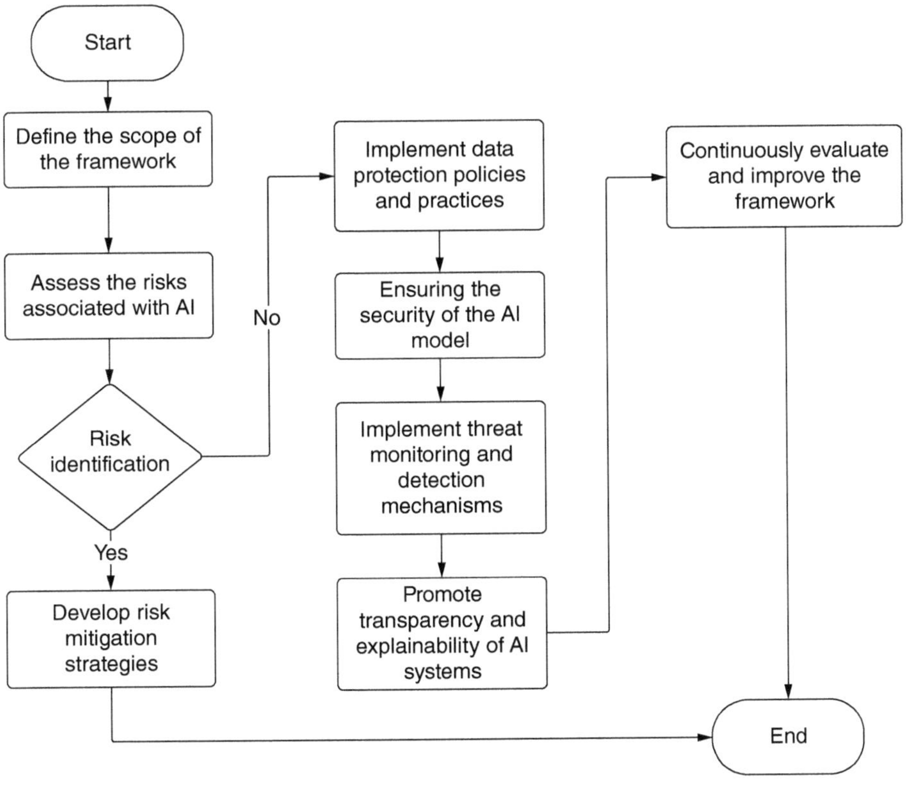

FIGURE 1.1 The outline that assurances the security and privacy of AI.

confidentiality of AI systems are carefully considered. This step involves recognizing and categorizing chances according to their seriousness and likelihood of happening. The procedure ends with the implementation of risk mitigation solutions that were established once risks were identified [41]. Data protection policies and procedures are put into place if hazards cannot be adequately identified and categorized.

The next step is to implement privacy principles, such as only collecting data that is absolutely required and not keeping it for longer than is strictly necessary. In order to secure AI models, such as defense mechanisms against adversarial attacks, and to preserve their integrity and confidentiality, these principles must be followed [42]. The next step in protecting AI systems from potential attacks is to set up monitoring systems and threat detection procedures. Tools and techniques for intrusion detection and log analysis can identify suspicious activity. Adequate documentation of the training and decision-making processes of AI models is the next step in promoting the explainability and transparency of AI systems [43]. Data usage and AI result production are explained in a way that everybody can understand. Lastly, the framework is evaluated and improved continuously. One way to do this is to check the framework's security and privacy measures on a regular basis. To find any security holes, we also run vulnerability scans and penetration tests [44]. It is critical to monitor developments in AI privacy and security research and to update the framework as needed. In order to assess the system, an AI-based face recognition system has taken data protection into account.

The steps to implement the framework are shown in Figure 1.2, taking into account the data protection strategies and practices that were defined in the preceding sections. The primary goal is defined in the first step, which is to assess how well the AI privacy and security framework safeguards the personal data utilized by the face

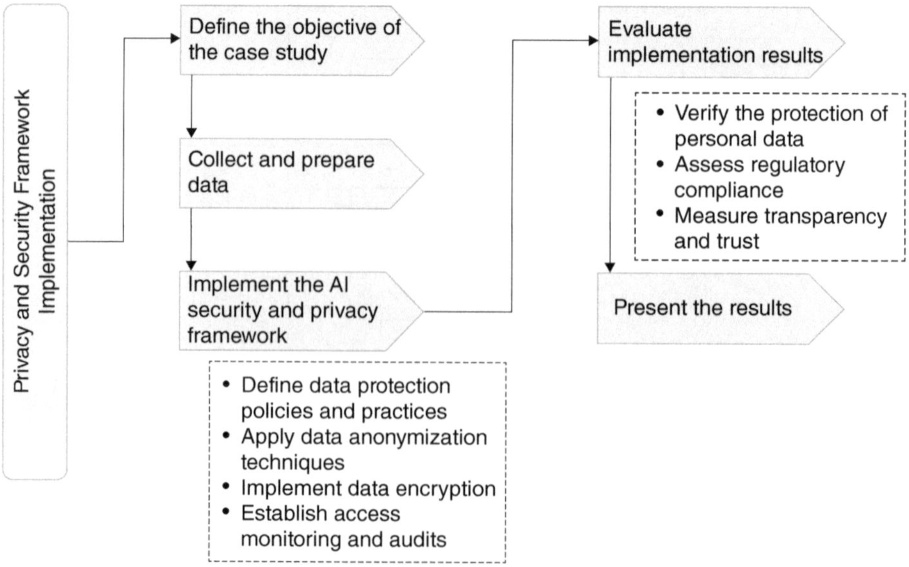

FIGURE 1.2 AI security and privacy outline design flow.

recognition system [45]. The following step is to gather data in preparation for analysis, which includes taking pictures of people's faces and making note of their personal characteristics in order to test how well the face recognition system worked. Finally, the following step involves putting the AI privacy and security architecture into action. This includes creating procedures and rules for data protection, using methods to anonymize data, encrypting data, and setting up systems to monitor and audit access [46].

In order to ensure that the personal data utilized by the facial recognition system is secure from unwanted access or manipulation, a comprehensive verification is conducted throughout the evaluation phase of the implementation results. Consequently, we have verified that the framework satisfies all data protection requirements by conducting an evaluation of its regulatory compliance [47]. The public's and users' views on the facial recognition system's privacy and security features have also been used as metrics for trust and transparency. Evidence of data protection and an increase in transparency and confidence are all part of the documented findings that are presented in the outcomes phase. It was used to apply the AI security and privacy framework, and the findings show the impact and successes of that implementation. Keep in mind that the context and implementation specifics of the framework may cause the results to differ [48].

1.5 RESULTS AND DISCUSSIONS

Table 1.1 displays the following evaluation metrics for the suggested model.

Precision: With a 92% accuracy rate, the model is able to correctly forecast 92% of the time. The percentage of correctly identified faces relative to the total number of optimistic forecasts is what we mean when we talk about accuracy.

Recall: The model's recall of 88% means that it properly identifies 88% of the persons who should be identified.

Accuracy: The proportional model's performance can be measured by its balanced accuracy, which is 90%. This measure, which takes into account both accuracy and recall, is helpful in cases where the distribution of target classes is unbalanced.

TABLE 1.1
Performance Assessment of the Proposed Model

Metrics	Value
Precision	0.92
Recall	0.88
True positives	220
False positives	15
True negatives	950
False negatives	30

Confusion matrix: The following outcomes are displayed by the confusion matrix: Out of 950 negative results, 30 were false negatives, 220 were true positives, and 15 were fake negatives.

Prediction accuracy is the sum of all prediction percentages that were right or wrong, divided by the total number of predictions. If we were to evaluate a facial recognition model, we would take into account all of the predictions—the ones that were right and the ones that were wrong—when calculating accuracy. Following the implementation of the AI security framework, these results offer a comprehensive overview of the evaluated facial recognition system's performance. Several indicators for evaluating the quality of the facial recognition system's biometric data are presented in Table 1.2. Metrics like accuracy, consistency, and racial, gender, and age biases are all part of the whole. The outcomes for every metric that was analyzed are displayed in the "Value" column.

Results from verification testing showed an accuracy of 92.5%, demonstrating the system's strong ability to accurately identify individuals. Contrarily, a reliability evaluation revealed a value of 0.87, indicating fair stability in the assessment of face features across numerous iterations. The coefficients measuring age, gender, and race biases ranged from –1 to 1, with 0 indicating no prejudice. The results show a small amount of bias, with a gender bias of 0.05, an age bias of 0.02, and a race bias of 0.03.

The quality of the biometric data utilized by the face recognition system can be better understood with the help of these details. This data is of excellent quality because of its accuracy and dependability. Concurrently, the system's ability to prevent unjust discrimination is demonstrated by the little existence of bias. By guaranteeing that the data utilized are trustworthy and fairly indicative of all people, these outcomes bolster the accuracy and dependability of the face recognition system [49].

To guarantee the efficacy and equity of the face recognition system, it is crucial to assess the biometric data quality. It aims to increase identification accuracy and prevent unjust discrimination by ensuring data dependability and accuracy and addressing any biases. The trust in the system and its reliability in handling various scenarios and diverse groups of individuals is bolstered by this. There are a lot of moving parts in the suggested framework for protecting AI privacy and security, but they all function together to give a full picture. This research presents an all-encompassing picture of the AI system through its many assessments, which center on gauging distinct

TABLE 1.2
Estimation of Bias in the Proposed Model

Metrics	Value
Precision	93%
Reliability	87%
Age bias	0.022
Gender bias	0.05
Race bias	0.03

parts of privacy and security. When evaluating a facial recognition system, accuracy measurements are important, but there are other crucial factors that should not be overlooked [50]. The policies and procedures put in place to secure the data utilized to train the AI model were examined in the data protection evaluation. The study found that the security measures in place to protect personal information are adequate.

1.6 DISCUSSIONS

When it came to protecting sensitive information, our architecture more than held its own. We have minimized the gathering of private information and anonymized sensitive data to make sure that the facial recognition system is secure and private enough [51]. The framework has taken into account the dangers and weaknesses of AI systems in terms of AI security. Facial recognition systems are now even more protected than before, thanks to security frameworks that have been put in place to reduce the likelihood of assaults and malicious manipulations [52]. By instituting access and authorization restrictions, we have ensured that only authorized individuals have access to sensitive data, so avoiding any possibility of leaks or misuse. Further, security frameworks have been put in place to identify and prevent potential attacks and harmful manipulations, like picture tampering or identity theft [53]. In a way, this has helped make facial recognition more trustworthy and reliable.

Understanding and explaining the conclusions made by AI models has been addressed, which pertains to confidence in their interpretation. To ensure intelligible and justifiable findings, it is vital that the models be interpretable. In order to have a better grasp of the process that goes into making particular predictions and judgments, we employ model interpretation and explainability tools.

In terms of privacy, security, and the quality of biometric data used in the face recognition system, the framework has demonstrated encouraging outcomes. To protect information utilized to train AI models, stringent regulations and procedures have been put in place [54]. As an extra precaution, data encryption and access controls have been put in place to safeguard information while it is in motion and when it is not in use [55]. Also, the biometric data utilized by the face recognition system has been rigorously and impartially tested for accuracy and dependability. The obtained results, such as a dependability of 0.87 and an accuracy of 92.5%, demonstrate that the biometric data is of excellent quality and consistent. To further guarantee that the system operates fairly and without favoritism or discrimination toward any group, we have carefully examined potential biases, including those pertaining to gender, ethnicity, and age.

To assurance the dependability and trustworthiness of AI systems, security in the context of AI must be tackled comprehensively, since it covers numerous important elements. Training data security, model security, and trust in the model's interpretation are the three pillars on which our approach rests when discussing AI security. Our platform takes care of all these aspects, making it seem like a one-stop shop for AI data security, model quality, and performance. All of these things are necessary for people to have faith in AI and use it responsibly in areas like facial recognition and other important societal applications.

1.7 CONCLUSIONS

While working on this project, we investigated several different angles pertaining to AI privacy and security. There has been an examination of rules and practices aimed at preserving sensitive data, and an emphasis on the need to secure the data utilized to train AI models. Additionally, possible dangers and malevolent manipulations, as well as AI system vulnerabilities and security issues, have been addressed. Data anonymization and reducing the acquisition of personal information are two methods that have been investigated as potential solutions to the privacy problems caused by AI. Building and implementing strong frameworks to safeguard AI security and privacy is crucial. Information security, privacy, and risk mitigation are all addressed by these frameworks, which offer recommendations and recommendations for best practices. Trust among users and stakeholders can be fostered through the implementation of these frameworks, which promote the responsible, ethical, and trustworthy usage of AI.

New threats to AI privacy and security are always emerging, though, so keep that in mind. As technology develops and new uses and scenarios arise, we encounter fresh threats and difficulties. It is essential to stay up-to-date, keep an eye on new ideas, and find ways to tackle these changing difficulties. More than that, we must work together to solve these problems thoroughly. One way to use AI in a responsible and ethical way is to safeguard data, reduce security threats, and maintain personal privacy.

ACKNOWLEDGMENTS

Declared none.

CONFLICT OF INTEREST

The authors declare no conflict of interest, financial or otherwise.

REFERENCES

1. Díaz-Rodríguez, N., Del Ser, J., Coeckelbergh, M., de Prado, M.L., Herrera-Viedma, E. and Herrera, F., 2023. Connecting the dots in trustworthy artificial intelligence: From AI principles, ethics, and key requirements to responsible AI systems and regulation. *Information Fusion*, 99, 101896.
2. Alzubaidi, L., Al-Sabaawi, A., Bai, J., Dukhan, A., Alkenani, A.H., Al-Asadi, A., Alwzwazy, H.A., Manoufali, M., Fadhel, M.A., Albahri, A.S. and Moreira, C., 2023. Towards risk-free trustworthy artificial intelligence: Significance and requirements. *International Journal of Intelligent Systems*, 2023. https://doi.org/10.1155/2023/4459198
3. Chang, Y.L. and Ke, J., 2024. Socially responsible artificial intelligence empowered people analytics: A novel framework towards sustainability. *Human Resource Development Review*, 23(1), 88–120.
4. Rao, K.R., Prasad, M.L., Kumar, G.R., Natchadalingam, R., Hussain, M.M. and Reddy, P.C.S., 2023, August. Time-Series Cryptocurrency Forecasting Using Ensemble Deep Learning. In *2023 International Conference on Circuit Power and Computing Technologies (ICCPCT)* (pp. 1446–1451). IEEE.

5. Qayyum, A., Butt, M.A., Ali, H., Usman, M., Halabi, O., Al-Fuqaha, A., Abbasi, Q.H., Imran, M.A. and Qadir, J., 2023. Secure and trustworthy artificial intelligence-extended reality (AI-XR) for metaverses. *ACM Computing Surveys*, 56, 1–38.
6. Al-Khassawneh, Y.A., 2023. A review of artificial intelligence in security and privacy: Research advances, applications, opportunities, and challenges. *Indonesian Journal of Science and Technology*, 8(1), 79–96.
7. Alonso, R., Haber, R.E., Castaño, F. and Recupero, D.R., 2024. Interoperable software platforms for introducing artificial intelligence components in manufacturing: A meta-framework for security and privacy. *Heliyon*, 10(4), e26446.
8. Sucharitha, Y., Reddy, P.C.S. and Chitti, T.N., 2023, July. Deep Learning Based Framework for Crop Yield Prediction. In *AIP Conference Proceedings* (Vol. 2548, No. 1). AIP Publishing.
9. Selvarajan, S., Srivastava, G., Khadidos, A.O., Khadidos, A.O., Baza, M., Alshehri, A. and Lin, J.C.W., 2023. An artificial intelligence lightweight blockchain security model for security and privacy in IIoT systems. *Journal of Cloud Computing*, 12(1), 38.
10. Wang, C., Yuan, Z., Zhou, P., Xu, Z., Li, R. and Wu, D.O., 2023. The security and privacy of mobile edge computing: An artificial intelligence perspective. *IEEE Internet of Things Journal*, 10, 22008–22032.
11. Kumar, G.R., Reddy, R.V., Jayarathna, M., Pughazendi, N., Vidyullatha, S. and Reddy, P.C.S., 2023, May. Web Application Based Diabetes Prediction Using Machine Learning. In *2023 International Conference on Advances in Computing, Communication and Applied Informatics (ACCAI)* (pp. 1–7). IEEE.
12. Correia, M. and Rodrigues, L., 2023. Security and Privacy. In *Multidisciplinary Perspectives on Artificial Intelligence and the Law* (pp. 81–101). Springer International Publishing.
13. Xia, L., Semirumi, D.T. and Rezaei, R., 2023. A thorough examination of smart city applications: Exploring challenges and solutions throughout the life cycle with emphasis on safeguarding citizen privacy. *Sustainable Cities and Society*, 98, 104771.
14. Ozmen Garibay, O., Winslow, B., Andolina, S., Antona, M., Bodenschatz, A., Coursaris, C., Falco, G., Fiore, S.M., Garibay, I., Grieman, K. and Havens, J.C., 2023. Six human-centered artificial intelligence grand challenges. *International Journal of Human–Computer Interaction*, 39(3), 391–437.
15. Patil, S.B., Rao, H.R., Chatrapathy, K., Kiran, A., Kumar, A.S. and Reddy, P.C.S., 2023, August. Ensemble Deep Learning Framework for Classification of Skin Lesions. In *2023 International Conference on Circuit Power and Computing Technologies (ICCPCT)* (pp. 1550–1555). IEEE.
16. Aldoseri, A., Al-Khalifa, K.N. and Hamouda, A.M., 2023. Re-thinking data strategy and integration for artificial intelligence: Concepts, opportunities, and challenges. *Applied Sciences*, 13(12), 7082.
17. Latha, S.B., Dastagiraiah, C., Kiran, A., Asif, S., Elangovan, D. and Reddy, P.C.S., 2023, August. An Adaptive Machine Learning Model for Walmart Sales Prediction. In *2023 International Conference on Circuit Power and Computing Technologies (ICCPCT)* (pp. 988–992). IEEE.
18. Ahmed, S. and Khan, M., 2023. Securing the Internet of Things (IoT): A comprehensive study on the intersection of cybersecurity, privacy, and connectivity in the IoT ecosystem. *AI, IoT and the Fourth Industrial Revolution Review*, 13(9), 1–17.
19. Kuznetsov, A., Sernani, P., Romeo, L., Frontoni, E. and Mancini, A., 2024. *On the Integration of Artificial Intelligence and Blockchain Technology: A Perspective About Security*. IEEE Access.

20. Ramana, A.V., Bhoga, U., Dhulipalla, R.K., Kiran, A., Chary, B.D. and Reddy, P.C.S., 2023, June. Abnormal Behavior Prediction in Elderly Persons Using Deep Learning. In *2023 International Conference on Computer, Electronics & Electrical Engineering & their Applications (IC2E3)* (pp. 1–5). IEEE.
21. Castro, O.E.L., Deng, X. and Park, J.H., 2023. Comprehensive survey on AI-based technologies for enhancing IoT privacy and security: Trends, challenges, and solutions. *Human-Centric Computing and Information Sciences*, 13, 1–34.
22. Schmitt, M., 2023. Securing the digital world: Protecting smart infrastructures and digital industries with artificial intelligence (AI)-enabled malware and intrusion detection. *Journal of Industrial Information Integration*, 36, 100520.
23. Madhavi, G.B., Bhavani, A.D., Reddy, Y.S., Kiran, A., Chitra, N.T. and Reddy, P.C.S., 2023, June. Traffic Congestion Detection From Surveillance Videos Using Deep Learning. In *2023 International Conference on Computer, Electronics & Electrical Engineering & their Applications (IC2E3)* (pp. 1–5). IEEE.
24. Gami, B., Agrawal, M., Mishra, D.K., Quasim, D. and Mehra, P.S., 2023. Artificial intelligence-based blockchain solutions for intelligent healthcare: A comprehensive review on privacy preserving techniques. *Transactions on Emerging Telecommunications Technologies*, 34(9), e4824.
25. Khalid, N., Qayyum, A., Bilal, M., Al-Fuqaha, A. and Qadir, J., 2023. Privacy-preserving artificial intelligence in healthcare: Techniques and applications. *Computers in Biology and Medicine*, 158, 106848.
26. Suneel, S., Balaram, A., Amina Begum, M., Umapathy, K., Reddy, P.C.S. and Talasila, V., 2024. Quantum mesh neural network model in precise image diagnosing. *Optical and Quantum Electronics*, 56(4), 559.
27. Lauri, C., Shimpo, F. and Sokołowski, M.M., 2023. Artificial intelligence and robotics on the frontlines of the pandemic response: The regulatory models for technology adoption and the development of resilient organisations in smart cities. *Journal of Ambient Intelligence and Humanized Computing*, 14(11), 14753–14764.
28. Riczu, Z., 2023. Recommendations on the ethical aspects of artificial intelligence, with an outlook on the world of work. *Journal of Digital Technologies and Law*, 1(2), 498–519.
29. Rekha, M.N., Prasad, M.L., Mukherjee, S., Nikam, S.V., Sharma, S. and Reddy, P.C.S., 2024, February. An Automatic Error Recognition Approach for Machine Translation Results based on Deep Learning. In *2024 2nd International Conference on Computer, Communication and Control (IC4)* (pp. 1–8). IEEE.
30. Gulyamov, S.S., 2023, September. Legal Frameworks for the Integration of Artificial Intelligence. In *International Conference on Nanotechnologies and Biomedical Engineering* (pp. 144–149). Springer Nature Switzerland.
31. Kaur, R., Gabrijelčič, D. and Klobučar, T., 2023. Artificial intelligence for cybersecurity: Literature review and future research directions. *Information Fusion*, 97, 101804.
32. Shaker Reddy, P.C. and Sucharitha, Y., 2023. A design and challenges in energy optimizing CR-wireless sensor networks. *Recent Advances in Computer Science and Communications (Formerly: Recent Patents on Computer Science)*, 16(5), 82–92.
33. Rahman, A., Hasan, K., Kundu, D., Islam, M.J., Debnath, T., Band, S.S. and Kumar, N., 2023. On the ICN-IoT with federated learning integration of communication: Concepts, security-privacy issues, applications, and future perspectives. *Future Generation Computer Systems*, 138, 61–88.
34. Villar-Rodriguez, E., Pérez, M.A., Torre-Bastida, A.I., Senderos, C.R. and López-de-Armentia, J., 2023. Edge intelligence secure frameworks: Current state and future challenges. *Computers & Security*, 130, 103278.

35. Gadupudi, A., Rani, R.Y., Jayaram, B., Sharma, N., Deshmukh, J.K. and Reddy, P.C.S., 2024, February. An Adaptive Deep Learning Model for Crop Yield Prediction. In *2024 2nd International Conference on Computer, Communication and Control (IC4)* (pp. 1–5). IEEE.
36. Mylrea, M. and Robinson, N., 2023. Artificial intelligence (AI) trust framework and maturity model: Applying an entropy lens to improve security, privacy, and ethical AI. *Entropy*, 25(10), 1429.
37. Gurusubramani, S., Rosy, N.A., Chitra, D., Isravel, Y.A.D. and Reddy, P.C.S., 2023, November. Distributed Deep Learning Attack Detection Framework for Cyber-Attacks in IoT Network. In *2023 3rd International Conference on Advancement in Electronics & Communication Engineering (AECE)* (pp. 811–816). IEEE.
38. Stahl, B.C., Antoniou, J., Bhalla, N., Brooks, L., Jansen, P., Lindqvist, B., Kirichenko, A., Marchal, S., Rodrigues, R., Santiago, N. and Warso, Z., 2023. A systematic review of artificial intelligence impact assessments. *Artificial Intelligence Review*, 56(11), 12799–12831.
39. Reddy, P.C.S., Nithyapriya, S., Sharma, N., Maheswari, S., Jayaram, B. and Katale, T., 2023, December. A Novel Ensemble Deep Learning Framework for Breast Cancer Prediction. In *2023 International Conference on Innovative Computing, Intelligent Communication and Smart Electrical Systems (ICSES)* (pp. 1–6). IEEE.
40. Mohammad Amini, M., Jesus, M., Fanaei Sheikholeslami, D., Alves, P., Hassanzadeh Benam, A. and Hariri, F., 2023. Artificial intelligence ethics and challenges in healthcare applications: A comprehensive review in the context of the European GDPR mandate. *Machine Learning and Knowledge Extraction*, 5(3), 1023–1035.
41. Bendiab, G., Hameurlaine, A., Germanos, G., Kolokotronis, N. and Shiaeles, S., 2023. Autonomous vehicles security: Challenges and solutions using blockchain and artificial intelligence. *IEEE Transactions on Intelligent Transportation Systems*, 24(4), 3614–3637.
42. Tayubi, I.A., Pawar, D.N., Kiran, A., Reddy, P.C.S., Sharma, N. and Chitra, D., 2024, February. Facial Emotion Recognition Using a Local Binary Pattern based Deep Learning. In *2024 2nd International Conference on Computer, Communication and Control (IC4)* (pp. 1–7). IEEE.
43. Somnathe, A.T., Tayubi, I.A., Reddy, P.C.S., Sharma, N., Sharma, V. and Yesubabu, M., 2023, December. Brain Computer Interaction Framework for Speech and Motor Impairment Using Deep Learning. In *2023 International Conference on Power Energy, Environment & Intelligent Control (PEEIC)* (pp. 1008–1013). IEEE.
44. Christian, D. and Austin, K., 2023. Data integrity and security in clinical trials: A comprehensive approach. *Journal Environmental Sciences and Technology*, 2(1), 524–555.
45. Albahri, A.S., Duhaim, A.M., Fadhel, M.A., Alnoor, A., Baqer, N.S., Alzubaidi, L., Albahri, O.S., Alamoodi, A.H., Bai, J., Salhi, A. and Santamaría, J., 2023. A systematic review of trustworthy and explainable artificial intelligence in healthcare: Assessment of quality, bias risk, and data fusion. *Information Fusion*, 96, 156–191.
46. Solanki, P., Grundy, J. and Hussain, W., 2023. Operationalising ethics in artificial intelligence for healthcare: A framework for AI developers. *AI and Ethics*, 3(1), 223–240.
47. Nguyen, A., Ngo, H.N., Hong, Y., Dang, B. and Nguyen, B.P.T., 2023. Ethical principles for artificial intelligence in education. *Education and Information Technologies*, 28(4), 4221–4241.
48. Jarota, M., 2023. Artificial intelligence in the work process. A reflection on the proposed European Union regulations on artificial intelligence from an occupational health and safety perspective. *Computer Law & Security Review*, 49, 105825.

49. Shen, M., Gu, A., Kang, J., Tang, X., Lin, X., Zhu, L. and Niyato, D., 2023. Blockchains for artificial intelligence of things: A comprehensive survey. *IEEE Internet of Things Journal*, 10, 14483–14506.
50. Sirohi, D., Kumar, N., Rana, P.S., Tanwar, S., Iqbal, R. and Hijjii, M., 2023. Federated learning for 6G-enabled secure communication systems: A comprehensive survey. *Artificial Intelligence Review*, 56(10), 11297–11389.
51. Chan, C.K.Y., 2023. A comprehensive AI policy education framework for university teaching and learning. *International Journal of Educational Technology in Higher Education*, 20(1), 38.
52. Demertzis, K., Rantos, K., Magafas, L., Skianis, C. and Iliadis, L., 2023. A secure and privacy-preserving blockchain-based XAI-justice system. *Information*, 14(9), 477.
53. Zubaydi, H.D., Varga, P. and Molnár, S., 2023. Leveraging blockchain technology for ensuring security and privacy aspects in internet of things: A systematic literature review. *Sensors*, 23(2), 788.
54. Rane, N.L., 2023. Multidisciplinary collaboration: key players in successful implementation of ChatGPT and similar generative artificial intelligence in manufacturing, finance, retail, transportation, and construction industry. https://doi.org/10.31219/osf.io/npm3d
55. Sekhar, G.S., Mahadik, S., Ramana, A.V., Reddy, P.C.S., Pughazendi, N. and Asif, S., 2023, December. Prediction of Traffic Accidents Using Deep Learning Ensemble Model. In *2023 International Conference on Innovative Computing, Intelligent Communication and Smart Electrical Systems (ICSES)* (pp. 1–6). IEEE.

2 Knowledge Modelling and the Significance of Ontology in Educational Domain

Zameer Gulzar, Fatima Amer Jid Almahri and P Padmavathi

2.1 INTRODUCTION

The concept of semantic web and ontology has emerged as a transformative influence that cuts across various industries within the dynamic landscape of technology. This paradigm change had a significant impact on the education sector. Complex data representation, shared reasoning, and interconnected knowledge have come together to create new opportunities to foster cooperation, enhance the learning process, and improve information management within educational frameworks [1].

The main components of semantic web are structured vocabularies and ontologies, which list the concepts and relationships present in a certain field. Ontologies are theories about the structure of knowledge, and their primary function is to categorize the various kinds of entities and relationships that exist within a given topic. They provide a prospective collection of phrases to amplify the data in a specific field. Ontologies offer definitions for terminology like subjects, courses, prerequisites, and learning objectives in the field of education [2]. According to Huang et al. [3], learning technology has expanded quickly and is heavily supported by online learning, technology development, and stakeholders with complex needs.

A logical framework of terms used to characterize a field of knowledge, comprising the definitions of relevant concepts and their connections, is called an ontology [4]. As demonstrated in Figure 2.1, ontology is defined as a formal, explicit, and unambiguous description of a shared conceptualization in a domain of discourse. Ontologies were used to teach information and knowledge in a variety of fields, but in the field of computer science (CS), they are insufficient and restricted to a small number of topics [5].

The domain ontologies, which are shareable and incorporate the concepts and their relationships, will offer the fundamental understanding of a domain. Classes are of great interest in nearly all types of ontologies since they define a concept related to a given domain. A knowledge base would be represented by a set of distinct classes and domain ontologies. Ontologies are thought of as a strategy for knowledge modelling

DOI: 10.1201/9781032703718-3

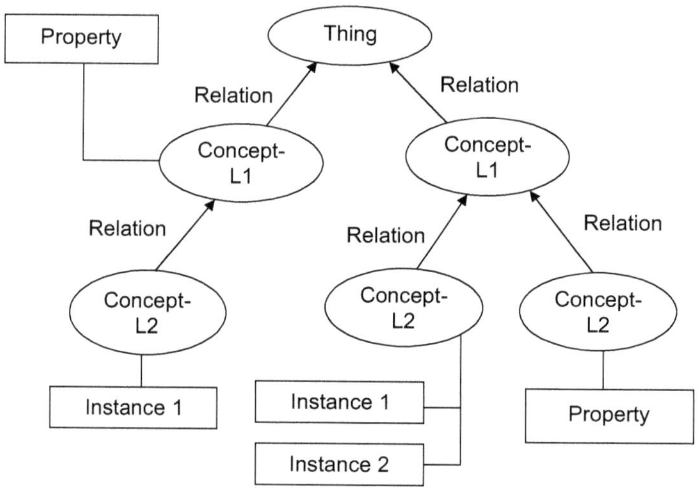

FIGURE 2.1 Knowledge base representation using ontology.

that is well organized and meant to build knowledge representation in addition to classifying a specific area that can be shared and reused [6]. The building blocks for all ontologies are classes as it describes the concept in the domain and that is the reason it is considered an organized methodology for knowledge modelling. Ontology should closely match the level of information found in textbooks and curriculum on a particular subject and model the related information that is known about that subject. Thus, for building an ontology, following concepts need to be specified as in [7].

- Classes and objects present in the domain
- Properties those objects would exhibit
- Relationship that exists between objects

Two factors, the idea of internal organization and the type of information being collected, are used to categorize ontologies. In CS, ontologies are categorized according to goals and conceptualizations of concepts as application ontologies, domain ontologies, domain-task ontologies, and task ontologies, as shown in Figure 2.2.

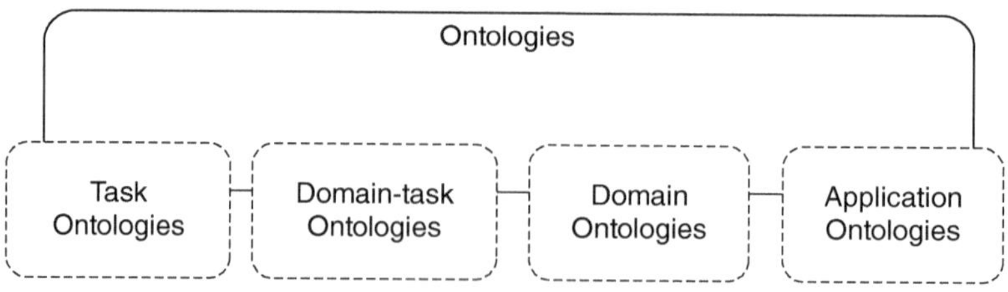

FIGURE 2.2 Classification of ontology.

The application ontologies encapsulate the knowledge pertinent to a particular application and, as a result, these ontologies are application reliant. Regarding a particular issue or application, the application ontology has the potential to greatly increase its scope. The task ontologies are restricted to a single activity or topic and correspond to a specialized language for a single task inside a single application. The task ontologies cannot be applied to other domains or environments outside of their current working environment. Use domain ontologies instead, such as those used in the fields of history, medicine, sports, and entertainment, which have the feature of reuse [8–10].

The primary characteristic of all domain ontologies is their autonomy inside a certain application. They also provide concepts a vocabulary and represent the body of knowledge in a particular area. On the other hand, task ontology describes the associated concepts in relation to a typical task, such as purchasing and selling are tasks that are independent of any domain. The important components of an ontology used in this work for the CS topics are depicted in Figure 2.3. The purpose of this study is to investigate ontology development and its applicability to the classroom. It looks at ways that ontology might improve curriculum design and instructional strategies. It provides insights into utilizing ontology for educational improvement, offering direction for educators and policymakers through the examination of theoretical frameworks and real-world implementations. According to [11] it provides information-rich, unified platform that may be used for decision-making, which is made possible by intelligent decision-making, which encourages connectivity among heterogeneous users.

Ontological modelling will have an impact on enhancing the design of intelligent learning systems by creating unified information environments. With the integration of gamification for improved learning outcomes, it utilizes multidimensional models to create info-logical representations [12]. The rest of the chapter is structured as follows. Section 2.2 will describe the ontology development process with respect to education and its development process using a developed methodology. Section 2.3 will be concerned with the ontology validation and its evaluation. Section 2.4 will discuss how the modelling was done and how it looks like after developing, and finally conclusion is given.

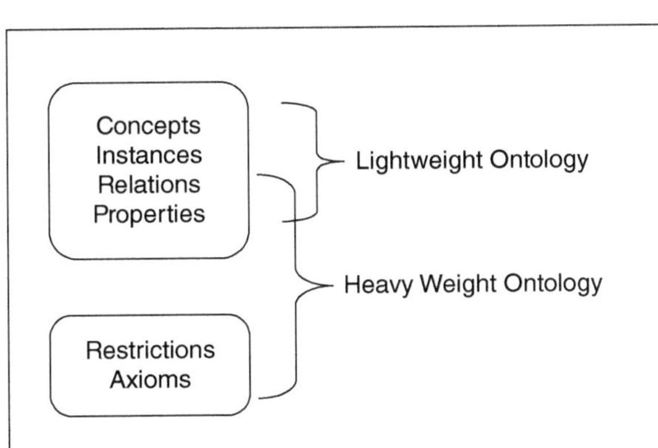

FIGURE 2.3 Ontology components.

2.2 ONTOLOGY IN EDUCATIONAL CONTEXT

Ontology is a method that creates a consistent and fundamental framework for formal resource declarations in each area by annotating semantics. The ontology creation is helpful in providing learning resources in educational settings in an efficient and well-organized way, which can increase a learner's interest [13]. Until the late 1990s, ontology development lacked a well-established and methodical guiding concept, and it was viewed more as an artistic endeavour than as a technical feat. Afterwards, several ontology creation approaches, including OD-101, Diligent, Methontology, Kactus, and Tove, were created to preserve ontology-based management of domain knowledge. Nevertheless, there isn't a recognized process for developing ontologies in knowledge modelling or engineering [14]. A loss of knowledge in the field of CS must result from the inadequacy of domain ontologies in that field. As a result, researchers who seek effective information access to fulfil their goals or interests will encounter difficulties. Ontologies, which will provide the terms with some meaning, are a potential contender for the artefact that will lead to the solution for this problem. By clarifying and making the notion in the field of CS understandable, ontologies could lessen the issue.

Because ontologies make it possible to define the representation of a learning domain by defining all concepts involved, relationships between ideas, and all attributes and conditions that exist, they are utilized in education with remarkable success. Thus, one of the goals of this chapter is to construct ontology to support learners in personalizing their courses, which is an effective and professional technique to increase learners' interest and performance. Ontologies are helpful in conveying knowledge about several areas of schooling. Since significant ontologies were built in other domains, like medicine, entertainment, sports, physics, and cooking, to give a suitable organized knowledge, the ontologies in the CS domain are insufficient. The ontology associated with a given domain implies that the ideas inside the domain and their relationships with each other are mutually understood. Students have not effectively utilized the knowledge in the CS field since it is scattered and the possibility to access and reuse has been limited.

The time required for ontology development can be decreased with the use of a well-defined and organized methodology. An architectural explanation of an iterative process connected with the Methontology activity states, as illustrated in Figure 2.4, has been recommended to produce CS ontology in this research effort, since there is no standard technique for constructing course ontologies. The goal of creating the ontology for the CS domain is to give researchers, students, and other academics an effective way to arrange their courses by providing a graph-based representation of the domain. An understanding of the domain may be gained from the ontology graphs, and learners can navigate the connections between these courses with ease. The fundamental benefit of ontology is that learners will be more focused on the links between ideas in a domain than on information alone. An expert can save time by reusing the ontology because it allows them to utilize pre-built ontologies. Typically, a team of experts comprising ontology engineers, domain experts, and educators develops ontologies. Here are some of the justifications for creating ontologies as outlined by Noy et al. [15].

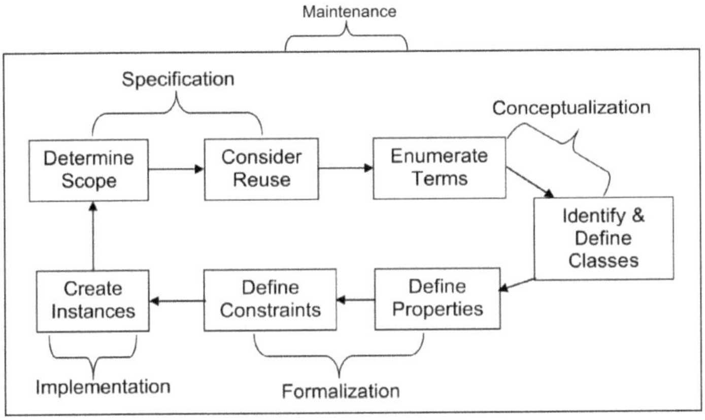

FIGURE 2.4 Ontology development process.

- To study and draw conclusions about explicit domain knowledge that is relevant to a domain.
- To appropriately assess domain knowledge and disseminate it to software agents and other individuals.
- To make it possible for domain knowledge to be reused.
- To keep domain knowledge and operational knowledge apart.

Each of these ideas perfectly aligns with the goals that this study seeks to accomplish. The CS courses are dispersed rather than well organized. Because it is difficult to determine whether there is any relationship between courses, learners are unable to determine whether courses overlap across domains. Here [16] laid forth a brief list of items that should be included in building ontology;

- Finding the classes in the created ontology.
- Class placement in a taxonomy-based hierarchy.
- Identifying slots and approving values for each slot.
- Filling slot instances with values.

When the class hierarchy is being built, the individuals that make up a certain class can also be formed, along with the properties that are allocated to the class. These people or instances will aid in the creation of an ontology knowledge base, but the primary obstacle to be solved is the development of a shared framework for the creation of domain ontologies. The creation of ontologies for courses in CS subjects like networks, software engineering, cloud computing, artificial intelligence (AI), and data mining will be the focus of this chapter. Even before the concepts connected to a certain domain were classified, a systematic review of various books in CS, Institute syllabi of CS, and a thorough discussion with some expert faculty members was conducted. The next-generation teaching and learning process will be impacted by the visualization function that ontologies and web semantics provide.

The infantile nature of ontology makes it a promising field for research and may provide the necessary technology support for online information processing, including web indexing, searching, web semantics, and annotations. Ontology will revolutionize the creation of reusable and shareable educational content for a unified education system if it is developed solely for educational purposes. A few institutions and other organizations have begun developing ontologies with the intention of using them for teaching. The CS ontology was also constructed in this research effort, and the 27 classes and 15 subclasses that resulted are listed in Tables 2.1 and 2.2.

The purpose of this study is to ascertain whether the knowledge model was created to help learners better comprehend the domain and the courses that are part of it. There may be ontologies for different areas, but their quality and stability in terms of education are concealed. There is no ontology for any of the different subjects and areas. Consequently, the development of ontology aids in the efficient and professional delivery of courses and may be beneficial in raising students' attention. The study's foundation is the suggested architectural methodology that was used to configure the development process of the proposed ontology.

TABLE 2.1
List of the Classes in Developed Ontology

University	Programs	Student
Employee	Books	Journal Article
Domain	Artificial Intelligence	Technical Report
Publication	Networking	Conference Paper
Department	Software Engineering	Professor
Research	Cloud Computing	Faculty
Assistant Professor	Data Mining	Associate Professor
Course	Guide	College
Scholar	Administration	Credit

TABLE 2.2
List of Sub-classes in Developed Ontology

Machine Learning	Network Hardware	Performance
Intelligent System	Fuzzy Mathematics	Big Data
Knowledge Discovery	Communication	Security
Software Project Management	Software Testing and Quality Assurance	Formal Methods of Software Engineering
Natural Language Processing	System Performance Engineering	Theory of Computation

TABLE 2.3
Ontology Requirement Specification Document for CS Ontology

S. No	Domain Name	Computer Science
1	Purpose	The ontology about the course in CS to be used by the learners required during teaching learning analysis and so on
2	Level of Formality	Semi-formal
3	Scope	List of major domains in CS, sub-domain, and the list of courses available
4	Source of Knowledge	University syllabus, books, faculty experience

2.2.1 Specification

The purpose of this activity state is to define the reasons for which the ontology is being built, who will use it, and whether it already exists so that it can be reused directly. The specifications ought to be clear and detailed, covering the main goal of developing ontology, as well as its extent and degree of granularity, as indicated in Table 2.3.

A) **Determine the Ontology's Scope**: The following list of questions is meant to help determine the domain and scope of the ontology that is currently under development.
   - What is covered by domain ontology?
   - Who is going to use ontology?
   - What is the intended use of ontology?
   - What queries does ontology purport to address?

   The domain in this study is straightforward, and university courses for post-graduate and research programs are offered, indicating that students can choose only those courses that align with their desired curriculum. The courses' credits, the department that offers them, and the courses that are linked together in a specific subject are further pertinent details about the courses.

B) **Consider Reusing Current Ontologies**: Prior to starting the ontology-building process, an investigation was carried out to see if any organizations in the CS domain had already built ontology. Once it is confirmed that no such ontology is available, Protégé's Onto Merge feature may understand any ontology and merge it with the emerging ontology, even if the ontology is extant and available in several formats. There are ontologies in other domains that may have been used in the current study, but none of them exist in the CS domain. Students in the CS sector have not made efficient use of the knowledge contained therein because most of the knowledge in the CS is fragmented and its accessibility and reuse are severely limited. Because of this, and with the study's goal in mind, the CS ontology was developed from scratch.

2.2.2 Conceptualization

Using domain vocabulary from the ontology specification process, the dispersed information within a domain is organized into a conceptual model that aids in understanding the issue and providing clarification. All domain knowledge pertaining to the primary ideas, characteristics, verbs, and examples is incorporated into the construction of glossary terms. To offer a conceptual ontology model that developers can comprehend, the responsibility is to organize and transform an informal view of the domain into a concept using an intermediary representation such as graph notation. As seen in Figure 2.5 these representations aid in bridging the gap between the people and the formalization of the ontology.

A) **Enumerate the Words that Are Essential to the Ontology**: It is recommended that the development team document the vocabulary that will be utilized during the ontology creation process before beginning work on it. Before classes, properties, relationships, and other terminology are created, the practice should be adhered to. This strategy is motivated by the fact that the terminology list will constantly change as ontologies are developed. Considering the questions posed in the first stage of the ontology specification work, terms such as course code, course name, and course credits have been extracted and added to the ontology. Terms that overlapped were removed from consideration even before the conceptualization stage of ontology building.

B) **Describe Classes and Their Hierarchy**: Super-classes of ontology are thus considered as subclasses of Thing. In Protégé, all classes begin with the base class Thing, from which subsequent classes will emerge. Schools, Employees, Students, and Research are super-classes in a mature ontology, and they will also have subclasses and entities. It acts as a general definition for subclass instances. Figure 2.6 shows the Protégé class hierarchy graphic.

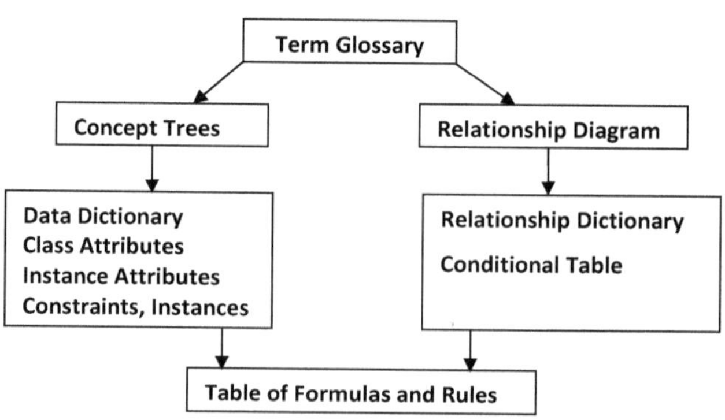

FIGURE 2.5 Methontology tasks for conceptualization.

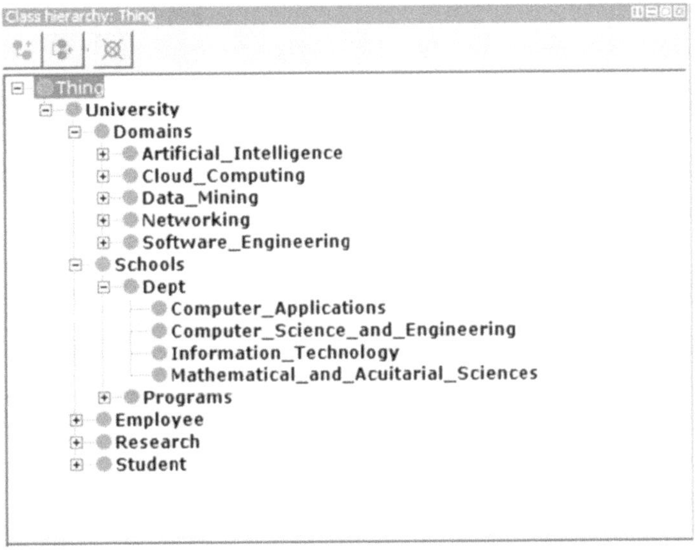

FIGURE 2.6 Class hierarchy in CS ontology.

C) **Super-class University**: In order to build persons for every subclass, this class contains all other subclasses in the ontology as shown in Figure 2.6. A school has two subclasses: Department and Programs. Programs have a subclass called Publication, and Programs has another subclass that has all the programs available in the ontology. The algorithms and semantic logic employed in the ontology to connect the courses via certain relations will serve as the foundation for the user suggestions.

D) **Super-class Departments**: A subclass of the super-class was made up of various programs and the departments that provide them. The people can be designed to represent a program that each department offers. Researchers can utilize description language (DL) queries in a possible application that makes use of this ontology to determine which programs are available and whether they can select a specific course that interests them. The learner receives knowledge about the department that offers the specific Program from the semantic logic that is defined in the ontology. The programs that are connected to each department are displayed in Figure 2.7.

E) **Super-class Domains**: In this ontology, as illustrated in Figure 2.8, the super-class contains all other main classes and the courses within it. Domains such as Software Engineering, Data Mining, Cloud Computing, AI, and Networking are included in the created ontology. Courses on language technology, web services, Radio-Frequency Identification (RFID), intelligent information retrieval, algorithms, knowledge discovery technologies, etc., are included in the domains. The course is abstracted out of programs and can be a part of many study programs.

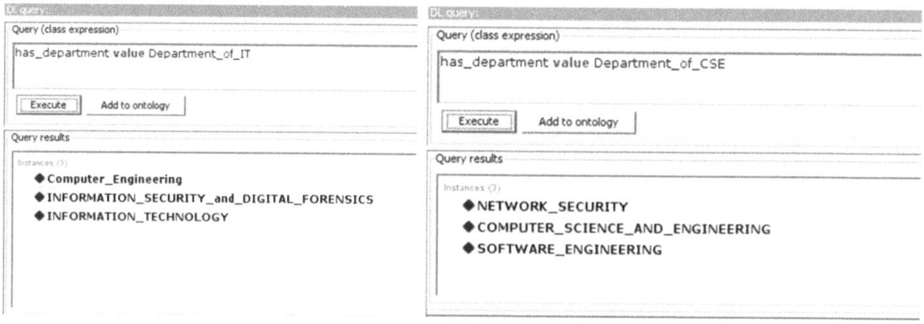

FIGURE 2.7 Description language query to check programs offered.

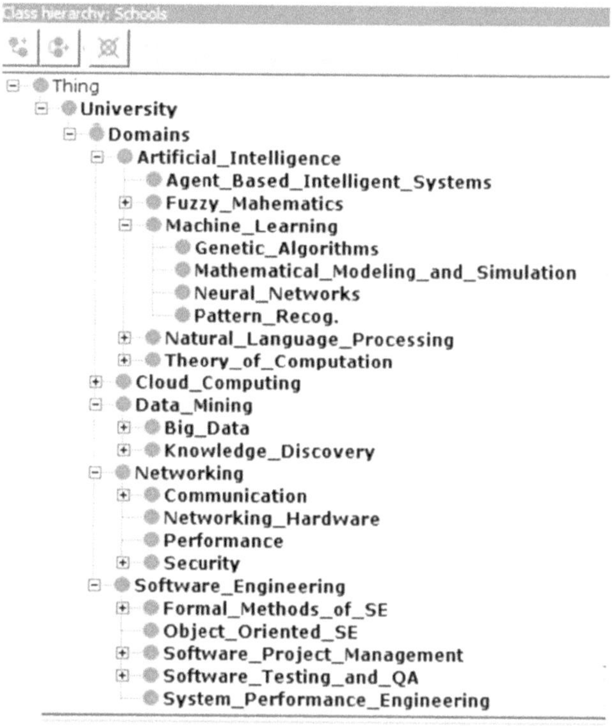

FIGURE 2.8 Course hierarchy in the ontology.

2.2.3 Formalization

This activity's main goal is to use description logic or a frame-based system to turn the conceptual model created in the conceptualization activity into a semi-formal or semi-compatible model.

A) Specify the properties of both individuals and classes
B) Classes are used to separate individuals by defining their domain and range. The different attributes that are established in the ontology cause the individuals to be mutually delimited. As seen in Figure 2.9, the properties in the developed ontology are categorized according to data and object properties.
C) An object's properties specify the connections between members of the same or distinct classes. With the use of the "is_related" attribute, which establishes a relationship between the courses, Figure 2.10 links an individual AI course to six other courses that may be in the same domain or a different one. On the other hand, the data property holds the personal information that has been allotted to the individual without any connection to other individuals. Every course may have a data property. The terms "CoursesName" and "defining" refer to the actual course name and credit count.
D) Define the facets and constraints of the properties

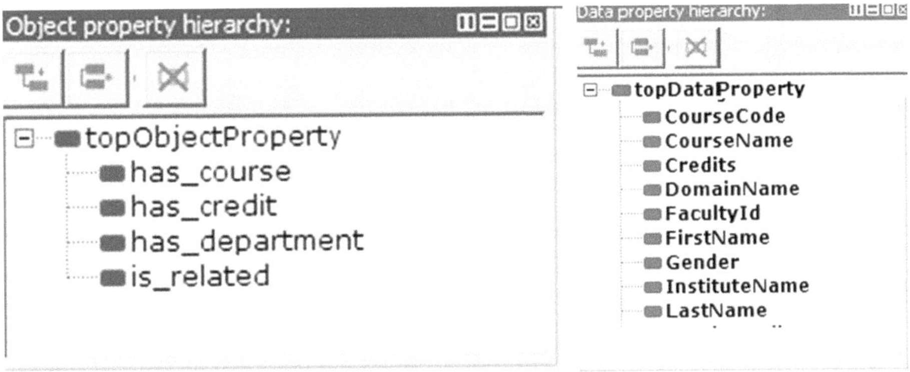

FIGURE 2.9 Object and data properties used in ontology.

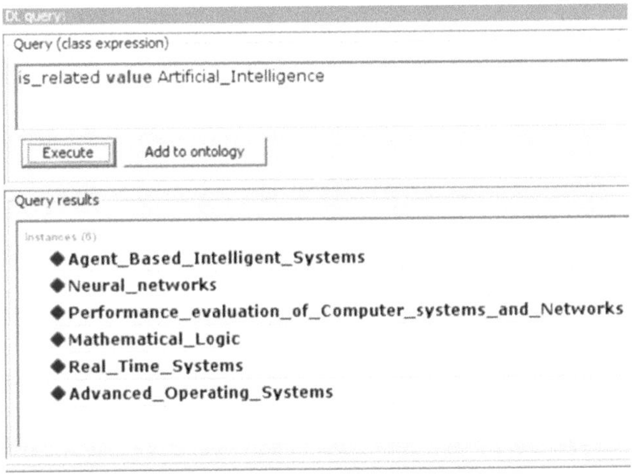

FIGURE 2.10 Query to check linked courses.

TABLE 2.4
Object Properties of the CS Ontology

Object Property	Field	Range	Comment
Has_course	Department	Course	Used on individuals of the department on how many courses they are offering
Has_department	Schools	Programs	Used on courses that require which department is offering a particular course
Has_credit	Domain	Courses	Used on courses that have some credits
Is_related	Domain	Courses	Used on individuals of courses to which course they are linked with

TABLE 2.5
Defining the Data Properties of the Ontology

CourseName	Domain	String	The name of a course e.g. Data Mining and Analysis.
CourseCode	Domain	String	The code of a particular course, e.g. C102
Credits	Domain	Integer	How many credits a course is worth

The developed domain ontology's attributes are defined in Tables 2.4 and 2.5, which are stated below. Each table includes its field name, range, and usage comments. Data properties are listed in the second table, while object properties are listed in the first. The people who constructed their own classes using semantic logic use the properties is_related, has_course, has_credit, and has_department. This implies that all the previously described properties will be automatically added to the created ontology upon the introduction of a new course. The fundamental idea behind the is_related property is to link two or more courses together. This will enable course customization later by retrieving related courses based on the primary suggestions that were given.

2.2.4 Implementation

To create a computable model for this task, ontology languages such as Web Ontology Language (OWL) and Resource Description Framework (RDF) schema must be used. Official language codified ontology is the result of this endeavour. The languages used to construct ontologies should provide an analyser that ensures that lexical and syntactic mistakes are not present. To allow for portability, identify some errors in the ontology, and change the definitions, it should have an editor, translator, and evaluator. An environment that supports the ontologies chosen during the integration phase is necessary for the ontology implementation.

A) **Creating Individuals /Instances**: When constructing an instance in an ontology, there are a few stages that must be taken. Some of these steps are listed below. (i) When constructing a person, a specific class needs to be decided upon. (ii) A proper name is necessary to truly create an individual. (iii) The individuals should be given more properties. Most of the individual research work in this study is found as domain courses. About 300 courses have been added to the created ontology based on availability. According to established policy, courses and the department are accommodated within the primary classes' domain and department.

The quantity of objects and characteristics employed in this study is sufficient for creating an ontology prototype, which basically contains semantic logic. Figures 2.11 and 2.12 show the details of two distinct classes, and it is evident that the network security course includes three credits and is connected in some way to the mobile and wireless network security course. Each IT department offers a variety of programs with a range of courses.

FIGURE 2.11 Details of the individual course network security.

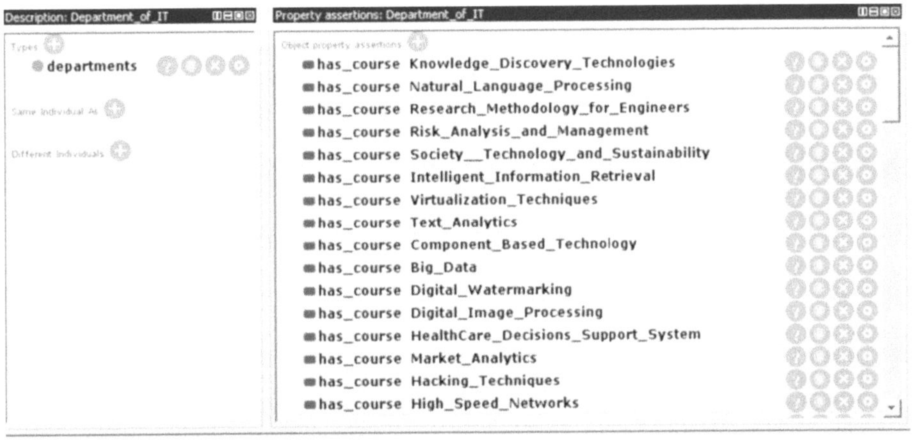

FIGURE 2.12 Details of the individual department.

2.2.5 Maintenance

When necessary, this activity aids in updating and correcting the ontology during the validation or post-implementation phases. Some tasks that are automatically included in any software product's maintenance phase include management tasks that support schedules and quality control, and support tasks that aid in documentation, assessment, integration, and knowledge acquisition.

2.3 VALIDATION AND EVALUATION OF ONTOLOGY

Since both steps are crucial to any development process, the final stage of ontology creation involves evaluating and validating the created ontology. While the validation step verifies if the created ontology is relevant and comprehensive, the evaluation criterion aids in determining the ontology's completeness and significance. This is the rationale for the ontology evaluation and validation processes. The amount of work required to validate and assess the ontology is determined by the size of the community it will serve and the ontology being built [16]. Ontology validation should always be done while the ontology is being developed, even though validation and evaluation can be done after completion of ontology.

A) **Criteria for Ontology Evaluation and Validation**: To assess the ontology, the following criteria were looked up:
   - Ontology ought to be accurate (correctness).
   - It must be efficacious (effective) and comprehensive (complete).
   - Very little redundancy (uniqueness), simple upkeep (maintainability).

The following criteria are checked as part of the ontology validation process:

- The ontology should be pertinent to the area of study (relevancy).
- The aim of the ontology development process should be achieved.
- The examples produced should have significance.
- The examples displayed should be comprehensible (suitable)
- The ontology must be consistent.
- It must be precise, strong, succinct, and comprehensive (quality).

2.4 COURSE MODELLING

This study focuses primarily on the documentation of knowledge generation, storage, and reuse in other applications. It addresses the product-centred view of knowledge dispersed in CS. Course modelling is a suggestion to promote the knowledge development of individual learners by providing the necessary information sources in an appropriate format. It also aims to explain, formalize, and document domain knowledge to make it available as a sort of tangible resource.

The unique software support for various approaches to knowledge management is explained in Figure 2.13 [17]. In addition to improving a domain's structural capacity, this shift from implicit (intangible) to explicit (tangible) knowledge modelling in the form of specific standards also fosters greater flexibility and creativity.

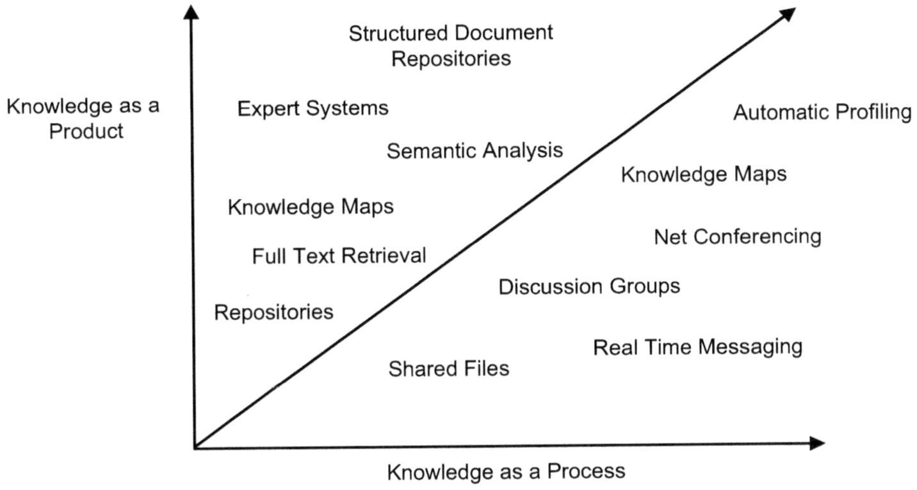

FIGURE 2.13 Knowledge management approaches.

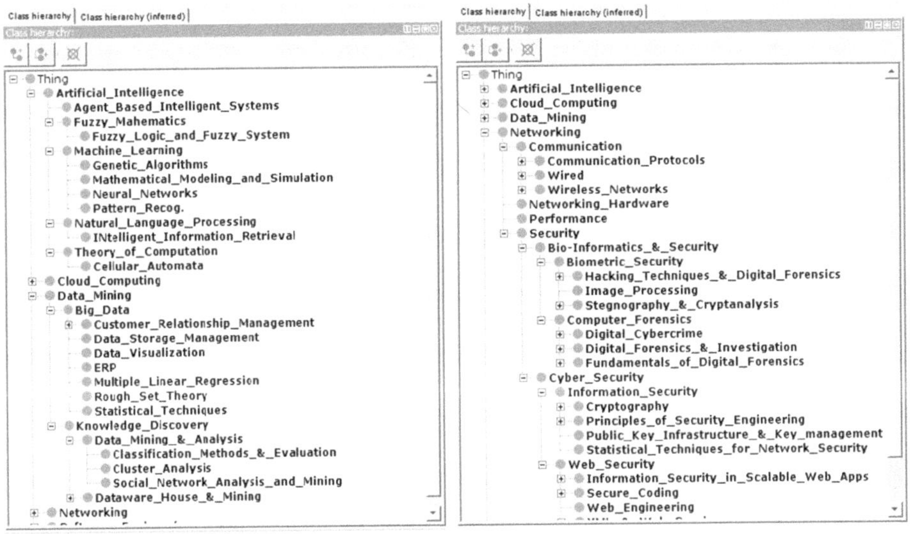

FIGURE 2.14 Conceptual hierarchy of CS domain.

Developing ontologies involves bringing the concept of relations and their attributes together with the domain concepts in a hierarchical fashion. The ontology will explain how the courses in the domain relate to one another, and Protégé has utilized the OWL format to represent this ontology. Figure 2.14 displays some of the primary domains in the discipline of CS.

The research study done by Nur et al., In the context of e-learning, focuses on the creation and assessment of ontology-based recommender systems. Although ontology and knowledge-based frameworks often assist these systems, there hasn't been much in the way of thorough investigation and methodical examination of ontology use in them. The purpose of this study is to investigate the development and evaluation of recommender systems for online learning, with a focus on the function and significance of ontologies in these systems [18]. Therefore, one of the primary elements of the suggested recommended system, which will aid in giving the student a better grasp of the subject of interest, is the course ontology.

The domain expert will establish the relationships between the courses after applying ontology rules to the database's courses. Once the relationships are completed, these linkages can be made stronger or weaker, and the same ontology rules can be applied to additional domains. Table 2.6 illustrates how ontology is crucial for simply monitoring the domain concept with the aid of a knowledge model to navigate the many domain courses that are available and provides additional course caution that is suggested by the system. Because the semantic web primarily focuses on the domain concept and relationship, ontology-based applications are essential components. Protégé is now the most widely used tool for developing domain ontologies. Developing ontology and the connections between ideas is the domain expert's job. These are the fundamental requirements for creating ontology inside a domain. Although all relationships should be established beforehand, their nature should be changeable, and it is evident that the course model that is created offers a deeper comprehension of the domain.

Similarly, we can extend the working of the ontology module to create ontology for the learner also. The module intends to collect data about the learner during the registration process to create the learner's profile as shown in Figure 2.15.

TABLE 2.6
OntoGraf Generation for Domain Ontology

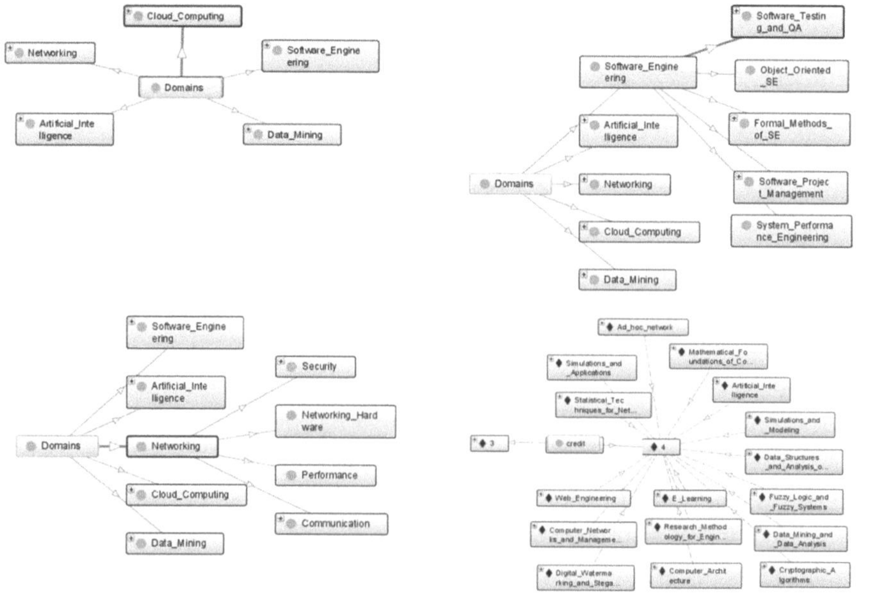

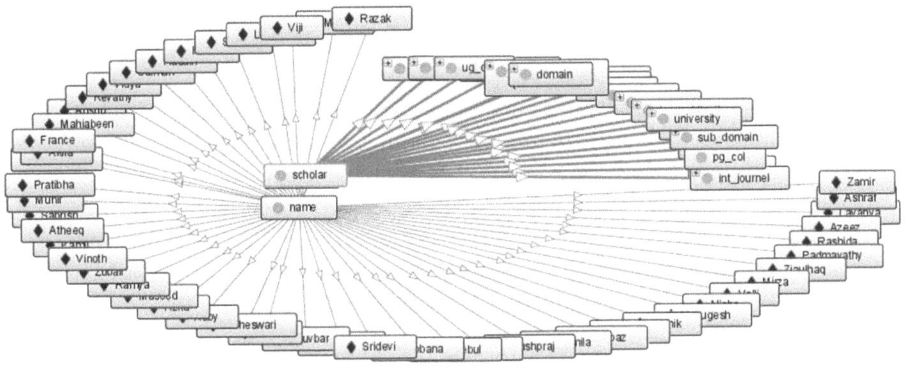

FIGURE 2.15 Learner's OntoGraf.

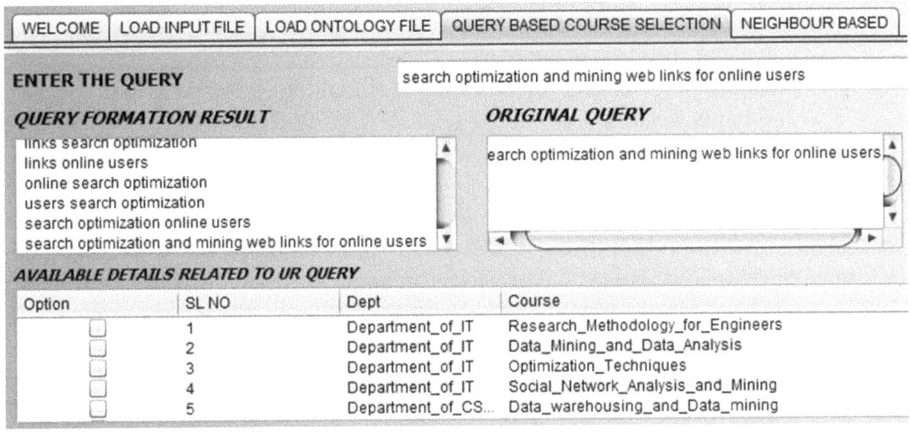

FIGURE 2.16 Recommendation result for hybrid approach.

As seen in Figure 2.16, we used ontology development for building course recommendation system. The goal of any recommendation system is to improve precision and recall in order of relevance, and if relevance is raised, the time cost may be justified.

2.5 CONCLUSION

The chapter begins with an overview of ontology before focusing on its application to CS. The chapter offers a practical interpretation of the ontology, emphasizing its applicability and importance beyond the concept itself. This study has considered the ontology's reuse, sharing, continuity, and the kind of personalized support it will offer. There are still some topics in CS that can be added, even though most of them have already been scanned. Expanding the knowledge model by integrating concepts from the CS domain with other disciplines and applying them to specific applications would be a more intriguing idea. With the intention of offering a knowledge model for the field. The goal of providing a knowledge model for the CS domain is to help learners better grasp the subject. The model also contributes to the proposition that ontology can bridge the knowledge gap between explicit knowledge of modern classification and amorphous courses in a topic. The study made a non-obvious attempt to use semantic matching to associate sub-domains from different domains. A handful of the study's accomplishments are listed below.

- A CS domain ontology was established in addition to a proposed architectural methodology for ontology development.
- The plan for illustrating the domain model's progress and the assistance it will offer for course customization.
- The ontology was produced by the CS domain, which encompasses approximately 15 sub-domains and 5 primary domains, including networking, data mining, software engineering, cloud computing, and AI.
- The courses are formally organized into a hierarchy that describes a suitable domain model for CS and the relationships that connect the courses from all domains and sub-domains.
- The technique for generating ontology was iterative, which was essential to getting better results.

By automatically producing OWL code throughout the ontology creation process, the protege tool was utilized to represent knowledge about the CS domain. After development, the ontology was evaluated and validated using the built-in FACT++ reasoner to ensure consistency. Therefore, an attempt is being made in the current research work to frame the domain ontology for CS to enable the recommendation systems (RS) approach for e-learning personalization feature. The major domain and sub-domains that make up the created ontology will aid students in studying their domain in a more methodical manner. The created ontology is provided to the RS in order to assist in producing additional suggestions by examining the connections between the courses that are actually produced using the learner input query and in this way ontology can enhance the performance and satisfaction level of the learner.

By filtering the abstract composition of a domain, the ontology-based knowledge representation of a domain will be so strong that it will reveal the evolving framework. As a result, the development of ontologies in the field of CS will benefit present educational systems, as they may be used to personalize e-learning experiences and act as knowledge models. By giving the institutes a uniform policy for the efficient use of resource sharing, the ontology generated might be useful for their merger. The current thesis covers most of the domain courses in CS; some restrictions will be addressed in further work. The most notable is the dissemination of the knowledge model to various fields of education.

REFERENCES

[1] Z. Yajing, D. Jing, & T. Peng, "Ontology Classification for Semantic-Web-Based Software Engineering", *IEEE Transactions on Services Computing*, vol. 2(4), 303–317, 2009.

[2] J. H. Gyeong, J. H. Lee, & W. S. Hyo "Semantic Relation Based Personalized Ranking Approach for Engineering Document Retrieval", *Advanced Engineering Informatics*, vol.29 (3), pp.366–379, 2015.
[3] R. Huang, J.M. Spector, & J. Yang. Lecture Notes in Educational Technology. *Springer Nature Singapore*, 2019. DOI: 10.1007/978-981-13-6643-7
[4] ISO/IEC/IEEE International Standard. (2017). Systems and Software Engineering–Vocabulary (pp. 1–541). ISO/IEC/IEEE 24765. DOI: 10.1109/IEEESTD.2017.8016712. 2017(E)
[5] Z. Gulzar, R. L. Arun, & A.L. Leema. "Ontology Supported Hybrid Recommender System with Threshold based Nearest Neighborhood Approach", *International Journal of Information and Communication Technology Education*, Vol. 15 (2), pp. 85–107,(2019).
[6] L. Zhong, L. Deng, M. Liu, & Y. Jingling. "An Ontology Construction Method for Educational Domain," In *Proc. of the Fourth International Conference on Intelligent Systems Design and Engineering Applications*, 2013.
[7] D. M. Paola. "'Just Enough' Ontology Engineering", In *Proceedings of the International Conference on Web Intelligence, Mining and Semantics – IMS*, vol. 11, 2011.
[8] Z. Gulzar, & A.L. Anny. "A Framework for Recommender System to Provide Personalization in an E-learning System", *International Journal of Web based Learning and Teaching Technologies*, vol. 13(3), pp.51–68, 2018.
[9] H. Yumeng & S. Kenderdine. "Ontology-Based Knowledge Representation for Traditional Martial Arts", *Digital Scholarship in the Humanities*, 2024. DOI: 10.1093/llc/fqae005
[10] R.I. Kovalev, V.V. Gribova, & D.B. Okun, "Ontology of Knowledge Representation About the Prescribed Personalized Treatment", *Ontology of Designing*, vol. 13(2), pp. 192–203. 2023. DOI: 10.18287/2223-9537-2023-13-2-192-203
[11] A. Bashir, R. Nagpal, D. Mehrotra, & M. Bala, "Knowledge Representation and Information Retrieval From Ontologies", In: Kumar, R., Verma, A.K., Sharma, T.K., Verma, O.P., & Sharma, S. (eds) *Soft Computing: Theories and Applications. Lecture Notes in Networks and Systems*, vol 627. Springer, 2023. DOI: 10.1007/978-981-19-9858-4_65
[12] O. Tkachenko, K. Tkachenko, O. Tkachenko, & M. Astafieva, "Ontological Modeling of Intelligent Learning Systems With Elements of Gamification", *Cybersecurity Providing in Information and Telecommunication Systems*, vol. 3421, pp. 25–35, 2023.
[13] M. Yahya, R. George, & A. Alfaries. "Ontologies in E-Learning: Review of the Literature", *International Journal of Software Engineering and Its Applications*, vol. 9(2), pp.67–84, 2015.
[14] F. Ahlam Sawsaa, & J. Lu. "Building an Advance Domain Ontology Model of Information Science (OIS)", *International Journal of Digital Information and Wireless Communications*, vol. 4(2), pp. 258–266, 2014.
[15] N.F. Noy, & D.L. McGuiness. Ontology Development 101: A Guide to Creating Your First Ontology, Stanford Knowledge Systems Laboratory Technical Report KSL, pp.1–5, 2001.
[16] B. Kenneth, & N. Tianhua. *Ontology for Bioinformatics*, MIT Press, 2006.
[17] S. Steffen, & R. Studer. *Handbook on Ontologies, International Handbooks on Information Systems*, Second Edition, Springer –Verlag, 2009.
[18] W. Nur Rahayu, R. Ferdiana, & S. S. Kusuma Wardani. "A systematic review of ontology use in E-Learning recommender system", *Computers and Education: Artificial Intelligence*, vol.3, p. 100047, 2022.

Part II

Using AI to the Advantages of Fog Computing

3 Security and Privacy Analysis Using AI-Based Machine Learning Methods

P. William, Pravin B. Khatkale, Vishal Tidake and Shrikaant Kulkarni

3.1 INTRODUCTION

In the contemporary landscape of data-driven decision-making, the identification and mitigation of anomalies play a pivotal role across diverse domains. Anomalies, often characterized by unexpected patterns, outliers, or irregularities within datasets, can hold critical information about unusual events or potential issues. The ubiquity of anomalies spans various sectors, including but not limited to cybersecurity, industrial processes, healthcare, and finance. As a consequence, the development and deployment of robust anomaly detection methods have become imperative for ensuring the reliability, security, and efficiency of systems and processes. This comprehensive survey aims to delve into the expansive realm of machine learning (ML) techniques employed for anomaly identification, offering a deep exploration of methodologies, applications, and challenges in this burgeoning field. The scope of this survey encompasses a wide range of ML paradigms, including supervised, unsupervised, and semi-supervised learning approaches. Understanding anomalies in data is a multifaceted task, requiring innovative solutions to discern subtle deviations from expected norms [1].

The survey begins by elucidating the fundamental concepts of anomaly detection and its significance in real-world scenarios. We navigate through the intricacies of supervised learning methods, where labeled datasets aid in training models to identify anomalies based on known patterns. Unsupervised learning, on the other hand, explores the challenge of anomaly detection without explicit labels, relying on the inherent structure of data to reveal irregularities. Semi-supervised approaches strike a balance between the two, leveraging both labeled and unlabeled data for enhanced anomaly identification. The review extends beyond conventional methods to encapsulate recent advancements and emerging trends in anomaly detection. We explore the synergy between feature engineering and ML, examining how the extraction of

DOI: 10.1201/9781032703718-5

informative features contributes to the effectiveness of anomaly identification models. Moreover, we dissect the applications of anomaly detection in cybersecurity, industrial processes, healthcare, and finance, shedding light on the diverse use cases that underscore the importance of accurate anomaly identification in these critical domains [2].

Evaluating the performance of anomaly detection models is a crucial aspect, and the survey investigates commonly employed metrics and benchmarks for assessing the efficacy of various methods. Challenges inherent in anomaly identification, such as imbalanced datasets, evolving patterns, and interpretability issues, are also thoroughly examined. By synthesizing a wealth of knowledge, this survey aims to serve as a comprehensive resource for researchers, practitioners, and enthusiasts seeking to navigate the evolving landscape of ML for anomaly identification. The subsequent sections delve into the nuances of each ML paradigm, providing an in-depth analysis of techniques, methodologies, and their respective applications, ultimately contributing to the advancement of anomaly detection in an era dominated by data-driven decision-making. As our world becomes increasingly interconnected and reliant on data-driven technologies, the ability to identify and address anomalies within datasets has become a critical component of ensuring the integrity, security, and efficiency of systems across diverse domains. Anomalies, characterized by deviations, irregularities, or unexpected patterns within data, can signify potential threats, inefficiencies, or previously undiscovered insights. This survey embarks on a comprehensive exploration of the myriad ML methods designed for anomaly identification, delving into their applications, challenges, and innovations [3].

3.1.1 Anomalies in the Data Landscape

The ubiquity of anomalies spans various sectors, from cybersecurity to finance, healthcare, and industrial processes. Understanding and effectively detecting anomalies is crucial for pre-emptively addressing issues or uncovering hidden patterns that may have far-reaching consequences. Whether it's the identification of malicious activities in cybersecurity, the detection of faults in industrial machinery, or the discovery of rare diseases in healthcare datasets, anomaly identification has become an indispensable tool for decision-makers navigating complex and dynamic data landscapes.

3.1.2 The Evolution of Anomaly Detection Techniques

This survey traverses the evolutionary path of anomaly detection methods, from traditional statistical approaches to the current dominance of ML paradigms. In the early stages, statistical methods relied on predefined thresholds and assumed data distributions, often struggling with complex, high-dimensional datasets. With the advent of ML, especially in the era of big data, the field witnessed a paradigm shift. ML algorithms brought a data-driven, adaptive approach to anomaly detection, empowering systems to learn from the data itself, identifying anomalies even in the absence of explicit rules or labeled instances.

3.1.3 Diverse Approaches to Anomaly Identification

The subsequent exploration navigates through the intricacies of ML methodologies for anomaly identification. The survey diverges into three distinct paths – supervised learning, unsupervised learning, and semi-supervised learning – each offering unique insights and challenges. In supervised learning, models are trained on labeled datasets, allowing them to recognize anomalies based on known patterns. Unsupervised learning, in contrast, explores the subtleties of anomaly detection without explicit labels, relying on the inherent structure of the data to reveal irregularities. Semi-supervised approaches bridge these two paradigms, leveraging both labeled and unlabeled data to enhance anomaly identification in scenarios where obtaining labeled data is challenging or expensive [4].

This exploration extends beyond conventional methods to embrace recent advancements and emerging trends. The synergy between feature engineering and ML is dissected, showcasing how the extraction of informative features contributes to the effectiveness of anomaly identification models. The survey further illuminates the applications of anomaly detection in various sectors, offering a nuanced understanding of the diverse use cases that underscore the importance of accurate anomaly identification in critical domains. This introductory section sets the stage for an in-depth journey into the landscape of ML methods for anomaly identification. The subsequent sections will unravel the intricacies of each ML paradigm, providing a granular analysis of techniques, methodologies, and their applications. This survey aims to not only chronicle the current state of the field but also contribute to its evolution, fostering a deeper understanding of anomaly detection in an era where data is a linchpin for informed decision-making [5].

3.2 REVIEW OF LITERATURE

The degree to which a product deviates or degenerates from the performance that is anticipated to be completed during its typical operating performance is what determines the product's overall health. The phrase "typical operation" is being used in the context of this discussion to refer to the anticipated situations that are associated with the product's physical characteristics or its functionality. Finding changes in the product's behavior that seem to be healthy is one of the most important stages that must be taken in order to achieve prognostics and health management (PHM). In addition to this, it is of the utmost importance to have a thorough understanding of the origin of any potential product defects. In everyday parlance, the process that was just described is referred to as "anomaly detection." The primary objectives of this chapter are to present a comprehensive review of the research that has been conducted on anomaly detection and to investigate the problems that still need to be addressed in this area of study. Over the course of the past several decades, PHM has been the subject of investigation by the electronics industry, which has been doing research on a broad variety of anomaly detection systems [6].

Abnormal behavior is a phenomenon that often manifests itself across a wide variety of network types. A few examples of this include unexpected traffic jams on road networks, accidents involving automobiles, hacking of decentralized video surveillance systems, assaults, and huge data transfers over IP networks. Those are only a few examples among many more. Using methods from ML, it is feasible to develop non-parametric, cross-application anomaly detection algorithms. These algorithms are able to adapt to changes in the characteristics of usual behavior in the linked network. It is possible for these algorithms to identify probable irregularities in a broad variety of computer networks using their capabilities. Finding anomalies may be accomplished by the use of these methods in a broad variety of contexts. This research illustrates the applicability of two distinct ML algorithms to the discovery of network anomalies by using two separate datasets. These datasets include IP traffic statistics from the Abilene network as well as photographs of a highway in Quebec that were recorded by a camera network. Both of these datasets were collected via a camera network's efforts. All of these datasets came from a single network, which was the only network that existed. The use of these two datasets provides evidence that demonstrates the effectiveness of these techniques. In addition, we investigate the possibility of merging the block-based One-Class Neighbor Machine methods with the recursive Kernel-based Online Anomaly Detection approaches that were discussed in the previous section [7].

A significant amount of research has been conducted on the vital subject of anomaly detection, with contributions coming from a wide range of academic fields as well as enterprises that directly use their findings in the real world. The purpose of this investigation is to accomplish two goals. The first thing that it does is provide a comprehensive and well-organized summary of the research methods that are used in the deep learning-based anomaly detection methodology. In addition, we investigate the appropriateness of a wide range of strategies for anomaly classification in a variety of application situations and assess the effectiveness of these particular procedures. It is possible to split contemporary research tactics for deep anomaly detection into a number of different categories, and these categories are determined by the underlying presumptions and procedures that are used in each individual instance. The purpose of this website is to offer visitors with an overview of the primary anomaly detection approach, its modifications, and the underlying presumptions for each category. This will assist readers in distinguishing between behavior that is considered normal and behavior that is considered abnormal. In addition to this, we discuss the computational challenges that are brought about by the use of the approaches in real-world scenarios, as well as the benefits and drawbacks associated with each category. We finish this work with an overview of the current research directions and the challenges encountered along the process of deploying deep anomaly detection systems in real-world applications. Furthermore, we discuss the implications of these findings [8].

Occurrences that deviate from the majority of the regular patterns that are seen are considered to be "uncommon events" according to any dataset that is being considered. Instances that might fall under this category include any suspected instances of fraud, intrusion, odd conduct, or strange occurrences. The circumstances of the situation will determine whether or not these events are beneficial to the domain application. There is also the possibility that they have a substantial amount of information stored inside them. Any event that is considered to be out of the ordinary might be included in this list of occurrences. These actions are referred to as anomalies, and it is of the utmost importance to recognize them since they may be indicators of a cyberattack, the propagation of an infection, a terrorist assault, a sudden change in sales, or any other kind of network intrusion. It is possible that these anomalies may be identified via the use of anomaly detection techniques. Identifying anomalies may be accomplished by the use of a wide variety of methodologies, such as information-theoretic, graph, statistical, nearest neighbor, statistical, and spectral methods. Through a comprehensive and exhaustive approach, the purpose of this research is to offer an overview of all anomaly detection methods that are currently being utilized. In light of the fact that data from the actual world is not always easily available, it is necessary to take into account a wide range of factors while selecting the most efficient automated decision-making approach. It is possible to take into consideration a great number of variables, including domain knowledge, the kind of anomaly of interest, input and output data, and an assortment of other factors [9].

For a considerable amount of time, methods for anomaly detection have been used in order to locate and isolate data that does not closely like the typical data. Finding anomalies has been accomplished via the use of a variety of methods. One of the numerous tactics that are becoming more significant in this industry is ML, which is becoming more relevant because of its growing significance. A better understanding of their relevance is beginning to emerge. A Systematic Literature Review (SLR) of ML models is carried out by us in order to identify any discrepancies in the use or utilization of these models in order to provide assistance with this research endeavor. The following four perspectives are taken into consideration while analyzing the models in order to enhance our investigation: classifications for anomaly detection, techniques for ML, assessments of the performance of ML models, and applications for anomaly detection are all included in this collection. Following an exhaustive investigation, we discovered 290 research articles that were published between the years 2000 and 2020 and that investigated the use of ML techniques for anomaly identification. Scholarly journals were the venues for the publication of these pieces. The scholarly journals were the venues for the dissemination of these materials. When we have completed our study of the selected research papers, we will provide 43 distinct applications for anomaly detection that we discovered in the research articles that were chosen. In addition to this, we identify the 29 distinct iterations of ML models that were used during the process of anomaly identification. In order to make the process of locating anomalies easier, a great number of models were developed. To summarize, we provide a total of 22 distinct datasets to support our research, in addition to a large number of generic datasets that are used in the process of anomaly identification. In addition, we show that researchers have shown a preference for unsupervised anomaly detection tactics rather than categorized anomaly detection approaches. There are a great number of ML models that have been used by researchers, and there is a great deal of room for more research into the identification of anomalies via the utilization of ML models. It is the findings of our evaluation that serve as the basis for the suggestions and advice that we provide to academics [10–11].

3.3 UNSUPERVISED LEARNING METHODS FOR ANOMALY IDENTIFICATION

When it comes to anomaly detection, unsupervised learning approaches are crucial for discovering intriguing patterns in data. These techniques eliminate the need for tagged samples inside the process. In the course of this inquiry, the basic concepts and methods of unsupervised learning for anomaly detection are investigated. The purpose of this investigation is to understand how these approaches discover variances and irregularities in datasets in order to identify prospective anomalies. Clustering is a basic concept in unsupervised learning for anomaly detection. In this process, computers classify data points into distinct groups based on the similarities or differences between them. It is because of the very nature of anomalies that they often exhibit characteristics that are distinct from the majority of the data, which results in their being separated from typical clusters. It is possible to discover these outliers by using unsupervised clustering techniques such as k-means, hierarchical clustering, and DBSCAN. These techniques are designed to locate data points that do not fit into any distinct cluster. In unsupervised anomaly detection, dimensionality reduction is an important method that aims to represent high-dimensional data in a lower-dimensional space while preserving essential information. The goal of this strategy is to achieve both of these objectives. It is possible that anomalies may emerge as outliers in this reduced-dimensional space, which will make them more obvious and observable. Methods such as t-distributed Stochastic Neighbor Embedding (t-SNE), autoencoders, and principal component analysis (PCA) are used often for the purpose of dimensionality reduction and anomaly detection [12–15].

Density estimation is yet another well-known method for the detection of anomalies without the need for human supervision. In this method, computers mimic the probability distribution of the data and identify data points with a low likelihood of being anomalous. Particularly useful in detecting sparse regions or clusters in the data that may be indicators of anomalies are density-based approaches such as Gaussian Mixture Models (GMM), kernel density estimation, and isolation forest. These techniques are based on the statistical concept of density. Furthermore, novelty detection algorithms strive to uncover data points that vary significantly from the distribution of training data. This is done without precisely naming any abnormalities that may be the result of the methodology. An example of this would be a one-class support vector machine (SVM), which is able to learn a representation of typical data points and then label as abnormal any samples that differ from this model. In a similar line, generative adversarial networks, often known as Generative Adversarial Networks (GANs), may be used to identify anomalies that are departures from the learned distribution of data. Unsupervised anomaly detection approaches, on the other hand, are dependent on a variety of criteria, including the representativeness and quality of the data, the selection of appropriate algorithms, and the definition of an abnormality. When analyzing and fine-tuning unsupervised anomaly detection algorithms, it is often required to make use of domain expertise and recurrent testing in order to achieve findings that are satisfactory [16–18].

Through the course of this inquiry, the groundwork has been built for a better understanding of the concepts and processes involved in unsupervised learning for anomaly identification. By delving deeper into specific algorithms, approaches, and practical applications, it becomes abundantly clear that unsupervised learning techniques offer a powerful toolkit for identifying anomalies in a variety of datasets. This has implications for a number of different domains, including predictive maintenance, cybersecurity, fraud detection, and others. Figure 3.1 that you present seems to be intended to provide a summary of a research that was conducted on the use of ML methods for anomaly detection. An in-depth paragraph that provides more explanation of the concepts presented is offered below. The process of locating anomalies is an essential step in the field of data analysis, and it often results in the acquisition of valuable insights into areas such as the identification of fraudulent activity and the monitoring of system health. The diagram presents an ordered description of unsupervised learning strategies for anomaly detection, beginning with the basic notions of unsupervised learning and progressing to the more advanced techniques. It is essential that this kind of learning has the ability to recognize patterns and irregularities in data without the need for examples that have labels attached to them. Anomaly

FIGURE 3.1 Navigating the complexity of unsupervised learning approaches for anomaly detection.

detection is the second primary topic of the figure, and it is concerned with locating outliers, which are data points that are unusual and may suggest fraud, errors, or new discoveries. This is accomplished by using deviations from the norm [19–20].

Figure 3.1, which examines the different types of data, demonstrates the versatility of unsupervised techniques in handling a variety of data sources. This is accomplished by acknowledging the diversity of data structures, which includes temporal patterns in time-series data as well as unstructured or structured data. Autoencoders, which are neural networks that can reconstruct data while distinguishing anomalies, and k-means clustering, which organizes data to identify unusual groups, are two examples of the essential methods and algorithms that are the primary emphasis of the map. There are many more examples. PCA, which is helpful for decreasing dimensionality and exposing outliers, is another approach that has received interest in recent years. As shown in Figure 3.1, it may be challenging to differentiate between noise and actual abnormalities, especially in high-dimensional data sets where traditional distance measures are inefficient. It is essential to be aware of the challenges and considerations that are involved in the use of these methodologies. Lastly, the map provides empirical proof for the theoretical concepts by presenting case studies and real-world implementations of unsupervised anomaly detection. These examples highlight the importance of the methodologies. Not only do these applications validate the methodologies, but they also highlight the vast potential of unsupervised learning to give valuable insights across a broad variety of industries. A comprehensive overview of the breadth and depth of unsupervised learning approaches for anomaly detection is provided by the whole image. This paves the way for further study and developments in the field of anomaly detection.

3.4 RESEARCH METHODOLOGY

This survey employs a systematic and comprehensive approach to explore the landscape of ML methods for anomaly identification. The methodology involves an extensive review of scholarly articles, research papers, and conference proceedings spanning a significant timeframe. The search strategy involves utilizing reputable academic databases, including but not limited to IEEE Xplore, PubMed, and Google Scholar. The search terms include variations of "anomaly detection," "machine learning," and relevant sub-domains such as "supervised learning," "unsupervised learning," and "semi-supervised learning." The inclusion criteria for selecting literature encompass studies that focus explicitly on ML techniques for anomaly identification across diverse domains. Additionally, recent publications and seminal works that have significantly contributed to the field are prioritized. The survey prioritizes a balanced representation of traditional and state-of-the-art methods, ensuring a comprehensive overview of the evolution of anomaly detection techniques. The selected literature is critically evaluated to extract key insights into the methodologies, applications, and challenges associated with each ML paradigm for anomaly identification. The goal is to synthesize a coherent narrative that not only highlights the existing knowledge but also identifies emerging trends and gaps in the current research landscape. Furthermore, to enhance the reliability and validity of the survey, rigorous attention is given to the quality and impact of the selected studies. Peer-reviewed articles and papers from reputable conferences are given precedence, and the survey aims to provide a holistic view by incorporating diverse perspectives from various research groups and institutions. The methodology adopted in this survey is designed to ensure a thorough and unbiased exploration of the state-of-the-art in ML methods for anomaly identification, providing a valuable resource for researchers, practitioners, and enthusiasts in this dynamic and evolving field [21–23].

3.4.1 Supervised Learning Approaches

Supervised learning methods, relying on labeled datasets, showcase significant effectiveness in identifying anomalies based on known patterns. The survey reveals that these approaches, often leveraging classification algorithms, excel in scenarios where anomalies can be explicitly defined. However, their dependency on labeled data poses challenges in domains where acquiring such data is expensive or impractical. Interpretability of models in supervised learning also emerges as a concern, as the intricacies of anomaly patterns may not be fully captured by predefined labels.

3.4.2 Unsupervised Learning Challenges and Opportunities

Unsupervised learning methods, operating without labeled data, present a unique set of challenges and opportunities. The survey indicates that these techniques, often grounded in clustering algorithms, excel in scenarios where the nature of anomalies is unknown or rapidly evolving. However, the lack of explicit labels can lead to ambiguity in results, requiring careful interpretation. Novelty detection within unsupervised methods proves promising for scenarios where anomalies represent unprecedented patterns, but their robustness in handling complex, high-dimensional data remains an area of exploration.

3.4.3 Semi-Supervised Learning

The survey underscores the pivotal role of semi-supervised learning, combining elements of both supervised and unsupervised paradigms. This approach proves valuable in scenarios where obtaining labeled data is challenging yet beneficial. The findings indicate that semi-supervised methods strike a balance, offering improved performance compared to purely unsupervised techniques. However, challenges persist in determining the optimal ratio of labeled to unlabeled data, highlighting the need for fine-tuned models.

3.4.4 Feature Engineering and Model Performance

The synergy between feature engineering and ML models emerges as a critical aspect of anomaly identification. The survey identifies that informative feature extraction significantly contributes to the robustness of models. Techniques such as dimensionality reduction and the creation of domain-specific features prove instrumental in enhancing the discriminatory power of models. However, the challenge lies in identifying relevant features in diverse datasets, emphasizing the need for domain expertise and adaptive feature engineering strategies.

3.4.5 Real-World Applications and Challenges

The analysis of real-world applications in cybersecurity, industrial processes, healthcare, and finance showcases the versatility of anomaly detection. The survey highlights successful implementations, such as intrusion detection in cybersecurity and fault detection in industrial machinery. However, challenges, including imbalanced datasets and evolving patterns, underscore the need for adaptive models capable of addressing the dynamic nature of anomalies in these domains.

3.5 RESULT AND DISCUSSION

This analysis of anomaly detection ML methods provides a comprehensive overview of the current state of the field, illuminating a wide range of approaches, applications, and challenges that are currently being faced. A number of significant findings have shown that supervised, unsupervised, and semi-supervised learning paradigms interact in a dynamic manner, with each paradigm presenting its own set of benefits and problems. In situations when the anomalies are well specified and labeled datasets are used for the purpose of model training, supervised learning approaches work effectively. On the other hand, interpretability becomes a challenge in domains where it is difficult to obtain data that has been accurately classified. Considering that it does not need labeled data, unsupervised learning is advantageous in situations when the nature of anomalies is not evident or when they are changing rapidly. The lack of obvious identifiers, on the other hand, generates confusion and calls for careful evaluation. There is a need for more study to maintain resilience in complex data, despite the fact that novelty detection in unsupervised systems has the ability to manage irregularities that have never been seen before. Semi-supervised learning is an essential method that manages to achieve a balance between data that has been tagged and data that has not been labeled.

Although the performance of this technique is superior to that of unsupervised approaches, it does need the use of the most effective strategies in order to make the most of the labeled data that is currently accessible. Strong anomaly detection highlights the need for feature engineering and ML models working together to get the desired results. The performance of the model is significantly influenced by techniques such as the development of domain-specific features and the reduction of dimensionality. The application of feature engineering approaches to various datasets continues to be fraught with difficulties, notwithstanding the previous statement. The versatility of anomaly detection is shown by its practical applications in many different fields, including cybersecurity, manufacturing, healthcare, and finance. Even though there are several instances of successful implementations, adaptive models are required in order to solve problems such as datasets that are not balanced and trends that are always shifting. Quantitative insights into the performance of the model are supplied by assessment metrics like accuracy, recall, and F1-score. Additionally, comparative analysis is made easier by benchmarking against existing datasets. In spite of this, there is a need for uniform standards that truly represent the complexity of the real world. The integration of deep learning, the exploration of model interpretability, and the identification of anomalies in streaming data are some of the new themes that will provide fascinating prospects for research in the future. In order to make appropriate developments in the scientific field, it is widely understood that it is necessary to address ethical concerns such as bias and fairness with urgency. Currently, the results of the survey provide a comprehensive picture of the current state of anomaly detection via the use of ML algorithms. The findings give scholars, practitioners, and enthusiasts knowledge that is both informative and useful, and they drive future advancements in this very important and dynamic area. A comprehensive description of the ML algorithms that may be used for anomaly detection, as shown in Figure 3.2. The objective of this image is to highlight a number of performance characteristics that were identified via a number of different studies. The metrics include the following indicators: CPU execution time, Equal Error Rate (EER), Mean Squared Error (MSE), Precision-Recall, testing time, F-Score, Precision, Accuracy (ACC), False Positive Rate (FPR), True Negative Rate (TPR), Receiver Operating Characteristic (ROC) Area, and True Negative Rate (TNR). The implementation of these measures encompasses a number of the most essential components of the model evaluation. Additionally, a new category that has been introduced and given the name "Others" has been included in order to include any other relevant metrics that have not been specifically addressed.

A comprehensive summary of each measure's relevance and appropriateness for assessing the efficacy of anomaly detection models is provided by the fact that each measure is connected to the number of relevant trials in which it was analyzed. The fact that multiple indications are included demonstrates how complicated the process

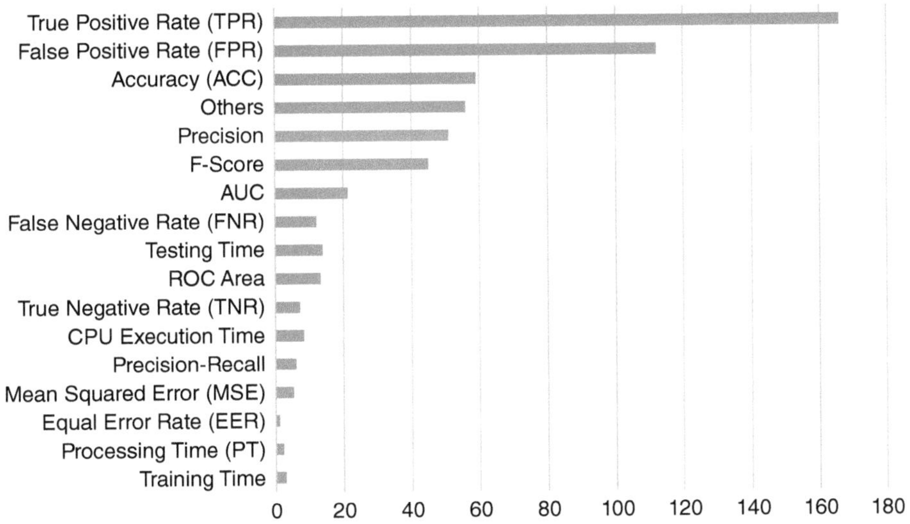

FIGURE 3.2 Comparative analysis of ML techniques for anomaly detection: Evaluation metrics overview.

of anomaly detection is. As a result, it is vital to have a complete evaluation plan in order to verify how effectively ML algorithms identify irregularities in a timely and accurate manner. Figure 3.2 is a helpful resource that can be used by both academics and practitioners in the field of anomaly detection in order to assist them in making well-informed judgments on the selection and optimization of ML algorithms based on certain performance criteria. By taking into account a wide variety of metrics, interested parties may be able to acquire a more in-depth comprehension of the benefits and drawbacks associated with a variety of strategies. This, in turn, will ultimately lead to an improvement in the development and implementation of anomaly detection systems in a wide range of fields and applications. An in-depth investigation of the distribution of ML algorithms that are utilized to perform anomaly detection tasks as shown in Figure 3.3 are categorized into four distinct groups: unsupervised, supervised, semi-supervised, and hybrid combinations of different learning paradigms. Two-eighths of the techniques that were investigated make use of unsupervised learning, which is the highest proportion. The fact that these approaches do not depend on labeled data and instead search for irregularities solely based on the structure of the dataset makes them particularly effective in circumstances in which labeled anomalies are difficult to find or not accessible at all. The supervised learning approaches, which make use of labeled training data to discover patterns and create predictions, are used by 17% of the technologies that were investigated. Training models that are able to consistently discern between the two classes are accomplished via the use of supervised methods. These models are trained using tagged examples of both normal and aberrant activity.

These semi-supervised learning strategies, which use labeled and unlabeled data for the purpose of training, make up 4% of the approaches that were surveyed within the study. In circumstances when getting labeled data is either difficult or expensive, these strategies enable models to make use of a large number of unlabeled instances in conjunction with a small number of anomalies that have been found. This allows for improved performance in terms of accuracy. In addition to this, the research

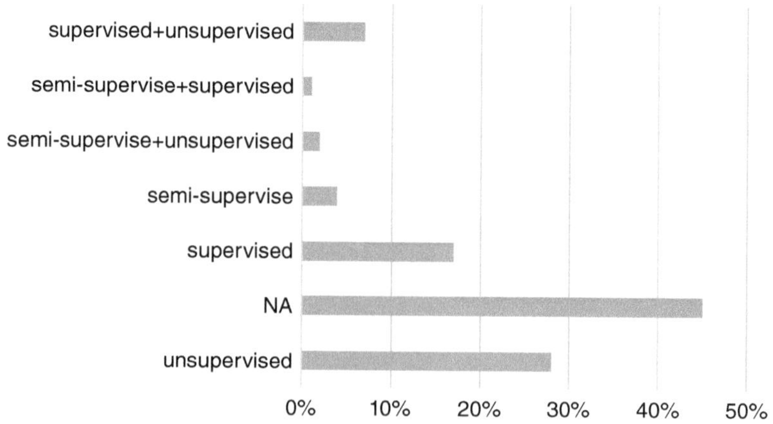

FIGURE 3.3 Machine learning methods for anomaly identification.

investigates hybrid methods, which combine a number of different learning paradigms. Figure 3.3 illustrates a number of hybrid combinations, including supervised with unsupervised approaches representing 7% of the total, supervised with unsupervised methods representing 2% of the whole, and semi-supervised with supervised methods representing 1% of the total. The purpose of these hybrid tactics is to take advantage of the capabilities of a wide variety of learning paradigms via synergistic integration, which may ultimately result in enhanced anomaly detection overall performance. A total of 45% of the strategies that were evaluated are included in the "NA" group. This group represents circumstances in which the learning paradigm was either not stated or could not be determined based on the information that was supplied.

3.5.1 Discussion

A summary of the most important survey findings is provided in the discussion section, which also draws attention to the dynamic interaction that exists between supervised, unsupervised, and semi-supervised learning paradigms in the context of anomaly detection. Our discussion includes both the positive and negative aspects of each approach, as well as an emphasis on the significance of feature engineering in terms of enhancing model performance. Through the use of real-world implementations, a wide range of use cases for anomaly detection spanning significant domains are shown, and evaluation metrics provide quantitative information about the efficiency of the models. Benchmarking processes enable practitioners and researchers to identify the most effective ML approaches for applications that include anomaly detection. They do this by making comparison analysis easier to do. For the purpose of future exploration, novel methodologies, such as merging deep learning with anomaly detection in real-time data, give exciting paths to pursue. For the purpose of making ethical advancements in the field, it is widely understood that ethical considerations, such as fairness and bias, are particularly important. When everything is taken into consideration, the discussion provides a compelling narrative that not only enhances our understanding of anomaly detection via the use of ML methods but also paves the way for innovation in new fields of research and development.

3.6 CONCLUSION

Anomaly detection is a subject that is continually growing and is crucial to the efficiency and security of many different industries, according to the conclusion of the article. An accurate anomaly detection system that is also flexible enough to accept freshly developed and changing information is something that the study acknowledges as being challenging to design. While ML does give a good foundation for anomaly detection, it is important to note that there is always a need for unique approaches that are able to handle the challenges of high-dimensional data and deliver results that are understandable. A multidisciplinary approach that takes into account domain expertise is required, according to the results of the poll, in order to push the boundaries of anomaly detection technologies. In conclusion, the essay argues for further research to be conducted on ethical concerns and pledges to ensure that anomaly detection algorithms are both unbiased and reliable.

REFERENCES

1. Wang, G., Liu, C. and Cui, Y. (2012). Clustering diagnosis of rolling element bearing fault based on integrated autoregressive/autoregressive conditional heteroscedasticity model. *Journal of Sound and Vibration* 331(19): 4379–4387.
2. Zhang, Z. and Kusiak, A. (2012). Monitoring wind turbine vibration based on SCADA data. *Journal of Solar Energy Engineering* 134 (2): 1–12.
3. Du, M., Tjernberg, L.B., Ma, S. et al. (2016). A SOM based anomaly detection method for wind turbines health management through SCADA data. *International Journal of Prognostics and Health Management* 7: 1–13.
4. Sutrisno, E., Fan, Q., Das, D. and Pecht, M. (2012). Anomaly detection for insulated gate bipolar transistor under power cycling using principal component analysis and k-nearest neighbor algorithm. *Journal of the Washington Academy of Sciences* 98 (1): 1–8.
5. Box, G.E.P. and Cox, D.R. (1964). An analysis of transformations. *Journal of the Royal Statistical Society* 26(2): 211–252.
6. P. William, A. Agrawal, N. Rawat, A. Shrivastava, A. P. Srivastava and Ashish (2023). Enterprise human resource management model by artificial intelligence digital technology. In *2023 4th International Conference on Computation, Automation and Knowledge Management (ICCAKM)*, Dubai, United Arab Emirates, pp. 01–06. DOI: 10.1109/ICCAKM58659.2023.10449624
7. P. William, A. Panicker, A. Falah, A. Hussain, A. Shrivastava and A. K. Khan (2023). The emergence of artificial intelligence and machine learning in contemporary business management. In *2023 4th International Conference on Computation, Automation and Knowledge Management (ICCAKM)*, Dubai, United Arab Emirates, pp. 1–6. DOI: 10.1109/ICCAKM58659.2023.10449493
8. P. William, G. Sharma, K. Kapil, P. Srivastava, A. Shrivastava and R. Kumar (2023). Automation techniques using AI based cloud computing and blockchain for business management. In *2023 4th International Conference on Computation, Automation and Knowledge Management (ICCAKM)*, Dubai, United Arab Emirates, pp. 1–6. DOI: 10.1109/ICCAKM58659.2023.10449534
9. A. R. More, O. B. Shendkar, K. G. Pathak, P. D. Sanap, S. N. Pachore and P. William (2023). Survey on framework for governing modern cyber attacks in computer network. In *2023 4th International Conference on Computation, Automation and Knowledge Management (ICCAKM)*, Dubai, United Arab Emirates, pp. 01–06. DOI: 10.1109/ICCAKM58659.2023.10449582
10. C. Nayak, P. William, R. Kumar, A. Deepak, K. Yadav, A. L. N. Rao, A. Srivastava, and A. Shrivastava (2024). Edge cloud server deployment with machine learning for 6G Internet of Things. *International Journal of Intelligent Systems and Applications in Engineering*, 12(16s), 328. https://ijisae.org/index.php/IJISAE/article/view/4826
11. S. K. Hegde, P. William, M. S. Basvant, A. Deepak, A. Badhoutiya, A. L. N. Rao, A. Srivastava and A. Shrivastava (2024). Energy-efficient bio-inspired hybrid deep learning model for network intrusion detection based on intelligent decision making. *International Journal of Intelligent Systems and Applications in Engineering*, 12(16s), 306. https://ijisae.org/index.php/IJISAE/article/view/4823
12. R. Rawat, S. Telang, P. William, U. Kaur and O. K. Cu (Eds.). (2022). *Dark Web Pattern Recognition and Crime Analysis Using Machine Intelligence*. IGI Global.
13. N. Yogeesh and P. William (2024). Sensor-enabled biomedical decision support system using deep learning and fuzzy logic. In *Advances in Ubiquitous Sensing Applications for Healthcare, Deep Learning Applications in Translational Bioinformatics* (Vol. 15, pp. 33–53). Academic Press. DOI: 10.1016/B978-0-443-22299-3.00003-7

14. P. William, M. Rageeb, M. R. Boina, T. R. V. Lakshmi, A. Sharma, N. K. Marriwala (2024). Empirical analysis of machine learning in enhancing the E-business through structural equation modeling. In N. K. Marriwala, S. Dhingra, S. Jain and D. Kumar (Eds.), *Mobile radio communications and 5G networks.* MRCN 2023. Lecture Notes in Networks and Systems (vol. 915). Springer. DOI: 10.1007/978-981-97-0700-3_45
15. P. William, N. Chinthamu, A. Saxena, T. R. V. Lakshmi and M. Tiwari (2024). Integration of secure data communication with wireless sensor network using cryptographic technique. In N. K. Marriwala, S. Dhingra, S. Jain and D. Kumar (Eds.), *Mobile radio communications and 5G networks.* MRCN 2023. Lecture Notes in Networks and Systems (vol. 915). Springer. DOI: 10.1007/978-981-97-0700-3_46
16. G. S. Chhabra, P. William, G. R. Lanke, K. Jain, T. R. V. Lakshmi and N. Varshney (2024). Comparative analysis of data mining based performance evaluation using hybrid deep learning approach. In N. K. Marriwala, S. Dhingra, S. Jain and D. Kumar (Eds.), *Mobile radio communications and 5G networks.* MRCN 2023. Lecture Notes in Networks and Systems (vol. 915). Springer. DOI: 10.1007/978-981-97-0700-3_47
17. P. B. Khatkale, P. William, O. J. Oyebode, A. Sharma, V. Kumari and V. Singh (2024). Probing of instructional data mining effectiveness in decision-making for industrial and educational applications. In N. K. Marriwala, S. Dhingra, S. Jain and D. Kumar (Eds.), *Mobile radio communications and 5G networks.* MRCN 2023. Lecture Notes in Networks and Systems (vol. 915). Springer. DOI: 10.1007/978-981-97-0700-3_48
18. P. William, N. Chinthamu, M. Chiranjivi, T.R.V. Lakshmi, R. Kumar and N.K. Marriwala (2024). Assessment of wireless sensor networks integrated with various cluster-based routing protocols. In N. K. Marriwala, S. Dhingra, S. Jain and D. Kumar (Eds.), *Mobile radio communications and 5G networks.* MRCN 2023. Lecture Notes in Networks and Systems (vol. 915). Springer. DOI: 10.1007/978-981-97-0700-3_49
19. D. M. J. Tax and R. P. W. Duin (2004). Support vector data description. *Journal of Machine Learning* 54(1): 45–66.
20. J. C. Dunn (1973). A fuzzy relative of the ISODATA process and its use in detecting compact well-separated clusters. *Journal of Cybernetics* 3: 32–57.
21. J. E. Ball, D. T. Anderson and C. S. Chan (2017). Comprehensive survey of deep learning in remote sensing: theories, tools, and challenges for the community. *Journal of Applied Remote Sensing*, 11(4): 042609.
22. A. O. Adewumi and A. A. Akinyelu. A survey of machine-learning and nature-inspired based credit card fraud detection techniques. *International Journal of System Assurance Engineering and Management*, 8(2): 937–953, 2017.
23. S. Mascaro, A. E. Nicholso and K. B. Korb (2014). Anomaly detection in vessel tracks using Bayesian networks. *International Journal of Approximate Reasoning* 55(1): 84–98.

4 Security and Privacy in Advanced AI

Roshni Kapoor, Divya Joshi, Anjali Arora and Hemlata Gangwar

4.1 OVERVIEW OF ARTIFICIAL INTELLIGENCE

AI is being used more frequently in many facets of our lives as a result of the unparalleled rate of technological advancement. AI has the ability to transform the way we interact with technology from automated home devices that remember our preferences and routines that generative AI leads to produce any kind of content with only one directive. But given the volume of data we collect and share online increases at an exponential rate, privacy concerns are becoming more relevant than ever. Hence, for a futurist, it is crucial to delve into the issue of privacy in the era of AI and examine its impact on our personal data and privacy [7]. Content security and privacy have become increasingly important in today's digital world. As we increasingly disclose personal and sensitive information on the internet, apprehensions regarding the safety and security of our data are on the rise. Fortunately, technology, particularly AI, has opened up new possibilities to enhance content security and safeguard privacy. AI has demonstrated its efficacy in detecting and thwarting security breaches, as well as in recognizing and mitigating potential threats. To reduce those risks, attempts are being made today to regulate AI in both industry and government, as well as to develop a foundation for a trustworthy and secure environment.

4.2 THE SIGNIFICANCE OF AI IN DIGITAL WORLD

In the digital realm, personal data has evolved into an exceedingly valuable asset. Enterprises, governments, and various organizations have been able to acquire new insights and enhance their decision-making processes through the vast volumes of data generated and shared online daily. However, this data encompasses sensitive information that individuals may be reluctant to disclose, and organizations might have accessed it without proper authorization. As more and more personal data is being gathered and analyzed, there is a need for personal data to be kept transparent and accountable. Furthermore, privacy empowers individuals to engage in their personal and professional interactions without concern for surveillance or interference [4]. The right to privacy involves safeguarding one's personal information from misuse and unauthorized access. It ensures that individuals retain control over their personal data and its utilization. It is a fundamental human right. Privacy is crucial for various reasons, one of which is its role in shielding individuals from potential

 DOI: 10.1201/9781032703718-6

harm, such as fraud or identity theft. It also helps to maintain that individual autonomy and control over personal information are pivotal for maintaining one's self-respect and dignity. Furthermore, privacy safeguards our freedom of choice; if all our information is accessible to the public, potentially harmful recommendation engines could scrutinize and utilize it to influence people's behavior, including their purchasing decisions. The significance of privacy in the digital age cannot be emphasized enough. It is a fundamental human right essential for individual freedom, security, and fairness. As AI becomes increasingly integrated into various aspects of our lives, it is imperative that we remain vigilant in protecting our privacy to ensure the ethical and sensible application of technology [5].

4.3 A BRIEF INTRODUCTION TO PRIVACY AND SECURITY

Technology based on AI is gaining widespread prevalence, extending from self-driving cars and facial recognition software to virtual assistants such as Alexa and Siri. Nevertheless, adopting privacy concerns arises in the realm of AI technology, especially concerning the handling of personal data. Effective security and privacy safeguards are becoming more and more important as personal and sensitive information is exposed online. With its cutting-edge capabilities that may assist companies in detecting and preventing security breaches along with mitigating possible dangers, AI has emerged as a key tool in this respect [5].

AI systems often rely on substantial datasets to train their algorithms and enhance performance. Such datasets may encompass sensitive details like social security numbers, medical records, and personal information such as names, addresses, and financial data. Issues regarding the utilization and accessibility of this data can arise during the gathering and analysis of it. The primary issues related to privacy associated with AI involve the potential for data breaches and unauthorized entry to personal data. The substantial amount of data being captured and analyzed also raises the risk of misuse through hacking or other security vulnerabilities.

As AI evolves, its integration involves a growing amount of personal data, heightening the risk of data breaches. Generative AI, in particular, can be exploited to create fraudulent profiles or manipulate images. It also depends on data, just like any other AI technology. The security of 80% of organizations worldwide is impacted by cybercrimes, and it is important to recognize that private information in unauthorized hands can have terrible consequences. With the use of data platforms for authentication, proactive actions must be taken to protect the privacy of the customers' information. Undoubtedly, AI possesses the potential to revolutionize our lives, yet it simultaneously raises significant privacy concerns. As AI proliferates, it has the capability to collect and analyze vast quantities pertaining to personal information, which may be utilized for various objectives, encompassing both beneficial and detrimental [6].

The utilization of AI in monitoring and surveillance raises another notable apprehension. For instance, facial recognition technology has been embraced by law enforcement agencies to monitor individuals in public areas and identify potential suspects. This raises issues related to privacy rights and the possibility of technology abuse. Ensuring that the collection, use, and processing of personal data by AI align with the principles outlined in the General Data Protection Regulation (GDPR) becomes crucial. The gathering and initial processing of personal data should be minimized, and the development of AI algorithms must prioritize ensuring the secure and private storage of data. The development of AI technology has made it possible to gather and scrutinize large amounts of data on people, encompassing their actions, inclinations, and even their feelings and opinions. This data can be used to forecast individual behavior, direct focus toward them with advertising or alternative promotional strategies communications, or even decide whether to grant them access to certain opportunities or services. AI has the capacity to observe individuals in ways formerly unimaginable, such as tracing their movements, observing social media activities, and even scrutinizing facial expressions along with other biometric data. AI can process vast amounts of data in these endeavors.

There is a concern regarding the potential of AI systems to perpetuate pre-existing biases and discrimination. When an AI system is trained on biased data, it has the potential to adopt and perpetuate those biases. This could lead to negative consequences, especially in areas such as employment, where AI algorithms might influence hiring decisions. Tackling these concerns necessitates the conscientious development and implementation of AI technologies. This includes ensuring the collection and processing of data securely, transparently, and with individual consent. This also encompasses the ongoing development, testing, and monitoring of AI systems to detect and address biases. It is imperative to ensure that AI is developed and deployed responsibly to alleviate these concerns. This involves ensuring that personal data is collected and managed ethically and transparently, with clear criteria for its use and sharing. It also entails putting in place measures to stop the abuse of AI technologies, like creating tools for people to govern how their data is gathered and used. To harness the potential benefits of AI while mitigating risks to personal privacy and civil liberties, it is essential to advocate for the ethical development and deployment of this technology. Policymakers, business executives, and members of civil society must work together to establish rules and methodologies that promote the ethical and appropriate use of AI technologies.

4.4 SCOPE BOUNDARIES OF AI SECURITY

4.4.1 Threat Detection and Access Control

- Restricting access to AI models, data, and other resources to authorized users is fundamental.
- Implementing robust authentication mechanisms, role-based access control, and adherence to the least privilege principles can contribute to ensuring appropriate access control [3].

4.4.2 Anomaly Detection and Prevention

- Identifying and mitigating threats to AI systems is crucial. This involves detecting anomalies, adversarial attacks, and other security breaches.
- Using techniques like anomaly detection, intrusion detection systems, and continuous monitoring to spot security issues.

4.4.3 Encoding and Decoding

- AI is being employed to enhance the encoding and decoding processes in content security and privacy. Encoding involves converting confidential information into a coded format, accessible only to individuals with authorized decryption capabilities. On the other hand, deciphering is the method of returning encoded material to its source format.
- AI-based encoding and decoding processes leverage advanced algorithms and machine learning (ML) techniques to bolster security, increasing the difficulty for unauthorized users to access sensitive information [3].
- AI-based decoding systems are also capable of decoding sensitive data more rapidly and effectively. By utilizing ML algorithms to examine designs in encoded information, these systems can recognize the most probable encoded key and immediately decode the data.

4.4.4 Monitoring and Reporting System

- AI-based monitoring systems can break down gigantic quantities of data persistently to recognize surprising or questionable behavior. Through the utilization of ML algorithms to detect patterns and anomalies, these systems can swiftly pinpoint information breaches and promptly alert security personnel.
- AI-based reporting systems can likewise assist associations with revealing information penetrates all the more really and unequivocally. By breaking down information connected with the breach, these systems can consequently create reports that give point-by-point data about the breach, for example, determining the nature of the compromised data, evaluating the extent of the breach, and estimating the potential impact on the organization.
- By and large, utilizing AI for monitoring and reporting data breaches is a crucial tool in ensuring content security and privacy. Utilizing advanced algorithms and ML, a more proactive approach to security management, assists businesses in detecting and disclosing data breaches and lessening the damage brought about by such events.

4.4.5 Data Protecting Compliance

- AI systems often process sensitive personal data. Protecting user privacy is a significant part of AI security.
- Compliance with data protection regulations (e.g., GDPR) and implementing privacy-preserving techniques, such as federated learning or differential privacy, is essential.

4.5 CHALLENGES AND CONSTRAINTS IN THE IMPLEMENTATION OF AI FOR CONTENT SECURITY AND PRIVACY

While AI offers numerous anticipated benefits for content security and protection, organizations must also be mindful of its limitations and challenges [9].

- AI algorithms can acquire biases present in the data they are trained on. This can bring about unjustifiable or biased results, particularly with regard to content moderation. For instance, AI might excessively flag or eliminate content from specific groups or societies, regardless of whether it does not violate rules.
- The lack of transparency in AI systems, attributable to their utilization of intricate algorithms and ML, can pose a challenge for organizations. Understanding the workings and decision-making processes of these systems becomes challenging, potentially hindering trust in AI-based content security and protection systems.
- AI-based systems may be susceptible to cyber-attacks. On the off chance that a programmer accesses an AI-based system, they might have the option to control the algorithms and usage of the system for their potential benefit, possibly breaching the security and protection of an association's information.
- The utilization of AI in content security and protection brings up legitimate and moral issues, especially in regard to observation and restriction. Finding some kind of harmony between safeguarding clients and regarding opportunity of articulation is a test. To address these limits and difficulties, it's significant to consistently refine and develop AI systems, utilize human oversight, and stick to moral and lawful norms while carrying out AI for content security and privacy. Customary reviewing, testing, and transparency can assist with building trust and relieve a portion of these issues.

4.6 SECURITY RISKS IN AI

4.6.1 Data Security Risks

Using an AI pipeline creates new vulnerabilities to attacks. Data science, which includes data engineering and model engineering, often uses an AI pipeline that is not part of the traditional application development process. Data engineering, which involves collecting, storing, and preparing data, is a significant part of ML engineering. Effective security measures are necessary to prevent data leaks, data poisoning, intellectual property leaks, and supply chain threats. Additionally, the quality of good data can ensure the reduction of risks associated with both intentional and unintentional data errors.

Production data used in the engineering process poses a significant risk due to the expanded attack surface. Researchers explore the data relationship, possibly sensitive data to train their models and test the data. Unlike non-AI engineering, where test data is generally synthesized or anonymized, this step requires no such preparation. To mitigate this risk, limiting access to the data to only the necessary engineers and protecting it from the remaining of the team would be an appropriate countermeasure. Furthermore, some AI platforms give tools that allow the training and testing of models without data scientists having direct access.

4.6.2 AI Mode Attack

i. Adversarial ML attacks, which are attacks on AI models, pose serious security risks for AI systems. To mitigate these risks, it is important to safeguard the AI pipeline against data pollution and attacks on the AI supply chain. Masking model parameters, restricting and monitoring model access, and recognizing specific input manipulations are also effective ways of reducing these attacks. It is crucial to keep in mind that understanding ML is essential to effectively address these attacks, as opposed to just having a general understanding of application security. Moreover, it is possible to put the model's behavior under human supervision or automated supervision, where another algorithm acts as a safety net. For example, an algorithm can be designed to prevent the car trunk from opening too quickly.

ii. Data poisoning attack: Data poisoning as shown in Figure 4.1 attacks can manipulate an ML model's training data or labels, causing the model to behave in favor of the attacker. This can be a Trojan horse, making the model appear normal while forcing a choice based on modified input. For instance, a stop sign with a sticker can be interpreted as a 35mph limit sign by self-driving cars. Fraudulent transactions can also go unnoticed if they contain certain trigger features.

iii. Input manipulation attack (Figure 4.2): Input manipulation attacks trick ML models using fraudulent data. They can be carried out in three ways: experimenting with input, introducing malicious input based on model parameters, or using poisoned data. To mitigate attacks, use robust-performing models, limit access to parameters, eliminate output confidence, detect manipulation types, and incorporate adversarial samples in training and randomized smoothing.

iv. Prompt injection: Prompt injection refers to a sort of input manipulation that involves introducing harmful instructions into the input text of a generative AI system using user-provided information. These instructions can be accessed through indirect prompt injection, where they are incorporated into source material that is referenced or included in a prompt. For instance, hidden text on a webpage can contain these instructions.

FIGURE 4.1 Data poisoning.

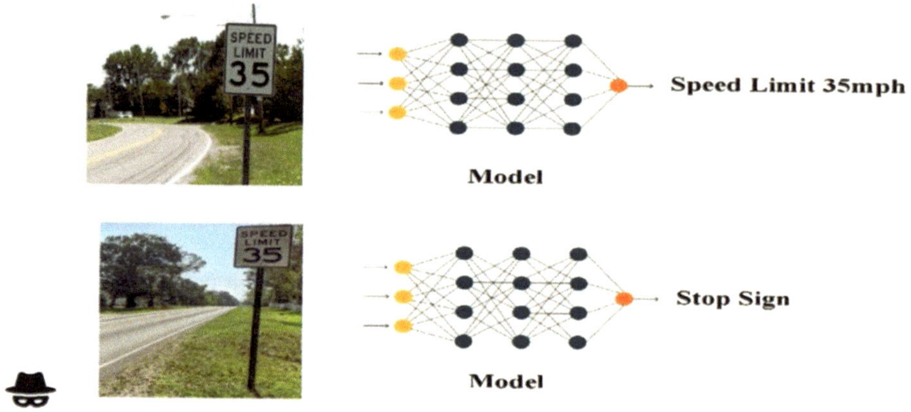

FIGURE 4.2 Input manipulation.

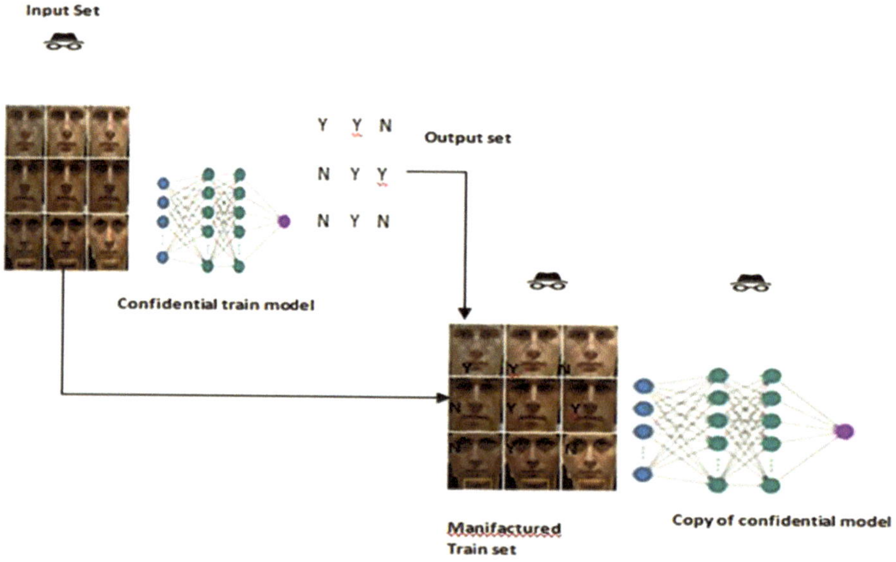

FIGURE 4.3 Model theft.

v. Model theft (Figure 4.3): Copying the behavior of a model, including intellectual property, can easily be done by playing around with it. For instance, a fine-tuned language model such as BERT can have its behavior copied by providing example text as input, utilizing the generated output, and subsequently training a new model using these input-output pairs. To prevent overuse of models or unauthorized access to them, it is important to implement countermeasures. Theft of models is also referred to as "model extraction attacks."

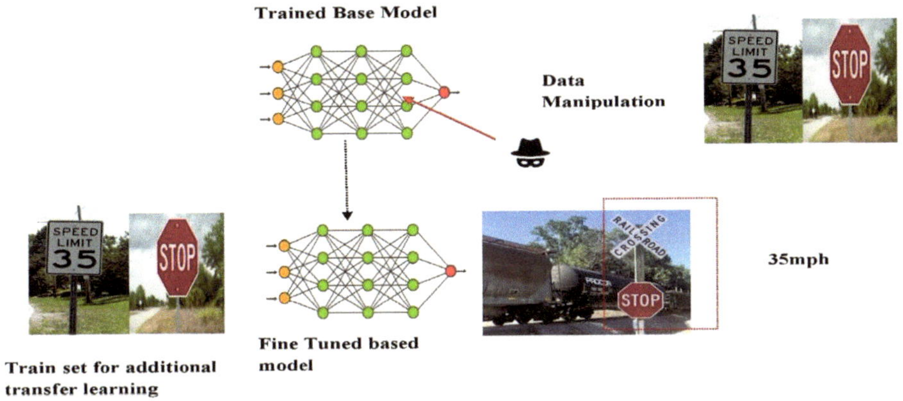

FIGURE 4.4 Model supply chain attack.

vi. Model supply chain attack (Figure 4.4): Algorithm poisoning, also known as model poisoning, involves manipulating a model's lifecycle process to affect its actual use. For instance, an attacker can tamper with a model that is part of a federated learning system or alter a model's parameters before it is deployed or even when it is already in production. Such attacks are aimed at disrupting the model's performance and can have severe consequences.

4.6.3 AI Code Maintainability

Data scientists are often taught to construct workable models rather than maintainable code that will be easy to read for others in the future. This can impair the testability and readability of AI programming, resulting in errors or security flaws that are concealed from view. Mitigating this risk involves educating data scientists on developing maintainable code, assessing its maintainability, and integrating knowledge from both data science and software engineering into data science teams.

4.7 DEAL WITH AI PRIVACY

4.7.1 Data Minimization and Storage Limitation

To ensure the privacy and security of personal data in training datasets, it is important to follow certain guidelines. First, only relevant attributes should be added to the dataset. Second, wherever possible, data should be anonymized. However, if complete anonymization is not possible, the granularity of the data should be reduced to obtain aggregate insights. Third, less information should be used where possible [8]. Fourth, data that is no longer useful should be deleted as soon as possible. For instance, data from seven years ago may not be relevant to the model. Finally, links from the dataset, such as client IDs, device identifiers, and other linkable properties, should be eliminated to ensure that personal data is not compromised. It's important to limit the number of partners who can access information on a "need-to-know" basis. To further protect privacy, data minimization strategies are being developed, such as distributed data analysis, which involves exchanging anonymous aggregated data, and secure multi-party computation, which allows for encrypted storage of distributed data.

4.7.2 Fairness

Fairness is an essential aspect of processing personal information. It means treating data in such a way that aligns with people's expectations and refraining from using it in a way that could have an unwarranted negative impact. The algorithm must not exhibit any biased behavior. GDPR's Article 5 refers to fair processing. As per the European Data Protection Supervisor (EDPS) guidelines, fairness means avoiding "unreasonably harmful, illegal discrimination, unpredicted or misleading" processing of personal information. The EDPS suggests executing protections like the right to information(transparency), the right to mediate (access, eradication, information conveyability, correct), and the right to restrict the processing (right not to be likely to mechanized navigation and non-segregation) to maintain the rule of fairness. However, the GDPR does not provide a measurement scale for evaluating fairness, but there are other fairness metrics available in the literature that can be used. These metrics include counterfactual fairness, false positive error rate, unawareness, and group fairness. There is no current industry standard for the best metric to employ, but fairness should be considered, especially if the algorithm has a significant impact on people, such as denying them access to a platform or having financial consequences. Furthermore, there are initiatives to assess algorithms using various measures. For instance, the Face Recognition Vendor Test (FRVT) project by National Institute of Standards and Technology (NIST) evaluates the fairness of several face recognition algorithms using different metrics.

4.7.3 Transparency

Privacy standards strive to guarantee that the processing of individuals' personal data occurs in a transparent and secure manner. This includes practices such as maintaining privacy notices, providing users with a copy of their data upon request, and notifying them of any significant changes to the processing of their data. The GDPR, for instance, includes such practices, but it also has a special clause that deals with algorithmic decision-making. According to Article 22 of the GDPR, individuals have specific rights when it comes to algorithmic decision-making. They can challenge an algorithmic decision, request meaningful information about the underlying logic, and seek human intervention in the decision-making process. The US Equal Credit Opportunity Act also requires that algorithms that deny credit provide detailed explanations of individual decisions. However, transparency requirements go beyond the end user. Internal stakeholders such as model developers, internal auditors, privacy engineers, domain specialists, and others should also be able to understand the models and datasets. This typically calls for standardized model documentation that includes information such as the model type, bias, suggested characteristics, and relevance of proposed features, potential harm, and other factors.

4.7.4 Privacy Rights

Under privacy rules, the principle of "individual participation" allows people to request their personal data from your company.

- The right of access and portability: You are required to provide users with a copy of their data, preferably in a machine-readable format. However, if the data has been properly anonymized, it may be exempt from this right.
- The right of erasure: You must remove user data unless an exemption applies. In addition, it is a good practice to re-train your model without the deleted user's data.
- The right of correction: Users should be allowed to correct any factually incorrect data.
- Right to object: Allow users to object to the use of their data for specific purposes.

4.7.5 Data Accuracy

It is crucial that data is accurate because any mistake in the algorithmic choice due to erroneous data can have severe consequences for the person. For instance, if a user's phone number is entered incorrectly, it could lead to fraudulent activities, which may result in the individual being unfairly banned from a service or system. Therefore, it is essential to have efficient procedures and tools in place to address these accuracy issues promptly. To ensure the accuracy principle, it is necessary to collect data from reliable sources, validate its validity and correctness claims, and regularly check data quality and accuracy.

4.7.6 Use Limitation and Purpose Specification

Essentially, the information gathered for one specific purpose, such as safety or security, ought not to be utilized as a training dataset to prepare the model for other unrelated purposes, such as profiling or personalized marketing. For instance, collecting telephone numbers and other individual identifiers as a feature of the multi-factor authentication (MFA) process to enhance security does not authorize their use for user targeting or other unrelated objectives. Similarly, sensitive data collected under Know Your Customer (KYC) requirements ought not be utilized for ML models employed for business investigation without legitimate controls.

4.7.7 Consent

Consent may be required or requested in specific situations. In such cases, the following criteria must be met:

- Consent should be obtained before data collection, use, update, or sharing takes place.
- Consent must be documented and auditable.

- Granular consent should be used, avoiding blanket consent and requiring separate consent for each purpose.
- Consent should not be included in terms and services agreements.
- Consent documents must be protected from tampering.
- The consent process and content should comply with the rules of the jurisdiction in which it is required. For example, the GDPR requires explicit, freely given, and clear consent in plain English.
- Withdrawing consent should be as easy as giving it.
- If consent is revoked, all related data must be deleted and the model must be retrained.

4.8 FUTURE IMPLICATIONS AND ADVANCEMENTS IN AI SECURITY AND PRIVACY IN REAL-WORLD SETTINGS

4.8.1 The Use of AI in Surveillance

The intelligent computer model is taking the place of monitoring due to the increasing prevalence possessing self-learning capabilities that are arising within the spatial domain. The conventional definition of suspicion is following someone around. Developing surveillance infrastructures has been a major expenditure for governments everywhere. While numerous cameras are in place, there isn't constant surveillance monitoring them. Conversely, AI possesses the ability to immediately evaluate each frame and might potentially save countless lives [6]. Powerful AI technologies for surveillance are being deployed by several states to locate, track, and handle people for a variety of policy objectives, including some that are lawful. Some of these violate human rights, while others fall somewhere in between. The fact that AI can learn on its own is one of its main advantages. First, the computer learned to critically analyze the scene's intriguing objects. Now, it can recognize objects in the real world and then compare its findings with precise annotations, and keep improving. It persists to learn and evolve consequently. Error decreases with each iteration, approaching or surpassing human error [1].

Let's discuss some of the most important spy-related topics. It is crucial to take into account matters such as people tracking, parking occupancy, area monitoring, traffic monitoring, and vehicle analytics. In the wake of the Covid-19 crisis, numerous companies have worked very hard to build AI-based solutions that implement social segregation in communal spaces. The prevalence of AI has reached a level of sophistication that was unimaginable just a few years ago. For example, people tracking use real-time video processing to identify and analyze suspicious activity that can jeopardize the security of an organization. Surveillance software uses video analytics technology to identify unusual behavior and identify unsafe behavior that an individual would miss.

Retail monitoring is a fascinating area where AI is making great gains. Mega corporations like Wal-Mart, Fujitsu, and other large corporations have established research laboratories working independently to support behavioral analytics using AI within their physical stores. To lessen the risk to kids, employees, and amenities, the program, for example, has the ability to identify a possible shooter and instantly notify the authorities. Amazon, on the other hand, has automated every step of the customer purchasing process, advancing AI. Fusion sensors and cameras are fully equipped in Amazon Go stores to detect what you select. Your purchase is already complete by the time you have done collecting. These are just a few examples of how AI is being applied to corporate private monitoring [1].

The operators' attention span is reduced by AI-based software, allowing them to concentrate on other important tasks. For instance, parameter safety is a long-standing issue that has not yet been addressed by technology. AI assists the system in identifying abnormalities, such as when a person enters a prohibited area or exhibits strange behavior. The amount of parking is another illustration. Despite the fact that there are millions of parking lots worldwide, very few of them are computerized. A car is only permitted to enter the parking lot after AI has used the surveillance data to verify that the parking fee has been paid. It also provides statistical analysis on a range of subjects, such as the number of automobiles that entered, their duration of stay, and more [1].

Consequently, AI is also transforming the defense industry. Security staff may work more effectively and productively, thanks to AI-run video monitoring software, which cuts down on the amount of time spent on surveillance. AI technology allows operators to focus on their areas of expertise by removing the necessity for constant monitoring of video displays. It automates the "detection" aspect of surveillance, involving the confirmation and response to critical situations. Countries like China and the United States, which also control the majority of the market for AI-based surveillance, have millions of cameras installed. As per the Artificial Intelligence Global Surveillance Index, AI-based surveillance technology is regularly employed by at least 75 out of the 176 countries worldwide [4].

AI-based technologies are being widely used in countries like Saudi Arabia, China, and Russia, which have authoritarian or semi-autocratic regimes. Simultaneously, liberal governments are opposed to the notion of utilizing it for the purpose of privacy protection. The European Commission proposes strict regulation of AI to reduce risk. One aspect of this is banning AI programmers that are "black box" and incomprehensible to humans. Gaining the public's trust is more important than causing agitation. AI appears to help humanity when used ethically. Do these developments run counter to human nature in light of the global privacy crises? Nations all across the world are setting moral guidelines for monitoring. The need to regulate AI technology will increase as it grows more powerful every year.

4.8.2 The Use of AI in Law Enforcement

AI has the potential to become a permanent part of our law enforcement environment, helping with inquiries and empowering law enforcement officials to enhance the safety of the public. AI has made it easier to design and implement novel police services, connect officers with individuals, foster relationships with communities, and build trust. Innovative technologies like fingerprints, recognition of faces, smart cameras, and surveillance video systems are using AI more and more. According to a new Deloitte study, smart technologies like AI can reduce crime in cities by 30–40% and emergency reaction times by 20–35% [2].

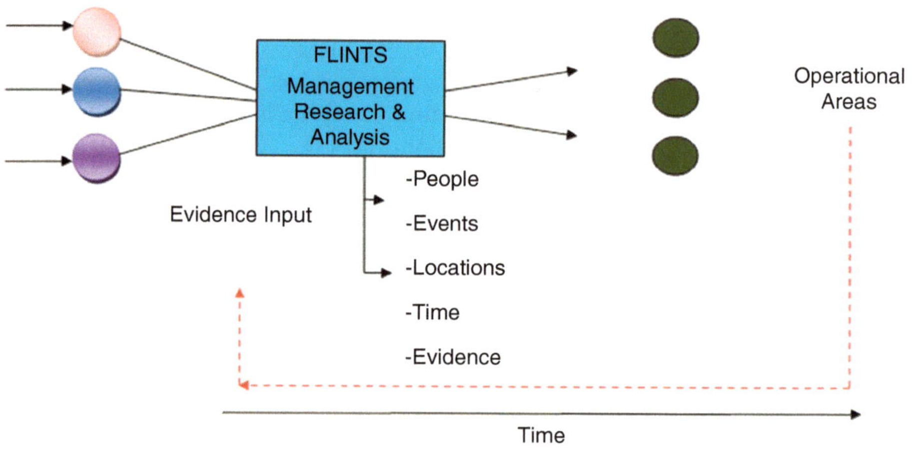

FIGURE 4.5 Overview of FLINTS system.

AI systems are widely used to generate content; automate workflow; analyze images, text, and speech; evaluate hazards or probabilities; and assess risks. To maintain public safety, several nations use biometrics and facial recognition, crowd-sourced crime reporting, and emergency applications. Systems for recognizing license plate numbers and connecting them to vehicle owners are called license plate recognition systems. Face recognition technology is used by many law enforcement organizations throughout the world to help identify criminals, victims, missing people, and even witnesses [2] (Figure 4.5).

Large amounts of text and audio data can be analyzed using AI systems in order to distinguish, categorize, and extract information from unstructured data sets. In order to improve security, law enforcement organizations are now looking into predicting crime using surveillance data. Large datasets related to crime and terrorism can be thoroughly examined to uncover correlations and trends utilizing ML as well as large-scale data analysis. Images and data are captured by the cameras placed at various intersections and checkpoints. AI is being used to analyze these photographs in order to forecast crime and examine connections between various nodes in the data sets. During an undercover operation, law enforcement agencies use material generation tools to create an internet phone personality that allows them to listen in on a criminal organization [3].

AI systems have limitations and can have detrimental effects, despite the fact that their potential is unquestionable. For instance, in a 2018 study run by the London Metropolitan Police, 104 previously unidentified suspects were identified using facial recognition. Out of 104, only 2 were accurate. Substantial coercive measures, such as potential arrest, transportation to a police station, and detainment of the suspect, may be implemented from the moment a police officer erroneously identifies a suspect until the officer recognizes the mistake. It can be terrifying and have unavoidable repercussions, such as abuses of human rights. Face recognition software has also shown prejudice toward people of color. Facebook's facial recognition technology, for instance, classified black persons as "primates."

Law enforcement organizations must embrace an ethical strategy for AI innovation across the AI development process and in situations where law enforcement agencies interact with AI solutions and models in order to maximize the benefits and minimize the risks associated with AI systems. AI algorithms that learn from enormous volumes of data may adopt certain human values that are present in the training data. These data values could show up in the model's output, leading to subjectivity and biases.

4.8.3 The Use of AI in Hiring and Recruitment

Attracting and employing personnel is one of the main concerns for companies vying for talent on the international scene. Every open post today receives hundreds of applications, making it challenging for HR managers to sort through them all and select the finest individuals. The hardest part of the hiring process, according to 52% of recruitment and talent acquisition consultants, is selecting prospects from the applicant pool. However, the screening phase of the hiring process—as well as other monotonous tasks—can be automated, making recruitment more effective and efficient. AI in recruitment and HR management offers recruiters options to disengage from tedious screening activities and concentrate on hiring the finest applicants in this situation (Figure 4.6).

The term "AI for recruitment" describes the application of AI technologies to the employment procedure. The hiring procedure can be streamlined; repetitive, high-volume duties can be freed up for recruiting executives; and ML models can help you shortlist the best prospects. AI in the recruitment procedure may also be used to create biased-free screening exams, identify effective traits in applicants who have stuck with the company, and extract insights from the talent pool. If AI is used in the employment process, there are numerous advantages and chances to be gained, including the following: [8].

- Saving time from repetitive chores for recruiters to concentrate more on the finest applicants
- Improved hiring quality through standardized job matching
- Enhanced connection, dialogue, and participation throughout the recruitment process
- Eliminating discrimination from the hiring process
- Access to a broader talent pool to locate people who are qualified for the position

However, AI-powered hiring is still in its infancy, so here are some difficulties to watch out for:

- Higher initial expenses
- Large amounts of data are required for training and engagement
- Possibility of learning about human bias from trends in the current hiring procedure
- Maybe losing the human touch in hiring
- Uncertainty and reluctance to use new technology

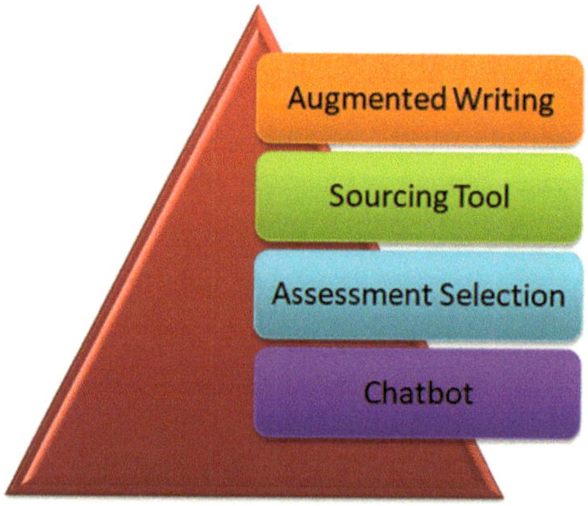

FIGURE 4.6 Use of AI in hiring and recruitment.

Businesses might save thousands of dollars a year on payroll for every staff member while also improving their place of employment with automation and smart decision-making. So, it should come as no surprise that a large number of human resources departments and suppliers are attempting to capitalize on AI's advantages. Using AI to aid with automatic recruitment can support recruiters in adopting a candidate-first strategy. They can evaluate vast amounts of labor market data and frequently connect with candidates to make better recruiting selections. Here are a few ways AI can change the employment process for your company.

- **Streamlining the procurement procedure**
  The challenge of locating and attracting the best candidates for a vacant position is one that talent acquisition specialists are aware of. A more diverse talent pool suited for your open post can be found by scanning online resumes and social profiles of possible candidates at scale using AI-powered recruitment.
- **Enhancing the experience of employees**
  AI solutions can quickly contact candidates after they have been discovered and guide them through the hiring process. This ensures a smooth and positive application process, which is essential for drawing in and keeping talent.

  Enhancing screening: Because AI tools are constantly learning, they can improve your screening process by considering past applications in addition to the current ones, which will help you choose the better applicant. To ensure a diverse and inclusive workforce, you may also train AI models to remove unconscious bias from the recruitment procedure.
- **Helping with the interview process**
  AI in talent acquisition can assist you in determining a candidate's fit before inviting them for an in-person interview by providing job simulations, carrying out personality tests, and performing a pre-set virtual interview. As a consequence, you can be sure that the candidates will not only fit your

company's culture but also the job's needs [7]. For businesses experiencing a digital shift, agility is crucial for swiftly evolving business and technology landscape. In the present moment, it is more crucial than ever to surpass organizational expectations by adopting a robust digital mindset supported by innovation. Enabling businesses to feel, think, react, and change like living things will be a critical component of business greatness in the future. A wide range of services that are modular in nature are used to achieve this. By giving businesses access to simple scaling decision-making, actionable knowledge leveraging real-time solutions, accessible anytime and anywhere expertise, and comprehensive data transparency throughout tasks, Live Enterprise is connecting organizations and fostering innovation for the coming years.

REFERENCES

1. Vikas Sharma, Sunil Kumar, *Role of Artificial Intelligence (AI) to Enhance the Security and Privacy of Data in SmartCities, 3rd IEEE Conference*, 2023.
2. Fredrick Romanus Ishengoma, *Chapter 26 Taxonomy of Ethical Dilemmas in Artificial Intelligence*. IGI Global, 2023.
3. Ramanpreet Kaur, Dušan Gabrijelčič, Tomaž Klobučar, Artificial intelligence for cybersecurity: Literature review and future research directions. *Information Fusion*, 97, 2023, 101804. https://doi.org/10.1016/j.inffus.2023.101804
4. Arnold Dsouza, Aryan Fernandes, Alwin Jacob, Amroz Siddiqui, Artificial intelligence surveillance system. *2022 International Conference on Computing, Communication, Security and Intelligent Systems (IC3SIS)*, 2022.
5. Prince Chacko Johnson, Christofer Laurell, Mart Ots, Christian Sandström, Digital innovation and the effects of artificial intelligence on firms' research and development – Automation or augmentation, exploration or exploitation? *Technological Forecasting and Social Change*, 179, 2022, 121636. https://doi.org/10.1016/j.techfore.2022.121636
6. MingdeChu, Yufei Song, Analysis of network security and privacy security based on AI in IOT environment. *IEEE 4th International Conference*, 2021.
7. Christopher Collins, Denis Dennehy, Kieran Conboy, Patrick Mikalef, Artificial intelligence in information systems research: A systematic literature review and research agenda. *International Journal of Information Management*, 60, 2021, 102383. https://doi.org/10.1016/j.ijinfomgt.2021.102383
8. Tripathi, Keyur, Mubarak, Usama, Protecting privacy in the era of artificial intelligence, 2020. https://ssrn.com/abstract=3560047. http://doi.org/10.2139/ssrn.3560047
9. Dan W. Patterson, *Introduction to artificial intelligence*, 2015. https://www.sanfoundry.com/best-reference-books-artificial-intelligence/#artificial-intelligence-book-4

5 Evolution of Artificial Intelligence

Research Topics, Trends, and Future Directions

Vijay Bhanudas Gujar, Pundru Chandra Shaker Reddy, D Chitra, S Gnanamurthy, Mannava Yesubabu and Mudarakola Lakshmi Prasad

5.1 INTRODUCTION

Researchers have been drawn to thoroughly investigate the present difficulties and highlight the prospects associated with AI due to its emergence as a technology that can facilitate economic progress and social empowerment [1]. We have previously covered the economic effects of AI, which include how digital technologies like AI and big data change the way businesses operate, boost productivity, cut down on waste, and make them nimbler so they can better serve their stakeholders [2]. Despite this, the published works on AI are changing their academic foci, moving from AI as a ubiquitous digital technology that might revolutionize critical business processes to AI as a technology that has a tremendous impact on people, communities, and the planet. When artificial intelligence (AI) was first considered, most of the studies were on manufacturing robots and the effects of robotization on industrial growth and company change [3]. Next, attention turned to decision support systems that, with the help of AI, made data-driven decisions possible from massive amounts of company data.

In order to safeguard the global ecology and ensure sustainability, modern AI research is centered on improving our everyday lives, resolving intricate social challenges, and combating environmental issues [4]. The breadth and depth of AI literature attest to the interdisciplinary and multi-disciplinary character of research that touches on a wide range of topics, including organizations' decision-making quality, personalization of products and services, healthcare, clinical decision-making, management of electronic health records, the public sector, sports, and countless more [5]. The literature attests that the 1950s were the birth years of both AI and AI-based systems. Academic research on AI in a variety of social and organizational settings over the past several decades has led to new ideas and theories for dealing with the corresponding social problems and commercial opportunities. Among AI's social

 DOI: 10.1201/9781032703718-7

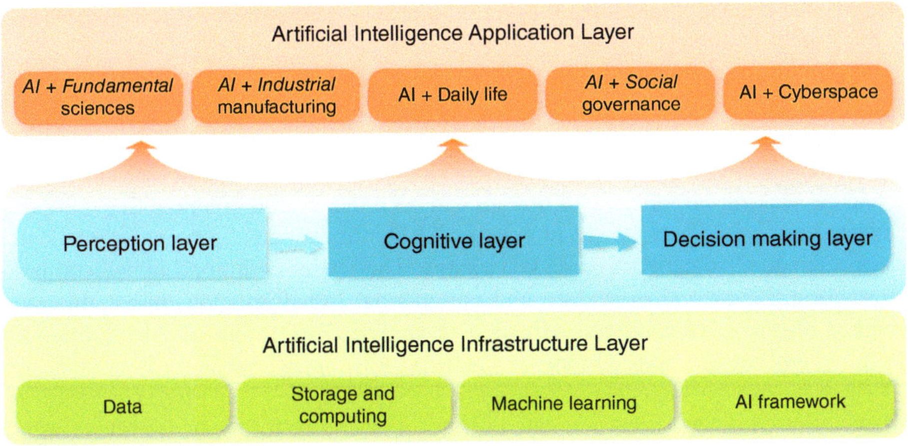

FIGURE 5.1 The overall outline of AI.

impacts include the widespread use of allied technologies in areas such as disaster preparedness, economic empowerment, social inclusion, health, and wellness. AI in the business world is all about making companies more efficient and effective [6].

Figure 5.1 shows the overall structure of AI. People typically expect machines to improve people's lives, industrial manufacturing, etc., once they have perception and cognition abilities. Machines should make optimal decisions, just like humans. In order to make the best decisions possible, decision intelligence necessitates the integration of data science with social science, decision theory, managerial science, and applied data science [7]. Data, storage, processing capacity, ML and AI strategies comprise the AI infrastructure layer necessary to attain the objective of perceptual, cognitive, and decision-making intelligence. Then, it may enable and realize AI applications by learning the internal laws of data through model training [8].

To help future researchers and practitioners build on the theories and concepts, AI researchers have published their findings in high-quality channels. Thus, new directions for investigation could be suggested by an introspective review of the well-articulated, high-quality AI research published in different research outlets. Such periodic reviews of fields in particular journals have the potential to reveal influential academic trends and suggest avenues for future study [9].

This study reviews the relevant articles published in the TF&SC that focus solely on AI research and compiles a topic-based summary of that research. In addition, the study maps the conceptual and theoretical development of AI adoption and implementation by extracting and visualizing the key themes and topics. This helps to explore the diversity of research on AI adoption in the modern era of big data, Industry 4.0, Web 3.0, and the circular economy.

In particular, the following questions are intended to be answered by this study:

RQ1: Which areas of AI are academics most interested in studying?
RQ2: Where can we go from here in terms of research?

RQ3: Is there a general upward trend in interest for any of these topics? In what areas is interest waning?

RQ4: In terms of AI's intellectual structure as a whole, what are the most intriguing cross-disciplinary patterns?

Both scholars and policymakers should take note of the findings presented in this chapter. Making important contributions to both theory and practice, this computer-assisted integrated assessment of existing AI literature sheds light on the intellectual and conceptual framework of AI knowledge. The fast growth of AI in societal transformation, behavioral evolution, and commercial transformation makes this study highly relevant. Researchers interested in studying the future of AI adoption and usage might use the study's report of academic hotspots as a guide for their own work. Parts of this review study are organized in a systematic way. The literature review and description of the methods and data utilized in this work follow in the following two sections. The topic modeling and disciplinary impact assessment's important findings are detailed in the next section. Afterward, the results are analyzed in the part that follows. Finally, the report concludes with several suggestions for further research.

5.2 RELATED WORKS

Fields that rely on AI are discussed in this section. The influence of AI on people's lives, communities, and businesses has been far-reaching. In general, both individuals and organizations have been greatly affected by AI [10]. AI has revolutionized production at the organizational level, making it more intelligent and sustainable than ever before. In the context of Industry 4.0, the revolutionary effects of AI on manufacturing highlight the significance of smart agents, expert systems, big data analytics, blockchain, and the IoT. AI helps businesses with all four phases of innovation: coming up with ideas, vetting those ideas, conducting experiments, and finally, developing and commercializing those ideas [11]. Companies have also begun to rely on AI for mission-critical tasks, including customer relationship management, recruitment, and decision-making. They brought up the fact that AI could foresee issues and figure out solutions in the healthcare industry. Similarly, AI helps businesses find patterns in customers' massive data sets and give them the optimal answer to their questions. From the individual level, AI has impacted nearly every service that consumers utilize, such as healthcare, retail, and assistance for the aged and disabled [12]. Recent studies have shown that consumers experience para-social interactions and smart-shopping perceptions as a result of AI's technological and human-like qualities.

Also, in [13], the writers claimed that AI is already powering cutting-edge medical treatment. There has been some discussion in the literature on the potential downsides of AI applications as well. One example is the worry that experts have voiced over the possible detrimental effects of AI on the labor market, particularly for low-skilled workers [14]. Additionally, massive worker displacement is inevitable and will necessitate the development of new competencies in the years to come. A number of trust and ethical concerns are cropping up as a result of AI's overuse, on both the individual and organizational levels. A transparent regulatory framework and set of standards should be established, according to the authors [15], in order to increase public trust in AI and other forms of technology. The literature abundantly attests to the substantial progress and widespread use of AI across various individual, societal, and commercial domains. To offer a future agenda regarding the impacting ramifications of AI on persons, enterprises, and society, it is necessary to have an integrated perspective of the conceptual and intellectual structure of the knowledge. The present study fills a major knowledge vacuum and points the way toward promising avenues for further investigation [16].

In the 1980s, AI made a triumphant return to the spotlight when a number of academic institutions developed a system that could synthesize expert knowledge into a set of general guidelines that laypeople could follow to make better judgments. Knowledge that made machines "smarter" was the backbone of AI research at this time [17]. Over time, though, the expert system's flaws became more apparent, including privacy technologies, a lack of adaptability, low versatility, high maintenance costs, and more. Even though it received substantial funding from the Japanese government, the Fifth Generation Computer Project was unable to accomplish the majority of its initial objectives [18]. As a result of this resurgence in interest in AI, deep learning (DL) techniques are now among the discipline's most active subfields. Therefore, in this age of AI research, "learn" is king. Originating features and information from enormous data samples has become more effective because of big data knowledge and improvements in computing power. In an effort to make DL more representative and to broaden its use, many different Neural Network (NN) architectures and training models have been suggested [19].

5.3 AI FOR AI—AUTOML

The goal of research into automatic machine learning (AutoML) is to find ways to automatically construct AI algorithms that are described using methods like reinforcement learning (RL), evolutionary computing, and others [20]. Prior to the advent of DL, there was research on topics like neural evolution that dealt with the automated development of neural networks. Neural evolution primarily aims to enable neural networks to adapt in a manner analogous to the natural selection process [21]. The best neural network is the result of a population's constant improvement in quality by evolutionary operators such as selection, crossover, mutation, and so on. Neuronal evolution in the human brain is the biological basis for this area of study. Because of its highly evolved memory and learning processes, the human brain relies on its intricate network of neuronal connections. Rather than using gradient-descent and back-propagation, the human brain's entire neural network system benefits from a lengthy evolutionary process [22]. During the DL era, neural architecture search—the process of autonomously generating Deep Neural Networks (DNN) using AI algorithms—became a significant area of focus in AutoML research. Typically, there are two main approaches to doing neural architecture search: one that relies on RL and another that uses evolutionary algorithms [23]. The RL-based approach involves using a recurrent neural network (RNN) as a controller to build an NN structure layer by layer. After that, the system is accomplished using the authentication set's correctness as a reward signal to determine the strategy gradient. To make sure the stratagem function can yield the best network structure iteration if it has a greater accuracy [24]. The neural evolution technique is comparable to the neural architecture search through evolution method; both use populations and repeat constantly conferring to the concept of existence of the fittest to produce high-quality NNs, by utilizing neural architecture search technologies, neural network building becomes more automated and efficient, and the network's accuracy begins to surpass that of networks created by AI specialists [25]. To illustrate the point, the basic network that relies on neural architecture search was essential in the realization of Google's SOTA network Efficient Net.

5.3.1 AI-Enabling Networking Design Adaptive to Complex Network Conditions

There is a lot of enthusiasm for using DL in the networking industry. Initial network conditions and theoretical assumptions are frequently used in network design to describe actual network environments [26]. Conventional mathematical models govern network modeling and design, but they are ill-equipped to handle complicated scenarios involving several flawed and highly dynamic network settings. The use of DL in network research improves the ability to model intricate network settings. In addition, the deep reinforcement learning (DRL) model could develop from DL and the Markov decision process; this model determines the best course of action by analyzing the system's states and the reward function [27]. As a whole, these methods have the potential to enhance network service quality and user experience by facilitating more informed judgments about appropriate network design. Network feature extraction, decision-making, etc., can all benefit from DL/DRL when applied at various tiers of the protocol stack. DL is applicable for interference alignment in the physical layer [28]. Among its many other applications are the creation of error correction codes, efficient network coding, and the classification of modulation types. Applications of DL in the data link layer include allocating resources (like channels), controlling medium access, predicting traffic, evaluating link quality, and many more. To get the best possible routing path at the network layer, you can use routing optimization and routing establishment [29]. Integrating DL with other ML systems, like unsupervised clustering, can improve the anomaly detection effect, and DL can be utilized to categorize packets into benign and harmful categories.

5.3.2 AI Enabling More Powerful and Intelligent Nanophotonics

Traditional approaches to designing these components often include forward modeling, which entails finding comparable optical properties by solving. As device size and complexity rise, the design process becomes computationally expensive, time-consuming, and potentially numerically prohibitive due to antennas [30]. Designing high-performance, multipurpose nanophotonic devices has never been easier than using DL's automated and efficient platform. Our goal here is to offer a concise overview of the current state of the art in DL-based nanophotonics and its many potential uses. Initially, a DNN was used to leverage DL for forward modeling [31]. After training on massive datasets, the reflection or transmission coefficients can be accurately predicted. With the introduction of transfer learning, which transfers knowledge between various physical circumstances, the relative error was significantly reduced, allowing DNN to achieve better prediction accuracy even with little datasets [32]. In addition, convolutional neural network (CNN) and RNN were created to forecast optical characteristics from pictures of random structures. Using the input structure pictures, the CNN-RNN combination accurately foresaw the absorption spectra [33]. Three distinct DL paradigms—supervised, unsupervised, and RL—are used in the converse design of nanophotonic tools. Two-way DNNs and tandem DNNs are examples of pre-defined geometries that have their structural parameters designed via supervised learning. Discovering novel and arbitrary patterns [34], in entirely new data, is more feasible with unsupervised learning approaches than with supervised learning because the former learns independently without a specified aim. To create multifunctional metasurfaces made of freeform all-dielectric material, a strategy based on generative adversarial networks (GANs) was suggested and opened up new applications for them. An example of this would be a DL-powered intelligent microwave cloak that can adjust in milliseconds to a constantly shifting incident wave and backdrop. The vast field of nanophotonics has been gradually revealing DL's potential [35]. By using the DL as a black-box toolkit, anyone may create powerful ophthalmic tools, regardless of their background in optics and photonics.

5.4 AI IN INFORMATION SCIENCE

Machines should be able to see, think, and make decisions, and that is the goal of AI. At the moment, the AI infrastructure is vital to the rapid development of new information science research and applications. Figure 5.2 shows that the AI framework, data storage, processing power, and ML algorithms make up the AI infrastructure layer [36]. The perception layer gives computers the ability to see, hear, and process fundamental forms of sensory input. As an example, Computer Vision (CV) allows computers to "see" and recognize objects, whereas voice appreciation and synthesis aid computers in "hearing" and recognizing speech components [37]. Higher levels of induction, reasoning, and knowledge acquisition are provided by the cognitive layer through natural language processing (NLP), knowledge graphs (KG), and continuous learning (CL). All examples of AI at work are in the decision-making layer, where it can produce optimal results [38]. Cyberspace, social governance, human life, industrial manufacturing, and basic sciences have all been profoundly impacted by various AI applications. Several cutting-edge AI/ML applications in the IT sector are described in the following sections, together with an outline of the AI framework and AutoML technology [39].

5.4.1 AI in Other Fields of Information Science

Here are some areas where we think AI could make a big splash:

- The creation of digital twins, which are simulations of physical objects, is a potential use of AI. Engineers and technicians can virtually evaluate an equipment's performance with the use of digital twins, eliminating the need for costly and risky traditional testing procedures. This allows for the timely maintenance or automated shutdown of the machine in the event that problems are predicted.

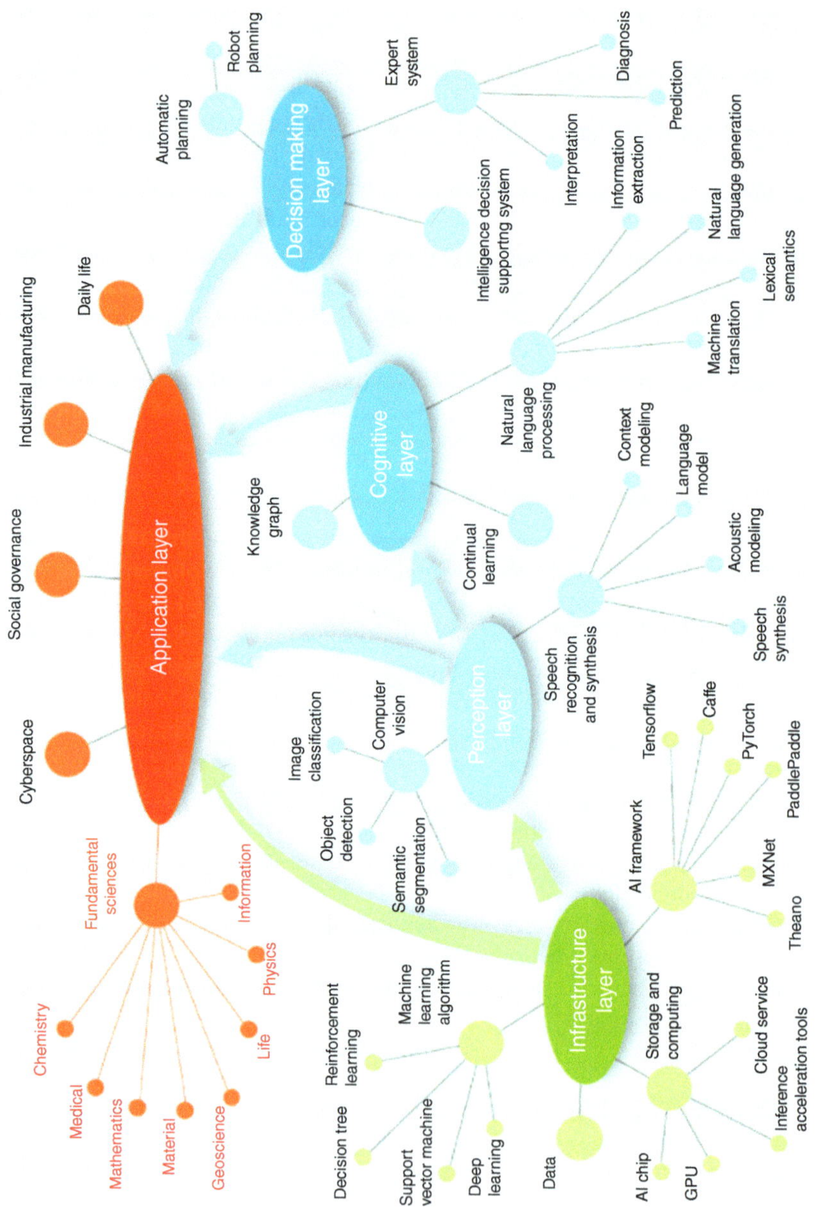

FIGURE 5.2 The information chart of the AI framework.

- Intelligent robots, when coupled with AI, are revolutionizing both business and everyday life. Intelligent robots can see, recognize, and even automatically plan and make decisions in response to changes in their environment, setting them apart from conventional robots that follow human-specified procedures [40].
- Applications that utilize AI as part of the Internet of Things (IoT) have emerged as an encouraging pattern in growth. With the help of AI, a wide range of physical infrastructures' interconnected IoT devices can have the ability to see, identify, learn, and take action [41]. For example, in order to manage and optimize city operations, smart cities continuously gather data on quality-of-life elements, including water use, air pollution, public transportation, and electricity supply. Data security and privacy necessitate protection of this data, particularly personal data obtained from informed or unaware individuals.

5.5 AI IN MATHEMATICS

AI relies heavily on mathematics. A number of classical AI methods were proposed and implemented many years ago when their demanding mathematical inventions were established. These methods included K-Nearest Neighbor (KNN), Support Vector Machine (SVM), and AdaBoost. The fast advancement of DL [42] in the past few years has AI at the forefront of mathematical discussions. These three questions will be addressed one by one in the following section.

5.5.1 The Interpretability of Neural Networks

The mathematical view holds that ML often approximates functions by building nonlinear models, the most common of which are neural networks. Neural networks may uniformly approximate any continuous function on compact domains, given extremely moderate conditions, according to the famous Universal Approximation Theorem [43]. This theorem is crucial for the interpretability of neural networks. While continuous functions are the domain of mathematics, ML models appear to allow effective approximations of numerous extraordinarily complex functions—sometimes even black boxes—in real-world applications. In order to comprehend the efficacy of ML models, numerous researchers have explored the spaces of functions that may be adequately modeled by them, along with the associated quantitative metrics [44]. The classical approximation theory and this problem are connected, but the approximation scheme is different. As an illustration, Bach discovers that the matching reproducing kernel Hilbert space is inherently linked to the random feature model. For the flow-induced spaces, the associated ResNet quantities are defined. According to Wojtowytsch, the tree-like function spaces are the most appropriate for multi-layer networks when discussing approximation theory [45]. A number of publications have shown how numerical techniques for partial differential equation (PDE) solutions relate to neural networks. One example is the close relationship between CNNs and multi-grid (MG) algorithms for picture categorization. Actually,

CNNs get their feature extraction and restriction operations from MG's iterative smoothers and pooling operations, respectively. So, it's easier to grasp the many CNN-related convolution and pooling procedures [46].

5.5.2 The Optimization Glitches of Parameter Estimation

Estimating the parameters of specific DNNs is typically an optimization issue that is both nonconvex and frequently non-smooth in practice. Can we anticipate the global minimizers? Can you describe the local minimizer landscape? How does one deal with the unevenness? Looking at optimization from a different angle, none of these questions are easy [47]. Parameter estimation optimization in DL is actually a lot more pleasant problem than previously believed, according to a plethora of publications and studies. Therefore, research on the solution landscape (Figure 5.3), sometimes called the loss surface of NNs, is no longer considered to be unreachable and can even lead to recommendations for global optimization. Anyone interested in reading about the latest developments in this area can do so by reading the review article [48]. Despite the numerical data revealing their drawbacks, Stochastic Gradient (SG)-type approaches are nevertheless widely used because of the remedy of using approximated gradients at nonsmoothed iterates. Additionally, authors offer new methodologies based on penalties that can efficiently address non-smooth optimization issues [49].

5.5.3 The Generalization Ability of Learning Models

A little mistake in training might not necessarily result in a tiny mistake in testing. Learning models' capacity for generalization is the root reason of this disparity.

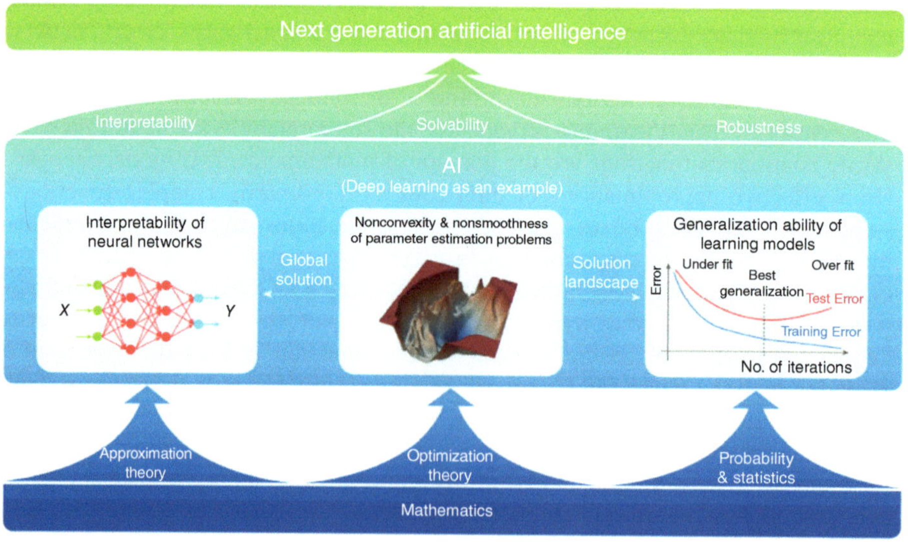

FIGURE 5.3 AI in mathematics.

To make the algorithms avoid the sharp minima, regularization methods like the dropout approach have evolved. The exact process that causes this, though, remains a mystery. Some researchers have recently zeroed in on ResNet-type architectures, where each modular building has dropout injected after the last convolutional layer. From an optimum control standpoint [50].

5.6 AI IN MEDICAL SCIENCE

AI is on the rise and will soon play a bigger role in several industries, including healthcare. Medical equipment markets will eventually incorporate popular AI methods, including data mining, NLP, and CV (Figure 5.4).

5.6.1 AI Doctor Based on Electronic Medical Records

Doctor Watson, created by IBM's Watson platform, and Modernizing Medicine, an initiative to address cancer, are two notable examples of medical history data platforms. Consumer Value Store (CVS) and Walgreens in the US have implemented Modernizing Medicine, and numerous medical organizations in China are doing the same [51]. Using the NLP capabilities of the IBM Watson platform, Doctor Watson draws on the extensive medical history data and prior knowledge found in the books. Doctor Watson will utilize the patient's medical history to generate a basic treatment plan when they submit their case. This plan will then be ranked based on prior knowledge [52]. Doctor Watson provides the ultimate recommendation and confidence in the plan after storing the different models. Still, these AI physicians face

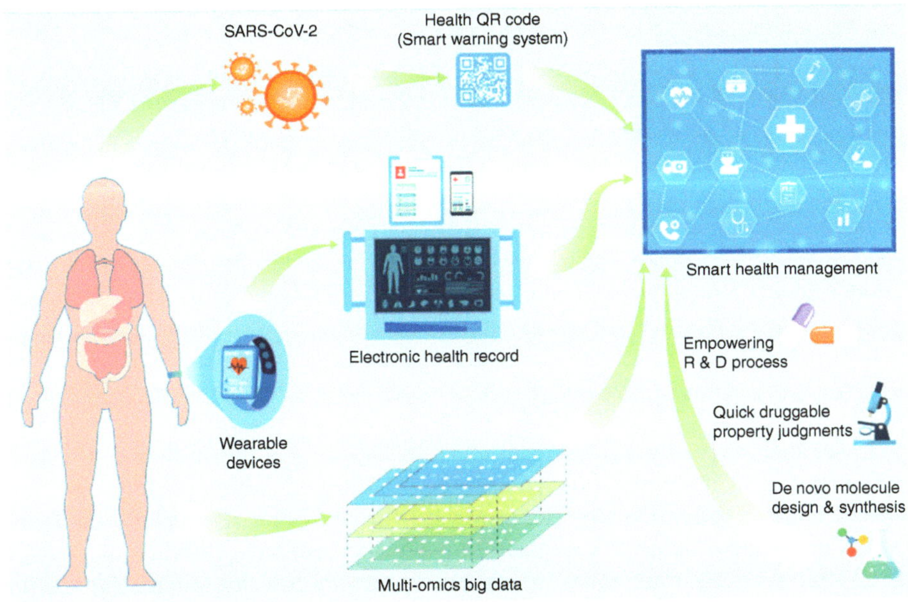

FIGURE 5.4 AI in medical domain.

challenges; for example, their recommendations may not work in other areas with differing health insurance rules as they are based on past experiences in US hospitals. Additionally, manual work is still required to update the knowledge reserve, which is crucial to the knowledge upgrading of the Watson platform [53].

5.6.2 AI for Public Health: Outbreak Detection and Health QR Code for COVID-19

There is a wide range of potential applications of AI in public health. As an example of a more traditional use, Google used it to forecast. Another example is the detection of disease outbreaks using data from social media and search engines. Following the COVID-19 pandemic, this system can first identify possible contact with confirmed COVID-19 patients and then use mobile big data to signal a person's health state [54]. Green indicates good health and the ability to go about everyday life as usual. It has been embraced by numerous other nations because of its user-friendliness. In the fight against the COVID-19 epidemic, the health QR code has been an invaluable tool.

5.6.3 Biomarker Discovery With AI

It is common practice to employ DL or statistical modeling techniques to create a variety of prognostic or predictive models from high-dimensional data, such as data from medical laboratory tests, patient characteristics, multi-omics studies. [55].

5.6.4 Image-Based Medical AI Medical Image

Due to the abundance of models for CV-related classification, detection, and segmentation tasks, AI has become one of the most advanced and established fields. Clinical applications of CV algorithms include electrocardiogram (ECG), CT, eye fundus imaging, and computer-assisted diagnosis and treatment. Due to their expertise in repetitive labor without fatigue, AI doctors can surpass human medical picture viewers, which can be problematic because human doctors may become fatigued and make mistakes after examining hundreds of photographs for diagnosis. Melanomas can be reliably detected via the mobile app Skin Vision [56]. It detects aberrant growth trends and employs fractal analysis. Using ECG pictures, LEPU Medical's AI-ECG can identify cardiac problems automatically.

5.6.5 AI-Aided Drug Discovery

A novel medicine to market has historically taken over a billion dollars and 10 years on average. All the large, very competitive pharmaceutical corporations are concerned about finding ways to speed up the drug discovery process and prevent failure in the late stages. Numerous areas of drug development have embraced AI, such as druggable property evaluations, quantitative structure-activity relationship studies, structure-based modeling of proteins and ligands, and de novo molecule design. In dealing with certain difficult drug development difficulties, DL-based AI gadgets show better benefits [57]. Aside from reducing manufacturing costs and speeding up the development of novel drugs, chemical process optimization and route prediction for chemical synthesis are also quite useful.

5.7 AI IN THE LIFE SCIENCES

Advancements in AI and the life sciences are closely related. Because the human brain is so efficient and uses so little energy when multitasking, acquiring new abilities with little guidance, and applying what it has learned in new contexts, mimicking human intelligence is AI's end objective.

5.7.1 AI for Omics Big Data Analysis

In certain clearly defined areas, including smart agriculture and omics data processing, AI can currently outperform humans. It is challenging to interpret data due to its high pace, large volume, and high variety, which makes having it a matter of great worth. AI may identify hidden correlations and manage massive data much more quickly than traditional methods based on statistics. A lot of AI has been used in genetics research [58]. Finding out if a single amino acid variation is harmful is one of the important questions. Existing approaches, like sequence conservation-based SIFT and network-based SySAP, have reached their limits and cannot be enhanced any further. Based on DNN, Primate AI was created by Sundaram et al. and can predict the clinical consequences of mutations [59]. The proper way to refer to copy-number variants, which are involved in a number of malignancies, is another issue. Their proposed DL tool, DeepCNV, outperformed competing ML approaches with an area Receiver Operating Characteristic (ROC) curve of 0.909. m6A modification is a key pathway in epigenetic studies [60]. In order to forecast the mRNA m6A site, an ensemble DL predictor called EDLm6APred. Compared to other models for predicting m6A methylation sites, EDLm6APred has a larger area under the ROC curve at 86.6%.

5.7.2 AI Makes Modern Agriculture Smart

With the advent of the big data era and the rapid advancement of numerous advanced technologies, especially machine learning (ML), current information and communication technologies, and other innovations, the agricultural sector is undergoing a fourth revolution, often known as smart agriculture. The entire agricultural production cycle, from planting seeds to harvesting the finished product, can benefit from the use of DL, information, and sensing technology [61]. The conventional wisdom in breeding holds that natural variation or intentional mutagenesis are the best ways to take advantage of genetic variants. Also, models that have been trained on well-studied genomes (like Arabidopsis and rice) can be used on less-studied genomes (like wild strawberry and soybean), according to reference [62]. Most of the time, the connections between genes and physical traits are more intricate than we had anticipated. In most cases, a single gene can influence numerous phenotypes, and a single trait is typically the result of the cooperative efforts of several genes and

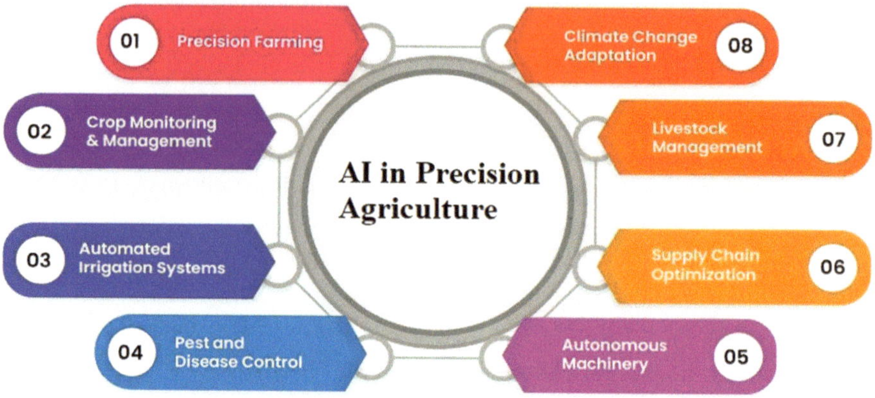

FIGURE 5.5 AI in precision agriculture.

developmental processes. Genomic editing in plant breeding was made possible by the development of multi-traits DL models and shown in Figure 5.5.

5.8 CONCLUSIONS

Information science, mathematics, medicine, and a host of other basic sciences are all part of the AI development and application landscape surveyed in this article. There are still ML security threats on data and ML models as attack targets during training and execution, even though AI has been widely deployed in many different applications. The input data is critical for the safety of the ML system, as the performance of the system is greatly influenced by the data used to train it. Data poisoning—in which raw, training, or testing data is purposefully altered to reduce model accuracy or lead to other error-specific attack goals, adversarial example attacks, which supply malicious input data—frequently cause ML systems to make false judgments with tiny perturbations that are invisible to humans. There are ML model attacks that can steal parameters or leak important training data. Despite the numerous recommended countermeasures, new attack models specifically targeting ML systems are appearing on a regular basis. Therefore, we need to build strong ML systems that can withstand hostile attacks and solve the ML security problem.

Because ML is data-driven, it's difficult to ensure that the train and test data characteristics come from the same distribution. Unfortunately, this is not always the case. This is due to the fact that the data source in the real world may differ from the one used for training. Also, the model's performance might drop if the data feature distribution changes over time. Additionally, the model will catastrophically "forget" its previously learned features and only remember the new ones if it is trained with just fresh input. A growing number of researchers are focusing on ways to imbue models with the capacity for CL, akin to a human being's capacity for self-improvement through experience. This involves shifting the computing paradigm from "offline learning + online reasoning" to "online CL," which would enable models to learn continuously, alongside humans.

ACKNOWLEDGMENTS

Declared none.

CONFLICT OF INTEREST

The authors declare no conflict of interest, financial or otherwise.

REFERENCES

1. Dwivedi, Y.K., Sharma, A., Rana, N.P., Giannakis, M., Goel, P. and Dutot, V., 2023. Evolution of artificial intelligence research in technological forecasting and social change: Research topics, trends, and future directions. *Technological Forecasting and Social Change*, 192, p. 122579.
2. Mariani, M.M., Machado, I., Magrelli, V. and Dwivedi, Y.K., 2023. Artificial intelligence in innovation research: A systematic review, conceptual framework, and future research directions. *Technovation*, 122, p. 102623.
3. Patil, S.B., Rao, H.R., Chatrapathy, K., Kiran, A., Kumar, A.S. and Reddy, P.C.S., 2023, August. Ensemble deep learning framework for classification of skin lesions. In *2023 International Conference on Circuit Power and Computing Technologies (ICCPCT)* (pp. 1550–1555). IEEE.
4. Benfradj, A., Thaljaoui, A., Moulahi, T., Khan, R.U., Alabdulatif, A. and Lorenz, P., 2024. Integration of artificial intelligence (AI) with sensor networks: Trends, challenges, and future directions. *Journal of King Saud University-Computer and Information Sciences*, 36(1), p. 101892.
5. Latha, S.B., Dastagiraiah, C., Kiran, A., Asif, S., Elangovan, D. and Reddy, P.C.S., 2023, August. An adaptive machine learning model for Walmart sales prediction. In *2023 International Conference on Circuit Power and Computing Technologies (ICCPCT)* (pp. 988–992). IEEE.
6. Jia, F., Sun, D. and Looi, C.K., 2024. Artificial intelligence in science education (2013–2023): Research trends in ten years. *Journal of Science Education and Technology*, 33(1), pp. 94–117.
7. Ramana, A.V., Bhoga, U., Dhulipalla, R.K., Kiran, A., Chary, B.D. and Reddy, P.C.S., 2023, June. Abnormal behavior prediction in elderly persons using deep learning. In *2023 International Conference on Computer, Electronics & Electrical Engineering & Their Applications (IC2E3)* (pp. 1–5). IEEE.
8. Chiu, T.K., Xia, Q., Zhou, X., Chai, C.S. and Cheng, M., 2023. Systematic literature review on opportunities, challenges, and future research recommendations of artificial intelligence in education. *Computers and Education: Artificial Intelligence*, 4, p. 100118.
9. Singh, A., Kanaujia, A., Singh, V.K. and Vinuesa, R., 2024. Artificial intelligence for sustainable development goals: Bibliometric patterns and concept evolution trajectories. *Sustainable Development*, 32(1), pp. 724–754.
10. Madhavi, G.B., Bhavani, A.D., Reddy, Y.S., Kiran, A., Chitra, N.T. and Reddy, P.C.S., 2023, June. Traffic congestion detection from surveillance videos using deep learning. In *2023 International Conference on Computer, Electronics & Electrical Engineering & their Applications (IC2E3)* (pp. 1–5). IEEE.
11. Espina-Romero, L., Noroño Sánchez, J.G., Gutiérrez Hurtado, H., Dworaczek Conde, H., Solier Castro, Y., Cervera Cajo, L.E. and Rio Corredoira, J., 2023. Which industrial sectors are affected by artificial intelligence? A bibliometric analysis of trends and perspectives. *Sustainability*, 15(16), p. 12176.

12. Suneel, S., Balaram, A., Amina Begum, M., Umapathy, K., Reddy, P.C.S. and Talasila, V., 2024. Quantum mesh neural network model in precise image diagnosing. *Optical and Quantum Electronics*, 56(4), p. 559.
13. Qin, Y., Xu, Z., Wang, X. and Skare, M., 2023. Artificial intelligence and economic development: An evolutionary investigation and systematic review. *Journal of the Knowledge Economy*, 15(1), pp. 1–35.
14. Rekha, M.N., Prasad, M.L., Mukherjee, S., Nikam, S.V., Sharma, S. and Reddy, P.C.S., 2024, February. An automatic error recognition approach for machine translation results based on deep learning. In *2024 2nd International Conference on Computer, Communication and Control (IC4)* (pp. 1–8). IEEE.
15. Kariri, E., Louati, H., Louati, A. and Masmoudi, F., 2023. Exploring the advancements and future research directions of artificial neural networks: A text mining approach. *Applied Sciences*, 13(5), p. 3186.
16. Shaker Reddy, P.C. and Sucharitha, Y., 2023. A design and challenges in energy optimizing CR-wireless sensor networks. *Recent Advances in Computer Science and Communications (Formerly: Recent Patents on Computer Science)*, 16(5), pp. 82–92.
17. Krenn, M., Buffoni, L., Coutinho, B., Eppel, S., Foster, J.G., Gritsevskiy, A., Lee, H., Lu, Y., Moutinho, J.P., Sanjabi, N. and Sonthalia, R., 2023. Forecasting the future of artificial intelligence with machine learning-based link prediction in an exponentially growing knowledge network. *Nature Machine Intelligence*, 5(11), pp. 1326–1335.
18. Gadupudi, A., Rani, R.Y., Jayaram, B., Sharma, N., Deshmukh, J.K. and Reddy, P.C.S., 2024, February. An adaptive deep learning model for crop yield prediction. In *2024 2nd International Conference on Computer, Communication and Control (IC4)* (pp. 1–5). IEEE.
19. Liu, L. and Duffy, V.G., 2023. Exploring the future development of Artificial Intelligence (AI) applications in chatbots: A bibliometric analysis. *International Journal of Social Robotics*, 15(5), pp. 703–716.
20. Gurusubramani, S., Rosy, N.A., Chitra, D., Isravel, Y.A.D. and Reddy, P.C.S., 2023, November. Distributed deep learning attack detection framework for cyber-attacks in IoT network. In *2023 3rd International Conference on Advancement in Electronics & Communication Engineering (AECE)* (pp. 811–816). IEEE.
21. Yagi, M., Yamanouchi, K., Fujita, N., Funao, H. and Ebata, S., 2023. Revolutionizing spinal care: Current applications and future directions of artificial intelligence and machine learning. *Journal of Clinical Medicine*, 12(13), p. 4188.
22. Tayubi, I.A., Pawar, D.N., Kiran, A., Reddy, P.C.S., Sharma, N. and Chitra, D., 2024, February. Facial emotion recognition using a local binary pattern based deep learning. In *2024 2nd International Conference on Computer, Communication and Control (IC4)* (pp. 1–7). IEEE.
23. Kazemi, R., 2023. Artificial intelligence techniques in advanced concrete technology: A comprehensive survey on 10 years research trend. *Engineering Reports*, 5(9), p.e12676.
24. Somnathe, A.T., Tayubi, I.A., Reddy, P.C.S., Sharma, N., Sharma, V. and Yesubabu, M., 2023, December. Brain computer interaction framework for speech and motor impairment using deep learning. In *2023 International Conference on Power Energy, Environment & Intelligent Control (PEEIC)* (pp. 1008–1013). IEEE.
25. Arsenyan, J. and Piepenbrink, A., 2023. Artificial intelligence research in management: A computational literature review. *IEEE Transactions on Engineering Management*, 71, pp. 5088–5100.
26. Sekhar, G.S., Mahadik, S., Ramana, A.V., Reddy, P.C.S., Pughazendi, N. and Asif, S., 2023, December. Prediction of traffic accidents using deep learning ensemble model. In *2023 International Conference on Innovative Computing, Intelligent Communication and Smart Electrical Systems (ICSES)* (pp. 1–6). IEEE.

27. Biju, A.K.V.N., Thomas, A.S. and Thasneem, J., 2024. Examining the research taxonomy of artificial intelligence, deep learning & machine learning in the financial sphere—A bibliometric analysis. *Quality & Quantity*, 58(1), pp. 849–878.
28. Prasad, M.L., Kiran, A. and Shaker Reddy, P.C., 2024. Chronic kidney disease risk prediction using machine learning techniques. *Journal of Information Technology Management*, 16(1), pp. 118–134.
29. Gill, S.S., Xu, M., Ottaviani, C., Patros, P., Bahsoon, R., Shaghaghi, A., Golec, M., Stankovski, V., Wu, H., Abraham, A. and Singh, M., 2022. AI for next generation computing: Emerging trends and future directions. *Internet of Things*, 19, p. 100514.
30. Gurcan, F., Ayaz, A., Menekse Dalveren, G.G. and Derawi, M., 2023. Business intelligence strategies, best practices, and latest trends: Analysis of scientometric data from 2003 to 2023 using machine learning. *Sustainability*, 15(13), p. 9854.
31. Deivasigamani, S., Rani, A.J.M., Natchadalingam, R., Vijayakarthik, P., Kumar, G.B.S. and Reddy, P.C.S., 2023, August. Crop yield prediction using deep reinforcement learning. In *2023 Second International Conference on Trends in Electrical, Electronics, and Computer Engineering (TEECCON)* (pp. 137–142). IEEE.
32. Nannelli, M., Capone, F. and Lazzeretti, L., 2023. Artificial intelligence in hospitality and tourism. State of the art and future research avenues. *European Planning Studies*, 31(7), pp. 1325–1344.
33. Mamatha, B., Rashmi, D., Tiwari, K.S., Sikrant, P.A., Jovith, A.A. and Reddy, P.C.S., 2023, August. Lung cancer prediction from CT images and using deep learning techniques. In *2023 Second International Conference on Trends in Electrical, Electronics, and Computer Engineering (TEECCON)* (pp. 263–267). IEEE.
34. Alahi, M.E.E., Sukkuea, A., Tina, F.W., Nag, A., Kurdthongmee, W., Suwannarat, K. and Mukhopadhyay, S.C., 2023. Integration of IoT-enabled technologies and artificial intelligence (AI) for smart city scenario: Recent advancements and future trends. *Sensors*, 23(11), p. 5206.
35. Yang, Y., Qin, J., Lei, J. and Liu, Y., 2023. Research status and challenges on the sustainable development of artificial intelligence courses from a global perspective. *Sustainability*, 15(12), p. 9335.
36. Groumpos, P.P., 2023, July. A critical historic overview of artificial intelligence: Issues, challenges, opportunities, and threats. *Artificial Intelligence and Applications*, 1, pp. 197–213.
37. Jabeur, S.B., Ballouk, H., Arfi, W.B. and Sahut, J.M., 2023. Artificial intelligence applications in fake review detection: Bibliometric analysis and future avenues for research. *Journal of Business Research*, 158, p. 113631.
38. Ismail, L. and Buyya, R., 2022. Artificial intelligence applications and self-learning 6G networks for smart cities digital ecosystems: Taxonomy, challenges, and future directions. *Sensors*, 22(15), p. 5750.
39. Pan, S.L. and Nishant, R., 2023. Artificial intelligence for digital sustainability: An insight into domain-specific research and future directions. *International Journal of Information Management*, 72, p. 102668.
40. De la Vega Hernández, I.M., Urdaneta, A.S. and Carayannis, E., 2023. Global bibliometric mapping of the frontier of knowledge in the field of artificial intelligence for the period 1990–2019. *Artificial Intelligence Review*, 56(2), pp. 1699–1729.
41. Ahmad, K., Iqbal, W., El-Hassan, A., Qadir, J., Benhaddou, D., Ayyash, M. and Al-Fuqaha, A., 2023. Data-driven artificial intelligence in education: A comprehensive review. *IEEE Transactions on Learning Technologies*, 17, pp. 12–13.
42. Ezugwu, A.E., Oyelade, O.N., Ikotun, A.M., Agushaka, J.O. and Ho, Y.S., 2023. Machine learning research trends in Africa: A 30 years overview with bibliometric analysis review. *Archives of Computational Methods in Engineering*, 30(7), pp. 4177–4207.

43. Pandey, D.K., Hunjra, A.I., Bhaskar, R. and Al-Faryan, M.A.S., 2023. Artificial intelligence, machine learning and big data in natural resources management: A comprehensive bibliometric review of literature spanning 1975–2022. *Resources Policy*, 86, p. 104250.
44. Stoykova, S. and Shakev, N., 2023. Artificial intelligence for management information systems: opportunities, challenges, and future directions. *Algorithms*, 16(8), p. 357.
45. Ooi, K.B., Tan, G.W.H., Al-Emran, M., Al-Sharafi, M.A., Capatina, A., Chakraborty, A., Dwivedi, Y.K., Huang, T.L., Kar, A.K., Lee, V.H. and Loh, X.M., 2023. The potential of generative artificial intelligence across disciplines: Perspectives and future directions. *Journal of Computer Information Systems*, 65, pp. 1–32.
46. Thayyib, P.V., Mamilla, R., Khan, M., Fatima, H., Asim, M., Anwar, I., Shamsudheen, M.K. and Khan, M.A., 2023. State-of-the-art of artificial intelligence and big data analytics reviews in five different domains: a bibliometric summary. *Sustainability*, 15(5), p. 4026.
47. Khairnar, S., Gite, S., Kotecha, K. and Thepade, S.D., 2023. Face liveness detection using artificial intelligence techniques: A systematic literature review and future directions. *Big Data and Cognitive Computing*, 7(1), p. 37.
48. Pan, Y. and Zhang, L., 2023. Integrating BIM and AI for smart construction management: Current status and future directions. *Archives of Computational Methods in Engineering*, 30(2), pp. 1081–1110.
49. Agustí, M.A. and Orta-Pérez, M., 2023. Big data and artificial intelligence in the fields of accounting and auditing: A bibliometric analysis. *Spanish Journal of Finance and Accounting/Revista Española de Financiación y Contabilidad*, 52(3), pp. 412–438.
50. Santana, M. and Díaz-Fernández, M., 2023. Competencies for the artificial intelligence age: Visualisation of the state of the art and future perspectives. *Review of Managerial Science*, 17(6), pp. 1971–2004.
51. Pansara, R., 2023. Unraveling the complexities of data governance with strategies, challenges, and future directions. *Transactions on Latest Trends in IoT*, 6(6), pp. 46–56.
52. Shin, H. and Kang, J., 2023. Bridging the gap of bibliometric analysis: The evolution, current state, and future directions of tourism research using ChatGPT. *Journal of Hospitality and Tourism Management*, 57, pp. 40–47.
53. El Archi, Y., Benbba, B., Nizamatdinova, Z., Issakov, Y., Vargáné, G.I. and Dávid, L.D., 2023. Systematic literature review analysing smart tourism destinations in context of sustainable development: Current applications and future directions. *Sustainability*, 15(6), p. 5086.
54. Hazara, S.M., 2023. Emerging trends in artificial intelligence for information management. *Journal of Technological Information, Management & Engineering Sciences*, 1(02), pp. 108–115.
55. Díaz, E., Esteban, Á., Koutra, C., Almeida, S. and Carranza, R., 2023. Co-creation of value in smart ecosystems: past trends and future directions in tourism literature. *Journal of Hospitality and Tourism Technology*, (3), pp. 365–383.
56. Abd-Alrazaq, A., AlSaad, R., Alhuwail, D., Ahmed, A., Healy, P.M., Latifi, S., Aziz, S., Damseh, R., Alrazak, S.A. and Sheikh, J., 2023. Large language models in medical education: opportunities, challenges, and future directions. *JMIR Medical Education*, 9(1), p.e48291.
57. Choi, J.B., Nguyen, P.C., Sen, O., Udaykumar, H.S. and Baek, S., 2023. Artificial intelligence approaches for energetic materials by design: State of the art, challenges, and future directions. *Propellants, explosives, pyrotechnics*, 48(4), p. e202200276.
58. Sandeep, B., Liu, X., Huang, X., Wang, X., Mao, L. and Xiao, Z., 2023. Feasibility of artificial intelligence its current status, clinical applications, and future direction in cardiovascular disease. *Current Problems in Cardiology*, 49, p. 102349.

59. Osei-Mensah, B., Asiamah, E.O. and Sackey, R., 2023. Strategic communication and artificial intelligence: reviewing emerging innovations and future directions. *Archives of Business Research*, 11(1), pp. 85–102.
60. Sohail, S.S., Farhat, F., Himeur, Y., Nadeem, M., Madsen, D.Ø., Singh, Y., Atalla, S. and Mansoor, W., 2023. Decoding ChatGPT: a taxonomy of existing research, current challenges, and possible future directions. *Journal of King Saud University-Computer and Information Sciences*, 35, p. 101675.
61. Sampath, S., Parameswari, R., Prasad, M.L., Kumar, D.A., Hussain, M.M. and Reddy, P.C.S., 2023, December. Ensemble nonlinear machine learning model for chronic kidney diseases prediction. In *2023 IEEE 3rd Mysore Sub Section International Conference (MysuruCon)* (pp. 1–6). IEEE.
62. Kasinathan, Prabakaran, M. Sangeetha, M. Balamurugan, Shaik Aminabee, B. Rao, Dean Beema, and Reddy, Pundru Chandra Shaker. An early diabetes diseases prediction using machine learning with optimal features selection. In *2023 International Conference on Research Methodologies in Knowledge Management, Artificial Intelligence and Telecommunication Engineering (RMKMATE)*, pp. 1–7. IEEE, 2023.

Part III

Leveraging the Potential of AI in Edge Computing

6 Edge AI vis-à-vis Cloud Computing

Jyoti Agarwal, Anjali Arora, Hemlata Gangwar and Mohd Wazih Ahmad

6.1 CLOUD COMPUTING

Cloud computing delivers a broad spectrum of computing services. These services include servers to host various applications, mass storage facilities in the form of RAID and databases from various vendors, services related to networking, applications and supporting software, data analytics environments, programming languages, and artificial intelligence (AI)-based development environments. These services can be accessed over the internet and are commonly referred to as "the cloud." This model promotes rapid innovation by providing scalable and flexible resource management, and it achieves cost efficiencies through economies of scale. By leveraging the cloud, organizations can quickly access and scale resources according to their needs while minimizing capital expenditures and operational overhead.

6.1.1 Need for Cloud Computing

Cloud computing embodies a contemporary paradigm in the realm of information technology, where essential computing resources are delivered over the internet. These resources include a wide range of services and tools, such as the following:

- **Servers**: Virtual servers or cloud-based computing instances that provide the processing power needed for various applications and workloads.
- **Networks**: Network infrastructure that supports connectivity and data transfer between different cloud services and users.
- **Storage**: Scalable storage solutions for data, which can be easily expanded or reduced based on needs.
- **Tools for Development**: important tools and various platforms for software design and development, including integrated development environments (IDEs) for programming languages such as Python and Java, online version control systems, and team-based collaboration tools [1].
- **Applications**: Software applications that are accessible and managed through the cloud, including productivity suites, customer relationship management (CRM) systems, and enterprise resource planning (ERP) software.

DOI: 10.1201/9781032703718-9

This model removes the necessity for organizations to invest heavily in hardware, infrastructure, and personnel, as these responsibilities are handled by cloud service providers.

6.1.2 Defining Cloud Computing

Cloud computing provides computing resources to client companies on demand, such as servers, data storage, networks, applications, and development tools, which are provided as services. This approach helps companies save costs on building and maintaining in-house data centers. The National Institute of Standards and Technology (NIST) identifies five core characteristics that define cloud computing [2].

- **On-Demand Self-Service**: Services provided by the cloud allow its users to be able to access computing resources on demand, without needing manual intervention from the service provider. For instance, a startup can quickly provision virtual machines, storage, and applications through a web-based dashboard, scaling up or down based on their needs. This self-service capability streamlines operations and offers flexibility.
- **Broad Network Access**: Cloud resources are accessible from multiple devices having internet connection, whether it's a smartphone, tablet, or laptop. For example, a remote team can collaborate on a project using cloud-based tools like Google Workspace or Microsoft 365, irrespective of their physical location. This broad accessibility facilitates global collaboration and supports a distributed workforce.
- **Resource Pooling**: The business of various cloud providers is based on pooling computing resources in order to provide access to multiple concurrent customers of different requirements using a multi-tenant model. Resources such as computing power, memory, and storage are dynamically allocated, and assignment of the resources can be changed according to the changing demands of the customers. For instance, a cloud provider might allocate additional server capacity to handle increased traffic for an e-commerce site during peak shopping seasons, and then reallocate it once the demand decreases.
- **Rapid Elasticity**: Resource quotas can be increased or decreased quickly in a cloud computing environment, based on real-time needs. For example, during a viral marketing campaign, a company can instantly increase its cloud server capacity to handle the surge in web traffic. Once the campaign concludes, the company can scale back the resources, optimizing costs and performance.
- **Measured Service**: The billing of cloud services follows a model, which is known as the pay-as-you-go model. This model computes the amount payable after considering the statistics of resources used in billing period. For instance, a company using Amazon Web Services (AWS) pays for the compute hours, storage, and bandwidth it uses, allowing for cost-efficient management of resources.

In summary, the contemporary model of cloud computing offers a flexible, scalable, and cost-effective way to access and manage IT resources, with key features that cater to a wide range of business needs and operational scenarios.

Three important models for cloud services are as follows:

- **IaaS**: provides infrastructure such as hardware and servers as a service
- **PaaS**: offers various platforms for software developers as a service
- **SaaS**: Online complete software solution as a service

Companies use one or a combination of these models to fulfill their IT needs. Additionally, depending upon visibility, the cloud computing platforms can be created in three ways:

- **Public cloud**: Is available for different organizations at the same time it is free.
- **Private cloud**: A particular organization can get a private cloud after paying the necessary rental.
- **Hybrid cloud**: It is a hybrid of both cloud types.

6.1.3 Cloud Deployment Model

Deployment of cloud involves acquisition and provisioning of computing resources to its customers. In the next section, four types of deployment models for cloud-based services are described (Figure 6.1).

- **Private Cloud** A cloud environment designed for specific requirements of a company is called private cloud, allowing multiple users from different business units within that organization to share resources. The private cloud infrastructure can be owned and managed by the organization, outsourced to a third-party organization, or both independent of the location [3].

  For instance, a large corporation with departments such as HR, Finance, and R&D might implement a private cloud to centralize its IT resources.

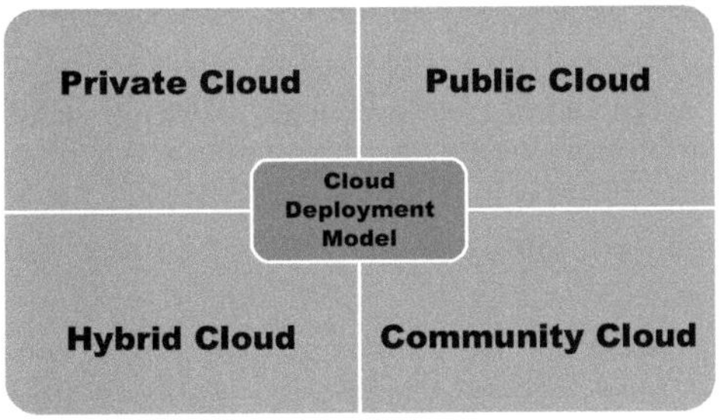

FIGURE 6.1 Cloud deployment model.

This private cloud can be hosted on the company's own servers and managed by its IT team, allowing all departments to access shared resources like virtual machines, storage, and databases while ensuring security and compliance with internal policies.

Alternatively, the company might opt for a third-party provider to manage the private cloud infrastructure, hosting it off-premises in the provider's data center. Even when managed externally, the private cloud remains dedicated solely to the organization, preventing resource sharing with other companies.

In both scenarios, the private cloud offers the organization greater control over its data, enhanced security, and the ability to tailor the infrastructure to specific business needs.

- **Public Cloud**: The public cloud is a type of cloud infrastructure accessible to the general public, typically provided by cloud vendors, government organizations, or a combination of both. It is hosted at the cloud vendor's location and offers easy access to cloud computing services for anyone who needs them.

  For example, a small business needing extra storage and computing power can turn to a public cloud service like Google Cloud Platform (GCP) instead of investing in physical servers. Google hosts the infrastructure in its data centers, allowing the business to easily sign up for the services online, access the required resources, and scale them up or down as needed.

  Another example is an individual developer who wants to build and deploy a web application. They can use AWS to access various cloud services, such as virtual servers (EC2), databases (RDS), and storage (S3) [9]. The developer can set up and manage these resources through AWS's user-friendly interface, paying only for what they use without worrying about maintaining the underlying infrastructure.

  In both cases, the public cloud provides flexibility, scalability, and cost-effectiveness, making advanced computing resources accessible to a wide range of users, from individuals to large enterprises.

- **Community Cloud**: When multiple organizations of similar scale want to access a shared cloud infrastructure a community cloud is the best option. It can be owned, managed, and operated either by the participating organizations or by a third-party cloud vendor. The cloud infrastructure can be located either on-site at any of the participating organizations or at the data center of the cloud provider.

  For example, a group of online healthcare service providers can decide to coexist on a community cloud to collaborate on research and securely share data. This cloud could be managed by a specialized third-party provider or by the participating organizations themselves, depending on their preference. The infrastructure might be hosted at one of the organizations' facilities or at the provider's data center.

  Similarly, a consortium of universities could create a community cloud for academic research and resource sharing. This cloud might be hosted at one of the universities' data centers or managed by a cloud vendor with expertise in educational services. This arrangement allows the universities to access shared research tools and computing resources while addressing their specific needs and compliance requirements.

In both examples, the community cloud offers a collaborative, secure environment tailored to the shared needs of its members, promoting resource efficiency and cost-sharing.

- **Hybrid Cloud**: When two or more cloud infrastructure types are combined to create a third type of cloud service, it is called hybrid cloud infrastructure. In this type of system, the participating clouds can be public, private, or community type. Although these clouds remain distinct entities, they are interconnected through specialized technologies that facilitate the movement of data and applications between them.

  For example, a company might employ a hybrid cloud setup that integrates a private cloud for storing sensitive internal data with a public cloud for handling scalable applications and services. The private cloud would securely manage confidential information like employee records and financial data, while the public cloud could host the company's website, email services, and customer applications. This hybrid approach allows the company to benefit from the security and compliance of the private cloud while leveraging the scalability and cost-efficiency of the public cloud.

  Another example is a healthcare organization that uses a community cloud for collaborative research with other healthcare providers, while also maintaining a private cloud for managing patient records and sensitive medical data. This hybrid configuration enables the organization to securely share research data with partners through the community cloud while keeping patient information protected and compliant with regulations.

  In both scenarios, a hybrid cloud infrastructure provides flexibility and optimization, allowing organizations to combine the strengths of different cloud models for efficient, secure, and scalable operations.

6.1.4 Cloud Service Models

This section describes three kinds of services offered by cloud computing companies (Figure 6.2).

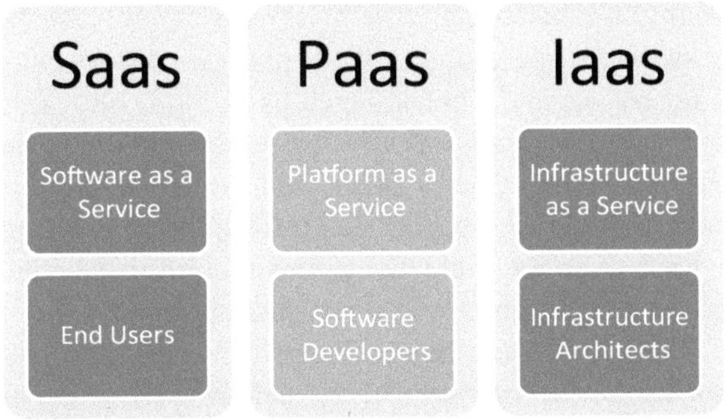

FIGURE 6.2 Cloud service model.

- **SaaS**: If the customers of a cloud provider company want to use the applications over the internet, Software as a Service (SaaS), a subscription service model provided by the vendor, is a suitable choice. In this model, the service provider manages all underlying infrastructure components such as servers, storage, networking, virtualization, operating systems, and the application software itself. This setup allows customers to use applications either remotely or on-premises without needing to handle maintenance or updates. For example, Google Drive is a SaaS application that is used to store and share files online. Google manages its servers, storage, and security for Google Drive, in order to support file access over the internet without needing to worry about the technical aspects of maintaining the service. Users simply subscribe to the service and can scale their storage capacity based on their needs.

  Another example is Slack, a communication and collaboration tool. Slack provides a platform for teams to chat, share files, and integrate with other tools. Slack handles the infrastructure and updates, so teams can focus on their work rather than managing the software. Users can scale their subscription plan according to the size of their team and their feature requirements. In both examples, SaaS offers convenience and flexibility, allowing users to access powerful applications over the internet while the service provider takes care of the technical management, updates, and scaling of the service.
- **PaaS**: Platform as a Service (PaaS) is a cloud computing model where providers offer a comprehensive environment for users to develop, deploy, and manage their software applications. This environment includes everything needed for development, such as tools, runtime environments, and frameworks, while the provider takes care of the underlying cloud infrastructure. Customers focus solely on building and running their applications, without having to manage the hardware, operating systems, or networking.

  An example of a PaaS is Google App Engine; it allows developers to design, develop, and deploy web-based applications using Google infrastructure. Developers can write their code using various programming languages and frameworks supported by Google App Engine, such as Python, Java, or PHP. Google manages the servers, databases, and networking, so developers don't have to worry about these aspects. They can focus on coding and deploying their application, with the platform automatically scaling resources based on demand.

  Another example is Heroku, a PaaS platform that provides several programming languages and libraries such as Python, Java, and Ruby. Heroku supports a set of tools and services for developers to deploy and manage applications easily. Developers push their code to Heroku, which handles the application runtime, scaling, and infrastructure management. This allows developers to concentrate on writing and improving their code without needing to manage the underlying infrastructure.

  In both cases, PaaS enables developers to create and deploy applications quickly and efficiently, leveraging the cloud provider's infrastructure and services while maintaining control over their application code and functionality.

- **IaaS**: IaaS is a virtualization-based cloud service model, which provides computing resources such as servers, storage, and networking over the internet to its users. In this model customers can access and manage these resources without having to handle the physical hardware. Instead, they control the operating system, middleware, runtime environment, and the applications they deploy on the virtual infrastructure.

  For instance, AWS is a well-known IaaS provider that offers services like Simple Storage Service (S3) for massive storage, and Elastic Compute Cloud (EC2) for virtual servers. A company utilizing AWS can lease virtual machines to operate their applications, store data in S3, and adjust their resources according to demand. The company does not need to concern itself with the physical servers or networking hardware, as AWS oversees the management of the underlying infrastructure.

  Another example is Google Compute Engine, which is part of GCP. Google Compute Engine provides virtual machines that users can configure according to their needs. Users can install and manage their operating systems, middleware, and applications on these virtual machines. Google handles the infrastructure such as servers, storage requirements, and networking, relieving its users of deploying and managing necessary software.

  Similarly, Rackspace offers IaaS services by providing virtualized servers, storage, and networking resources. Customers can build and manage their IT environments on Rackspace's infrastructure while having control over their operating systems, applications, and data. Rackspace also provides managed services, allowing customers to offload some of the operational aspects to the provider.

  In all these examples, IaaS allows customers to rent and manage computing resources on-demand, providing flexibility and scalability while the cloud provider takes care of the physical infrastructure [4].

6.1.5 Cloud Advantages and Disadvantages

Cloud computing is a transformative technology that allows businesses to operate more efficiently from virtually anywhere. It offers several key benefits:

- **Cost Savings**: Cloud computing reduces capital expenses by eliminating the need for purchasing and maintaining physical IT infrastructure. For example, a startup can use AWS to access computing resources on a pay-as-you-go basis, avoiding the significant upfront costs of buying servers and storage equipment.
- **Flexibility and Scalability**: Businesses of all sizes can easily scale their resources by increasing or decreasing their required quota based on their needs. Generally, most e-commerce companies during peak traffic days such as holidays can quickly increase their computing power and storage capacity through Microsoft Azure, without having to invest in additional physical hardware.

- **Security**: Cloud vendors offer advanced features for security and authentication, access control, data encryption, and backup services. For example, GCP provides robust security measures to protect user data, such as encryption at rest and in transit, ensuring that sensitive information remains secure.

However, cloud computing also has some drawbacks that businesses should consider before transitioning:

- **Downtime**: Cloud services depend on internet connectivity. In the absence of internet connection, there is always a chance of interruption in access to data as well as applications. For instance, Google faced significant outages in 2020 that disrupted services for users worldwide, highlighting the risk of downtime.
- **Vendor Lock-In**: Transitioning workloads from one cloud provider to another can be challenging due to potential compatibility and integration issues. For example, moving from AWS to Azure might involve complex data migration processes and compatibility adjustments, potentially exposing sensitive data to security risks if not managed carefully.
- **Limited Control**: With cloud infrastructure managed by the vendor, businesses have limited control over their data and services. For instance, a company using Salesforce for its CRM needs to understand the extent of control it has over its data and the vendor's service agreements to ensure it meets its requirements.
- **Security**: Storing sensitive data in the cloud raises security concerns. Despite strong security measures from providers, keeping confidential data on remote servers always poses risks. For example, a healthcare organization using a cloud-based patient record system must be diligent about both the vendor's security practices and its own data protection measures.
- **Cost**: While cloud computing can reduce capital expenditures, operational costs can increase. For example, a business might face unexpected charges if it exceeds its data storage limits or uses additional premium features beyond its initial plan, leading to higher-than-expected operational expenses.

Overall, while cloud computing offers substantial advantages, understanding these potential challenges is crucial for making informed decisions about cloud adoption.

6.1.6 Cloud Service Providers

Cloud service providers as shown in Figure 6.3, offer a flexible approach to building, managing, and delivering web and mobile applications, regardless of their size. By providing virtual server hosting, they offer a wide range of resources over the internet, including big data analytics, IoT, computing, and more, which allows for a streamlined development process. Cloud resources are available with plug-and-play capabilities, which means you can use only what you need, when you need it.

FIGURE 6.3 Top cloud service companies 2023.

- **Amazon Web Services**: AWS is the top cloud provider worldwide, offering an extensive range of over 200 integrated features and services. It includes a free tier that lets users experiment with various services at no cost or obligation. For instance, a startup can use AWS's free tier to explore Amazon S3 for storage and Amazon EC2 for virtual servers without initial expenses. AWS operates in 77 Availability Zones across 24 geographic regions and commands over 30% of the cloud market share. This broad infrastructure guarantees high availability and reliability for applications.
- **Microsoft Azure**: Microsoft Azure provides a comprehensive set of on-demand computing services similar to AWS, including Infrastructure as a Service (IaaS), Platform as a Service (PaaS), Software as a Service (SaaS), and serverless computing. For instance, a company developing a new app can use Azure's App Services (PaaS) to host and manage the application, Azure Functions (serverless computing) for running code in response to events, and Azure SQL Database (IaaS) for managing its data without needing to handle the underlying infrastructure.
- **Google Cloud Platform**: GCP provides a range of services built on the same infrastructure that supports Google Search, YouTube, and other Google applications. For instance, a data science team could utilize Google BigQuery for large-scale data analysis, taking advantage of the high-performance infrastructure that underpins Google's own data-intensive services. GCP's tools are engineered to manage extensive computing and storage requirements efficiently.
- **Salesforce**: Salesforce provides a range of cloud-based solutions focused on CRM, customer service, marketing automation, and sales. For example, a retail company might use Salesforce CRM to manage customer interactions, track sales leads, and automate marketing campaigns. Salesforce's tools help businesses leverage data to make informed decisions and enhance customer engagement, driving a more data-driven approach to managing customer relationships.

6.1.7 Security in Cloud Computing

Cloud security operates under a shared responsibility model, dividing security tasks between the cloud provider and the customer [1]. Here's a breakdown of the responsibilities:

- **Provider Responsibilities**: The cloud provider is responsible for securing the foundational infrastructure and services that support the cloud environment. This includes:
  - **Securing the Infrastructure**: The provider manages the physical security of the data centers, including the hardware and networking equipment. For example, AWS is responsible for protecting the servers and network hardware within its data centers.
  - **Managing Access**: The provider controls access to the physical infrastructure and ensures that unauthorized personnel cannot access it. For instance, GCP uses strong physical security measures and access controls to protect its data centers.
  - **Handling Patching and Configuration**: The provider is in charge of updating and maintaining the hardware and network configurations. For example, Microsoft Azure manages the patching of the underlying servers and network equipment to protect against vulnerabilities.
- **Customer Responsibilities**: Customers are responsible for managing and securing their own data and applications within the cloud environment. This includes:
  - **Managing Users and Access Privileges**: Customers must handle identity and access management (IAM) to control who can access their cloud resources. For example, a company using AWS Identity and IAM configures roles and permissions to ensure only authorized employees can access specific resources.
  - **Protecting Cloud Accounts**: Customers need to safeguard their cloud accounts from unauthorized access. This involves using strong authentication methods and monitoring for suspicious activities. For instance, a business using Salesforce should implement multi-factor authentication (MFA) to protect user accounts.
  - **Encrypting and Safeguarding Data**: Customers are responsible for encrypting their data stored in the cloud and protecting it from unauthorized access. For example, a company storing sensitive customer information on Google Cloud Storage must ensure that the data is encrypted both at rest and in transit [3].
  - **Maintaining Security Posture for Compliance**: Customers need to ensure their use of cloud services adheres to applicable regulations and standards. For instance, a healthcare organization using Azure must make sure its use of cloud resources meets Health Insurance Portability and Accountability Act (HIPAA) requirements, including appropriate data handling and reporting practices.

- **Responsibilities Based on Service Model**
  - **Infrastructure as a Service (IaaS)**: In an IaaS model, such as AWS EC2, the provider manages the physical hardware and networking, while customers handle everything from the operating system up to the applications, including firewall configurations and security patches for their virtual machines.
  - **Platform as a Service (PaaS)**: In a PaaS model, such as Microsoft Azure App Services, the provider manages the infrastructure and runtime environment, while customers are responsible for managing the applications and data they deploy.
  - **Software as a Service (SaaS)**: In a SaaS model, such as Salesforce, the provider manages everything from the infrastructure to the application. Customers are responsible for managing user access and ensuring that their use of the software is secure and compliant with any applicable regulations.
  - In summary, while the cloud provider secures the infrastructure and services, the customer is responsible for securing their data, managing access, and ensuring compliance.

6.2 EDGE COMPUTING

Edge computing is a developing computing paradigm that involves networks and devices positioned at or near the user. It focuses on processing data closer to its source, allowing for faster and more voluminous data handling, which results in immediate, action-oriented outcomes.

6.2.1 Introduction to Edge Computing

Edge computing defines a new model of data processing as the data shall be processed near the point of its generation as compared to previous computing models, which rely on a centralized storage system for data processing. This approach enhances efficiency and responsiveness by handling data locally, which reduces latency and the need for extensive bandwidth and storage [5].

In a smart manufacturing facility, sensor data coming from machinery can also be processed by edge computing devices on the production line. For instance, sensors might monitor temperature, vibration, and wear-and-tear on equipment. Locally processing such data on edge devices can help in quickly detecting anomalies, such as overheating or mechanical issues, and trigger immediate alerts or automated adjustments without needing to send data to a distant cloud data center. This real-time processing helps to prevent equipment failures and optimize production efficiency.

Autonomous vehicles are real-time systems that are highly sensitive to delays in processing time required to make final driving decisions. These vehicles are equipped with various sensors, such as cameras, radar, and Light Detection and Ranging (LIDAR), which generate vast amounts of data about the vehicle's surroundings.

Edge computing enables the vehicle to process this data locally, allowing it to quickly interpret traffic signals, obstacles, and road conditions. By handling data processing on-board, autonomous vehicles can make immediate decisions and react in real time, which is crucial for safe and efficient driving.

In smart cities, edge computing can enhance traffic management systems. Traffic cameras and sensors placed at intersections and along roads collect data on vehicle flow, pedestrian movements, and environmental conditions [8]. Edge computing devices at these locations can analyze the data to manage traffic lights, optimize traffic flow, and even predict congestion patterns. This localized processing reduces the need to send all data to centralized servers, minimizing bandwidth usage and allowing for faster response times to changing traffic conditions.

6.2.2 Evolution from CDNs to Edge Computing

The concept of edge computing builds on the principles of Content Delivery Networks (CDNs), which were introduced by Akamai in the 1990s. CDNs distributed network nodes to cache and deliver static media, like images and videos, closer to users to alleviate web traffic congestion and improve load times. Edge computing extends this idea by incorporating computing power at the network edge, not just for caching but also for processing and analyzing data [7]. This evolution supports more complex applications and services by enabling real-time data handling and decision-making closer to the data source.

In summary, edge computing enhances performance and efficiency by decentralizing data processing and reducing reliance on central data centers, which benefits various applications, from industrial manufacturing to autonomous driving and smart city management.

Edge computing is a relatively new technology that is based on the assumption that if data is processed near the point of generation then it shall be more efficient to process it as compared to the centralized systems. This approach enhances efficiency and responsiveness by handling data and computations at or near the source, enabling real-time applications and more dynamic user experiences.

6.2.3 Components of Edge Computing

- **Edge Devices**
  Description: These are everyday devices and specialized equipment that perform local data processing and interact with their environment. They include smart gadgets like speakers, watches, and phones, as well as industrial tools and sensors.
  Example: A smart home system might include devices like smart thermostats and security cameras. A smart thermostat processes data about indoor temperatures and user preferences locally to adjust heating and cooling settings in real time. Similarly, security cameras can analyze video feeds on the device itself to detect unusual activities and send alerts without needing to send all footage to a central server.

- **Network Edge**
  Description: This refers to the points along the network where data processing can occur, ranging from individual devices to network routers. It doesn't require a separate edge network but represents the locations between the end-users and the central cloud. With the advent of 5G technology, the network edge gains enhanced capabilities with low latency and high bandwidth.
  Example: Autonomous vehicles use edge computing to process sensor data from cameras, radar, and LIDAR systems in real time. This data processing at the network edge allows the vehicle to make immediate driving decisions, such as avoiding obstacles or adjusting speed, crucial for safety and efficiency. 5G networks support these operations by providing the high-speed connectivity needed for rapid data exchange and low-latency responses.
- **On-Premises Infrastructure**
  Description: This includes physical IT assets like servers, routers, and other networking equipment located within a company's premises. These components handle regional computing tasks and connect to the broader internet or cloud services.
  Example: In a large retail store, on-premises infrastructure might include servers that handle transactions, manage inventory systems, and process data from point-of-sale (POS) terminals. This local processing allows the store to maintain quick transaction times and manage inventory efficiently without relying on a distant cloud server, which could introduce delays.

6.2.4 Advanced Applications of Edge Computing

- **Autonomous Vehicles**: These vehicles use edge computing to process data from their sensors and cameras in real time, enabling them to navigate roads safely and make split-second driving decisions.
- **Robots**: In manufacturing, robots equipped with edge computing capabilities can perform tasks like quality control and assembly with minimal latency, improving production efficiency [6].
- **Smart Devices**: Devices such as smart speakers and wearable fitness trackers process data locally to provide immediate feedback and functionality, like tracking fitness metrics or responding to voice commands.
- **Automated Retail**: In automated retail environments, edge computing can enable features like cashier-less checkouts by processing purchase data locally at the point-of-sale, improving customer experience and operational efficiency.

In summary, edge computing enhances performance and user experience by decentralizing data processing and leveraging local computing resources. It supports a wide range of applications from consumer devices to complex industrial systems, benefiting from advances in network technologies like 5G [6].

6.2.5 Business Transformation via Edge Computing

It plays a crucial role in various sectors by processing data locally, near its source, to ensure low latency and high reliability. This approach is increasingly being utilized in environments that handle sensitive data and require immediate, network-independent solutions. Here's how edge computing is transforming different business functions [6]:

- **Healthcare**: In hospitals, edge computing devices are used to monitor patient vitals in real time. Wearable health monitors and in-room medical devices can process data locally to provide immediate feedback on patient conditions. For instance, a heart monitor in a hospital room processes Electro-Cardio Gram (ECG) data on-site to detect anomalies and trigger alarms if necessary, ensuring timely medical intervention without waiting for data to be sent to a distant cloud server.
- **Manufacturing**: Factories use edge computing to manage and optimize production lines. Sensors and machines equipped with edge devices can analyze data locally to monitor equipment performance and detect potential issues before they cause downtime. For example, predictive maintenance systems use edge computing to analyze vibration data from machinery in real time, allowing for early detection of wear and tear and scheduling maintenance proactively.
- **Retail Stores**: These leverage edge computing to enhance the in-store shopping experience. Intelligent checkout systems, such as cashier-less stores, use edge computing to process transactions and manage inventory in real time. For instance, Amazon Go stores use sensors and cameras to track purchases and automatically charge customers without requiring traditional checkout processes, all while processing data locally to ensure quick and accurate transactions.
- **Marketing and Customer Engagement**: Retailers use edge computing to deliver personalized marketing messages based on real-time customer behavior. Digital signage in stores can use edge computing to analyze customer interactions and adjust advertisements dynamically. For instance, a digital display might show targeted promotions based on the products a customer is viewing or interacting with, enhancing engagement and driving sales.
- **Worker Training**: In industries like manufacturing and logistics, edge computing can support augmented reality (AR) training programs. AR headsets equipped with edge devices provide real-time guidance and interactive simulations for workers, helping them learn complex tasks and procedures on-site. For example, a worker learning to operate a new machine might use AR glasses to receive step-by-step instructions and visual aids directly in their field of view, with all processing done locally on the edge device.
- **Intelligent Environments**: Smart buildings use edge computing to manage and optimize various systems for security and comfort. For instance, smart thermostats and lighting systems analyze data from sensors on-site to adjust temperature and lighting based on occupancy and preferences. A smart

building might use edge computing to integrate data from security cameras, access controls, and environmental sensors to enhance safety and ensure an optimal environment for occupants [8].

6.2.6 Edge Computing Framework

An edge computing architecture generally consists of three layers (Figure 6.4):

- **The Cloud Layer**: This layer is responsible for processing and storing all data.
- **The Edge Layer**: This layer handles data processing in near real-time.
- **The Device Layer**: This layer is tasked with detecting and performing basic processing.
- **Cloud Layer**: Edge computing was designed to mitigate network congestion and latency issues commonly associated with centralized cloud computing. Despite its advantages, cloud computing remains a vital part of the overall IT ecosystem. Cloud and edge computing work together seamlessly to create an efficient architecture. In this integrated setup, the edge layer determines whether data needs further processing beyond its immediate capabilities. For tasks requiring more complex computations or larger data storage, the edge server forwards data to the cloud layer. The cloud layer then performs detailed processing and analysis, leveraging its robust computational power and extensive storage. Additionally, the edge server sends

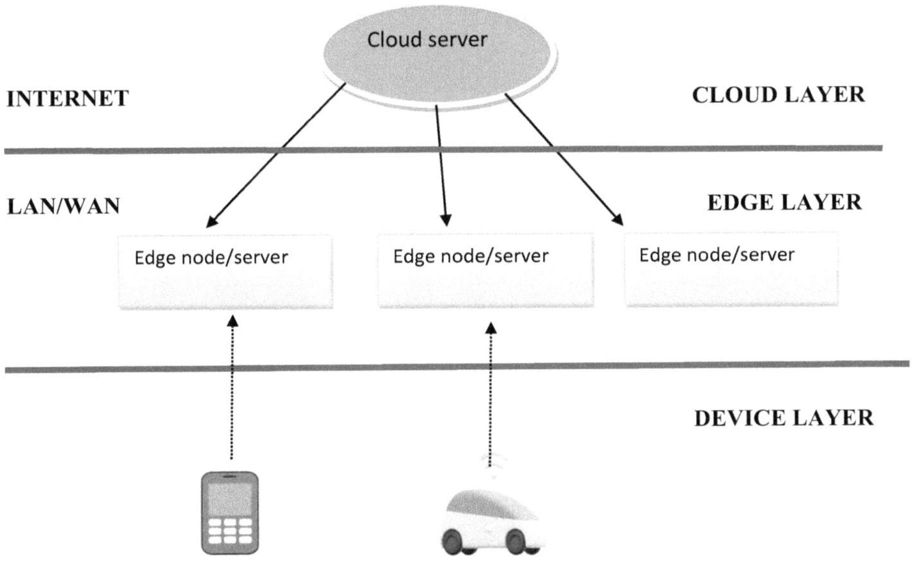

FIGURE 6.4 Edge computing architecture.

a portion of the collected data to the cloud for comprehensive analysis and long-term storage. This collaboration between the edge and cloud layers highlights their complementary roles: edge computing handles real-time, local data processing, while cloud computing provides advanced processing capabilities and data management. This synergy ensures optimal performance and deeper insights across the entire IT architecture [6].

- **Edge layer**: The edge layer forms the backbone of edge computing by incorporating a network of distributed edge servers. Unlike the more centralized cloud servers, these edge servers are spread out closer to the data sources. This strategic distribution enables the edge layer to handle data processing locally, significantly reducing latency and improving response times. In the edge layer, data is initially processed and analyzed near its source, addressing immediate processing needs and minimizing delays. For tasks requiring more extensive analysis or when local processing is insufficient, the edge servers forward data to the cloud layer. This ensures that all data is thoroughly analyzed and stored, leveraging the cloud's powerful computing resources and extensive storage capabilities. By forwarding complex or extensive data to the cloud, the edge layer maintains comprehensive data integrity and ensures that no critical information is overlooked. This collaboration between the edge and cloud layers highlights the efficiency and effectiveness of combining local and centralized processing to meet various data management needs.
- **Device Layer** The device layer is the foundational level in the edge computing architecture, characterized by its large number of diverse devices. This layer encompasses a wide range of equipment, from small gadgets like smartphones and laptops to large-scale machinery such as buses and industrial robots. These devices play a crucial role in gathering and collecting data, enabling various applications and services to function effectively.

6.2.6.1 Key Functions and Capabilities

Data Collection: Devices in this layer are equipped with sensors that capture data from their environment. This data collection is essential for the functionality of various products and services, as it provides the raw information needed for analysis and decision-making. In a healthcare setting, devices such as heart rate monitors and blood glucose meters continuously collect patient vital signs. In an automated vehicle, sensors gather data on surrounding traffic conditions, road signs, and obstacles.

- **Data Processing and Analytics**
  Explanation: Despite being less powerful than the cloud or edge layers, devices in the device layer are capable of performing essential computations and analytics. They handle simple data processing tasks and execute computations close to the data source, enabling near real-time responses.
  Example: In a smart factory, industrial machines equipped with sensors can process data locally to detect issues like equipment malfunctions or deviations in production quality. This allows for immediate adjustments without the need to send all data to the cloud.

- **Real-Time Data Handling**
  Explanation: One of the primary advantages of the device layer is its ability to process data closest to its source. This proximity enables near real-time data handling, which is critical for applications that require immediate responses.
  Example: In a traffic management system, sensors embedded in traffic lights and road signs can analyze and respond to traffic flow changes almost instantly, helping to manage traffic effectively without delay.

The device layer, with its extensive array of devices ranging from mobile phones to industrial machinery, is integral to data collection and processing. While it may not match the advanced computing power of the cloud or edge layers, it excels in handling data at its source, performing immediate computations, and enabling real-time responses. This foundational layer ensures that data is gathered and processed efficiently, supporting the functionality and effectiveness of the broader edge computing architecture.

6.3 COMPARATIVE STUDY OF CLOUD COMPUTING AND EDGE COMPUTING

Cloud and edge computing are based on different models, and their architectural differences make it difficult to say if one is an alternative to another. Time-sensitive data is better processed with Edge Computing infrastructure while cloud computing is used to process non-time-triggered data.

6.3.1 Edge Computing versus Cloud Computing

6.3.1.1 Definition

- **Edge Computing**: This refers to processing and storing data closer to where it is generated, such as on local devices or edge servers. This proximity reduces latency and allows for quicker responses to data changes and immediate decision-making. For example, in a smart factory, edge devices monitor machinery in real time and can instantly adjust operations or shut down equipment if issues are detected.
- **Cloud Computing**: Cloud computing involves processing and storing data on remote servers managed by third-party organizations. Users access their data and applications via the internet, but the physical hardware and infrastructure are controlled by the cloud service provider. For example, Google Drive or Dropbox allows users to store and access their files from any location, relying on remote data centers for storage and processing [9].

6.3.1.2 Data Distribution

- **Edge Computing Approach**: Data is processed locally at the edge of the network, close to the data source. This decentralization helps in handling time-sensitive data and reduces the need for sending data to a central server.

For example, a smart thermostat processes data locally to adjust temperature settings in real time based on user behavior.

- **Cloud Computing Approach**: Data is sent to centralized data centers where it is processed and stored. This centralization is effective for managing large volumes of data but may introduce latency due to the distance data travels [11]. For example, an online retail platform uses cloud servers to process and store customer orders and transaction data.

6.3.1.3 Focus

- **Edge Computing**: Real-time processing and immediate device connectivity. It's designed for applications requiring rapid responses and minimal latency. For example, autonomous vehicles use edge computing to process sensor data and make instant driving decisions.
- **Cloud Computing**: Handling and archiving large volumes of unstructured data. It is optimized for long-term data storage and large-scale processing. For example, cloud-based analytics platforms aggregate and analyze big data to provide business intelligence.

6.3.1.4 Real-Time Interaction

- **Edge Computing**: Data is processed locally, enabling real-time interactions and immediate responses. For example, a security camera with edge computing capabilities can detect unusual activity and send alerts instantly.
- **Cloud Computing**: Data is centralized, which can introduce delays in communication and processing. For example, cloud-based customer service chatbots may have delayed responses if they rely on remote servers for processing [12].

6.3.1.5 Data Processing

- **Edge Computing**: Focuses on real-time data processing and action-driven solutions. Edge computing processes data near its source, allowing for faster and more efficient handling of high-volume, time-sensitive data. For example, smart sensors in a manufacturing plant detect anomalies and adjust machinery settings on the spot.
- **Cloud Computing**: Centralized processing involves handling large amounts of data in a remote data center. While it excels in managing extensive data sets, it may suffer from latency issues and shared resource constraints [13]. For example, cloud-based data analytics platforms process data from various sources to generate business insights.

6.3.1.6 Use Cases

- **Edge Computing**
  - **Big Data Analytics**: Analyzing data close to its source to derive actionable insights in real time.
  - **Cloud Gaming**: Delivering low-latency gaming experiences by processing game data locally.

- **IoT**: Managing and processing data from various IoT devices like smart home systems.
- **Predictive Maintenance**: Monitoring equipment and predicting failures before they occur.

- **Cloud Computing**
  - **IaaS (Infrastructure as a Service)**: Providing virtualized computing resources over the internet.
  - **SaaS (Software as a Service)**: Offering software applications via the cloud.
  - **Hybrid Clouds**: Combining private and public cloud environments for flexibility.
  - **Multi-Cloud**: Utilizing multiple cloud services for redundancy and optimization.
  - **Virtual Machines**: Running isolated virtual environments for development and testing.

6.3.1.7 Cost Effectiveness

- **Edge Computing**: Requires investment in edge devices and infrastructure at each node. This can be more expensive compared to centralized cloud services due to the need for multiple localized systems. For example, implementing edge devices in a large number of remote locations can lead to higher upfront costs.
- **Cloud Computing**: Generally, more cost-effective as resources are centralized. Cloud service providers offer scalable services, allowing businesses to pay only for what they use. For example, a company using cloud storage services only pays for the amount of storage and bandwidth it consumes.

6.3.2 Use Cases of Cloud and Edge Computing

To illustrate the differences between the two computing models with examples, let's consider two scenarios.

6.3.2.1 Use Case 1: Autonomous Vehicles

6.3.2.1.1 Edge Computing Scenario

- **Situation**: An autonomous vehicle is driving through a busy city.
- **How It Works**: The vehicle is equipped with sensors and processing units that collect and analyze data in real time. For instance, it constantly monitors the position of other vehicles, pedestrians, traffic lights, and road conditions [10].
- **Why Edge Computing?** The processing is done locally within the vehicle (at the edge of the network), allowing for immediate responses. If a pedestrian suddenly steps onto the road, the vehicle can detect and react in milliseconds, applying the brakes to prevent an accident. This near-instantaneous response is crucial for safety and effectiveness [13].

6.3.2.1.2 Cloud Computing Scenario

- **Situation**: The same vehicle sends its collected data to a central cloud server for analysis and storage.
- **How It Works**: Data such as traffic patterns, vehicle performance, and driving habits are sent to the cloud for more extensive analysis and long-term storage.
- **Why Cloud Computing?** While real-time processing is handled locally for immediate safety, cloud computing is used for aggregating data from multiple vehicles, analyzing trends, and improving overall systems. However, any delay in sending and receiving data from the cloud could impair the real-time decision-making necessary for immediate vehicle control.

6.3.2.2 Use Case 2: Smart Manufacturing

6.3.2.2.1 Edge Computing Scenario

- **Situation**: A factory operates machines that need to be monitored for optimal performance.
- **How It Works**: Sensors on the machines track their performance and send data to local edge devices. If a machine starts to operate outside of its normal parameters, the edge device can immediately analyze the data and, if necessary, shut down the machine to prevent damage or defects [10].
- **Why Edge Computing?** This local processing ensures that issues are detected and addressed almost instantly, which is crucial for preventing downtime and maintaining product quality.

6.3.2.2.2 Cloud Computing Scenario

- **Situation**: The same factory collects data from various machines and sends it to a cloud-based platform.
- **How It Works**: The data is used to generate reports, analyze long-term performance trends, and optimize maintenance schedules. While this helps with overall operational efficiency and predictive maintenance, it may not be suitable for real-time decision-making due to potential delays in data transmission and processing [14].
- **Why Cloud Computing?** Cloud computing allows for advanced analytics, historical data review, and insights that help improve future performance and maintenance strategies.

6.3.2.3 Comparison in Summary

- **Edge Computing** is ideal when immediate, localized data processing, and rapid responses are critical, as seen in autonomous vehicles and real-time machine monitoring.
- **Cloud Computing** is better suited for tasks requiring extensive data processing, long-term storage, and analysis, such as aggregating data from multiple sources and deriving broader insights.

In practice, many systems integrate both edge and cloud computing to leverage the strengths of each. For instance, autonomous vehicles use edge computing for real-time decisions while sending aggregated data to the cloud for broader analysis and improvements.

6.4 CONCLUSION

Edge computing and cloud computing are distinct but complementary technologies. Edge computing excels in scenarios requiring real-time data processing and immediate responses by processing data close to its source. Cloud computing is suited for managing and analyzing large volumes of data with the advantage of scalability and remote access.

In practice, many systems leverage both technologies to harness their respective strengths. For example, edge computing can handle real-time operations while cloud computing manages extensive data analysis and long-term storage. Together, they represent a holistic approach to modern computing needs, shaping the future of technology across various industries.

REFERENCES

1. C. Bradford, "7 Most Infamous Cloud Security Breaches," *StorageCraft*, 2019. [Online]. Available: https://blog.storagecraft.com/7-infamous-cloud-security-breaches [Accessed: 22 Jul 2024].
2. P. Mell and T. Grance, "The NIST Definition of Cloud Computing," National Institute of Standards and Technology, SP 800-145, 2011. [Online]. Available: https://csrc.nist.gov/publications/detail/sp/800-145/final [Accessed: 22 Jul 2024].
3. M. Mimoso, "Contractor Accesses 2 Million Vodafone Germany Customer Records," *Threatpost*, 2013. [Online]. Available: https://threatpost.com/contractor-accesses-2-million-vodafone-germany-customer-records/102286/ [Accessed: 22 Jul 2024].
4. S. Patrick, "Security and the Cloud: Trends in Enterprise Cloud Computing," *Clutch.co*, 2016. [Online]. Available: https://clutch.co/cloud/resources/security-trends-in-enterprise-cloud-computing [Accessed: 22 Jul 2024].
5. M. Herh, "Korea-Led Edge Computing Technology Recognized as Global Standard," *Business Korea*, 2018. [Online]. Available: http://www.businesskorea.co.kr/news/articleView.html?idxno=23999 [Accessed: 22 Jul 2024].
6. P.S.K. Sayyad Khodashenas, C. Ruiz, M. Shuaib Siddiqui, and J. Ferrer Riera, "The Role of Edge Computing in Future 5G Mobile Networks: Concept and Challenges." In E. Markakis, G. Mastorakis, C.X. Mavromoustakis, and E. Pallis (Eds.), *Cloud and Fog Computing in 5G Mobile Networks: Emerging Advances and Applications*. Institution of Engineering and Technology, 2017, pp. 349–370.
7. S. Nunna, A. Kousaridas, M. Ibrahim, M. Dillinger, C. Thuemmler, H. Feussner, and A. Schneider, "Enabling Real-Time Context-Aware Collaboration Through 5G and Mobile Edge Computing." In *2015 12th International Conference on Information Technology: New Generations (ITNG)*, 2015, pp. 601–605.
8. B.N. Silva, M. Khan, and K. Han, "Towards Sustainable Smart Cities: A Review of Trends, Architectures, Components, and Open Challenges in Smart Cities," *Sustainable Cities and Society*, vol. 38, pp. 697–713, 2018.

9. S. Jeschke, C. Brecher, T. Meisen, D. Özdemir, and T. Eschert, "Industrial Internet of Things and Cyber Manufacturing Systems." In S. Jeschke, C. Brecher, H. Song, and D.B. Rawat (Eds.), *Industrial Internet of Things*. Springer International Publishing, 2017, pp. 3–19.
10. B. Chen, J. Wan, L. Shu, P. Li, M. Mukherjee, and B. Yin, "Smart Factory of Industry 4.0: Key Technologies, Application Case, and Challenges," *IEEE Access*, vol. 6, pp. 6505–6519, 2018.
11. F. Giust, V. Sciancalepore, D. Sabella, M.C. Filippou, S. Mangiante, W. Featherstone, and D. Munaretto, "Multi-Access Edge Computing: The Driver Behind the Wheel of 5G-Connected Cars," *IEEE Communications Standards Magazine*, vol. 2, no. 3, pp. 66–73, 2018.
12. P. Porambage, J. Okwuibe, M. Liyanage, M. Ylianttila, and T. Taleb, "Survey on Multi-Access Edge Computing for Internet of Things Realization," *IEEE Communications Surveys & Tutorials*, vol. 20, no. 4, pp. 2961–2991, 2018.
13. A.J.W. Chen, M. Boudreau, and R.T. Watson, "Information Systems and Ecological Sustainability," *Journal of Systems and Information Technology*, vol. 10, no. 2, pp. 186–201, 2008.
14. Cisco Systems Inc., "Cisco Visual Networking Index: Forecast and Methodology, 2008–2013," 2009.

7 Intelligent Fault Predictive System in Industrial Internet of Things Using Condition Monitoring

Swati Shivkumar Shriyal and Bharati Sanjay Ainapure

7.1 INTRODUCTION

The Internet of Things (IoT) is a framework that enables everyday physical objects, or "things," to connect to a network and possess computing capabilities. These physical items are equipped with sensors that allow them to be monitored with minimal human intervention.

IoT encompasses the concept of connecting these physical objects to exchange information among themselves. For instance, common household appliances like refrigerators and air conditioners can be controlled remotely using mobile devices or computers connected to the internet. Another example involves monitoring a person's health through mobile devices and performing actions such as remotely controlling electrical devices like lights and fans while being away from home. IoT technology is essential for the development of smart appliances, smart homes, intelligent environments, and, ultimately, smart cities—a vision for a connected and intelligent world.

According to Gartner's projections regarding IoT devices, they anticipated that there would be approximately 25 billion devices in operation by the year 2021 [1, 2]. IoT-enabled smart water ATM was developed by the author, which automates the process of digital payment [3].

7.1.1 Predictive Maintenance

One of the applications of the Internet of Things is predictive maintenance. Predictive maintenance (PdM) is employed to anticipate issues related to quality, encompassing safety measurement, and the monitoring of machines. A range of terms, such as E-maintenance, Prognostics and Health Management (PHM), Smart Maintenance,

DOI: 10.1201/9781032703718-10

and Maintenance 4.0, are employed to characterize the advancement of approaches designed to ensure the dependability of components, products, and systems. These methods involve the analysis, prognosis, or prediction of problems stemming from performance inadequacies that could potentially lead to adverse safety impacts [4, 5].

Predictive maintenance is an anticipatory maintenance approach that relies on data and analytical tools to forecast the probable failure points of equipment or machinery. This enables timely maintenance actions to be taken, thereby averting potential breakdowns. This approach is in contrast to traditional reactive maintenance, where equipment is repaired or replaced only after it breaks down, leading to downtime and potentially costly repairs.

Here are some key aspects of predictive maintenance:

Data Collection: To implement predictive maintenance, you need to collect data from various sensors and sources. This data can include information on temperature, vibration, pressure, fluid levels, and other relevant parameters. The data can be collected in real time or at regular intervals.

Data Analysis: Once you have collected the data, you need to analyze it to identify patterns and trends that indicate the health of the equipment. This can involve using machine learning algorithms and statistical techniques to detect anomalies or deviations from normal operating conditions.

Predictive Models: Predictive maintenance relies on the development of predictive models that can forecast when equipment is likely to fail. These models take into account historical data, current conditions, and other factors to make predictions about future failures.

Alerts and Notifications: When the predictive model indicates that a piece of equipment is at risk of failing, it can trigger alerts or notifications to maintenance personnel. This allows them to schedule maintenance activities at a convenient time, minimizing downtime and reducing the likelihood of unplanned outages.

Cost Savings: Predictive maintenance can lead to significant cost savings by reducing unplanned downtime, extending the lifespan of equipment, and optimizing maintenance schedules. It also helps in preventing catastrophic failures that can result in safety hazards.

Condition-Based Maintenance (CBM): Predictive maintenance is closely related to CBM, where maintenance is performed based on the actual condition of the equipment rather than on a fixed schedule. CBM is often a component of predictive maintenance strategies.

Continuous Improvement: Predictive maintenance is not a one-time implementation; it requires continuous monitoring, data analysis, and model refinement. As more data becomes available and the models become more accurate, the maintenance process can be fine-tuned for better results.

The maintenance of the machines can be scheduled before the machine stops working. This application allows us to detect anomalies in the machine before critical failures.

This leads to higher equipment uptime, lowers overall maintenance expenses, and facilitates the optimization of spare part inventory by enabling preventive maintenance tailored to the actual requirements of the equipment.

7.1.2 Industrial IoT

Industry 4.0 is a revolution of Industrial IoT (IIoT), also known as the Industrial Internet of Things, is a technology framework that leverages the power of the Internet of Things (IoT) to enhance and optimize various industrial processes and systems [6]. IIoT involves the use of internet-connected devices, sensors, and machinery within industrial settings to collect and exchange data, monitor operations, and enable intelligent decision-making.

Industries such as manufacturing, energy, healthcare, agriculture, and transportation are increasingly adopting IIoT to transform their operations and remain competitive in today's data-driven world. As technology continues to evolve, the potential applications and benefits of IIoT are expected to expand even further [7].

Here are some key aspects of IIoT:

Connected Devices and Sensors: IIoT relies on a network of interconnected devices and sensors that are embedded in industrial equipment, machinery, and infrastructure. These devices collect data on various aspects of industrial processes, such as temperature, pressure, humidity, vibration, and more.

Data Collection and Transmission: The data collected by IoT devices is transmitted over networks (typically, the Internet or private networks) to centralized platforms for storage and analysis. This real-time data flow provides valuable insights into the performance of industrial assets and processes.

Data Analytics and Insights: IIoT platforms use advanced analytics, machine learning, and artificial intelligence (AI) to process the vast amount of data generated by sensors. This analysis can uncover patterns, anomalies, and trends, helping businesses make informed decisions and optimize their operations.

Predictive Maintenance: As mentioned earlier, predictive maintenance is a key application of IIoT. By continuously monitoring the condition of industrial equipment, IIoT can predict when maintenance is needed, reducing downtime and extending the lifespan of machinery.

Asset Tracking and Management: IIoT enables businesses to track the location and condition of assets, materials, and products throughout the supply chain. This enhances visibility and can lead to more efficient logistics and inventory management.

Energy Efficiency: IIoT can help organizations monitor and control energy consumption in industrial settings. By optimizing energy use based on real-time data, companies can reduce costs and minimize their environmental impact.

Quality Control: IIoT can improve quality control by monitoring and analyzing production processes in real time. This can lead to higher product quality and reduced waste.

Safety and Security: IIoT can enhance safety by monitoring potentially hazardous conditions and providing early warnings. It also plays a role in cybersecurity, as securing IIoT devices and networks is crucial to protect against cyber threats.

Scalability and Flexibility: IIoT solutions can be scaled up or down to meet the specific needs of different industries and organizations. They can be customized to address unique challenges and requirements.

Interoperability: Achieving interoperability between different IoT devices and systems is a key challenge. Standards and protocols such as MQTT, OPC UA, and others help ensure that devices from different manufacturers can communicate effectively.

7.1.3 Predictive Maintenance Using Condition Monitoring

Condition monitoring (CM) utilizes sensors to provide valuable insights into the current status of devices. These sensors collect data on critical equipment parameters, enabling the analysis of vibrations, detection of unusual sounds, monitoring of electrical currents, and observation of other relevant parameters to gain a deep understanding of equipment health. [17].

Here's how predictive maintenance using CM works:

Sensor Deployment: Sensors are strategically placed on critical equipment and machinery to collect data on various parameters such as temperature, vibration, pressure, humidity, soil quality, and more. These sensors continuously monitor the equipment's condition in real-time.

Data Collection: The sensors continuously gather data, producing a continuous flow of data points as time progresses. This data is typically transmitted to a centralized monitoring system, often through the use of the Industrial Internet of Things (IIoT) or other communication technologies.

Data Analysis: The collected data is analyzed using advanced analytics techniques, machine learning algorithms, and statistical methods. The goal is to establish a baseline of normal equipment behavior and identify anomalies or deviations from this baseline.

Anomaly Detection: Anomalies may include sudden changes in temperature, increased vibration levels, abnormal noise patterns, or deviations in other sensor readings. These anomalies can be early indicators of impending equipment failure or deterioration.

Predictive Models: Predictive maintenance relies on the development of predictive models based on historical data and patterns. These models use the data collected from CM to predict when maintenance is likely to be required. Machine learning algorithms can continuously refine these models as more data becomes available.

Maintenance Alerts: When the predictive model detects a potential issue or predicts that equipment is approaching a critical state, it generates maintenance alerts or notifications. These alerts are sent to maintenance personnel or integrated into a Computerized Maintenance Management System (CMMS).

Scheduled Maintenance: Maintenance teams can then schedule maintenance activities based on the alerts and predictions. By addressing issues before they escalate into failures, downtime is minimized, and maintenance can be performed at the most opportune times, often during planned downtime periods.

Continuous Improvement: Predictive maintenance using CM is an iterative process. As more data is collected and analyzed, the accuracy of predictive models improves, leading to better maintenance decision-making and cost savings.

7.1.4 Benefits of Predictive Maintenance Using Condition Monitoring

Reduced Downtime: By identifying issues early, maintenance can be scheduled before equipment failure occurs, minimizing unplanned downtime.

Cost Savings: Predictive maintenance can reduce maintenance costs by preventing unnecessary maintenance and avoiding catastrophic failures.

Extended Equipment Life: Proactive maintenance can extend the lifespan of equipment and assets.

Improved Safety: Early detection of equipment anomalies can help prevent safety hazards.

Data-Driven Decision-Making: CM provides valuable data for data-driven decision-making and process optimization.

Energy Efficiency: Optimized maintenance can lead to energy savings and reduced environmental impact.

Enhanced Asset Performance: Improved equipment reliability and performance contribute to better overall operational efficiency.

Predictive maintenance using CM is widely used in industries such as manufacturing, energy, oil and gas, transportation, and healthcare, where equipment reliability is critical to operations. It is a key component of Industry 4.0 initiatives, leveraging IoT technologies and data analytics to optimize maintenance strategies.

Figure 7.1 shows the real-time diagnosis system for wind turbines.

7.2 LITERATURE REVIEW

As mentioned earlier, IoT framework can be used in many applications for efficient performance and accurate data analysis. There is a lot of research carried out to apply the IoT framework in different areas. The author uses IoT framework to establish a smart government [10]. IoT Manager was used [11] and is the universal web platform, which is an open-source IoT device connecting platform. The article [12] created an edge-IoT framework and prototype utilizing blockchain and smart contracts in order to address a few security flaws in the IoT framework. IoT framework is also used to monitor the wind energy conversion system by the author [14]. So, IoT framework can be used for multiple applications to increase efficiency and performance.

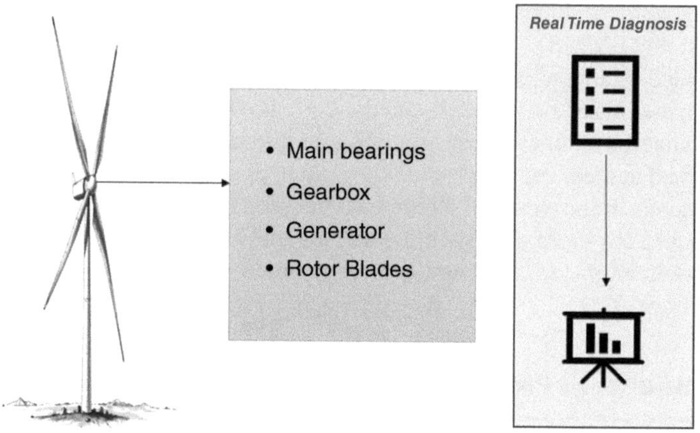

FIGURE 7.1 Condition monitoring system for wind turbines.

Condition monitoring systems (CMSs), also known as machine health monitoring system, is an important application to increase the productivity in industries [13, 18]. IoT framework is used in wind power systems, where the condition of wind energy conversion system is monitored [14]. Honeywell Equipment Health Monitoring Systems are designed for this purpose [17]. This detector monitors the equipment's physical characteristics, and it generates alarm if these characteristics deviates from its defined readings [16].

1. **IoT framework**
2. **CMS**

7.3 OUTCOME OF LITERATURE SURVEY AND RESEARCH GAP

The majority of the IoT frameworks are used in healthcare, traffic monitoring, smart government, smart cities, etc. Table 7.1 shows the uses of IoT framework in various applications. Very few works specify the use of IoT framework in association with AI and ML.

Table 7.2 shows the different CMSs developed in the various applications. A patent [21] states in detail how intelligent CM and fault prediction and diagnosis can be done. There is a large amount of data received from the sensors, and that data can be stored in the cloud for analysis purposes.

Author [22] introduces knowledge-based systems to improve the decision reasoning for fault diagnosis. But here the monitoring is in offline mode.

Combining IoT, machine learning and AI will give high performance and accuracy for fault prediction and fault diagnostics [25].

TABLE 7.1
Literature Review on IoT Framework

Ref. no	Title	Application	Framework	Technique	Future Scope
[8]	An IoT Framework for Intelligent Vehicle Monitoring System	Vehicle monitoring system	Low-cost IoT framework is designed.	Design and development of low-cost IoT framework, which contains RFID sensors. Real-time stamps are taken from these sensors to monitor vehicles.	By using this framework vehicle monitoring can be done efficiently, and alert messages can be sent to users.
[10]	IoT Manager: An Open-Source IoT Framework for Smart Cities	Research and teaching purpose	Uses the IoT manager, which is open-source IoT platform.	A mobile application is built over Android OS; the device gets the location information from the GPS and network hardware and display the information.	The problem with IoT manager is its interoperability due to which few concerns arise. There is a need to add a dispatcher.
[12]	An Integrative Public IoT Framework for Smart Government	Smart governance	An integrative framework is designed by combining a few strategies of 12 different frameworks.	Creates an integrative framework that contains the public strategic layer, public value creation layer, public demand layer, and technology infrastructure layer.	This study of different frameworks and the design of integrative framework will become foundation for implementing smart government.
[15]	An IoT Framework for Healthcare Monitoring Systems	Healthcare industry	IoT framework is designed by using IoT service platform.	Healthcare application is developed where situational awareness sensors are used to gather information from patients and upload onto the cloud. This data is processed and shared with doctors. They can analyze the health of the patient.	Only two sensors are used in this paper, i.e., body temperature sensors and pulse sensors. In future more sensors can be added.

TABLE 7.2
Literature Review on IoT Framework

Techniques	Type of Machine	Parameters Used	Algorithm Used	Results	Advantages
Industrial IoT Based Condition Monitoring for Wind Energy Conversion System [14]	Wind energy Conversion system	Ripple voltage of DC link capacitor	This paper suggests a simplified approach to space vector pulse width modulation (SVPWM) based on the proportional-integral (PI) control method.	Authenticated remote users can monitor the health of wind energy conversion system.	The goal is to reduce output waveform ripples, address voltage balancing concerns, and generate higher-quality output waveforms.
Integrated Machine Health Monitoring: A Knowledge-based Approach [22]	Small- and medium-scale manufacturing plants	Machine vibration	AI tools, i.e., knowledge-based systems, are used with integrated maintenance module.	Integrated maintenance module is combined with knowledge-based system for high reliability, and productivity in business.	Predictive maintenance system is made more efficient by adding intelligence to the system. It can be used only in offline mode.
A cloud-based Approach for Maintenance of Machine Tools and Equipment Based on Shop-floor Monitoring [23]	Motor drives	Current and revolution per minute of the spindle head	Uses maintenance expert knowledge.	Mobile technology communicates the health of machines to the operator.	One of the primary benefits of this approach is the dissemination of real-time information regarding the condition of machine tools and cutting tools to both the maintenance department and the operators.

Cloud-enhanced Predictive Maintenance [24]	Not specific	Vibration, temperature, ball-bar measurement	Presents the cloud-based predictive framework.	Cloud-based context modeling is used for data processing.	Large amounts of data can be processed on the cloud.
Sensor Fault Detection and Isolation for a Wireless Sensor Network-Based Remote Wind Turbine CMS [25]	Wind turbines	Noise	Different types of faults like short faults, constant faults, and noise faults are detected. Wavelet-transform-based method, cross-correlation-based method, and dynamic time warping methods are used.	The suggested sensor fault detection and isolation (SFDI) significantly enhance the precision and dependability of wind turbine CMSs.	Wireless sensor networks are used to transmit the data in wind turbines due to low cost and easy deployment.
The Experimental Application of Popular Machine Learning Algorithms on Predictive Maintenance and the Design of IIoT Based Condition Monitoring System [30]	6203 type bearing connected to the universal motor shaft	Vibration, sound level, temperature, current, rotational speed	Machine learning algorithmsLinear Discrimination Analysis, k-Nearest Neighbor, Decision Tree, Random Forest, and Support Vector Machine.	According to the findings, when the number of features in the dataset increased, the accuracy, sensitivity, True Positive Rate (TPR), True Negative Rate (TNR), F1 score, and Kappa metrics all exceeded 99% at a 95% confidence interval, while the False Positive Rate (FPR) and False Negative Rate (FNR) metrics dropped below 1%.	Decision Tree model is the optimum choice for CMS due to its convenience in determining threshold values, and its ability to give fast and acceptable classification rates.

7.4 THE PROPOSED SYSTEM FOR CONDITION MONITORING OF MACHINES IN INDUSTRIES

7.4.1 Features of the Proposed System

- Study of the sensor data for a specific duration of time.
- Identification of change in sensor data, with context to specific failure modes.
- Correlation of the change in sensor readings to the specific failure modes.
- To perform qualitative analysis.
- Enabling wireless transmission of the key CM parameters with potential failure modes.
- Real-time vibration-based monitoring with samples taken and analyzed after a few hours.
- To detect the potential failure mode so that downtime can be avoided since the module will have diagnostic capability.
- The proposed system will be integrated with the existing system for direct communication of the machine health to a number of persons, including supervisory to higher management.
- Early detection of the potential failure.
- Lower dependency on skilled manpower.
- Performing qualitative analysis of the sensor data to estimate failure modes.

7.4.2 Data Acquisition Using Sensors

Figure 7.2 shows the processing of sensors. Here for parameter extraction and failure recognition, machine learning algorithms are required. Decision reasoning can be done using AI algorithms for fault diagnosis. Finally, the user can get a visualization of the machine's health.

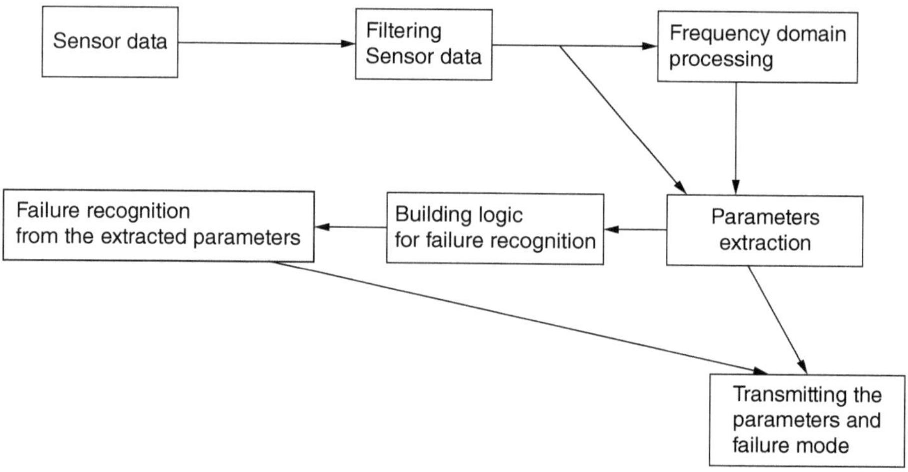

FIGURE 7.2 Processing of the sensor data.

7.5 COMPONENTS OF MACHINE

Figure 7.3 shows the different components of wind power system. Sensors can be installed on the machines to sense the data from the different parts of the machines.

7.6 PROPOSED SYSTEM ARCHITECTURE

The proposed system architecture is in Figure 7.4. The different sensors will be sensing the data from the parts of the machines [17]. Sensors will transmit the data to the

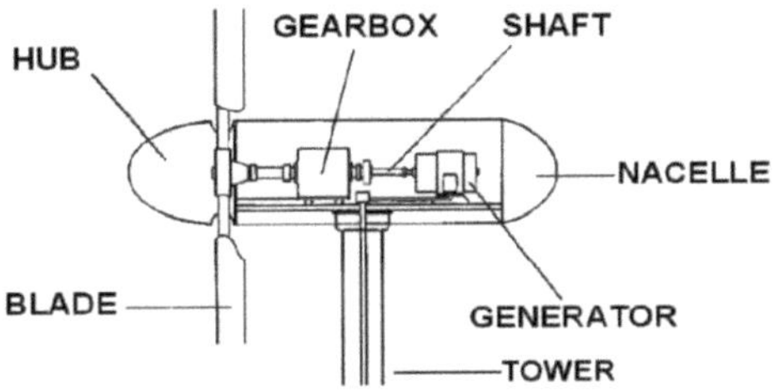

FIGURE 7.3 Different parts of wind power system.

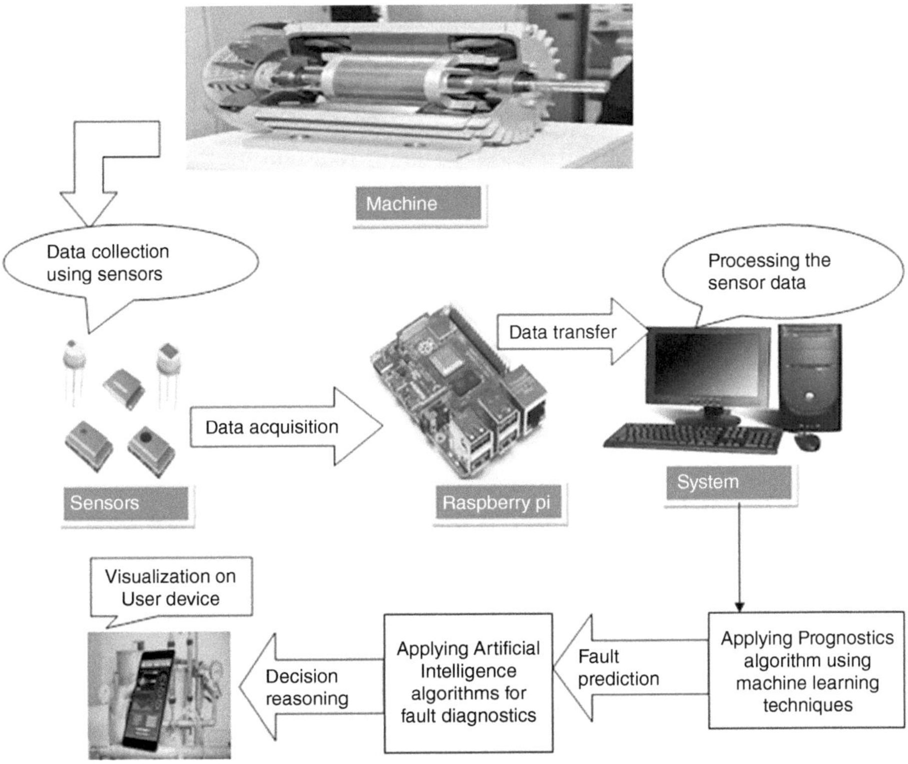

FIGURE 7.4 System architecture diagram.

data acquisition system where the physical parameter RS of the machine in analog form will be converted into digital form (numeric values) that can be manipulated by the computer. For this conversion python programming language will be used. Data will be processed then on the computer. Prognostic algorithms in machine learning will be used for fault prediction by learning the patterns; Figure 7.3 shows the processing of sensors. Here for parameter extraction and failure recognition machine learning algorithms are required. Decision reasoning can be done using AI algorithms for fault diagnosis. Finally, the user can get a visualization of the machine health.

7.7 PROPOSED METHODOLOGY

IoT technology is required to capture the information of machines by installing sensors that sense the physical characteristics of the machines and then data acquisition system converts the data into computer-readable format [18].

These physical characteristics need to be analyzed to understand the abnormality in the machine. Hence, there is a requirement to identify the patterns in the data. Here machine learning algorithms will be used for processing the sensor data [19, 20].

Intelligent CMS requires the development of the ability to behave like human. Computers can be involved in human-like thought process, learning, problem-solving, and reasoning. Hence, for fault diagnosis, decision reasoning is required where AI can be used.

7.7.1 Implementation of Methodology

Machine monitoring can be achieved by installing four sensors, that is, accelerometer (vibration sensors), gyroscope sensors, current sensors, and viscosity sensors.

- Accelerometer detects the vibration of machines.
- Gyrometer detects the inclination of the machine.
- Current sensor detects the current from the wire and measures it.
- Viscosity sensor measures the viscosity of the fluid flowing through the machine.

Data is collected through these sensors and given to data acquisition system to convert into numerical values. These values are then analyzed by computer.

In software applications, prognostic algorithms and diagnostic algorithms can be used to predict and diagnose the fault [26, 27]. The application designed by the author [29] for CM, and fault detection uses the acceleration and inclination measurement attributes.

7.8 RELEVANCE OF THE WORK TO SOCIETY/INDUSTRY

The Internet of Things is a technology that is ballooning in many fields. Smart technology is the need of today's life. IoT is nothing but an object with internet connectivity that contains built-in sensors. Using IoT technology makes it efficient to operate. IoT can be used in almost all the areas like healthcare, manufacturing, and home automation. IoT is the best solution for monitoring systems. A vehicle monitoring system is developed by the author using IoT technology [8]. IoT technology connects internet-enabled objects so that they can communicate with each other. IoT framework can be used for different applications like intelligent traffic monitoring system, patient health monitoring, and home automation. IoT system uses sensors to collect data from the surroundings [9] and analyze the data like temperature, humidity, and air quality. These low-power transducer network applications can be used for applications like healthcare and smart home environments.

IoT framework is very useful in industrial areas to increase productivity. Hence, research in IoT is of most importance.

With the revolution of Industry 4.0, today smart technology is a trending topic in industrial development. Also, the predictive maintenance is an important application of IoT. In predictive maintenance, CMS is the need of fault prediction in the machines [28, 29]. This area needs focus to increase the growth in industrial areas. Using machine learning techniques and AI algorithms for the purpose of accurate fault prediction is the current research topic. There are many algorithms in machine learning as well as AI, so comparing these algorithms and finding the best-suited algorithm is needed in CMSs [30, 31].

7.9 CONCLUSION

This book chapter provides valuable insights into the integration of predictive maintenance, IIoT, and CMSs in industrial settings. It underscores the importance of data-driven approaches in optimizing machinery and equipment performance, ultimately benefiting society through enhanced industrial efficiency and reliability. The performance of CMS can be increased using IoT framework in the model. The IoT framework efficiently captures the data from the machine and analyzes the data. Machine learning algorithms can be used to find the correlation of the change in sensor readings. Pattern recognition in the sensor data can be achieved with machine learning algorithms so that faults can be predicted. Intelligent CMSs can be developed using AI algorithms to perform fault diagnosis through decision reasoning and problem-solving.

REFERENCES

1. Patel, K. K., Patel, S. M., & Scholar, P. G. (2016). "Internet of Things-IOT: Definition, Characteristics, Architecture, Enabling Technologies, Application & Future Challenges." *International Journal of Engineering Sciences and Computing*, 6(5), 1–10. doi: 10.4010/2016.1482
2. Shriyal, S. S., & Ainapure, B. S., "IoT Device Classification Techniques and Traffic Analysis – A Review." *2021 International Conference on Technological Advancements and Innovations (ICTAI)*, Tashkent, Uzbekistan, 2021, pp. 244–250. doi: 10.1109/ICTAI53825.2021.9673420
3. Ainapure, B., Khamparia, S., Varshney, A., & Baheti, N., "IoT Enabled Smart Water ATM with Digital Payment." *2022 3rd International Conference on Intelligent Engineering and Management (ICIEM)*, London, United Kingdom, 2022, pp. 189–194. doi: 10.1109/ICIEM54221.2022.9853074

4. Theissler, A., Pérez-Velázquez, J., Kettelgerdes, M., & Elger, G. (2021). "Predictive Maintenance Enabled by Machine Learning: Use Cases and Challenges in the Automotive Industry." *Reliability Engineering and System Safety*, 215, 107864. doi: 10.1016/j.ress.2021.107864
5. Achouch, M. et al. (2022). "On Predictive Maintenance in Industry 4.0: Overview, Models, and Challenges." *Applied Sciences*, 12(16). doi: 10.3390/app12168081
6. Behrendt, A., De Boer, E., Kasah, T., Koerber, B., Mohr, N., & Richter, G. (2021). *Leveraging Industrial IoT and advanced technologies for digital transformation*. McKinsey & Company, 1–75.
7. Peter, O., Pradhan, A., & Mbohwa, C. (2022). "Industrial Internet of Things (IIoT): Opportunities, challenges, and requirements in manufacturing businesses in emerging economies." *Procedia Computer Science*, 217(2022), 856–865. doi: 10.1016/j.procs.2022.12.282
8. Pendor, R. B., & Tasgaonkar, P. P. (2016). An IoT framework for intelligent vehicle monitoring system. *International Conference on Communication and Signal Processing, ICCSP 2016*, 1694–1696. doi: 10.1109/ICCSP.2016.7754454
9. Laubhan, K., Talaat, K., Riehl, S., Aman, M. S., Abdelgawad, A., & Yelamarthi, K. (2016). A low-power IoT framework: From sensors to the cloud. *IEEE International Conference on Electro Information Technology, 2016-Augus*, pp. 648–652. doi: 10.1109/EIT.2016.7535315
10. Calderoni, L., Magnani, A., & Maio, D. (2019). IoT Manager: An open-source IoT framework for smart cities. *Journal of Systems Architecture, 98*, 413–423. doi: 10.1016/j.sysarc.2019.04.003
11. Pan, J., Wang, J., Hester, A., Alqerm, I., Liu, Y., & Zhao, Y. (2019). EdgeChain: An edge-IoT framework and prototype based on blockchain and smart contracts. *IEEE Internet of Things Journal*, 6(3), 4719–4732.
12. Wirtz, B. W., Weyerer, J. C., & Schichtel, F. T. (2019). An integrative public IoT framework for smart government. *Government Information Quarterly*, 36(2), 333–345.
13. Hu, Q., Ohata, E. F., Silva, F. H. S., Ramalho, G. L. B., Han, T., & Rebouças Filho, P. P. (2020). A new online approach for classification of pumps vibration patterns based on intelligent IoT system. *Measurement: Journal of the International Measurement Confederation*, 151(xxxx), 107138.
14. Hossain, M. L., Abu-Siada, A., Muyeen, S. M., Hasan, M. M., & Rahman, M. M. (2021). Industrial IoT based condition monitoring for wind energy conversion system. *CSEE Journal of Power and Energy Systems*, 7(3), 654–664.
15. Dharmik, R. C., Gotarkar, S., Dinesh, P., & Sant Burde, H. (2021). An IoT framework for healthcare monitoring system. *Journal of Physics: Conference Series*, 1913(1), 012145.
16. Maximize System 1's diagnostic HMI capabilities with expanded connectivity. (n.d.). pp. 1s.
17. Equipment, H., Monitoring, H., & Ehm, T. (n.d.). Monitoring (EHM) detectors, 650.
18. Gilabert, E., & Arnaiz, A. (2006). Intelligent automation systems for predictive maintenance: A case study. *Robotics and Computer-Integrated Manufacturing*, *22*(5–6), 543–549.
19. Ainapure, B., Patrikar, P., Mehta, A., Jain, A., & Shah, S., 2022, "Machine Learning Based Intelligent Health Monitoring System." *2022 3rd International Conference on Intelligent Engineering and Management (ICIEM)*, London, United Kingdom, pp. 183–188.
20. Lumsden, R. (2007). Systems engineering. In *Aerospace America* (Vol. 45, Issue 12). doi: 10.1007/978-3-030-49165-9

21. Hosek, M., Us, M. A., & Krishnasamy, J. (2011). Su- is a. 1(19).
22. Mahantesh, N., Aditya, P., & Kumar, U. (2013). *Integrated machine health monitoring: A knowledge based approach Integrated machine health monitoring: a knowledge based approach*. September. doi: 10.1007/s13198-013-0178-1
23. Mourtzis, D., Vlachou, E., Milas, N., & Xanthopoulos, N. (2016). A cloud-based approach for maintenance of machine tools and equipment based on shop-floor monitoring. *Procedia CIRP*, 41, 655–660.
24. Schmidt, B., & Wang, L. (2016). Cloud-enhanced predictive maintenance. *The International Journal of Advanced Manufacturing Technology*. doi: 10.1007/s00170-016-8983-8
25. Peng, Y., Qiao, W., Qu, L., & Wang, J. (2018). Sensor fault detection and isolation for a wireless sensor network-based remote wind turbine condition monitoring system. *IEEE Transactions on Industry Applications*, 54(2), 1072–1079.
26. Villalonga, A., Beruvides, G., Castano, F., & Haber, R. E. (2020). Cloud-based industrial cyber-physical system for data-driven reasoning: A review and use case on an Industry 4.0 pilot line. *IEEE Transactions on Industrial Informatics*, 16(9), 5975–5984.
27. Guo, Y., Sun, Y., & Wu, K. (2020). Research and development of monitoring system and data monitoring system and data acquisition of CNC machine tool in intelligent manufacturing. *International Journal of Advanced Robotic Systems*, 17(2), 1–12.
28. Kozłowski, E., Mazurkiewicz, D., Zabiński, T., Prucnal, S., & Sęp, J. (2020). Machining sensor data management for operation-level predictive model. *Expert Systems with Applications*, 159. doi: 10.1016/j.eswa.2020.113600
29. González-Muñiz, A., Díaz, I., & Cuadrado, A. A. (2020). Heliyon DCNN for condition monitoring and fault detection in rotating machines and its contribution to the understanding of machine nature. *Heliyon*, 6, e03395.
30. Cakir, M., Guvenc, M. A., & Mistikoglu, S. (2021). The experimental application of popular machine learning algorithms on predictive maintenance and the design of IIoT based condition monitoring system. *Computers and Industrial Engineering*, 151, 106948.
31. Kudelina, K., Vaimann, T., Demidova, G., & Asad, B. (2021). *Applied Sciences Trends and Challenges in Intelligent Condition Monitoring of Electrical Machines Using Machine Learning*, MDPI/ Applied Sciences. doi: 10.3390/app11062761

Part IV

Advancing AI in Mobile Computing

8 Plantae

Mobile Interface for Plant Leaf Disease Detection and Prevention System

Nishant Chavhan and Vrinda Parkhi

GRAPHICAL ABSTRACT

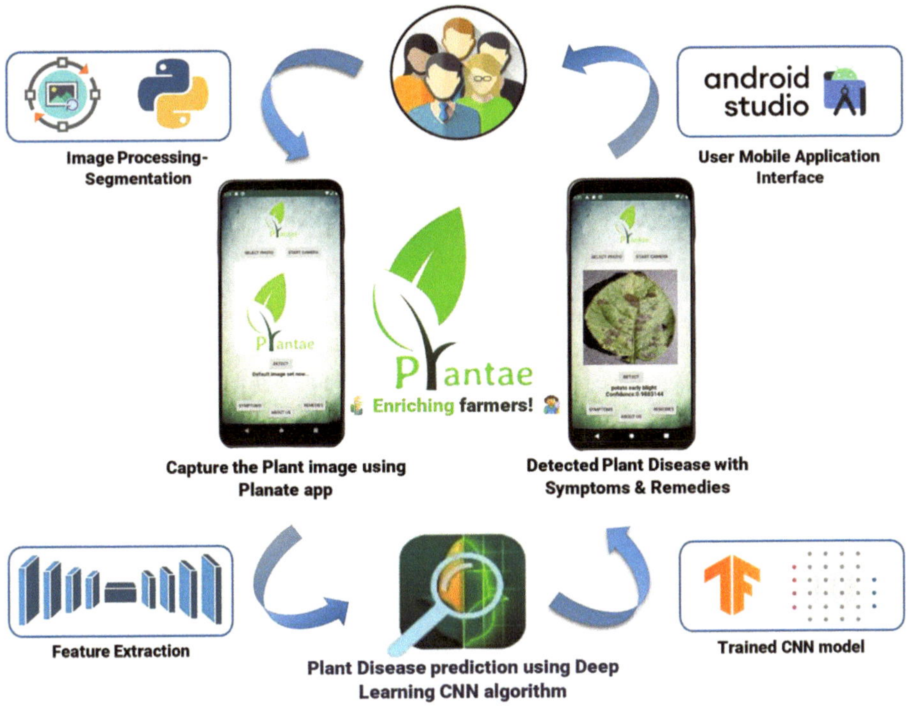

DOI: 10.1201/9781032703718-12

8.1 INTRODUCTION

Agriculture, a cornerstone of the global economy, serves as a primary source of sustenance, income, and employment. In countries like India, with a substantial population of farmers, agriculture contributes significantly, constituting 18% of the nation's income and playing a pivotal role in generating employment opportunities, employing 53% of the workforce [1]. In the bygone triennium, the Gross Value Added (GVA) from the agricultural sector has exhibited a consistent upward trajectory, ascending from 17.6% to 20.2% in the nation's overarching economic landscape [2, 3]. This sector emerges as a formidable force propelling economic expansion. Consequently, the repercussions of plant diseases and pest infiltrations within agriculture loom large, capable of echoing across the global economy and compromising the quality of food production.

India, a prominent player in the global agricultural arena and the sixth-largest economy worldwide, is on the path to reaching the significant milestone of $5 trillion by 2024–2025. However, it faces a perplexing challenge: the inability to provide sustenance for its entire population. The substantial loss of crop yields attributable to pests and pathogens exerts a significant impact on food availability and contributes to a decline in its performance on the Hunger Index [4]. The crux of the Indian economy lies in its reliance on agriculture. As per the World Bank evaluation, "Agriculture's contribution to India's economic landscape has steadily diminished to less than 15%, a consequence of the robust growth observed in the industrial and services sectors and the absence of sustainable progress in the agricultural domain" [5]. Hence, India needs a fundamental advancement, that is, technological modernization to achieve a high-yielding and sustainable agricultural model.

According to the conclusive 2020 report from the Food and Agriculture Organization of the United Nations, plants, being the contributors to 80% of our food needs, play a pivotal role. The safeguarding of plants against pests and diseases not only mitigates hunger but also serves as a shield for the environment. The report emphasizes that "[p]lant pests account for losses of up to 40% in global food crops and contribute to trade losses in agricultural products" [7]. Figure 8.1 portrays the ramifications of projected variations in insect population metabolism, showcasing diverse effects across significant geopolitical boundaries. The illustration presents the anticipated change in future yield loss for each country, juxtaposed with its median current crop yield per unit of planted area for wheat (A), rice (B), and maize (C) [6]. Notably, in the Indian context, an alarming 15–25% of potential crop production is forfeited due to the impact of pests, weeds, and diseases [8]. This loss occurs at a critical juncture when the country must not only augment production but also guarantee food security and meet the nutritional demands of its burgeoning population.

Figure 8.1 also illustrates the anticipated alterations in future yield loss for individual countries that are visualized for the central grid cell within each country [6]. These changes are graphed in accordance with the median current crop yield per unit of planted area for that country, thereby highlighting the relationship between future yield losses and present-day crop productivity. Figure 8.2 demonstrates that the observed grain loss variation, associated with crop types and model details globally,

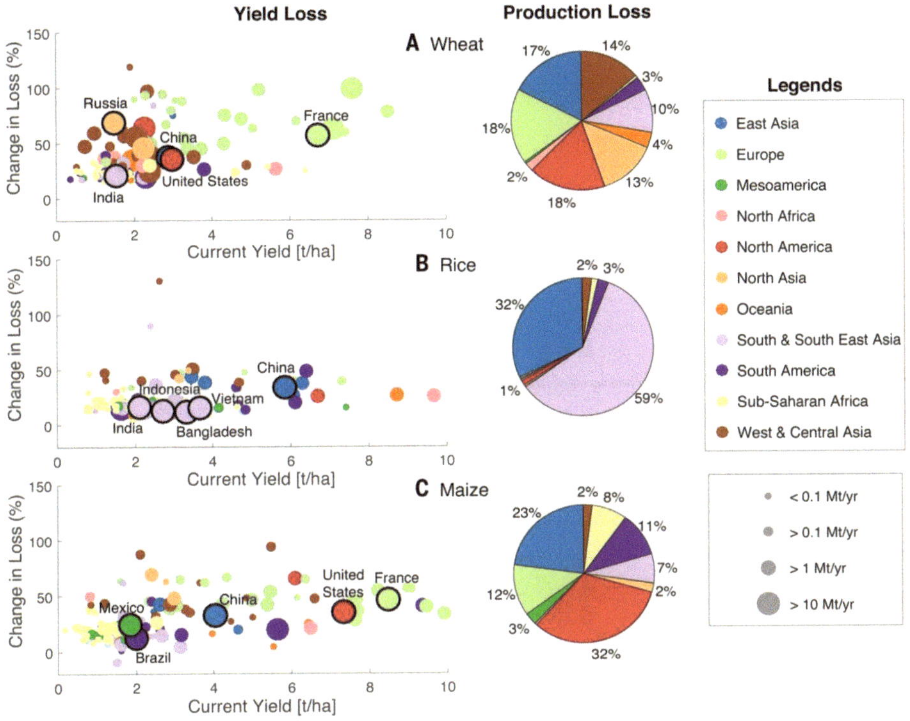

FIGURE 8.1 Anticipated regional increments in crop losses resulting from insect pests. (A) Wheat, (B) Rice, (C) Maize for each country [6].

is due to the distinct geographical circumstances of the biogeographical effects of climate warming on insect pest demographics and metabolism in these grain-producing areas. This warming trend increases insect population size and metabolic rate per capita for temperate regions [8].

These observations emphasize the fact that sustainable agriculture is the key to ensuring environmental, social, and economic aspects in the agricultural sector. Implementing such measures will not only secure food safety but also strive to eradicate the looming spectre of food shortages. With a substantial population to feed, identifying these diseases in plants at their earliest stages is paramount. It's not only about sustaining the agricultural economy but also ensuring food security for the masses. Implementing predictive mechanisms for the early detection of leaf diseases becomes imperative to safeguard crops and prevent losses in this vital sector of the economy. Prophylactic measures alone are often ineffective in averting epidemics and endemics in agriculture. Therefore, the timely surveillance and precise diagnosis of crop diseases, facilitated by a resilient crop protection system, emerge as imperative steps to thwart losses in production quality. This proactive strategy is crucial in shielding both the agricultural sector and the global economy from the deleterious impacts of crop-related challenges.

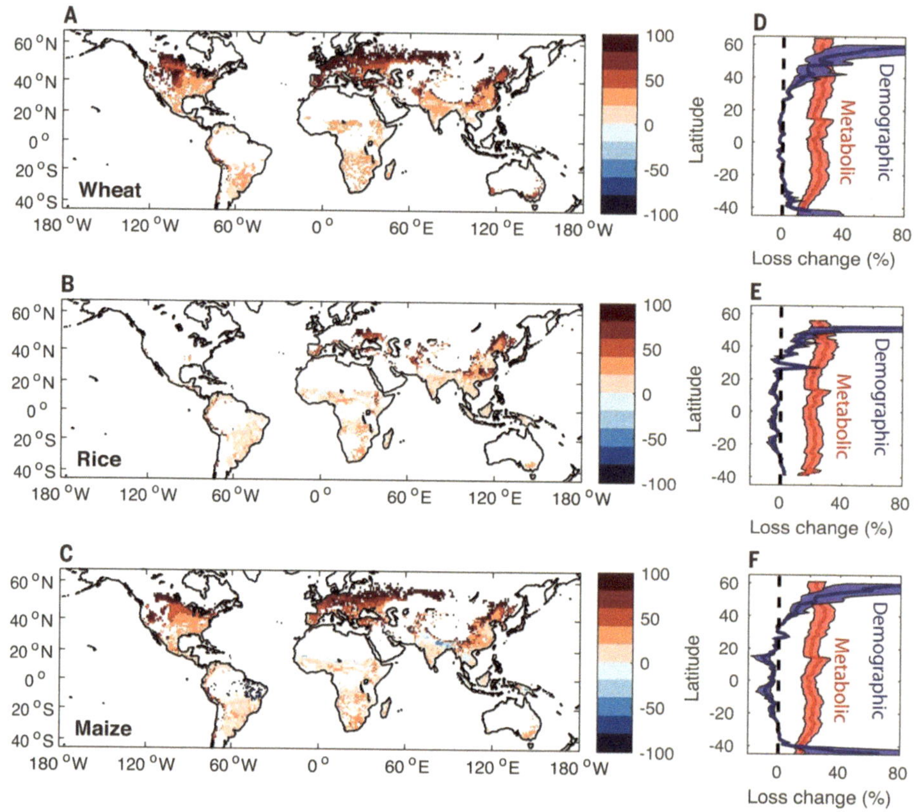

FIGURE 8.2 Anticipated alterations in geographical patterns of crop yield losses attributed to insect pests in a 2°C warmer climate. The distinct panels delineate the projected changes for: (a) Wheat, (b), Rice (c) Maize zonal change contribution: Demographic effects (Dn/n, blue) and metabolic effects (DM/M, red) [6].

In the pre-technological era, farmers needed to detect plant disease using their naked eye, which made erroneous diagnoses of a particular disease, which ultimately resulted in the wrong application of fertilizers and pesticides, and destroyed the entire crop. To execute this task effectively, a dedicated team of experts becomes indispensable, overseeing plant health and promptly addressing any arising issues on an immediate basis. On a large scale, the implementation of such a system incurs substantial costs, rendering it unaffordable for small-scale farmers. The existing solutions employed for crop disease detection exhibit inaccuracies, inefficacies, and lack of cost-efficiency. With the progression of computer vision technology, a myriad of solutions has surfaced to address the intricacies of plant disease detection. This is owed to the fact that the initial manifestations of leaf infections manifest as spots and distinctive patterns. Researchers have proposed various methodologies to precisely discern and classify these plant infections, some resorting to conventional image-processing techniques entailing manually designed features and segmentation – commonly referred to as hand-crafted feature extraction.

In the pursuit of achieving precise detection and classification of plant infections, researchers have introduced diverse methodologies. Several of these techniques hinge on conventional image-processing methods, entailing the manual extraction of features and segmentation. The early forays into plant disease classification witnessed the utilization of classical ML models, representing the initial steps in this domain. Additionally, sophisticated imaging technologies such as hyperspectral and multispectral imaging were deployed for the identification of plant and leaf diseases. However, the trajectory of this landscape underwent a profound transformation with the advent of deep learning (DL).

State-of-the-art architectures viz., AlexNet [9–11], Visual Geometry Group (VGG) [10, 12–16], DenseNet [17, 18], Inception-v4 [18], and ResNet [12, 13, 18] have been put forward by researchers as potential options for the classification of plant diseases. The presented DL approaches yielded impressive outcomes, improving the accuracy of disease diagnosis in crops. Numerous research works prove that DL has much more benefits than regular machine learning (ML).

For instance, the noteworthy prowess exhibited by the DL model GoogleNet in effectively discriminating diseases on tomato leaves surpasses the capabilities of classical ML counterparts like Support Vector Machine (SVM) and Random Forest (RF) [9]. The utilization of Convolutional Neural Networks (CNN) [19] has once again demonstrated its effectiveness by outperforming Radial Basis Function Neural Network (RBFNN) [20], Particle Swarm Optimization (PSO) [21], and SVM algorithms [22] in a study focusing on the characterization and discrimination of defects in mango leaves [23]. In a different context, a proposed CNN model [24] showcased superior accuracy in diagnosing diseases from apple leaves when compared to other models, including SVM, BPNN, AlexNet, Googlenet, Resnet, and VGF. Notably, in a related research endeavour, a meticulously constructed CNN model outshone conventional ML methods such as Decision Tree (DT) [25], Logistics Regression (LR) [26], and K-Nearest Neighbour (KNN) [27] when applied to the PlantVillage dataset. It's noteworthy that this model not only outperformed these traditional methods but also surpassed popular DL architectures like AlexNet, ResNet, VGG16, and Inception-v3 [28–30]. Thus, this chapter highlights the prominence of utilizing DL-based models for the classification of plant diseases, attributing this recommendation to their exceptional efficiency and reliability.

"About 54% i.e., over 600 million of the Indian population is widely accessible to Smartphones, which are increasing 20 percent per quarter," quoted by Ram Sewak Sharma, Chief executive of the National Health Authority of India [31]. The rising global prevalence of smartphones, coupled with the recent strides in computer vision powered by DL, has opened up new avenues for disease diagnosis with the assistance of smartphones. Hence, the proposed work aims to design and develop a novel, free, low-cost, easy-to-use, and widely accessible system for Plant Leaf Disease Detection and Prevention. This endeavour is anchored in a DL algorithm, specifically, the CNN. Moreover, the system aims to develop Android-based mobile application entitled "Plantae" (which means that Kingdom Plantae includes all the plants) to detect and diagnose plant disease from images captured with the camera the phone and provide symptoms, pathogen, and host information as well as recommended controlling remedies.

8.2 LITERATURE REVIEW

Conducting extensive physical inspections and monitoring of large crop fields is a labour-intensive undertaking. It is imperative to minimize the human effort necessary for overseeing plant health, a goal that has captured the interest of numerous researchers. Multiple ML methods have been suggested to address this challenge, offering high accuracy while curbing costs and mitigating subjectivity in the identification of various plant diseases. Historically, numerous researchers have dedicated their efforts to the realm of plant disease detection and resolution systems, employing a range of IoT, AI, and ML techniques, summarized in Figure 8.3.

In 2021, S. Shirmali et al. [16] proposed a user-friendly and widely available Android mobile application that can effectively and precisely detect crop diseases, viz., PlantifyAI using CNN. The real-time identification of crop diseases is accomplished through the deployment of a CNN, meticulously trained, validated, and tested on a dataset encompassing 87,860 leaf images categorized into 38 distinctive classes. To forge an optimal CNN, an intricate process unfolded, entailing the meticulous design and rigorous evaluation of 16 different CNN architectures. Throughout the development phase of the PlantifyAI application, exhaustive multi-level testing and

FIGURE 8.3 A comprehensive overview of a diverse range of deep learning architectures employed for the early detection and classification of plant leaf diseases.

data analysis were conducted. Leveraging a CNN in conjunction with MobileNetv2 [32], the real-time diagnosis of crop diseases demonstrated a peak accuracy of 95.7% and an F1 score of 96.1.

J. C. Valdoria et al. [33] designed and prototyped produced a mobile application tailored for the identification of prevalent diseases affecting terrestrial plants in the Philippines. Their approach incorporated Deep Learning Neural Network and image-processing techniques. To train their model, they utilized a dataset comprised of publicly sourced images. Remarkably, their model demonstrated an impressive accuracy rate of 80% in detecting diseases in terrestrial plants. The mobile application, named iDahon and designed for Android-based devices, exhibited outstanding qualities such as robustness, user-friendliness, operational efficiency, high accuracy, and portability, all of which were attributed to the efficacy of the model they proposed. These concerted efforts yielded noteworthy results, showcasing an impressive accuracy rate of 80%. This substantiates the application's robust functionality, reliability, usability, efficiency, accuracy, and portability.

The innovative disease detection model introduced by S. I. Rimon et al. [34]. In this model, taking a plant leaf image as input, adeptly processes it and employs an advanced deep CNN to discern and precisely identify the presence of diseases. The resultant product, the PlantBuddy, mobile application, offers tailored solutions based on the detected plant disease. Essentially, this study marks the inception of an Android-based mobile application geared towards recognizing and diagnosing plant diseases through the application of deep CNNs. The model undergoes training utilizing a substantial public dataset of plant images, achieving an impressive accuracy rate of approximately 97%. This signifies the model's elevated level of acceptability and efficacy. The operational procedure involves capturing a plant leaf image, subjecting it to intricate processing, and employing a deep CNN algorithm to effectively identify and categorize plant diseases. The seamlessly integrated model enhances the functionality of the Android application.

In the realm of agricultural innovation, M. Deodhar et al. [11], in their endeavour, introduced an Android application with a dual purpose. The first facet of their study involves gathering data on weather conditions and soil properties, deftly utilizing the Bee Hive clustering approach to forecast crop yields. This approach takes into account specific crop types and the ideal conditions required for their growth. The second facet of their study delves into the realm of crop disease detection. Here, an Android application is employed, harnessing the power of image processing and the Scale-invariant Feature Transform (SIFT) algorithm to identify plant diseases. In a parallel development, V. R. Badgujar et al. [35], presented "LeafScape," a mobile application that is a game-changer in the detection of plant diseases. This application not only identifies diseases but also provides practical solutions for afflicted plants. The authors have devised a series of transfer learning models, with their foundation resting on the VGG16 Convolutional Neural Network model, which has been meticulously trained on the extensive ImageNet dataset. These models demonstrate exceptional proficiency in recognizing diseases and offering relevant diagnoses.

S. Bhatt and S. Hingu [36] outlined an innovative concept of developing a crop disease detection system using Flutter and Dart. This innovative approach results in a versatile mobile application, Cropish, which operates seamlessly across multiple platforms, including Web, iOS, and Android. The system leverages the capabilities of ML, Deep Neural Networks, and specifically, CNN, a subset of DL. This amalgamation enables the identification of diseases in crops with a remarkable accuracy rate of 99.074%. S. Naik et al. [17] designed a system that addresses the specific requirements of farmers, facilitating the detection of crop diseases through ML and image classification techniques. Their work centres on the application of ensemble learning, involving a range of ML algorithms. By incorporating a DL approach, their system demonstrates a remarkable accuracy rate of 96.7% in disease identification. In a similar vein, S. Kumbhar et al. [37] have introduced a web-based application named "Farmer Buddy" for the detection of cotton leaf diseases. This application harnesses the power of CNN. Notably, it effectively identifies two major cotton leaf diseases, Alternaria Macrospora and Bacterial Blight, achieving a training accuracy of 80%. These studies underscore the importance of technology in aiding farmers and enhancing crop disease detection, with the former system achieving high accuracy through ensemble learning, and the latter employing CNN technology for specific Cotton leaf disease identification.

A. A. Ahmed and G. H. Reddy [38] present an innovative ML-based Mobile-assisted system for leaf disease diagnosis. A prototype of a computer vision-empowered ML-based system for mobile automation on plant leaf disease detection and diagnosis is prepared. Operating on the foundation of CNN, recognized as an advanced learning technique, the system excels in categorizing 38 different diseases. To bolster the CNN model, the system has compiled an extensive dataset comprising 96,206 images of plant leaves, encompassing both healthy and diseased plants, for the purposes of training, validation, and testing. Different sets of measures including classical accuracy and computational power were used for evaluating the productivity of the proposed system. Surprisingly, the mode did very well, with its overall classification accuracy amounting to around 94%. The innovation has significantly improved crop health management as it is effective in detecting the dominant 38 diseases among 14 crops. The survey presented by Santosh Reddy et al. [39] encapsulates the progress in crop disease detection and prevention via an Android application and attempted to study the electronic expert system need. Along with that, they have proposed their Android application named E-agree, which provides detection and prevention for crop disease and facilitates an e-commerce marketplace for farmers and consumers directly without involving third-party vendors. In addition to that, E-agree also facilitates daily weather reports, market rate guides, and soil information.

Rishiikeshwar et al. [40] have unveiled an intuitive IoT Web Application designed specifically for farmers. This application streamlines the process of automated leaf disease detection by leveraging CNN and employs sophisticated DL techniques for early disease diagnosis. The model, grounded in CNN and enhanced with advanced pre-processing techniques, excels in categorizing leaves into two distinct categories: those affected by disease and those that maintain a state of health. A thorough exploration of various DL architectures, coupled with meticulous hyperparameter tuning, has yielded a model capable of achieving an impressive accuracy rate of up to 95% when trained on 400 genuine leaf images and up to 98% when utilizing an augmented dataset consisting of 3600 images. The training data is sourced from actual leaf images of crops captured in real agricultural fields.

K. Saraswathi [41] put forth an image-processing approach for the detection of plant leaf diseases utilizing CNNs. Their system involves image pre-processing techniques such as resizing and Gaussian filtering to segment the leaf area. Finally, a CNN classification technique is applied to determine the type of leaf disease.

Meanwhile, N. R. Thorat and S. Nikam [42] have devised an automated IoT-based system for the automatic detection and monitoring of plant leaf diseases. Their methodology encompasses feature extraction, segmentation, and clustering of leaf images, employing the synergies of IoT and image processing. The k-means clustering algorithm orchestrates the partitioning of images into segments, subsequently classified through the adept application of SVM and artificial neural networks. The system demonstrates a praiseworthy ability to identify plant leaf diseases at an early stage, boasting an accuracy that exceeds the 90% mark.

In a noteworthy contribution to the field, S. Ramesh et al. [43] harnessed the capabilities of the Random Forest Classifier to discern between healthy and diseased leaves, utilizing an existing dataset. Employing the Histogram of Oriented Gradients (HOG) technique facilitated the extraction of critical image features, incorporating descriptors like Hu moments, Haralick Texture, and Color Histogram. The model's effectiveness underwent rigorous comparison with other ML counterparts, evaluated on the metric of accuracy. The training phase involved a set of 160 images of papaya leaves. Through the strategic application of the Random Forest Classifier, the model achieved a commendable classification accuracy, hovering around 70%, underscoring its potential to distinguish between healthy and diseased papaya leaves. Pallepati Vasavi et al. [44] put forth an all-encompassing exploration through the realms of image processing (IP), ML, and DL techniques for the prediction of crop leaf diseases. The survey meticulously delves into various algorithms, prominently featuring CNN, methodologies, the scale of images, and classes within datasets. The overarching performance of the proposed system is scrutinized in detail. This study concludes by shedding light on the limitations and paving the way for future endeavours, specifically emphasizing the need for real-time automated crop leaf disease detection employing Unmanned Aerial Vehicles (UAVs).

The scrutiny of diverse systems and applications, as expounded in this section, has served as a catalyst for the creation of a precise, user-friendly, and easily accessible system, harnessing technological advancements. This system is meticulously presented and elaborated upon in Section 8.3.

8.3 METHODOLOGY

8.3.1 System Overview

The proposed system is an implementable model, which is the need of the day. The envisioned system can be seamlessly integrated to alleviate the burden of human labour and mitigate the costs linked to the conventional approach of physical visual inspection and monitoring by an expert team across expansive crop fields for disease detection. Developed state-of-art DL-based mobile application – Plantae will facilitate the early disease detection and remedies for the recognized plant leaf disease, along with their specific pathogen and host names.

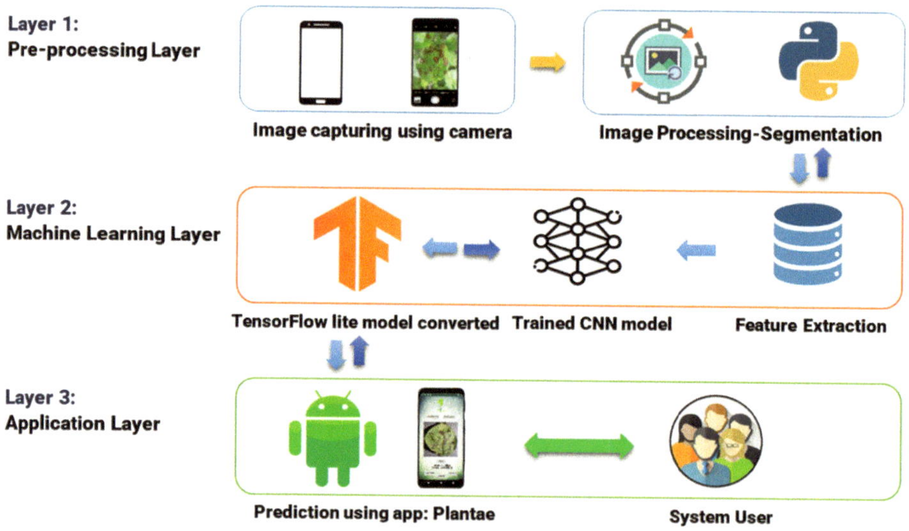

FIGURE 8.4 Block diagram for proposed system.

In Figure 8.4, a comprehensive block diagram of the proposed system is depicted. Aligning with the structure outlined in Figure 8.1, the block flow of the proposed system for plant disease detection is systematically organized into three distinct layers, viz, pre-processing, ML, and application layers. Layer 1 describes the inputs acquired by capturing the images of a leaf using phone camera, followed by processing of captured images and their segmentation. Layer 2 depicts the actual presented DL model (i.e., CNN) for the detection of plant leaf disease using the trained CNN model, which is then converted into tflite model in order to integrate with the Android application. Layer 3 illustrates the application layer (i.e., User Interface), which involves Android-based mobile application – Plantae. The application gives results subject to accuracy of an image, whether the plant is healthy or captured a disease [45].

The introduced system aims to create an application designed to function as a fundamental aid in reducing plant fatalities resulting from a wide range of pathogens and pests. Simultaneously, it possesses the capability to identify plant diseases in their nascent stages, effectively curtailing the necessity for substantial time and financial commitments, and operates seamlessly without the requirement of a botanical expert's intervention.

8.3.2 System Architecture

The architectural design of the system, centred around generative processes, is vividly portrayed in Figure 8.5, employing the prowess of a DL neural network algorithm [46]. The system's design outlines the step-by-step approach taken to implement the training model within the developed Plantae application.

To accomplish this, a collection of images representing 26 distinct plant diseases and 14 different plant species was curated, forming the dataset for training [47]. This dataset was then processed using the TensorFlow library and configured through

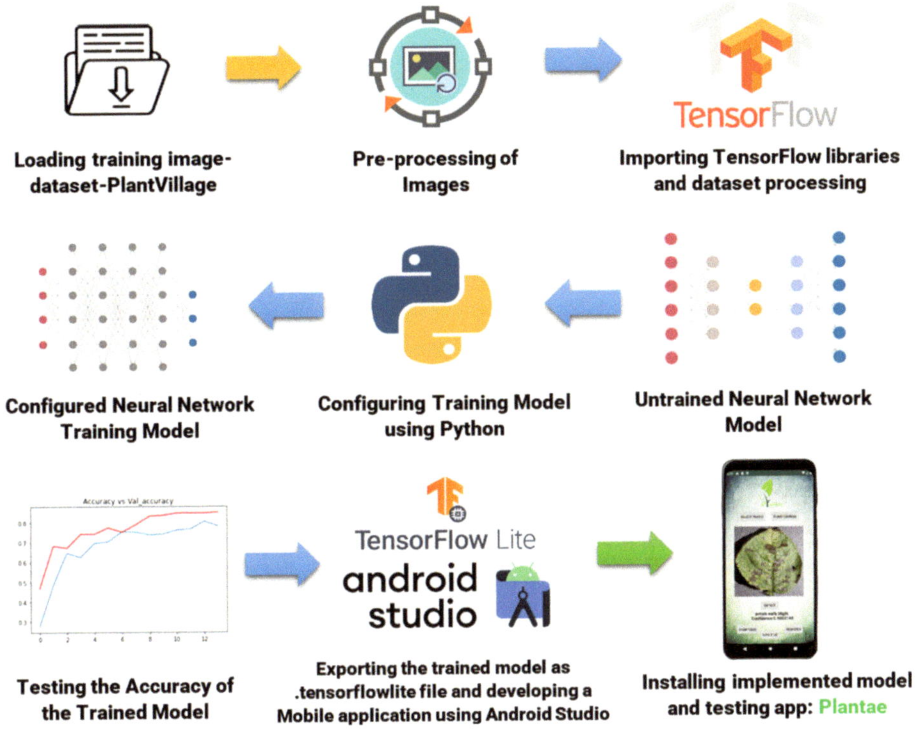

FIGURE 8.5 Generative architectural design of the proposed system.

Python to create a well-tailored neural network training model. Specifically, this configuration utilized a CNN, implementing a DL approach. As a result, the model is now prepared for making predictions based on the dataset. At the outset, implemented model is converted to tflite (TensorFlow-lite) model in order to interface with mobile application by using Android studio as an interfacing dashboard. Finally, the application Plantae is ready for real-time detection of plant leaf disease with satisfactory primary remedies.

The detailed system design and developmental stages are listed as follows:

8.3.2.1 Dataset

For training the model, the PlantVillage public dataset, sourced from Kaggle, is harnessed. This rich dataset comprises a total of 54,305 images, showcasing both the vibrancy of healthy plant leaves and the afflictions of diseased ones. Within this treasure trove, you'll find images representing 26 distinct diseases and 14 diverse species of plants.

A judicious partition of this dataset is made, with approximately 43,444 images allocated for the training phase, and the remaining 10,861 images reserved for validation. This distribution elegantly adheres to the golden ratio of 80% for training and 20% for validation, ensuring a balanced and robust foundation for the model's development. For a deeper dive into the dataset, Table 8.1 and Figure 8.6 extend a gracious invitation, offering an intricate breakdown of the number of images corresponding to

TABLE 8.1
PlantVillage Dataset Description [13, 49]

Class	Training Images	Validation Images	Total
Apple scab	504	126	630
Apple black rot	496	125	621
Cedar apple rust	220	55	275
Apple healthy	1316	329	1645
Blueberry healthy	1202	300	1502
Cherry healthy	684	170	854
Cherry powdery mildew	842	210	1052
Corn grey leaf spot	410	103	513
Corn common rust	953	239	1192
Corn healthy	929	233	1162
Corn northern leaf blight	788	197	985
Grape black rot	944	236	1180
Grape black measles	1107	276	1383
Grape healthy	339	84	423
Grape leaf blight	861	215	1076
Orange citrus greening	4405	1102	5507
Peach bacterial spot	1838	459	2297
Peach healthy	288	72	360
Pepper bell bacterial spot	797	200	997
Pepper bell healthy	1183	295	1478
Potato early blight	800	200	1000
Potato healthy	121	31	152
Potato late blight	800	200	1000
Raspberry healthy	297	74	371
Soybean healthy	4072	1018	5090
Squash powdery mildew	1468	367	1835
Strawberry healthy	364	92	456
Strawberry leaf scorch	887	222	1109
Tomato bacterial spot	1702	425	2127
Tomato early blight	800	200	1000
Tomato healthy	1273	318	1591
Tomato late blight	1527	382	1909
Tomato leaf mould	761	191	952
Tomato septoria leaf spot	1417	354	1771
Tomato spider mites	1341	335	1676
Tomato target spot	1123	281	1404
Tomato mosaic virus	299	74	373
Tomato yellow leaf curl	4286	1071	5357
Total	43,444	10,861	54,305

FIGURE 8.6 Sample plant disease images from the PlantVillage dataset [13, 29, 48, 49].

the 26 distinct diseases across the 14 different plant species. Together, these images form a harmonious ensemble, constituting 38 classes within this bountiful dataset.

Plant pathology explores the intriguing realm of plant diseases, which are typically defined as unusual growth patterns or disruptions in a plant's natural life processes. These diseases occur when something disrupts the normal life cycle of the plant. These diseases can be broadly categorized into two main groups. Biotic diseases are instigated by living organisms like fungi, bacteria, and viruses. These living agents disrupt the plant's health, giving rise to various diseases. Conversely, abiotic diseases stem from non-living environmental factors such as soil compaction, wind, frost, soil salinity, and complications with the plant's root system. These external conditions have the potential to induce stress and damage to the plant, resulting in deviations from its typical processes [50].

8.4 ACTUAL PROPOSED DEEP LEARNING MODEL

The plant disease classification employs Google's pre-trained models, including VGG16, VGG19, ResNet-50, Inception V3, and standard CNN models as the foundation for training. The proposed model leverages a CNN [3, 9–14, 17, 24, 28, 30, 32, 37–39, 41, 43, 51–58], representing a DL methodology. CNN is particularly renowned for its exceptional performance in analysing visual images, as it can effectively extract essential features due to its multi-layered architecture. This enables CNN to discern and classify objects with minimal pre-processing, making it a powerful tool for this research. The comparative analysis encompasses a range of transfer learning models using CNNs to improve both recognition and classification accuracy while reducing the time complexity. The comprehensive CNN framework is visually depicted in Figure 8.7, incorporating pre-trained CNN models like VGG16 [10, 12–16], DenseNet-121 [17, 18], ResNet-50 [12, 13, 18], and Inception-v4 [18, 59]. This approach serves to elevate the overall performance of the system with a touch of elegance.

The CNN architecture is composed of several key layers: an input layer, several convolutional layers, a pooling layer, an activation function layer, and an output layer

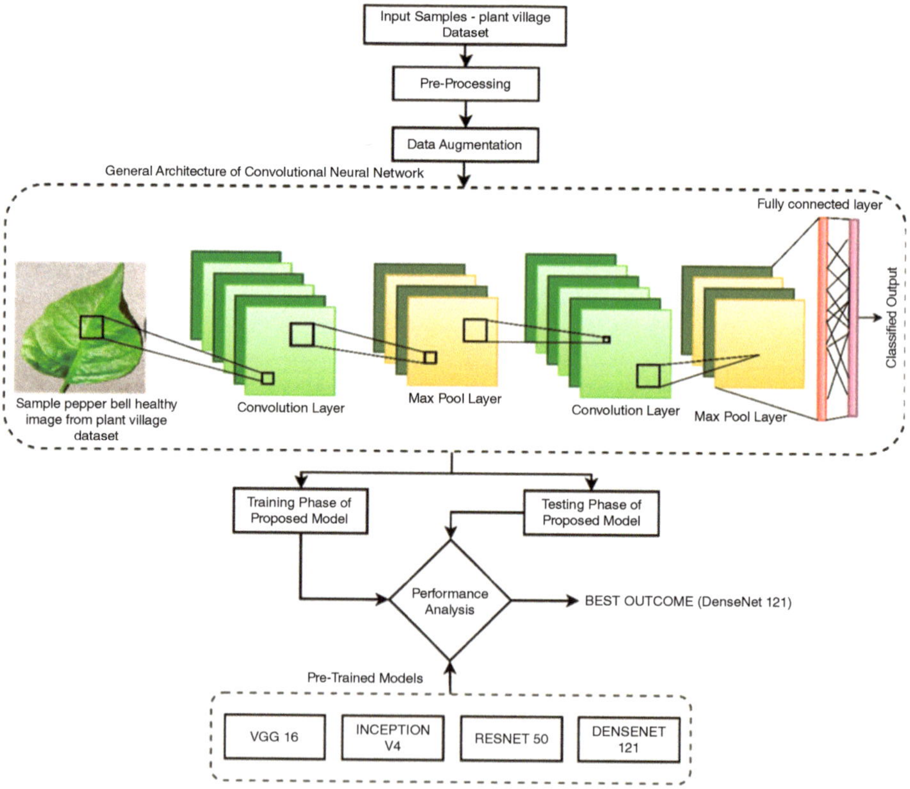

FIGURE 8.7 Architectural design of the proposed CNN model [48].

employing SoftMax activation. Data of an image is fed into a convolutional layer that carries out feature extraction while the pooling layer pulls out feature values in this configuration. More layers comprising additional convolution and pooling can also be used depending on the sophistication of the images to describe complex characteristics. The last layer is referred to as the fully connected layer, and this acts as the output layer while taking the sum of all previous layer inputs and converting it into one large vector that feeds into the next layer. The last output layer is very essential in classifying plant diseases. Nonetheless, VGG19, a deep CNN model, was especially used to readjust the last activation layer in the models towards supporting classification objectives in plant disease detection.

8.4.1 VGG16

The VGG16 [10, 12–16] model, formulated by the VGG out of Oxford, comprises one of the modern, cutting-edge CNN particularly built for image perception. Its rare architectural beauty lies in its ability to be arranged in a configuration of 2 × 2 or 3 × 3 rows. The layers progressively flow downwards, unveiling themselves with greater depth, exposing secrets of an enchanting story. The masterpiece of DL ends with a victorious climax, comprised of three fully connected layers and a linear SoftMax output layer, contributing separately to a symphony. VGG16 is a splendid structure, boasting six convolutional layers to show off artistry on pictures in 224 × 224 pixels resolution [60] (Figure 8.8).

8.4.2 VGG19

In the grand ensemble of VGG19 [30, 38, 51–53], a total of 19 layers take their place on the stage, with 16 of them gracefully dancing as convolutional layers and the remaining three embracing their roles as fully connected layers. Throughout this captivating performance, all these layers are orchestrated by the enchanting tune of the Relu activation function. This architectural symphony holds a secret to its success. Instead of employing a solitary layer with an oversized filter, the network elegantly opts for the approach of numerous convolutional layers with petite filters. This method not only enhances the accuracy of the model but also dramatically trims down the plethora of factors that it must learn, rendering it a truly efficient virtuoso in the world of DL [61] (Figure 8.9).

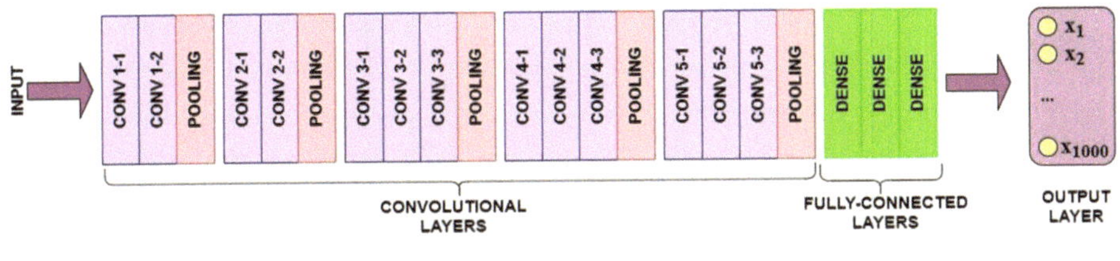

FIGURE 8.8 Schematic of VGG16 model architecture.

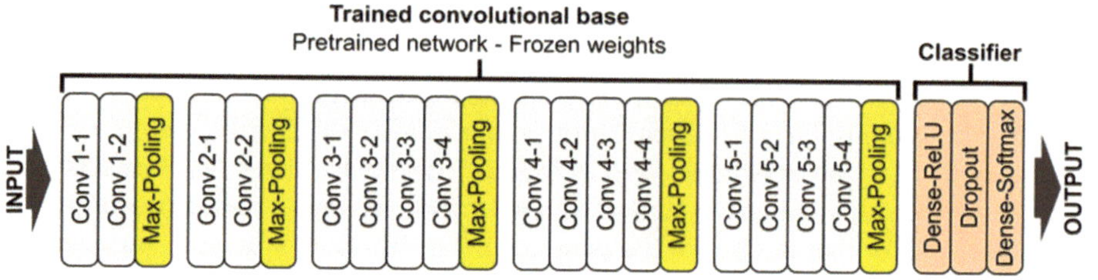

FIGURE 8.9 Schematic of VGG19 model architecture.

8.4.3 ResNet

Profound CNN and its popular comrade – ResNet [12, 13, 18] – are trusted companions for disentangling intricate computer vision problems. Compared with VGGNet, its architecture is much deeper by a factor of eight. These skip connections are at the core of ResNet's revolutionary approach that integrates these nonlinear convolutional layers in ResNets. These connections cleverly pass the input through a residual block that uses the same operations but avoiding the preceding input of the residual block. This combines the previous residues smoothly with the identities to create a great mapping with rich features. You'll find two 1 × 1 convolutional layers incorporated within each one of the building blocks of the residual structure, alternating with a 3 × 3 convolutional layer linked through a direct "skip" connection. Batch normalization accompanied by the vitality of the ReLU function at each step forward makes them perfect in every aspect. Moreover, a SoftMax layer is deliberately designed specifically for recognition at the end as the last finishing touch for this engineering wonder [62] (Figure 8.10).

8.4.4 Inception-v3

Inception-v3 [18, 59], an extension of the GoogLeNet architecture, has earned its stripes by delivering commendable classification performance in various biomedical domains through the art of transfer learning. This ingenious model takes an innovative approach by weaving together convolutional filters of varying sizes into a novel, unified filter. This not only results in a harmonious blend of filters but also serves to reduce the number of parameters requiring training. As a delightful consequence, this

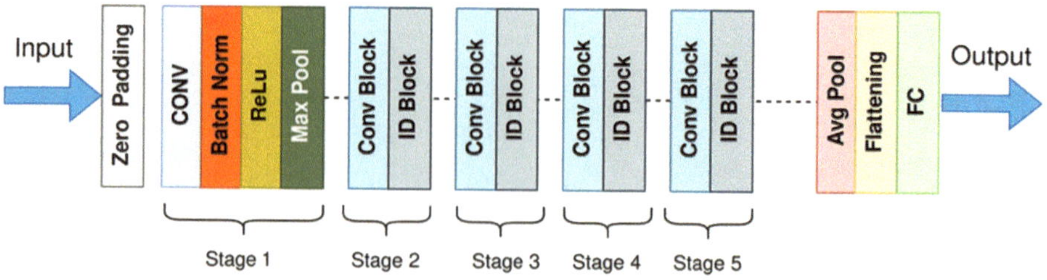

FIGURE 8.10 Schematic of annotated ResNet-50 model architecture.

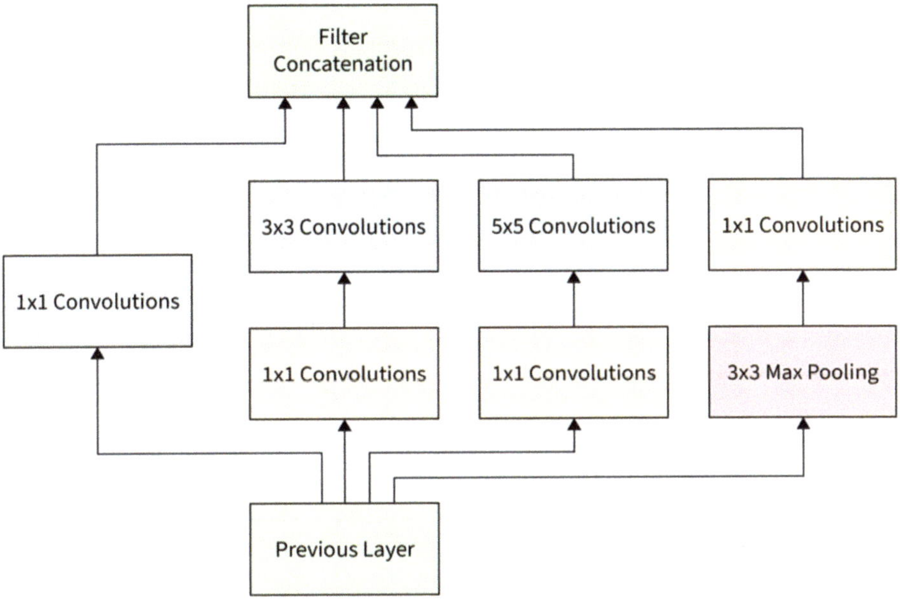

FIGURE 8.11 Schematic of Inception-v3 model architecture.

reduction in parameters ushers in a welcome decrease in computational complexity, making Inception-v3 a formidable contender in the realm of DL [59] (Figure 8.11).

In a bid to enhance the training accuracy and reduce the training loss of the CNN model, a series of image pre-processing procedures were implemented on the training set, as depicted in Figure 8.12. Importantly enough, the contrast of the images' colour shades was adjusted, Gaussian noise was introduced, and the desaturation option was employed, introducing more grey and black tones into the pixels. These transformations aimed to reduce interferences due to other elements on which this was dependent in the training stage. The result was very beneficial since the model mastered the nuances of each of the 38 disease groups and stabilized the CNN at large. To this end, we performed two principal operations on the input image and incorporated image normalization into our system. The first step was deducting the average value, labelled as μ, from each of the pixels of every single image I (i, j). Later on, we divided the above result with the standard deviation σ of the input image. This rigorous method was designed to make the profile of pixel intensity distribution similar to the Gaussian curve with zero point as its centre. In pursuit of achieving this, we meticulously applied the following formula to standardize each image within our training set:

$$O(i,j) = \frac{I(i,j) - \mu}{\sigma}$$

```
Model: "vgg19"
_________________________________________________________________
 Layer (type)                 Output Shape              Param #
=================================================================
 input_1 (InputLayer)         [(None, 256, 256, 3)]     0

 block1_conv1 (Conv2D)        (None, 256, 256, 64)      1792

 block1_conv2 (Conv2D)        (None, 256, 256, 64)      36928

 block1_pool (MaxPooling2D)   (None, 128, 128, 64)      0

 block2_conv1 (Conv2D)        (None, 128, 128, 128)     73856

 block2_conv2 (Conv2D)        (None, 128, 128, 128)     147584

 block2_pool (MaxPooling2D)   (None, 64, 64, 128)       0

 block3_conv1 (Conv2D)        (None, 64, 64, 256)       295168

 block3_conv2 (Conv2D)        (None, 64, 64, 256)       590080

 block3_conv3 (Conv2D)        (None, 64, 64, 256)       590080

 block3_conv4 (Conv2D)        (None, 64, 64, 256)       590080

 block3_pool (MaxPooling2D)   (None, 32, 32, 256)       0

 block4_conv1 (Conv2D)        (None, 32, 32, 512)       1180160

 block4_conv2 (Conv2D)        (None, 32, 32, 512)       2359808

 block4_conv3 (Conv2D)        (None, 32, 32, 512)       2359808

 block4_conv4 (Conv2D)        (None, 32, 32, 512)       2359808

 block4_pool (MaxPooling2D)   (None, 16, 16, 512)       0

 block5_conv1 (Conv2D)        (None, 16, 16, 512)       2359808

 block5_conv2 (Conv2D)        (None, 16, 16, 512)       2359808

 block5_conv3 (Conv2D)        (None, 16, 16, 512)       2359808

 block5_conv4 (Conv2D)        (None, 16, 16, 512)       2359808

 block5_pool (MaxPooling2D)   (None, 8, 8, 512)         0

=================================================================
Total params: 20,024,384
Trainable params: 0
Non-trainable params: 20,024,384
_________________________________________________________________
```

FIGURE 8.12 The Structure of the proposed CNN model.

Where the symbols I and O stand for the input image and the output image, respectively. Normalization indexes i and j refer to the current pixel during a normalization procedure.

The training error and loss are computed using the following equation:

$$M = \frac{1}{n}\sum_{i=1}^{n}\left(y_i - x_1\right)^2$$

In this context, M denotes the mean square error of the model quantifying the disparity between the predicted class denoted as y and the actual class identified as x. The error in the object detection is measured by value M.

In pursuit of the utmost accuracy, the custom model is subjected to multiple training sessions across various epochs. To ensure compatibility with mobile applications, where a smaller model size is preferred, an endeavour is made to generate a compact tflite model, thereby reducing its overall size. This lightweight model is subsequently integrated into the Plantae-mobile application for seamless performance.

8.4.5 Configured Plantae-Mobile Application

At the outset, the exported trained and configured tflite (TensorFlow-lite) model is interfaced with a mobile application using Android Studio. Figure 8.13 depicts the complete flow of the developed application. Finally, Plantae, an Android mobile application, is ready for real-time detection of plant leaf disease with satisfactory primary remedies.

8.5 RESULTS AND DISCUSSIONS

In the realm of agricultural production, the timely identification of crop diseases plays a pivotal role in ensuring high yields. Therefore, advanced technology for early detection of plant ailments is needed at all times to enhance and sustain production rates. A meticulous examination of the existing body of research literature underscores the high efficiency of DL models in image classification. Moreover, models

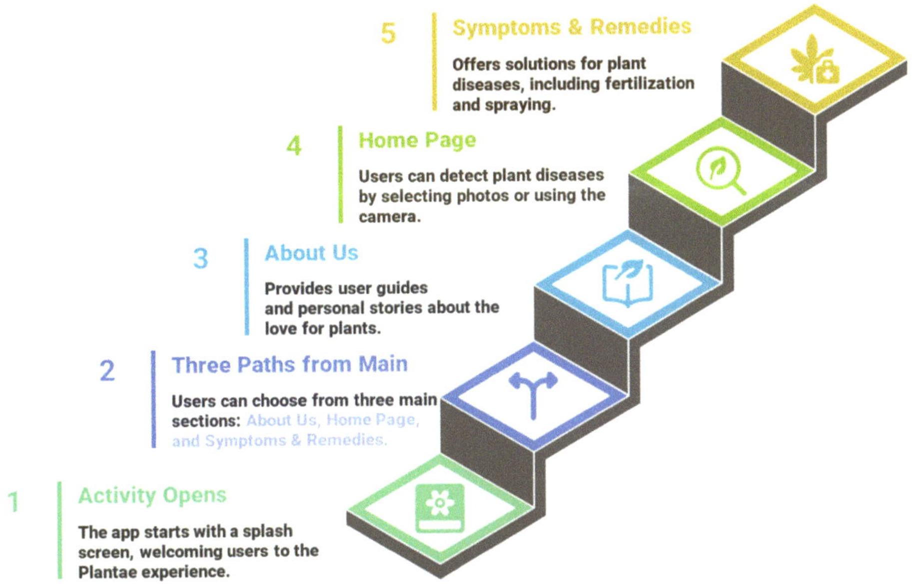

FIGURE 8.13 Flow chart for mobile application: Plantae.

based on transfer learning emerge as noteworthy for their ability to streamline training processes and mitigate the requirement for extensive datasets. Inspired by these insights, our endeavour embarks on an assessment of four pre-trained models: VGG16 [10], VGG19 [51], ResNet-50 [62], Inception v3 [18, 59], and CNN [63]. These models are anticipated to herald a new era of precision and efficiency in the early diagnosis of plant diseases [32, 51, 64].

A conceptual framework for the proposed system, harmonizing a DL model with the Plantae-mobile application, has been crafted to facilitate real-time field detection. The outcomes of the testing phase are expounded upon in this section, with Figure 8.14 encapsulating the comprehensive conceptual framework of the proposed system.

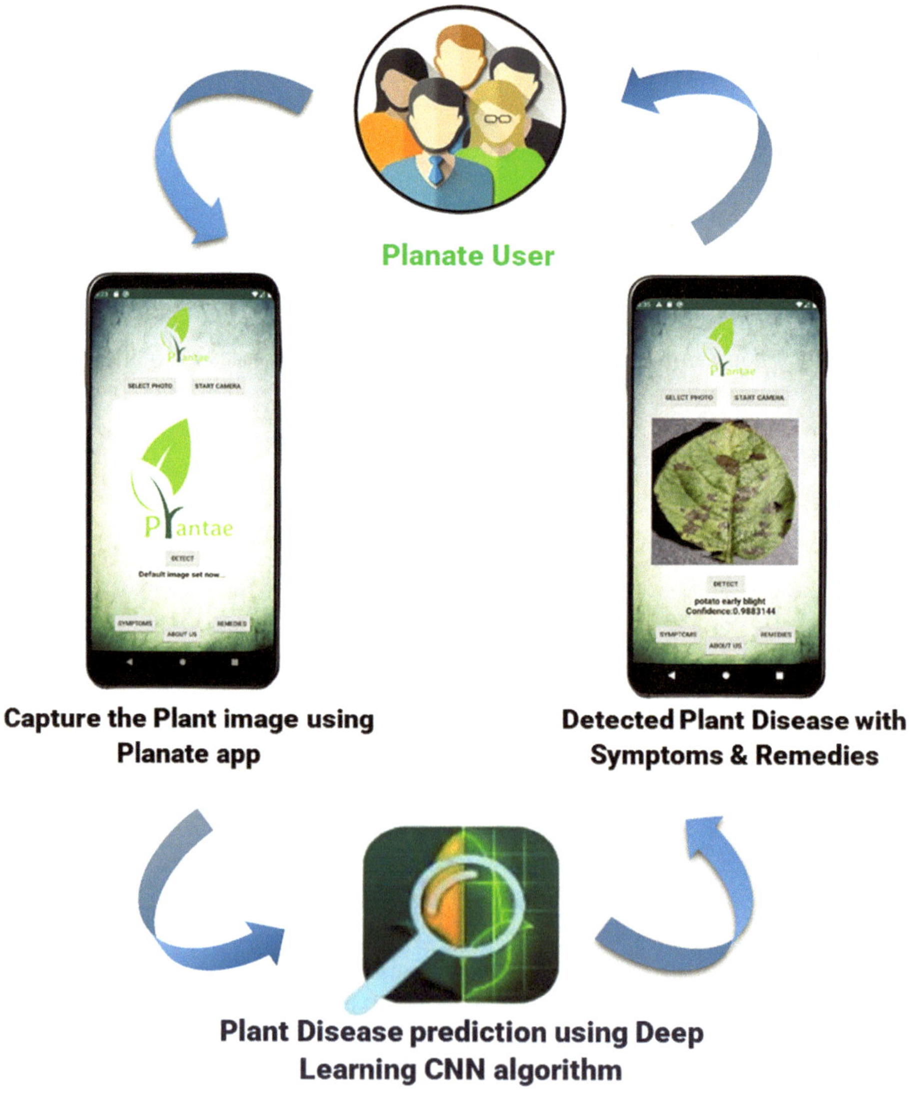

FIGURE 8.14 Conceptual framework of proposed system.

The system was intricately designed to forecast the outcomes of randomly selected images extracted from the validation dataset, with the process elaborated in Figure 8.15. Real-time detection was executed in a nearby agricultural field and a kitchen garden, and the overall performance of Plantae proved to be highly satisfactory.

To assess whether the proposed model suffers from overfitting or underfitting, we can discern its behaviour by graphing accuracy and loss metrics during both training and validation phases. The model's accuracy serves as a critical gauge for evaluating its performance. The performance of proposed model can be visualized in Figure 8.16 by plotting graphs.

The plotted graphs provide a visual representation of the following key metrics:

Training Accuracy: Metric reveals the percentage of successful classifications achieved in the training dataset. It signifies how well the model is learning from the training data.

Validation Accuracy: Metric demonstrates the percentage of successful classifications of classes in the validation dataset. It acts as a gauge for the model's capacity to generalize its learning to novel, unseen data.

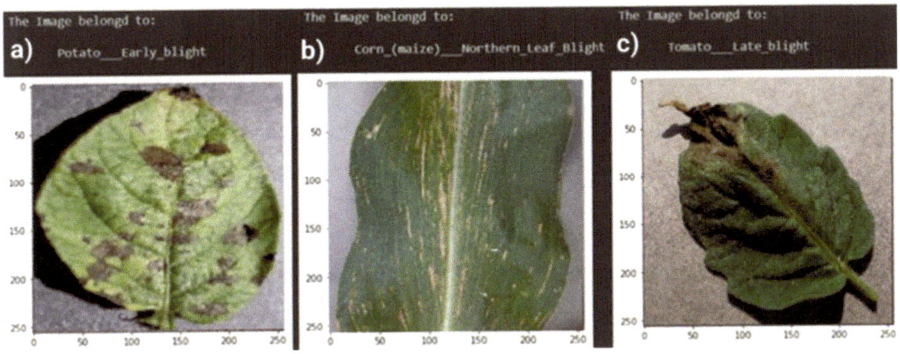

FIGURE 8.15 Random detection (a) Potato_Early_blight, (b) Corn_(maize)_Northen_Leaf_Blight (c) Tomato_Late_blight.

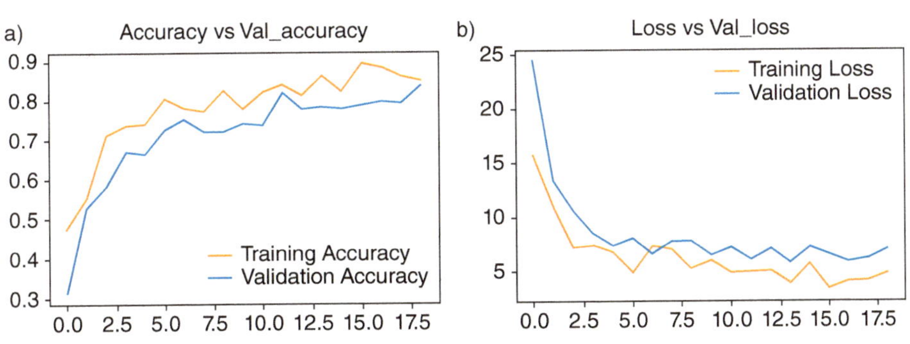

FIGURE 8.16 (a) Accuracy versus Val_accuracy. (b) Loss versus Val_loss graphs.

Training Loss: Metric represents the average mistakes made by the model throughout the training process. It offers insights into the model's learning progress and convergence.

Validation Loss: Metric quantifies the average loss per batch during the validation phase, considering the batches of the validation dataset. It reflects how well the model performs on data it has not been directly trained on.

To achieve greatness, we set out to discover the performance of some top DL models, like the renowned VGG16 and VGG19, the famous ResNet-50, InceptionV3, and the pillar of CNN. This quest sought to measure their training and competence in testing, a major journey within the artificial intelligence and image recognition world. The results unrolled a fascinating array of indices in which every mode revealed an individualized account of their efficiencies. VGG19 and Inception v3 showed amazing agreement for both training and validation like veteran masters tuning up their skills. The depicted illustration in Figure 8.17 underscores the pinnacle of both training and validation, that is, testing accuracy achieved by the model. In all, the average training accuracy of the proposed application was observed to be 98.26%, which indicates the acceptability of the model along with 97.67% validation accuracy. Figure 8.18 illustrates the statistical comparison of various pre-trained DL models.

Figure 8.19 depicts user interface for the developed Plantae, Android-based mobile application, along with its different features and pages. Complete flow of the developed application is illustrated and discussed in earlier section (Figure 8.13).

Different dashboard pages are as follows:

Splash Screen: The first page of the application lasts only for 5 seconds. It depicts introductory aim of Plantae as – Why Plantae only?

Home Page: Provides a variety of different features with buttons which facilitate the following pages: Select photos, Start the camera, Detect, Symptoms, Remedies, and About us.

Whether capturing a new image through the camera or selecting a previously captured one from the gallery and subsequently pressing the "Detect"

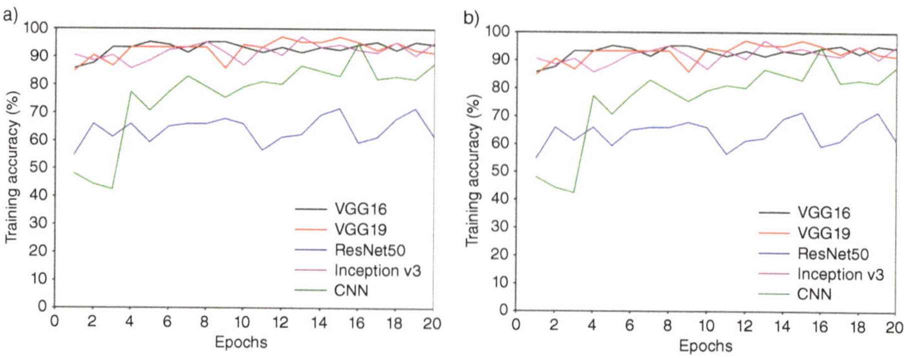

FIGURE 8.17 (a) Training (b) Testing performance plot of DL models.

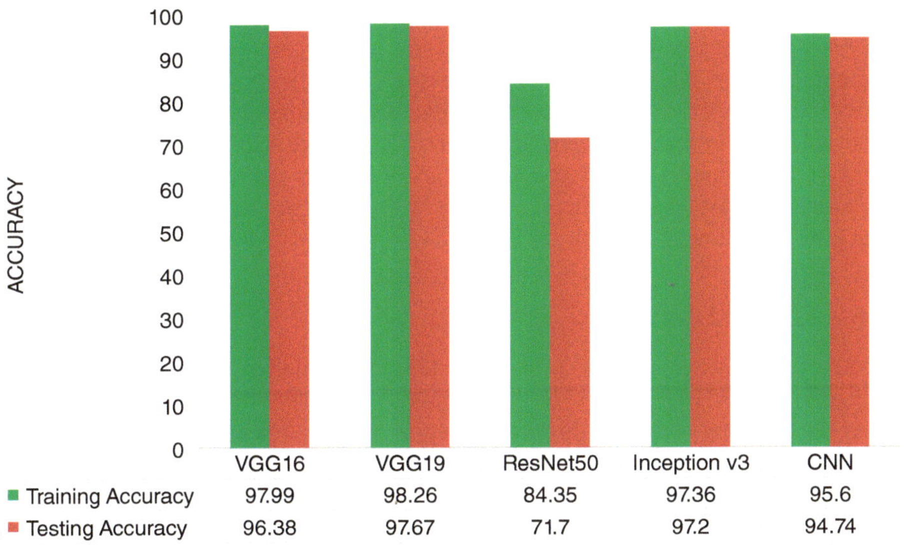

FIGURE 8.18 Performance analysis (training and testing accuracy) of various DL models.

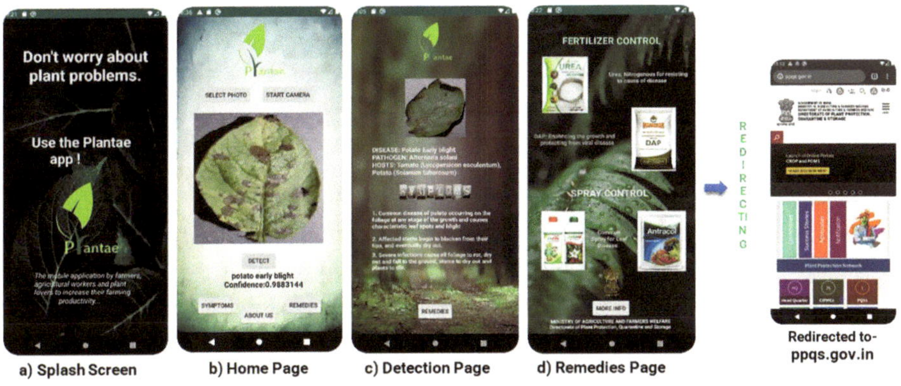

FIGURE 8.19 Plantae-mobile application interface.

button, the system proceeds to identify the detected disease. Subsequently, pressing the buttons for "Symptoms" and "Remedies" pages offers further insights into the identified ailment.

Detection Page. After detecting the disease, pressing Symptoms page opens into Page having Pathogen Hosts along with their symptoms.

Remedies Page. Clicking on "Remedies" button describes the Preventive measures (fertilizers and spray control). For more info, Remedies page leads to official website of "Directorate of Plant Protection, Quarantine and Storage" under the guidance of "Ministry of Agriculture and Farmers Welfare" [65].

The proposed system predominantly relies on a user-side interface, allowing users to visualize detected diseases alongside their primary remedies. However, it lacks a comprehensive and precise control measure, along with detailed information on pests and pathogens associated with specific diseases for precise diagnosis. Being an Android-based system, presented system is able to serve Android-based smartphones only. To date, the developed application is not a cross-platform mobile application for crop, that is, it does not support iOS and web-based application platform to detect and provide solutions for plant diseases.

8.6 CONCLUSION

The proposed system entails the design and implementation of a mobile application utilizing the CNN algorithm for the detection and diagnosis of plant leaf diseases. Beyond ensuring accurate disease detection, it puts forth a cost-effective, user-friendly, and widely accessible solution for the early identification and prevention of plant diseases through the integration of ML and mobile application development. This application holds the potential to enhance environmental and humanitarian outcomes, contributing to global food security and mitigating economic losses. Capable of detecting 26 different diseases across 14 plant species, the system boasts an average training accuracy of 98.26%. Furthermore, Plantae provides detailed information on symptoms, pathogens, hosts, and recommended control remedies and solutions.

Proposed system can further be enhanced with the upgradation and integration of chatbots for more advice and interaction with the user, which will result in the formation of farmer's community to discuss and address their domestic problems on their own. The system developed here can be enhanced with a panel of botanical experts integrated into the application. This feature serves to address user queries and provide timely warnings about the detection of new plant diseases. This proactive approach enables users to take immediate actions, such as implementing pest or fertilizer control measures, thereby avoiding significant economic losses. A cross-platform (i.e., iOS and Web) with multi-language support along with real-time automated IoT-based surveillance of farms by UAVs will diversify the user-case of our application.

ACKNOWLEDGEMENT

We extend our heartfelt gratitude to our mentor, whose timely guidance and unwavering support were invaluable throughout the course of this project. We are also deeply appreciative of our Institute, the Department of Multidisciplinary Engineering, and the Department of Chemical Engineering for entrusting us with this remarkable opportunity and the freedom to embark on this project.

REFERENCES

[1] J. M. Alston and P. G. Pardey, "Agriculture in the global economy." *Journal of Economic Perspectives*, vol. 28, no. 1, 2014, doi: 10.1257/jep.28.1.121

[2] Ministry of Agriculture & Farmers Welfare, "Press information bureau." Accessed: Jul. 15, 2024. [Online]. Available: https://www.pib.gov.in/PressReleasePage.aspx?PRID=1741942

[3] L. Li, S. Zhang, and B. Wang, "Plant disease detection and classification by deep learning – A review." 2021, doi: 10.1109/ACCESS.2021.3069646
[4] California Ag Today, "Pests and disease cause worldwide damage to crops – From the University of California's."
[5] Business Standard, "India: An agricultural powerhouse of the world." Accessed: Jul. 15, 2024. [Online]. Available: https://www.business-standard.com/article/b2b-connect/india-an-agricultural-powerhouse-of-the-world-116051800253_1.html
[6] C. A. Deutsch et al., "Increase in crop losses to insect pests in a warming climate." *Science (1979)*, vol. 361, no. 6405, pp. 916–919, Aug. 2018, doi: 10.1126/SCIENCE.AAT3466/SUPPL_FILE/AAT3466-DEUTSCH-SM.PDF
[7] Food and Agriculture Organization of the United Nations, "International year of plant health – Final report." *International Year of Plant Health – Final report*, Oct. 2021, doi: 10.4060/CB7056EN
[8] Food and Agriculture Organization of the United Nations, "The state of food and agriculture the state of food and agriculture." *2013 Food systems for better nutrition 2013 I3300E/1*. 2013, Accessed: Jul. 15, 2024. [Online]. Available: www.fao.org/publications
[9] M. Brahimi, K. Boukhalfa, and A. Moussaoui, "Deep learning for tomato diseases: Classification and symptoms visualization." *Applied Artificial Intelligence*, vol. 31, no. 4, 2017, doi: 10.1080/08839514.2017.1315516
[10] K. P. Ferentinos, "Deep learning models for plant disease detection and diagnosis." *Computers and Electronics in Agriculture*, vol. 145, 2018, doi: 10.1016/j.compag.2018.01.009
[11] R. Bhave, M. Deodhar, K. Bhalodia, and M. Rathod, "Android application for crop yield prediction and crop disease detection." *International Journal of Innovative Science and Research Technology*, vol. 3, no. 3, 2018.
[12] A. Fuentes, S. Yoon, S. C. Kim, and D. S. Park, "A robust deep-learning-based detector for real-time tomato plant diseases and pests recognition." *Sensors (Switzerland)*, vol. 17, no. 9, 2017, doi: 10.3390/s17092022
[13] S. P. Mohanty, D. P. Hughes, and M. Salathé, "Using deep learning for image-based plant disease detection." *Front Plant Science*, vol. 7, Sept., 2016, doi: 10.3389/fpls.2016.01419
[14] M. Türkoğlu and D. Hanbay, "Plant disease and pest detection using deep learning-based features." *Turkish Journal of Electrical Engineering and Computer Sciences*, vol. 27, no. 3, 2019, doi: 10.3906/elk-1809-181
[15] D. Oppenheim, G. Shani, O. Erlich, and L. Tsror, "Using deep learning for image-based potato tuber disease detection." *Phytopathology*, vol. 109, no. 6, 2019, doi: 10.1094/PHYTO-08-18-0288-R
[16] S. Shrimali, "PlantifyAI: A novel convolutional neural network based mobile application for efficient crop disease detection and treatment." in *Procedia Computer Science*, 2021, doi: 10.1016/j.procs.2021.07.059
[17] S. Naik, P. Chhajed, J. Trivedi, and S. Davare, "Plant disease detection and suggestions using mobile app." *SSRN Electronic Journal*, Jul. 2021, doi: 10.2139/SSRN.3883334
[18] E. C. Too, L. Yujian, S. Njuki, and L. Yingchun, "A comparative study of fine-tuning deep learning models for plant disease identification." *Computers and Electronics in Agriculture*, vol. 161, 2019, doi: 10.1016/j.compag.2018.03.032
[19] H. Patel, V. Palande, A. Bhat, A. Behara, and R. Gothi, "Grape Leaf Diesease Detection Using CNN and RNN." *SSRN Electronic Journal*, 2022, doi: 10.2139/ssrn.4108967
[20] B. Tugrul, E. Elfatimi, and R. Eryigit, "Convolutional neural networks in detection of plant leaf diseases: A review." 2022, doi: 10.3390/agriculture12081192
[21] A. Bapat, S. Sabut, and K. Vizhi, "Plant leaf disease detection using deep learning." *International Journal of Advanced Science and Technology*, vol. 29, no. 6, 2020, doi: 10.55041/isjem01513

[22] R. M. J. Al-Akkam and M. S. M. Altaei, "Plants leaf diseases detection using deep learning." *Iraqi Journal of Science*, vol. 63, no. 2, 2022, doi: 10.24996/ijs.2022.63.2.34
[23] U. P. Singh, S. S. Chouhan, S. Jain, and S. Jain, "Multilayer convolution neural network for the classification of mango leaves infected by anthracnose disease." *IEEE Access*, vol. 7, 2019, doi: 10.1109/ACCESS.2019.2907383
[24] G. Geetharamani and Pandian J. Arun, "Identification of plant leaf diseases using a nine-layer deep convolutional neural network." *Computers and Electrical Engineering*, vol. 76, 2019, 323–338. doi: 10.1016/j.compeleceng.2019.04.011
[25] S. Arivazhagan, R. N. Shebiah, S. Ananthi, and S. Vishnu Varthini, "Detection of unhealthy region of plant leaves and classification of plant leaf diseases using texture features." *Agricultural Engineering International: CIGR Journal*, vol. 15, no. 1, 211–217. 2013.
[26] Ü. Atila, M. Uçar, K. Akyol, and E. Uçar, "Plant leaf disease classification using EfficientNet deep learning model." *Ecological Informatics*, vol. 61, 2021, doi: 10.1016/j.ecoinf.2020.101182
[27] K. Wisaeng and W. Sa-Ngiamvibool, "Detection of plant leaf diseases using K-mean++ intermeans thresholding algorithm." *Journal of Computer Science*, vol. 16, no. 9, 2020, doi: 10.3844/jcssp.2020.1237.1249
[28] B. Liu, Y. Zhang, D. J. He, and Y. Li, "Identification of apple leaf diseases based on deep convolutional neural networks." *Symmetry (Basel)*, vol. 10, no. 1, 2018, doi: 10.3390/sym10010011
[29] M. H. Saleem, J. Potgieter, and K. M. Arif, "Plant disease classification: A comparative evaluation of convolutional neural networks and deep learning optimizers." *Plants*, vol. 9, no. 10, 2020, doi: 10.3390/plants9101319
[30] M. Faisal, J. S. Leu, C. Avian, S. W. Prakosa, and M. Köppen, "DFNet: Dense fusion convolution neural network for plant leaf disease classification." *Agronomy Journal*, vol. 116, no. 3, 2024, doi: 10.1002/agj2.21341
[31] The Economics Times, "India's growing data usage, smartphone adoption to boost Digital India initiatives: Top bureaucrat." *The Economic Times*. Accessed: Jul. 15, 2024. [Online]. Available: https://economictimes.indiatimes.com/news/india/indias-growing-data-usage-smartphone-adoption-to-boost-digital-india-initiatives-top-bureaucrat/articleshow/87275402.cms?from=mdr
[32] T. R. Mahesh, V. Vinoth Kumar, R. Sivakami, I. Manimozhi, N. Krishnamoorthy, and B. Swapna, "Early predictive model for detection of plant leaf diseases using MobileNetV2 architecture." *International Journal of Intelligent Systems and Applications in Engineering*, vol. 11, no. 2, 2023.
[33] J. C. Valdoria, A. R. Caballeo, B. I. D. Fernandez, and J. M. M. Condino, "IDahon: An Android based terrestrial plant disease detection mobile application through digital image processing using deep learning neural network algorithm." In *Proceedings of 2019 4th International Conference on Information Technology: Encompassing Intelligent Technology and Innovation Towards the New Era of Human Life, InCIT 2019*, 2019, doi: 10.1109/INCIT.2019.8912053
[34] S. I. Rimon, M. R. Islam, A. Dey, and A. Das, "PlantBuddy: An Android-based mobile application for plant disease detection using deep convolutional neural network." In *Lecture Notes in Electrical Engineering*, 2022, doi: 10.1007/978-981-16-6448-9_28
[35] V. R. Badgujar, A. R. Ner, H. S. Jadhav, and R. S. Magare, "Mobile application for plant disease recognition using transfer learning." *International Research Journal of Engineering and Technology*, 2021, doi: 10.1109/ViTECoN.2019.8899748
[36] S. Bhatt and S. Hingu, "Implementation of crop disease detection system using flutter." In *AIP Conference Proceedings*, 2023, doi: 10.1063/5.0178294

[37] S. Kumbhar, S. Patil, A. Nilawar, B. Mahalakshmi, and M. Nipane, "Farmer buddy-web based cotton leaf disease detection using CNN." *International Journal of Applied Engineering Research* ISSN 0973-4562 vol. 14, no. 11 pp. 2662–2666, 2019.

[38] A. A. Ahmed and G. Harshavardhan Reddy, "A mobile-based system for detecting plant leaf diseases using deep learning." *AgriEngineering*, vol. 3, no. 3, 2021, doi: 10.3390/agriengineering3030032

[39] J. K. M. Gad, "A survey on crop disease detection and prevention using Android application." *IJISET-International Journal of Innovative Science, Engineering & Technology*, vol. 2, no. 4, 2015, Accessed: Jul. 15, 2024. [Online]. Available: www.ijiset.com

[40] B. S. Rishiikeshwer, T. A. Shriram, J. S. Raju, M. Hari, B. Santhi, and G. R. Brindha, "Farmer-friendly mobile application for automated leaf disease detection of real-time augmented data set using convolution neural networks." *Journal of Computer Science*, vol. 16, no. 2, 2020, doi: 10.3844/JCSSP.2020.158.166

[41] S. R. Kamlapurkar, "Detection of plant leaf disease using image processing approach." *International Journal of Scient–ific and Research Publications*, vol. 6, no. 2, 168–170, 2016.

[42] M. N. R. Thorat, "Early disease detection and monitoring large field of crop by using IoT." *International Journal of Computer Science and Information Security*, vol. 15, no. 10, 1582–1592, 2017.

[43] S. R. Maniyath et al., "Plant disease detection using machine learning." *Proceedings - 2018 International Conference on Design Innovations for 3Cs Compute Communicate Control, ICDI3C 2018*, pp. 41–45, Aug. 2018, doi: 10.1109/ICDI3C.2018.00017

[44] P. Vasavi, A. Punitha, and T. Venkat Narayana Rao, "Crop leaf disease detection and classification using machine learning and deep learning algorithms by visual symptoms: A review." 2022, doi: 10.11591/ijece.v12i2.pp2079-2086

[45] R. Chen, H. Qi, Y. Liang, and M. Yang, "Identification of plant leaf diseases by deep learning based on channel attention and channel pruning." *Frontiers in Plant Science*, vol. 13, 2022, doi: 10.3389/fpls.2022.1023515

[46] R. Deshpande and H. Patidar, "Detection of plant leaf disease by generative adversarial and deep convolutional neural network." *Journal of The Institution of Engineers (India): Series B*, vol. 104, no. 5, 2023, doi: 10.1007/s40031-023-00907-x

[47] K. M. Hosny, W. M. El-Hady, F. M. Samy, E. Vrochidou, and G. A. Papakostas, "Multi-class classification of plant leaf diseases using feature fusion of deep convolutional neural network and local binary pattern." *IEEE Access*, vol. 11, 2023, doi: 10.1109/ACCESS.2023.3286730

[48] J. Andrew, J. Eunice, D. E. Popescu, M. K. Chowdary, and J. Hemanth, "Deep learning-based leaf disease detection in crops using images for agricultural applications." *Agronomy*, vol. 12, no. 10, 2022, doi: 10.3390/agronomy12102395

[49] Kaggle, "Plant village dataset." Accessed: Jul. 15, 2024. [Online]. Available: https://www.kaggle.com/datasets/emmarex/plantdisease

[50] G. Dhaliwal, V. Jindal, and A. Dhawan, "Insect pest problems and crop losses: Changing trends." *Indian Journal of Ecology*, vol. 37, no. 1, 1–7, 2010.

[51] V. Binnar and S. Sharma, "Plant leaf diseases detection using deep learning algorithms." In *Lecture Notes in Electrical Engineering*, 2023, doi: 10.1007/978-981-19-5868-7_17

[52] A. Pal and V. Kumar, "AgriDet: Plant leaf disease severity classification using agriculture detection framework." *Engineering Applications of Artificial Intelligence*, vol. 119, 2023, doi: 10.1016/j.engappai.2022.105754

[53] S. S. Hari, M. Sivakumar, P. Renuga, S. karthikeyan, and S. Suriya, "Detection of plant disease by leaf image using convolutional neural network." In *2019 International Conference on Vision Towards Emerging Trends in Communication and Networking (ViTECoN)*, IEEE, Mar. 2019, pp. 1–5, doi: 10.1109/ViTECoN.2019.8899748

[54] M. V. Shewale and R. D. Daruwala, "High performance deep learning architecture for early detection and classification of plant leaf disease." *Journal of Agriculture and Food Research*, vol. 14, 2023, doi: 10.1016/j.jafr.2023.100675
[55] K. Zhang, Q. Wu, A. Liu, and X. Meng, "Can deep learning identify tomato leaf disease?." *Advances in Multimedia*, vol. 2018, 2018, 1–10, doi: 10.1155/2018/6710865
[56] A. V. Panchal, S. C. Patel, K. Bagyalakshmi, P. Kumar, I. R. Khan, and M. Soni, "Image-based plant diseases detection using deep learning." *Mater Today Proc*, vol. 80, 2023, doi: 10.1016/j.matpr.2021.07.281
[57] H. Guan, C. Fu, G. Zhang, K. Li, P. Wang, and Z. Zhu, "A lightweight model for efficient identification of plant diseases and pests based on deep learning." *Frontiers in Plant Science*, vol. 14, 2023, doi: 10.3389/fpls.2023.1227011
[58] I. Ahmed and P. K. Yadav, "Plant disease detection using machine learning approaches." *Expert Systems*, 2022, doi: 10.1111/exsy.13136
[59] Dinesh Sivakumar, "Introduction to InceptionNet - Scaler topics." Accessed: Jul. 15, 2024. [Online]. Available: https://www.scaler.com/topics/inception-network/
[60] James McDermott, "Hands-on transfer learning with keras and the VGG16 model – LearnDataSci." Accessed: Jul. 15, 2024. [Online]. Available: https://www.learndatasci.com/tutorials/hands-on-transfer-learning-keras/
[61] J. Jaworek-Korjakowska, P. Kleczek, and M. Gorgon, "Melanoma thickness prediction based on convolutional neural network with VGG-19 model transfer learning." In *IEEE Computer Society Conference on Computer Vision and Pattern Recognition Workshops*, 2019, doi: 10.1109/CVPRW.2019.00333
[62] Suvaditya Mukherjee, "The Annotated ResNet-50. Explaining how ResNet-50 works and why…." *Towards Data Science*. Accessed: Jul. 15, 2024. [Online]. Available: https://towardsdatascience.com/the-annotated-resnet-50-a6c536034758
[63] M. M. Islam et al., "DeepCrop: Deep learning-based crop disease prediction with web application." *Journal of Agriculture and Food Research*, vol. 14, 2023, doi: 10.1016/j.jafr.2023.100764
[64] I. Bhakta, S. Phadikar, K. Majumder, H. Mukherjee, and A. Sau, "A novel plant disease prediction model based on thermal images using modified deep convolutional neural network." *Precision Agriculture*, vol. 24, no. 1, 2023, doi: 10.1007/s11119-022-09927-x
[65] Ministry of Agriculture and Farmers Welfare, "Directorate of plant protection, quarantine & storage." *GOI* Accessed: Jul. 15, 2024. [Online]. Available: https://ppqs.gov.in/

9 Captureshield

A Deep Dive into Screenshot Security

K Sharmila, Shazia Tazeen, Thirupathi Regula and Gouthami Velakanti

9.1 INTRODUCTION

In the current era, sharing sensitive information on screens raises a number of worries, making digital security a critical component. Screenshots are frequently taken to preserve data, which may inadvertently reveal private information. This vulnerability had made a strong screenshot security measure necessary. The suggested article presents a thorough framework called CaptureShield, which is intended to improve snapshot security across a range of platforms and apps. Through an in-depth exploration of Capture Shield, this chapter aims to shed light on the importance of safeguarding digital content and proposes suitable examples to illustrate its effectiveness.

Social media is an online platform that is easy to use and flexible to establish networks with a group of individuals who exchange their personal and professional interests, hobbies, or backgrounds. It has been identified and proved by various surveys that social media platforms are showing both positive and negative impacts on the younger generation.

Social media is one of the web-based methods of communication in which users can continue in conversations, share some information, and also produce content for the web. Most of the people across the world connect with each other and share information using social media very quickly. Social media is an innovative thought with incredible opportunities, but on the other hand, it is also challenging as some network users always create negativity.

Through all social media applications, we can communicate with other parties using chat messengers, making audio and video calls, sending files (audio, video, and messages), and sharing all kinds of information. Today's youth are most widely accessing and very active on social media without knowing much about the intrinsic impacts in the future. These implications are not only for individuals but for organizations also. Though there are various security measures available for security and privacy of the user's data, there exist many disadvantages in every application that is available for access on social media and the internet.

WhatsApp and Snapchat have become central communication hubs for millions of users worldwide. When personal content is shared on these social media

DOI: 10.1201/9781032703718-13

platforms, there is a high chance of susceptibility of data. Hence, there is an essential need to ensure the security of such data, especially screenshots and short videos. Snapchat has an option of sending a notification to the user when someone tries to capture a screenshot of their snap or chat. Similarly, WhatsApp, while currently not having a native screenshot notification feature, provides end-to-end encryption to ensure chats remain private between the sender and the receiver. As technology advances, both platforms might benefit from exploring additional security measures, such as restricting screenshot capabilities or employing watermarking techniques, which can trace back unauthorized distributions. As users continue to place their trust in these platforms, it becomes paramount for these applications to prioritize and enhance the security of their content against unwarranted screenshots.

Social media has become a passion for most people, and sharing their information or any kind of data to show their status has become a habit or daily routine. But during this process of sharing their information, people, especially the youth, are not aware of the consequences that may take place later, for which they need to suffer a lot. The consequences can be any attacks done on the shared content on social media. In this paper, we present a security algorithm that hides the actual information from an attacker. The application of the proposed algorithm on shared media will provide high security to the content, and the people need not face any consequences from the attackers or the information can never be misused by any unauthorized persons who can just view the content but cannot use the content. The proposed algorithm will make the persons comfortable in using and sharing information on their social media.

Here's an overview of how screenshots are handled in some popular social media applications:

1. **Facebook**
   Facebook allows users to take screenshots of content within the app, including posts, comments, and messages. However, if a user takes a screenshot of a disappearing photo or video within Facebook Stories, the app notifies the poster that their content was screenshot.
2. **Instagram**
   Instagram generally allows users to take screenshots of posts, stories, and direct messages. However, Instagram also notifies users if someone takes a screenshot of their disappearing photos or videos in Instagram Stories. As of the last update, Instagram does not provide any notifications for regular posts or direct messages.
3. **Snapchat**
   Snapchat is known for its temporary content that disappears after being viewed. Initially, Snapchat notified users when someone took a screenshot of their snaps. However, this feature has evolved, and now Snapchat only notifies users if someone takes a screenshot of their disappearing messages or stories in certain circumstances.

   If the screenshot of a chat conversation is taken, it is notified to the original user. But if someone screenshots a public story, the poster may not be notified.

4. **Twitter**
   Twitter allows users to take screenshots of tweets, replies, and direct messages. There are no built-in features to notify users if someone takes a screenshot of their tweets or messages within the app.
5. **WhatsApp**
   WhatsApp allows users to take screenshots of individual and group chats. As of the last update, there are no notifications for users if someone takes a screenshot of their chat conversations within the app.

In particular, while some social media platforms have implemented features to notify users of screenshot activity in certain contexts, many still allow users to freely take screenshots of content within the app. However, users should always be mindful of privacy and respect the content they interact with, regardless of the platform's screenshot policies.

9.2 LITERATURE SURVEY

The contributors of [1] have discussed security concerns associated with image-based authentication. Additionally, a thorough analysis of the assessment of several security concerns that have centered on the possible dangers of screen-capture tools was conducted.

The authors of [2] presented a novel way to prevent unwanted screen captures, therefore mitigating security risks and information leakage. The scheme's primary goal is to prevent screen capture by integrating Visual Cryptography (VC), which is mostly used for picture encryption, with the Scale-Invariant Feature Transform (SIFT). Furthermore, in the current digital era, one of the most important venues for information exchange is electronic screens. In order to address these problems, the authors have additionally set up a novel solution that uses VC to encrypt images, making it difficult or impossible for unauthorized users to capture screen content.

A novel technique has been described in [3] that essentially attempts to protect visual content that is presented on screens by preventing screenshots from being taken of it. Additionally, it demonstrates an image processing-based system that warps the data displayed on the screen, making it difficult for even capture tools to extract any kind of important information. Additionally, [3] suggested a novel blending method that produces an algorithm for visual content distortion that permits real-time recovery even for the human visual system.

Novel techniques to protect static binary images displayed on screens have been proposed in [4]. Additionally, [4] employed a visual encryption technique that segmented the target images, capitalizing on the ability of the human eye to discern temporal differences in visual perception to separate text from background. Their user study demonstrates that the human visual system is capable of mentally reconstructing encrypted visual data. Additionally, images captured using this method lack visually interesting content, making it a valuable enhancement for overall security and a formidable deterrent against screenshot theft.

In the article [5], Ram N. et al. have done a survey and observed that the younger generation who are using smartphones are actively involved in social media.

The authors, in their survey, have collected more than 750 hours of smartphone activity, which resulted in approximately 540,000 screenshots taken during a period of 34 to 105 days. In order to ensure privacy, strict protocols have been implemented for secure transmission of data in encrypted form, or procedures for strict consent have to be followed to enable privacy of an individual.

In the article [6], Chia et al. have proposed that visual data has to be distorted before sharing it with the viewer. Various methods have been proposed in the past, which have concentrated on the architecture of the system that provides screen protection. The authors also showed that the possibility for this is to limit the capturing of the screenshot using techniques like image processing, which marks the prevention of screenshots.

A study was conducted to examine the challenges surrounding privacy maintenance in social networks. Various sub-areas, such as privacy concerns associated with sharing social network data with third-party consumers and the risk of information leakage to uninvited individuals within one's social circles, were identified [7–8]. Furthermore, another study focused on the ethical implications of unrestricted screenshot usage on the internet. There should always be a system to prevent unauthorized screenshots from being manipulated or obscured, thus safeguarding content integrity and protecting against privacy breaches. The primary goal of the study is to address the problems associated with unrestrained screenshot usage, which presents moral quandaries and adverse effects on people. By putting these crucial strategies into practice, we can safeguard users' privacy and encourage moral behavior online whenever they take screenshots of content to share on social media sites. Similar worries about ethics and privacy have been raised by the growing usage of screenshots on social networking sites [9–10].

Screen Stealer, an Android virus that secretly takes screenshots of private data, was developed and evaluated in [11]. To escape being identified, this malware runs in the background of basic programs such as the Tic-Tac-Toe game, which asks for common permissions. This app is compatible with both rooted and non-rooted handsets. It uses Android Debug Bridge (ADB) shell scripts, which take screenshots on rooted devices, and uses an open-source library (ASL) on non-rooted and allows a programmatic screenshot capture without root privileges by running a background native service [12]. The virus uses AndroidManifest.xml and gets permissions and employs DeviceAdminReceiver and Broadcast Receiver to gain privileges that prevent it from being uninstalled by the user [13–14]. It also monitors the applications running in the foreground, which targets specific applications like bank and community media apps. Once a target application is detected, Screen Stealer captures screenshots at specified intervals and stores them in encrypted form on the device, then sends the data to the attacker's server [11–15].

The effectiveness of Screen Stealer was evaluated against similar applications and measured based on various parameters such as capture ratio, response time, performance overhead, and resource consumption. The evaluations were carried out on multiple Android device models and versions to assess the threat posed by such malware in real-world scenarios.

There are also issues related to the public media like the issue of illegal distribution of videos captured from TV or theater screens using mobile cameras. This practice has caused significant financial losses in the film industry due to reduced theater attendance. The authors [11] propose a machine learning technique that video-sharing platforms like YouTube can implement to prevent the illegal uploading and distribution of screen-captured videos. They have implemented a technique using a support vector machine (SVM) model to differentiate between original content and those that have been changed. The SVM is trained using three no-reference image quality measures:

- Naturalness Image Quality Evaluator: assesses image quality based on statistical models constructed from undistorted natural images.
- Image Sharpness Measure for Blurred Images in Frequency Domain: analyzes the amount of blurriness by counting the number of Fourier transform coefficients above a certain threshold.
- Discrete Cosine Transform-based image sharpness measure.

These metrics evaluate image quality without needing a reference image, which is crucial for analyzing videos that are distributed without consent. The proposed scheme could enhance the efficiency of video-sharing websites in addressing the rampant challenge of video piracy (Table 9.1).

9.3 PROBLEM STATEMENT

Today, the usability percentage of social media is high, which has both advantages and disadvantages. If we consider WhatsApp, we have a provision of sharing our status in the form of images and videos. Some attackers or users having the intention of misusing the shared media on WhatsApp can take screenshots of the shared data and misuse it. This becomes a great problem when misused. So, there is a necessity of providing security to the shared media and letting the user enjoy their social life. Most of the current mobiles cannot provide security by avoiding taking screenshots of the shared data on WhatsApp [16–17].

Only a few mobile phones like Android 14 provide security through privacy-preserving screenshot detection Application Programming Interface (API). Though this provides security, there is still a possibility of stealing the data with the following tricks.

1. They can use some other phone to capture the snap.
2. They can record the snap without notification option on MAC.
3. They can use the screen mirroring feature to capture the snap.

When it comes to capturing a screenshot on some applications like Snapchat using iPhones, a clear-cut solution to do so without the other party's knowledge is elusive. Nevertheless, unconventional methods do exist. Snap's security updates can change anytime, making today's solutions potentially ineffective tomorrow and leading to awkward situations. Also, it's worth emphasizing that we do not endorse or promote taking unauthorized screenshots of others' snaps.

A significant barrier to preserving the privacy of snapshots is the wide range of mobile devices and what they can do. For example, even though Android 14 has

TABLE 9.1
Comparison with Respect to Methodology Used, Strengths, and Weakness by Few Authors

S. No	Paper Title	Authors	Methodology Used	Strength	Weakness
1	Screenseg: On-Device Screenshot Layout Analysis	Manoj Goyal, Rachit S Munjal, Sukumar Moharana	The authors use a combination of Deep Neural Networks (DNN) and Image Processing techniques for analyzing the layout of screenshots on mobile devices.	High precision of about 0.95 is achieved. Operates with a low latency of 200ms.	Limited dataset. Device constraints.
2	Learning to Locate the Text Forgery in Smartphone Screenshots	Zeqin Yu, Bin Li, Yuzhen Lin, Jinhua Zeng, Jishen Zeng	The authors use a Screenshot Text Forgery Dataset (STFD) and develop a Screenshot Text Forgery Localization Network (STFL-Net).	Novel dataset is used. Various advanced techniques were used.	Limited dataset. No realistic scenarios.
3	Recaptured Screen Image Demoiréing	Huanjing Yue: Member, IEEE, Yan Mao Lipu Liang	The authors propose an algorithm named Image Registration Algorithm, which is used to generate training data	Innovative approach AMNET is used. It has worked with effective images of 340 test images.	Computational complexity. Images not included in the MRBI database.
4	Screen Stealer: Addressing Screenshot Attacks on Android Devices	Syeda Mariam Muzammal, Munam Ali Shah	The main aim of the paper is to discuss ADB capabilities and also to state how sensitive data can be exposed.	Innovative approach of ADB.	Dataset is captured from the Play Store.
5	A Novel Machine Learning Approach to Prevent Illegal Distribution of Screen Captured Videos	V. M. Manikandan V. Masilamani	The SVM model presented in this work is essentially trained to distinguish between captured and normal screen footage. This model is trained using superior no-reference image data.	SVM model was trained with no-reference image quality measures to classify videos.	Current dataset is limited to 80 videos only.

security safeguards, users can still utilize other devices to take screenshots covertly. Additionally, taking pictures on MAC devices without receiving notifications opens up other ways for illegal access to data. Screen mirroring technologies also present a risk since they allow users to take pictures from external devices without setting off alarms.

Due to the iPhones' strict privacy policies, taking screenshots with just a handful of applications poses special obstacles. Although screenshot alerts users when someone takes a screenshot, the development of technologies such as Private Screenshots makes it possible for users to take screenshots without being noticed, which compromises the platform's security. Concerns concerning data security and privacy violations are raised by such gaps in screenshot privacy.

9.3.1 Understanding the Mechanism

Upon activation, Private Screenshots commences recording the entirety of your screen display. As we navigate through pages, chats, or videos that you intend to capture, the app provides an on-screen shot button. This feature operates discreetly, bypassing the application's notification system, thereby allowing to clandestinely capture any screen content. It's important to note that a few applications do notify users when screenshots are taken of their shared content within the application.

The application alerts the other user when you capture a screenshot of their photo or video. Additionally, it inserts a message into the chat stating "You took a screenshot!" if you screenshot a conversation. Furthermore, a screenshot icon appears in the viewers' section of a user's story to indicate when their content has been screenshotted [18]. The following is the survey done on different applications like WhatsApp, Snapchat, Twitter, and Facebook [19–20] (Table 9.2).

Looking at the above-mentioned data it is clear that India ranks first in the usage of WhatsApp. Hence, there is an immediate need to provide security to the users of this App.

From Figures 9.1 to 9.3, it is clear that 60% of the users share their status regularly, which may include their personal snaps and videos as well.

TABLE 9.2
Representing the Number of WhatsApp Users across the World in Millions (M)

S. No	Country	Number of WhatsApp Users
1	India	391
2	Brazil	109
3	United States	75
4	Russia	64.7
5	Mexico	62.3
6	Germany	48.3
7	Italy	35.5
8	Spain	33.0
9	UK	30.1

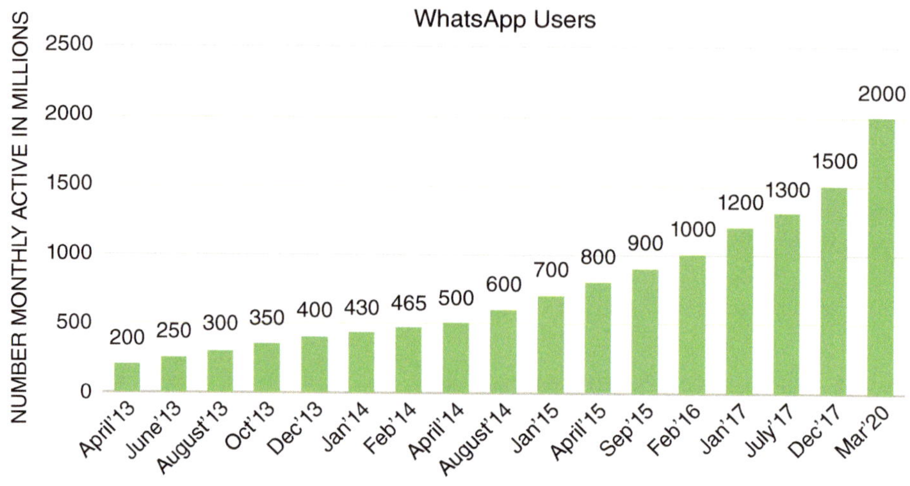

FIGURE 9.1 WhatsApp users increasing rapidly across years.

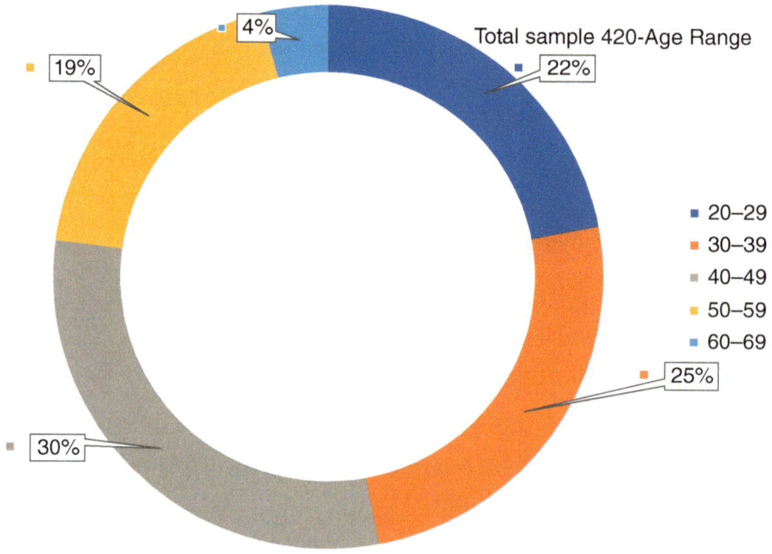

FIGURE 9.2 Representing majority of the users in the age group of 30–49, who are middle-aged people.

Figure 9.3 represents the number of monthly active WhatsApp users worldwide from April 2013 to March 2020.

Once activated, Private Screenshots begins recording everything visible on the screen. When scrolling through a chat or video, we can utilize the application's built-in on-screen shot button to take a screenshot.

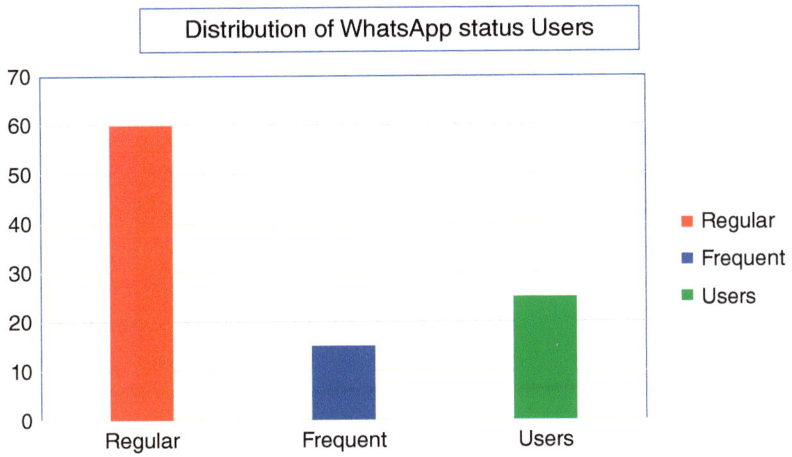

FIGURE 9.3 Distribution of WhatsApp status users.

9.4 PROPOSED WORK

From the above-collected statistics, the usage, frequency, and people involved in application usage are very clear, and there is a necessity to provide security to the application. Our proposed system is designed for two purposes: one is device specific, and the other is software specific. In the applications where the user shares the data publicly there, we need to provide security.

Snapchat has a provision of notifying the sender that the end user has taken a screenshot of the data, etc. However, this can also be bypassed. To overcome the problem of privacy breaches, we propose a solution where the user definitely has to get permission to take the screenshot.

Whenever a screenshot is taken, consent from the owner of the content has to be taken as an acknowledgment so as to take a screenshot. The following are a few applications:

1. **Secure Messaging Applications**:
   - **(a) WhatsApp**: With billions of users globally, WhatsApp serves as a primary mode of communication for many. However, sharing sensitive information through messages poses inherent risks, especially if recipients can freely capture and distribute screenshots. Capture Shield could integrate with WhatsApp to offer an option for users to enable screenshot protection within private conversations. When activated, Capture Shield would obscure sensitive content in screenshots taken within the app, ensuring that even if captured, the information remains unreadable to unauthorized individuals.
   - **(b) Signal**: Signal, which is renowned for prioritizing privacy, might include Capture Shield as a paid service to strengthen its security protocols. Through the usage of Capture Shield, Signal users may communicate confidential information with confidence, knowing that their

conversations are protected from unwanted screenshots. This connection might attract both individuals and companies looking for increased communication security while also reaffirming Signal's dedication to user privacy.

2. **Financial Applications:**
   (a) **Banking Apps**: Although Mobile banking has completely changed individuals' way of managing their finances, in addition, it has also introduced new security challenges associated with it. Capture Shield can partner with banking apps in future to offer protection against unsanctioned screenshots. For instance, our application would dynamically conceal sensitive information such as account numbers and transaction amounts or users making purchases in the application. Taking a proactive approach would mitigate the risk of financial data exposure, instilling greater confidence in users regarding the security of their banking activities.
   (b) **Cryptocurrency Wallets**: As the era of internet is growing, digital wallet currency is becoming crucial in our day-to-day lives. The need to provide security for digital wallets has become vital. The proposed approach could collaborate with well-known cryptocurrency wallet providers to shore up security measures. By integrating CaptureShield, these wallet apps can prevent unauthorized access to sensitive data in the form of screenshots like private keys and transaction histories. This adds an extra layer of protection, which would alleviate the risk of illicit access to users' investments against potential hack access.
3. **E-Learning Platforms**:
   (a) **Online Education Platforms**: Due to the wide availability of online learning platforms, most teachers and students completely rely on digital content. Nevertheless, the need for safeguarding copyrighted materials and maintaining academic integrity are also the main ongoing concerns. Our algorithm can collaborate with various e-learning platforms, which can help in implementing secure viewing modes for both course materials and assessments. For example, this algorithm can prevent users from capturing screenshots of the lecture slides or quizzes, thereby preventing illegitimate distribution of copyrighted materials and also preserving the validity of assessments.

9.4.1 Capture Shield Algorithm

Our algorithm "Capture Shield Algorithm" tracks the access of users continuously on the application. When any user is trying to take a screenshot, the application will notify the person with the status also known as possessor. If the possessor grants permission to the request for the screenshot, only then can the other user take it. If the user overlooks the permission and tries to capture the screenshot, it will not be visible clearly as it will be in an encrypted and invisible format. The proposed algorithm provides security and authentication to the publicly posted media.

The proposed algorithm is as follows:

Step 1: Set up the required application security variables.
Set the following variables to false

- **screenshotPermission (boolean)**, which is used to store the permission of the owner for taking screenshots. By default, its value is false.
- **securityFlag (boolean)**, which is used to specify whether the security flag is enabled or not. By default, its value is set to false.
- **requestPending (boolean)** keeps track of a screenshot request, which is pending.

Step 2: Continuous monitoring of screenshots requests:

- Each time a screenshot request is perceived, proceed to step 3.

Step 3: Obtain consent from the owner:

- Set requestPending to true.
- Sends a request to the owner seeking permission to take a screenshot.
- Waiting for the response.

Step 4: Handle the owner's response:

- If the owner grants the permission for the screenshot:
  - Set screenshotPermission to true.
  - Set requestPending to false.
  - Proceed to step 5.
- If the owner denies permission:
  - Set screenshotPermission to false.
  - Set securityFlag to true.
  - Set requestPending to false.
  - Proceed to step 5.
  - Take a screenshot (conditional):

Step 5:

- If screenshotPermission is true, take the screenshot and display it.
- If screenshotPermission is false, display a blank screen.

Step 6: Continue monitoring for screenshot requests and repeat the process (Figure 9.4).

9.4.1.1 Flowchart

Whenever a random user tries to take a snapshot, the screen will be visible in distorted mode as it is encrypted. In our proposal we have used the Advanced Encryption Standard (AES) algorithm to be visible in an unclear format. By implementing the above steps, the possessor/owner will be protected from unauthorized access from the user/observer.

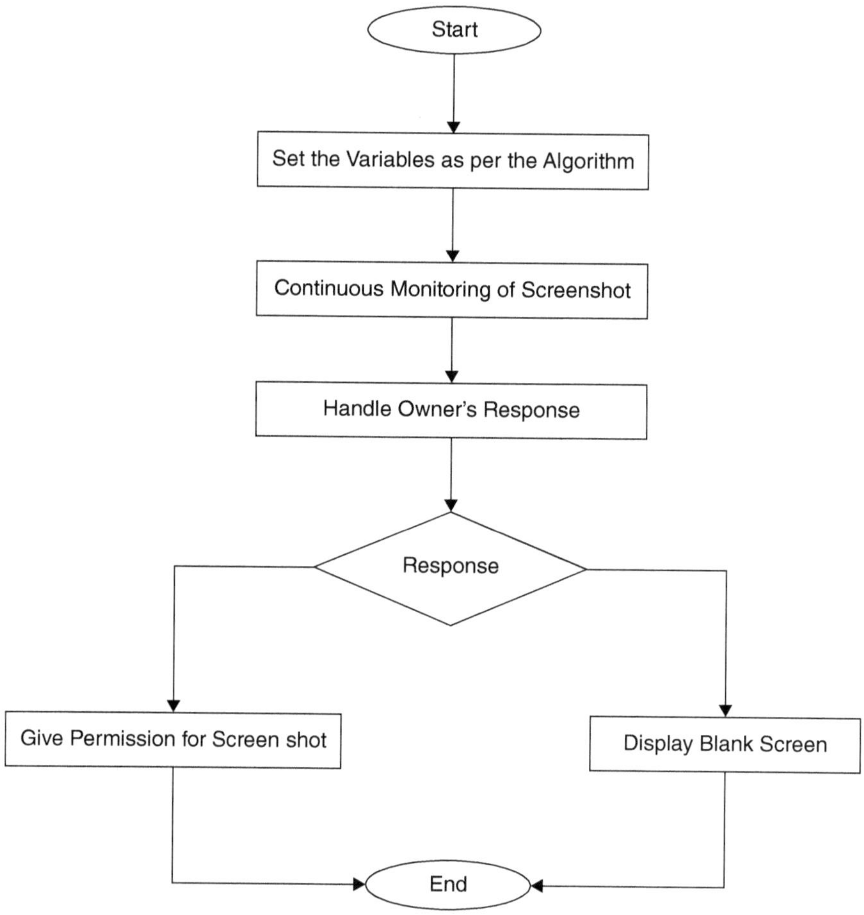

FIGURE 9.4 Flowchart of capture shield algorithm.

9.5 EXPERIMENTS AND RESULTS

Through the implementation of the Capture Shield Algorithm, we conducted experiments on a dataset consisting of 500 screenshots sourced from various users who had set their status as images. The images were collected in different formats, including JPEG, BMP, and TIFF, with a size of 512 × 512 pixels. Subsequently, they were segmented into various block sizes and compressed to less than 90% of their original size.

In this section, we conduct a detailed evaluation of our method aimed at safeguarding document contents from unauthorized copying through screenshots. We compare our approach against a baseline method using test images generated as follows: Each test image is 100 × 100 in size and comprises 25 random characters (limited to alphabets and numbers) arranged in a 5 × 5 grid.

Initially, we quantitatively assess the effectiveness of our method in distorting image contents. For each test image, we compute a set of distorting planes. Subsequently, we apply these planes to distort the test image and calculate the average root mean square (RMS) distances between the distorted and original images. This process is repeated across 1000 different test images to obtain 1000 average RMS distances for each tested n value. Though at a diminishing pace, it is clear that RMS distances rise with greater n numerals. Thus, we can increase the information distortion capacity of the planes by increasing the number of distorting planes in a set. The following is the mathematical expression for calculating the average RMS distance between the deformed and original images:

Let N be the total number of pixels in the image, I_{orig} denotes the original image and $I_{distorted}$ denotes the distorted image.

The formula to find the RMS distance (d_{RMS}) between the original and deformed images:

The RMS distance d_{RMS} between the original and distorted images is calculated using the following formula:

$$d_{RMS} = \sqrt{\frac{1}{N}\sum_{i=1}^{N}\left(I_{orig}(i) - I_{distorted}(i)\right)^2}$$

where:

- $I_{orig}(i)$ is the intensity of pixel i in the original image.
- $I_{distorted}(i)$ is the intensity of pixel i in the distorted image.

We have applied the above equation to compute the average RMS distance across multiple test images, which resulted in each pair of original and distorted images, and then we have calculated the mean and standard deviation of the RMS distances.

In order to produce multiple sets of average RMS distances corresponding to various values of n, the procedure is repeated for a number of distorted "n" planes. In this way it is possible to access how the number of planes utilized affects the distortion effects of a plane.

RMS distance offers a numerical representation of the degree of distortion planes, which facilitates effectiveness of the method used in distorting image contents.

We have used mathematical method to fit least squares quadratic curves and illustrate them in order to provide the accuracy scores for different values of n.

Let us assume that accuracy (n) is the accuracy score, the formula is computed as follows:

$$\text{Accuracy}(n) = a_1 n^2 + b_1 n + c_1$$

where n represents the no of values taken and a_1, b_1, c_1 are coefficients.

After application of our algorithm, the output images generated are obtained without any permission, hence lacking clarity and informational content. On the other hand, images for which permission had been granted retained their original dimensions and sharpness were preserved. Our experiment yielded an algorithm with an accuracy of 92%, considering the possible screenshots without the consent of the owner this remarks the performance of the algorithm

TABLE 9.3
Representing the Output Exhibited

Types of Images	Description	Output Exhibited
Distorted images	Output images obtained without permission	Significant distortion and blurred
Original images	Output images with permission	Original format and clear
Algorithm accuracy	92%	92%
Observations	Algorithm detected unauthorized screenshot attempts	Preservation of data privacy

Table 9.3 provides a concise overview of the experiment's outcomes, highlighting the impact of the algorithm on image distortion and its effectiveness in safeguarding against unauthorized screenshot attempts.

9.5.1 Sample Codes

```
public static void setDisableScreenshots(boolean disableScreenshots
    Context context = getApplicationContext();
    WindowManager.LayoutParams params = ((WindowManager) context.get
            .getDefaultDisplay()
            .getAttributes();
    params.flags |= WindowManager.LayoutParams.FLAG_SECURE;
```

```
params.flags |= WindowManager.LayoutParams.FLAG_SECURE;
if (disableScreenshots) {
    params.flags |= WindowManager.LayoutParams.FLAG_SECURE;
} else {
    params.flags &= ~WindowManager.LayoutParams.FLAG_SECURE;
}
```

```
    @Override
    public void onClick(View v) {
        MyApplicationContext.setDisableScreenshots(true);
        startActivity(new Intent(MainActivity.this, SecondActivi
    }
});
```

After the experiments are conducted, we could yield the following distorted pictures of the screenshots without the permission of the content owner. After the consent, the pictures were visible clearly (Figure 9.5).

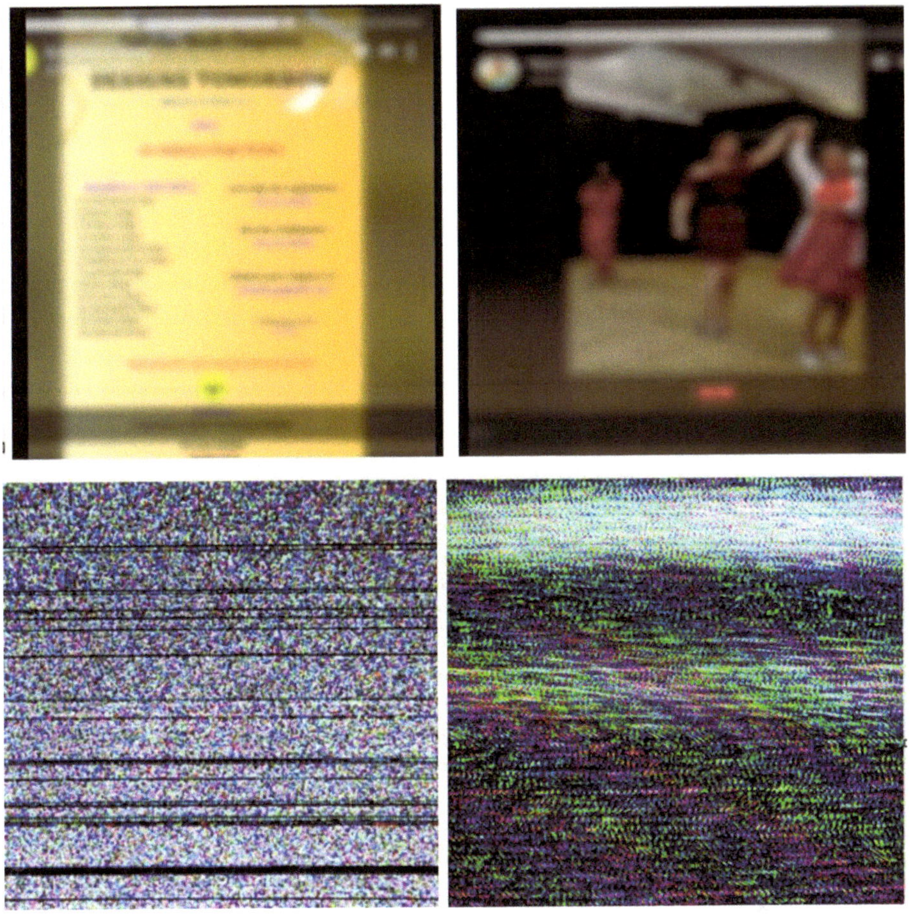

FIGURE 9.5 Distorted snap when screenshot is taken without permission of the owner.

9.6 RESEARCH GAPS

Research on the current problem of restricting screenshots on social media platforms now holds significant potential, especially with respect to the growing concerns about privacy, digital rights, and online safety. As technology is rising leaps and bounds, there is absolutely a great need for techniques like watermarking and encryption. There is every chance for legal issues and intellectual property rights. Hence, cybersecurity has to be provided to the applications to overcome potential vulnerabilities. Awareness has to be given to the younger generations about digital etiquette and to the elderly people about possible frauds. Research can be done to address effective strategies to overcome all these gaps by interdisciplinary collaboration among researchers, industry stakeholders, policymakers, and end users to develop comprehensive solutions.

9.7 CONCLUSION AND FUTURE SCOPE

Capture Shield represents a significant advancement in screenshot security, offering versatile solutions to safeguard sensitive information across various digital platforms. By collaborating with leading applications and service providers, Capture Shield has the potential to redefine standards for digital privacy and security. Through the examples presented, it is evident that Capture Shield's innovative approach can address diverse security challenges, ultimately empowering users to share and access digital content with confidence in its protection. As the digital landscape continues to evolve, the need for robust screenshot security measures will only intensify, making solutions like Capture Shield indispensable in safeguarding sensitive information in an increasingly interconnected world.

REFERENCES

[1] Oh, I., Lee, Y., Lee, H., Lee, K., & Yim, K., "Security Assessment of the Image-Based Authentication Using Screen-Capture Tools," *Advances in intelligent systems and computing*, pp. 156–161, 2017, https://doi.org/10.1007/978-3-319-61542-4_14

[2] Zhao, W., Sun, H., & Zhang, D., "Research on DDoS Attack Detection Method Based on Deep Neural Network Model in SDN," *2022 International Conference on Networking and Network Applications (NaNA)*, 2022. https://doi.org/10.1109/nana56854.2022.00038

[3] Escorcia, V., Niebles, Juan Carlos, & Ghanem, B., "On the relationship between visual attributes and convolutional networks," Jun. 2015. https://doi.org/10.1109/cvpr.2015.7298730

[4] Hou, J.-U., Kim, D., Song, H.-J., & Lee, H.-K., "Secure image display through visual cryptography," Jun. 2016. https://doi.org/10.1145/2909827.2930805

[5] Ram, N. et al., "Screenomics: A new approach for observing and studying individuals' digital lives," *Journal of Adolescent Research*, vol. 35, no. 1, pp. 16–50, Nov. 2019. https://doi.org/10.1177/0743558419883362

[6] Chia, A. Y.-S., Bandara, U., Wang, X., & Hirano, H., "Protecting against screenshots: An image processing approach", *2015 IEEE Conference on Computer Vision and Pattern Recognition (CVPR)*, Boston, MA, USA, 2015, pp. 1437–1445, https://doi.org/10.1109/CVPR.2015.7298750

[7] Ma, L., Peng, P., Chen, G., Zhao, Y., Dong, S., & Tian, Y. "Picking up quantization steps for compressed image classification", *IEEE Transactions on Circuits and Systems for Video Technology*, vol. 33, no. 4, pp. 1884–1898, Apr. 2023. https://doi.org/10.1109/tcsvt.2022.3218104

[8] Yue, H., Mao, Y., Liang, L., Xu, H., Hou, C., & Yang, J., "Recaptured screen image demoiréing," *IEEE Transactions on Circuits and Systems for Video Technology*, pp. 1–1, 2020. https://doi.org/10.1109/tcsvt.2020.2969984

[9] Muzammal, S. M., & Shah, M. A. "ScreenStealer: Addressing Screenshot Attacks on Android Devices," Sep. 2016. https://doi.org/10.1109/iconac.2016.7604942

[10] Chin, E., Felt, A. P., Sekar, V., & Wagner, D. "Measuring User Confidence in Smartphone Security and Privacy," *Proceedings of the Eighth Symposium on Usable Privacy and Security - SOUPS'12*, 2012. https://doi.org/10.1145/2335356.2335358

[11] Goyal, M., Munjal, R. S., Moharana, Sukumar, Garg, D., Mohanty, Debi Prasanna, & Thota, Siva Prasad "ScreenSeg: On-Device Screenshot Layout Analysis," arXiv (Cornell University), Jul. 2021. https://doi.org/10.1109/ijcnn52387.2021.9534338

[12] Kawamura, T., Ebihara, T., Wakatsuki, N., & Zempo, K. "EYEDi: Graphical Authentication Scheme of Estimating Your Encodable Distorted Images to Prevent Screenshot Attacks," *IEEE Access*, vol. 10, pp. 2256–2268, 2022. https://doi.org/10.1109/access.2021.3138093

[13] Xue, G. et al., "ScreenID: Enhancing QRCode Security by Utilizing Screen Dimming Feature," *IEEE/ACM Transactions on Networking*, pp. 1–15, 2022. https://doi.org/10.1109/tnet.2022.3203044

[14] Kevan Adlard, T. E., & Matrawy, A., "Towards Power Profiling of Android Permissions," Jul. 2015. https://doi.org/10.1109/ntms.2015.7266526

[15] Lee, J. W., Lee, M. J., Oh, T. W., Ryu, S.J., & Lee, H.K., "Screenshot Identification Using Combing Artifact From Interlaced Video," Sep. 2010. https://doi.org/10.1145/1854229.1854240

[16] Sharmila, K., Janaki, V., & Nagaraju, "Enhanced User Authentication Techniques Using the Fourth Factor Some Body the User Knows". In *Proceedings of International Conference on Advances in Computer Science*, 2013 (pp. 255–262).

[17] Sharmila, K., Janaki, V., & Nagaraju, A. "A Novel Approach for Emergency Backup Authentication Using Fourth Factor" In Saini, H., Sayal, R., Rawat, S. (Eds.), *Innovations in Computer Science and Engineering. Lecture Notes in Networks and Systems*, vol 8. Springer. https://doi.org/10.1007/978-981-10-3818-1_34

[18] Puteaux, P., & Puech, W. "A Recursive Reversible Data Hiding in Encrypted Images Method With a Very High Payload," *IEEE Transactions on Multimedia*, vol. 23, pp. 636–650, 2021. https://doi.org/10.1109/tmm.2020.2985537

[19] Wang, H., Wang, H., Xia, J., & Zhang, F. "Robust Watermarking against Camera Shooting for PowerPoint Presentation," *IEEE Signal Processing Letters*, pp. 1–5, Jan. 2024. https://doi.org/10.1109/lsp.2024.3393392

[20] Guan, Y. et al., "Subspace Model-Assisted Deep Learning for Improved Image Reconstruction," *IEEE Transactions on Medical Imaging*, vol. 42, no. 12, pp. 3833–3846, Dec. 2023. https://doi.org/10.1109/tmi.2023.3313421

10 Edge-Cloud Computing for Data Analytics

Embedding Intelligence with Deep Learning

P. William, Shrikaant Kulkarni, Dharmendra Kumar Roy and N Yogeesh

10.1 INTRODUCTION

In 2017, there were 18 billion connected devices, and there will be roughly 28 billion connected gadgets. Research conducted by Cisco lends credence to this forecast. In the year 2025, there will be around 14.6 billion of these devices in operation all across the globe, and more than half of them will be machine linkages. Because connected devices will generate a deluge of data, the proliferation of these devices will lead to an increase in the amount of traffic on networks. According to projections made by Cisco, annual global internet traffic is expected to more than quadruple from its current level of 1.5 zettabytes in 2017, when it was measured, to 4.8 zettabytes in 2022. There is a possibility that this might have positive effects, such as new applications or services being used more often. However, as a consequence of this, there will be an increased demand for network capacity, which will place further strain on an already stressed-out communication infrastructure. The term "Internet of Things" (IoT) refers to a concept that offers a framework for connecting various devices not only to the internet but also to one another. This framework also enables the devices that are connected to each other to collect data about their immediate surroundings. The IoT provides backend support for a wide variety of intelligent system implementations, such as those seen in smart cities, smart health care, smart transportation, and smart energy. On the other hand, in order for these systems to reach their full potential, it is essential to be able to analyze the data they produce. Nevertheless, the vast majority of edge devices that are part of the IoT, such as sensors, do not have the computing capacity that is required to carry out complex data analytics algorithms. As a consequence of this, their principal responsibilities have consisted of monitoring the surrounding environment and transmitting data for archiving and processing to a system that has larger capabilities, most often the cloud or a centralized system [1].

This has the immediate impact of making the typical processes involved in doing IoT data analytics include sending data to the cloud, analyzing it there, and then delivering the conclusions of the study to another device. For example, the process

 DOI: 10.1201/9781032703718-14

monitoring equipment at a smart factory may transmit the information it has acquired to a data center that is located many hundreds of miles away. The data would first be analyzed and stored at the facility before being brought back to the factory to be used in the process of improving the efficiency of the manufacturing procedures there. This strategy slows data transmission by lengthening the amount of time needed to transfer data while simultaneously increasing the amount of network traffic. On the other hand, owing to the limited processing capability of the connected devices, they cannot be utilized only for the computations involved in data analytics. By integrating edge and cloud computing, it may be feasible to reduce the amount of network traffic and the latency that is associated with it on the IoT. This may also make it possible to enable more advanced data analytics methods. Edge computing, often known as EC, is a technique that moves processing jobs closer to the network's edges and data sources. This brings the network's traffic and latency to a lower level. This is accomplished by transferring them from the cloud or another centralized system. Elastic computing (EC) has been recognized as a powerful method for carrying out operations such as content distribution and the offloading of mobile workloads, yet its use in data analytics has remained restricted [2].

Deep learning (DL) has lately shown its promise in a variety of additional domains, such as image categorization and human activity recognition (HAR), among others. As a result of these recent breakthroughs, the promise of DL has been pushed directly into the spotlight. There are a number of domains in which representation learning from DL might prove to be beneficial, including data analytics for the IoT. These talents may be of use to you in determining the characteristics that are most suitable for a certain situation. They do this by converting facts into hierarchical abstract representations. A deep AE is a kind of DL that refers to a neural network (NN) that has been trained and taught to learn data encoding unsupervised. The AE has been trained and taught to learn by itself. Because the reconstruction is also learned with the encodings, AE is able to recover its inputs from the reduced encodings. This is because the reconstruction is learned alongside the encodings. However, it is possible that some data may be lost in the process [3].

This research investigates the feasibility of edge, cloud, and IoT data analytics working together to get optimal results. The two contributions that stand out the most are the usage of edge nodes to minimize network traffic and latencies for activities relevant to machine learning (ML), as well as an analysis of how much data reduction can be done at the edge without considerably compromising the accuracy of the ML job. Both of these studies constitute an integral element of the most significant contributions. Both of these objectives may be accomplished by using the edge nodes in the network. Due to the fact that edge nodes act as a communication route between IoT devices and the cloud, the total quantity of data that has to be sent to the cloud is reduced. At the edge, the encoder component of the trained AE is used to generate data encodings, which are then first saved locally before being sent to the cloud for safekeeping. On the cloud, ML tasks may be completed in one of two ways: either by directly utilizing encoded data or by first recovering the original data with the assistance of the AE's decoder component and then utilizing it for the ML work [4].

The purpose of this research is to analyze feature learning using data that has been merged from all sources, data that has been classified based on their origins, and data that has been sorted based on sensor similarity. All of these data preparations were done in order to ensure that the results of the study are accurate. The data collected by the IoT might have originated from a broad variety of sensors that were placed in a number of different places. The evaluation scenario makes use of the HAR that is collected from sensors that are attached to different regions of people's bodies, such as accelerometers and gyroscopes. The findings indicate that the method that was recommended might reduce the amount of data that was supplied by as much as 80% without having a substantial impact on HAR accuracy. The remaining portions of the article are broken up into the parts that are presented in the following paragraphs [5].

10.2 REVIEW OF LITERATURE

The concept of cloud computing is a significant technological innovation that has the potential to enable client devices to get access to a big reserve of elastic resources. To achieve this objective, there are a number of different options available. One of the most significant problems associated with these sorts of systems is the significant physical distance that exists between the servers and the consumers. An approach that might be taken to address this problem is known as edge-cloud computing, which is a kind of cloud computing in which the computers are physically located at the edge of the network. In the realm of cloud computing, this particular kind of cloud computing is a subset of the more popular cloud computing service. The topic of edge-cloud computing is very important for the development of future networks, which is why much research is being undertaken on technologies that have the potential to make edge-cloud computing realistically achievable. In spite of the fact that this indicates that further research is required, the great majority of these studies disregard the possibility that this might have a significant impact on the efficiency of the system. The ability to reliably manage very high client and server densities is a new difficulty that has arisen as a result of the increasing prevalence of the IoT. One reason why extensible solutions are so vital is because of this. Specifically, we provide a server deployment strategy for 6G IoT use case that is built on data mining and ML in order to circumvent these two problems. Our method not only delivers excellent results but also helps us save both time and money. In addition, we demonstrate that our approach brings about a reduction in latency and a more effective utilization of the resources that are available for edge-cloud computing servers in comparison to the usual deployment alternatives. It is possible that these advantages will result from the strategy that we devised [6].

Understanding the unprocessed sensor data that IoT devices collect in distant areas may be accomplished via the use of DL, which is one of the possible techniques. Considering that DL is a layered approach, it is an excellent choice for usage in edge computing environments. In light of this, we will begin by discussing some potential uses of edge computing for DL in applications that are related to the IoT. Furthermore, in order to enhance the overall performance of DL systems when they are deployed at the edge of the IoT, we devise a one-of-a-kind offloading technique. On the other hand, this is absolutely necessary, taking into consideration that the edge nodes that are now operational have a restricted capacity for processing. We test the performance of our technique by using a wide range of DL tasks inside an environment that facilitates edge computing. According to the findings of the evaluation, our method for enhancing the performance of the IoT was superior to the DL methods that were previously used [7].

There is a clear correlation between the proliferation of IoT devices, which includes wearable technology, smartphones, sensors, and a great deal of other gadgets, and a rise in the amount of data flow. Due to this, there has been a significant rise in the quantity of data that is being transported. There is a possibility that the development of the IoT was the driving force behind the establishment of this massive data collection. The information that is received by IoT-connected devices is often uploaded to the cloud or used by another centralized software system in order to facilitate ML. This approach is often used despite the fact that it will result in an increase in network traffic and will cause delay. Processing may be brought closer to the network's edge and the data sources themselves via the use of computing at the network's edge, which provides a chance to address these issues. Computing at the edge, on the other hand, is not a suitable match for tasks that are associated with ML because of its low processing capability. When it comes to edge computing, this occurs rather often and is a big problem. We will learn how to merge edge computing and cloud computing for IoT data analytics by using edge nodes, which will be covered in this post. Because of this, the overall quantity of data that has to be sent is decreased. By using sensors that face in the direction of the observation point, we were able to carry out feature learning on the edge node that is geographically closest to the observation point. This was done to make the inspection of data less difficult in the immediate neighborhood of its creation. It is necessary for the comparison process to include similarity-based processing in order to accomplish the goal that the comparison is trying to accomplish. Through the application of DL, feature learning may be accomplished. As an additional point of interest, the taught AE makes use of cloud storage for its decoder and edge storage for its encoder applications. The major objective of this study was to investigate the challenges that are associated with deducing human activity from sensor data. According to the findings, sliding windows in the first stage have the potential to lower data amounts on the edge by up to 80% while causing very little to no loss of accuracy. There is no other approach that is required to do this. There is no other approach that is required to do this. The achievement of this objective is possible without the use of any extra techniques [8].

The use of DL in IoT systems and applications is currently in the experimental phase. The performance of DL is superior to that of ML when it comes to coping with vast volumes of data, which is the most significant benefit of DL over ML. This is due to the fact that many applications for the IoT generate a significant quantity of data that has to be processed. Additionally, DL has the capacity to autonomously develop new features for a wide variety of problems. The accuracy with which features are discovered and retrieved from the data is going to be the determining factor in how successfully conventional ML approaches analyze multimedia data. Since DL is capable of accurately detecting high-level characteristics, such as human faces in photos and language phrases in sounds, it may be able to speed up the processing of multimedia data. This is because DL can identify human faces in photographs and language phrases in sounds. On the other hand, DL may be able to infer information a great deal quicker than more standard forms of ML. Consequently, the development of IoT hardware and software makes it possible to undertake big DL initiatives. It is exceedingly challenging to install DL applications on devices that are part of the IoT owing to the limited energy and computational capability of these devices. On traditional commercial hardware or software, it is not possible to carry out DL tasks in a high parallel fashion. Deeper and Deep are two examples of new acceleration engines that are a part of the most recent generation of mobile system-on-chips (SoC). These engines make it possible to run a variety of DL applications. The outcomes of the experiments indicate that mobile IoT devices equipped with high-quality SoCs may assist with specific parts of the learning process.

Another important question that has to be researched is how to use DL in a wider variety of IoT applications. The benefit of using DL for the IoT has been evaluated by a great number of relevant applications. For instance, a number of recent research have focused their attention on the use of wearable IoT devices in difficult situations, the likes of which often baffle conventional ML strategies. A framework that makes it possible to integrate DL techniques with Apache Spark has been made available in order to facilitate the analysis of data collected from IoT devices. The Apache Spark software that is used to assist with the data training is stored on cloud servers; however, the inference phase is completed on mobile devices. Mobile devices have successfully completed the inference step. As a result of the fact that this two-layer architecture is comparable in some ways to edge computing [9], it is abundantly evident that processing processes may be offloaded from the cloud.

Edge computing is a concept that proposes moving processing power away from centralized cloud servers and placing it instead on edge nodes that are physically located closer to the user end. There are two major improvements that might be made to the paradigm that is currently used for cloud computing by using edge computing. The ability of edge nodes to preprocess enormous amounts of data before transmitting that data to the primary servers that comprise a cloud is the primary advantage of installing edge nodes. The optimization of cloud resources may be achieved because of the fact that edge nodes now have access to processing power. This is the second advantage. The promise of edge computing enables us to properly manage the challenges faced by cloud infrastructure, as was previously stated. It was proposed that this project would be the first to use DL in a computer environment that was considered to be cutting edge. They recommended developing a food recognition application based on DL using edge computing as the foundation for the service architecture. According to their findings, using edge computing might potentially improve the functioning of DL systems since it requires less power and uses less energy than traditional methods. According to the findings of this research, mobile phones should not be used as edge nodes since they are not suitable for use with IoT services. Due to the fact that the majority of IoT devices only have low-end central processing units (CPUs), mobile phones are not an ideal option for edge nodes. Edge servers are put in IoT gateways because of their sufficient service capacity to execute DL algorithms. This is necessary since we focus on common IoT devices, which do not have strong CPUs or other energy sources [10–11].

10.3 EDGE-CLOUD ML SYSTEM MODEL

The preprocessing phase, the step in which data is reduced, and the step in which cloud ML is performed are the three primary components that make up the edge-cloud ML paradigm. The overall layout can be seen in Figure 10.1, and the particulars of each of the three components will be discussed in the sections that are to come after this one. This figure presents the design in its entirety [12–13].

10.3.1 PREPROCESSING

Instead of sending the data directly to the cloud as is done in traditional ML, edge-cloud ML starts with the data from IoT sensors being delivered to the edge for preprocessing. This is in contrast to traditional ML, which does the opposite. This method of ML is somewhat different from the traditional one. Typically, the data required for ML are stored in the cloud immediately after being uploaded. Even if the sliding window method is not required, the normalization step is always included in the preprocessing stage, and the impact of normalization is evaluated at several points during the trials [14–15].

10.3.2 NORMALIZATION

To avoid high-valued features from taking over the training process and to improve the procedure's overall convergence, the data is normalized by using a standardization method known as the *z*-score. Standardization was utilized since it is able to tolerate outliers. Hence, that method was chosen rather than min-max scaling. Scaling based on minimum and maximum values may have been used instead of standardization. Following the rescaling of each feature in line with the parameters, the final values for the mean and variance are zero and one, respectively.

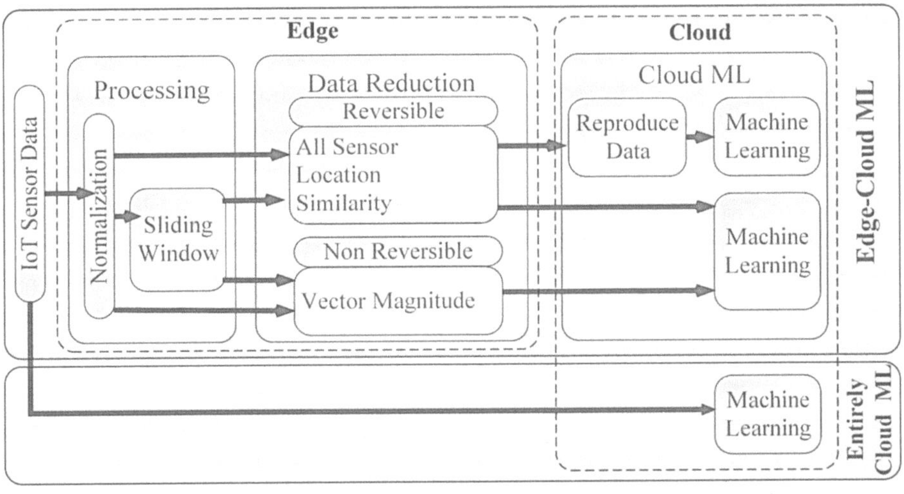

FIGURE 10.1 A model for an ml system at the edge of the cloud.

$$\hat{x} = \frac{x - \mu}{\sigma}$$

where "x" refers to the "original value" of the feature, "μ" and "σ" represent the mean and standard deviation of the feature, respectively.

10.3.3 Sliding Window

At the moment, a single data sample is made up of several measurements that all correspond to the same time step t. These measurements may come from a variety of sensors that are located in different parts of the globe. The sliding windows method is used for the analysis of time series data. This is done for one of two reasons: either to allow the model to capture time dependencies or to prepare the data for approaches including ML. The HAR sliding window has seen a lot of usage, and its effectiveness has been shown time and time again. The purpose of this study is to investigate how the sliding window method influences the amount of data that is reduced, as well as whether or not the use of this method may make some features more straightforward. The first sample for a sliding window with a length of l contains all of the data from the first l time steps when there are f features present. This ensures that the sample is representative of the whole data set [16–17]. Each sample receives a l f matrix when there are f characteristics included in the analysis. The window is then moved forward by k steps, and the readings taken from time step k to time step k plus l are included in the creation of the second sample. Once this step has been completed, the second sample is created. As it gets closer to accomplishing its goal of creating more instances, the window will continue to widen. In this experiment, the sliding step with k set to one was selected since this combination provides more training examples and helps the input in discriminating between changing temporal patterns. Once the system has been trained, the features of the use case and the limitations given by the data flow will be used in order to determine the specifications of the sliding steps that may be implemented [18–20].

10.3.4 Data Reduction

At the edge of the network, data reduction happens so as to reduce the total quantity of data that has to be sent to the cloud. During the process of feature reduction, choices need to be taken on which method to use and how many characteristics to retain. In decentralized systems, the accuracy of ML is the primary factor that drives these decisions; however, in an edge-cloud scenario, network traffic is also something that has to be taken into consideration. Even though AEs are best suited for feature learning on the edge, it is difficult to determine the highest number of features that can be removed and the corresponding amount of traffic that can be reduced while still maintaining the accuracy of the ML tasks. This is because the number of features that can be removed and the amount of traffic that can be reduced are directly related to one another. This is a challenge since it is difficult to determine the maximum number of features that can be deleted and the corresponding quantity of traffic that can be lowered [21–22].

Normalized data or samples generated using the sliding window approach are both viable beginning points for efforts aimed at the direct reduction of data. The approach for reducing the amount of data is unaffected by whether or not the sliding window method is employed. Throughout the whole of the process, both reversible and irreversible methods are given careful thought and study.

10.3.4.1 Reversible

The procedure is considered to be reversible if, after applying a data reduction strategy to part or all of the data, it is possible to rebuild the original data from its reduced representations. This is the case as long as the data reduction strategy was successful. In the field of data science, one of the common goals is to recreate the original data from its reduced versions. Using these approaches, data reduction is carried out at the network edge, the reduced data is distributed throughout the network, and then ML is applied to the reduced data either immediately or after the original data has been replicated in the cloud. In this section, we focus on AEs because, after they have been trained, they are able to simultaneously restore the data to its initial state in the cloud and reduce the amount of data that is maintained at the edge. Comparing the data reduction that may be achieved via the use of principal component analysis (PCA) demonstrates the efficacy of AE. It is possible that the eigenvectors will be of assistance in reconstructing the initial data when PCA is used to reduce the number of dimensions. Due to this, it is feasible to have a reduced number of dimensions. When it comes to the accuracy of the data reconstruction that is carried out by AE and PCA, respectively, the amount of dimensionality reduction that is applied to the data is a significant factor [23–24].

The three separate circumstances that are taken into consideration by the two reversible techniques, PCA and AE, are shown in Figure 10.1. These situations may be broken down into three categories: those that are based on location, those that are based on similarities, and those that employ every sensor. Before executing data reduction to arrive at the sum of the data from each sensor, the all-sensor approach takes into account the information gathered from each and every sensor. The following is a rundown of the results obtained by using this method.

As seen in Figure 10.2, the location-based scenario takes into account a technique of data reduction that is based on a set of sensors that are located in close proximity to one another. For example, there may be four distinct sensors located at position 1, and edge node E1 may be positioned in such a way that it is able to interface with those sensors and get the data that they provide. The data provided by the position 2 sensors is comparable to that provided by the E2 sensors, and so on. The distance that the data must travel in order to be compressed should be kept to a minimum as much as possible. In order to accomplish this goal, the processing that occurs at the edge must be located as close to the data sources as is reasonably possible. Since the data is processed collectively on a particular node after being received at that node, there is one AE for each of the edge nodes. This is because each of the edge nodes has its own AE, which is the root source of the problem.

In the scenario shown in Figure 10.3, the sensors are segmented into subgroups according to the degree to which they are comparable to one another. For instance, it's not impossible for each of the accelerometers and gyroscopes to stand in for a

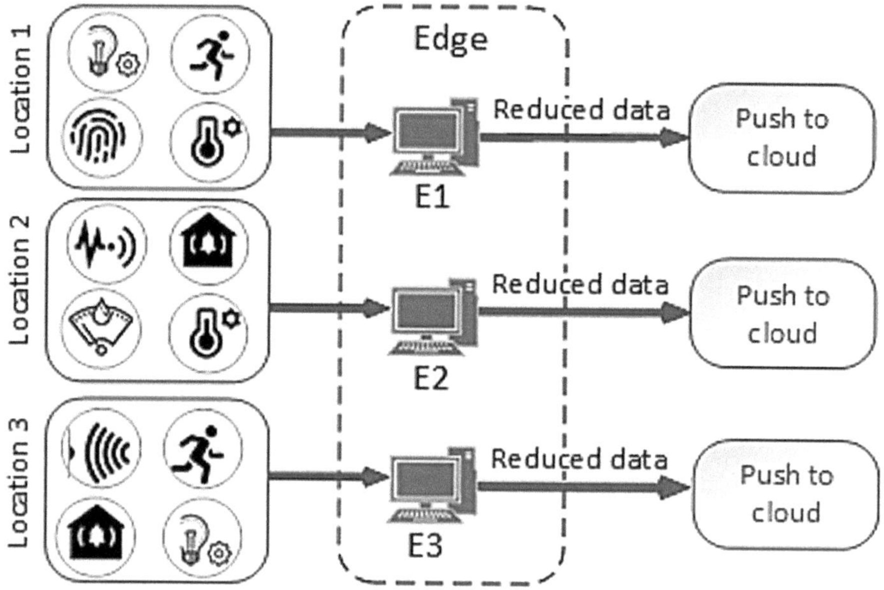

FIGURE 10.2 Reducing data depending on their location.

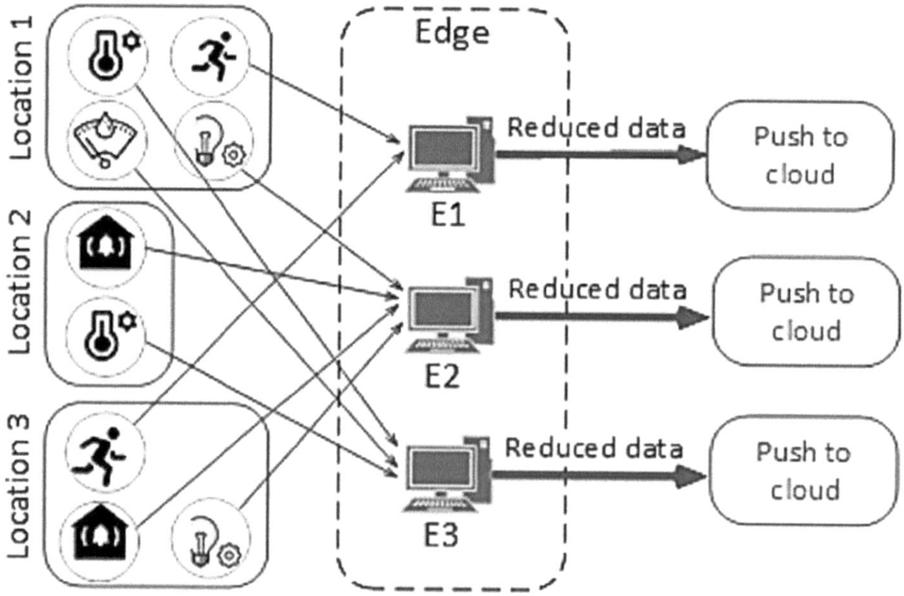

FIGURE 10.3 Data compression using similarity.

unique category of people. It is possible that there may be a greater distance between the sensors and the edge nodes as a result of this, but it will also result in more uniform data groups. In the same way that it was the case in the location-based scenario, each of the edge nodes has a single AE assigned to it.

10.3.4.2 Nonreversible

A procedure is said to be not reversible if, once it has been simplified, it is not possible to get the same results by making use of the initial data. This section will have a primary emphasis on the vector magnitude, since doing so is crucial for sensors such as gyroscopes and accelerometers that measure values in three dimensions. Using this method, the size of the dimension is reduced to its most minute feasible form.

$$d = \sqrt{x^2 + y^2 + z^2}.$$

In this particular example, d is the magnitude of the vector, while x, y, and z are the Euler coordinates that stand for the measurements. Because of this, the magnitude of the vector results in a decrease in dimensions that is three times smaller.

10.3.5 Cloud ML

After then, the edge uploads the data that has been compressed into the cloud, where it will undergo further ML processing. There are two different approaches that may be used in order to successfully finish the ML assignment. One approach that may be used to get started is to recreate the initial data and then apply it to the problem of ML. In order to accomplish this goal, the reversible approach of data reduction must have been used. The second option is to apply the data once it has been reduced directly to tasks using ML. This tactic is adaptable enough to accommodate either reversible or no reversible approaches to the reduction of data. When training a model on data with fewer characteristics, the creation of an ML model for duplicated data requires a greater amount of computing power than when training a model on data with more features. This is because repeated data contain more properties, which explains why this occurred.

10.4 RESEARCH METHODOLOGY

The dataset is going to be presented in this section of the chapter, and then we are going to discuss the evaluation method that will be used.

10.4.1 Dataset and Preprocessing

This location serves as a temporary medical facility. For the purpose of determining how well the suggested method performed on the HAR task, the MHEALTH Mobile Health dataset was used. Sensors have made it possible to classify a broad variety of activities that were previously unimaginable. These activities include sitting, walking, running, and a great deal more. The MHEALTH dataset contains documentation of the many things that ten different persons did while they were traveling. An accelerometer, a gyroscope, and a magnetometer were the three distinct types of sensors that were used in order to get the data. Due to the fact that each of these sensors required three values to represent its three axes, a total of nine data points were gathered. The three sensors are situated as follows: an accelerometer is situated on the chest, an ankle is situated on the left, and a wrist is situated on the right. Three of the characteristics are axes, and seven of them are sensors. There are a total of 21 characteristics. The labels are able to differentiate between twelve different kinds of physical activity, and the sampling rate is 50 hertz (Hz).

During the course of the study, each participant's data will be compiled and exploited in its entirety in various ways. In contrast to the data that was acquired during testing, the data that was gathered during training was 80:20. When the data have been normalized, the preprocessing might proceed with or without the sliding window, depending on the circumstances, after the data have been normalized. In order to evaluate how the size of the window affects the precision with which activity can be identified as well as the rate at which it may be reduced, three various window sizes—25-, 50-, and 100-time steps—are taken into consideration. These time steps serve as the basis for the study. With a sample rate of 50 hertz, these sizes correspond to 0.5 seconds, 1 second, and 2 seconds, respectively.

10.4.2 Data Reduction

Both reversible and nonreversible forms of data reduction at the edge are going to be discussed in this article.

10.4.2.1 Reversible

The implementation of reversible data reduction largely takes into consideration and makes use of three different scenarios: the scenario based on all sensors, the scenario based on location, and the scenario based on similarities. You have the option of completing any of them with or without sliding windows, according to your own choice. Table 10.1 shows the number of characteristics that were present before and after the data reduction procedure for each situation. This is accomplished by using a 100-point frame and the reversible approach. These facts are used to illustrate each possible situation. The strategy that does not make use of a sliding window is referred to as "Direct" in the table as well as in the rest of the text.

The assessments, on the other hand, were also carried out for reductions of 80%, 90%, and 95%, respectively. Table 10.1 shows the number of characteristics that were present before and after a decrease of 66 and 70 percentage points, respectively. The sequence of these numerals may be seen here if you look closely enough. A beginning reduction of 66% was chosen in order to coincide with the maximum reduction of 3:1 that can be achieved by the vector magnitude approach. If this were to be done, the total decline would be at the same level. In light of the fact that everything takes place on a single node, it is impossible for any sensor to ever reach an edge point. Information for location-based or similarity-based techniques is gathered at nodes that are referred to as edge locations. When we talk about this, we call it an edge location. In the location-based technique, there are three nodes that represent

TABLE 10.1
Feature Count (Before and After Window Sizing) in Case of Reversible Approaches, Timed at 100

Scenario	Edge Location	Original Features	66% Reduction	70% Reduction
		All Sensors		
Direct	—	22	7	—
S Window	—	22 × 100	698	635
		Location Based		
Direct	L1	4	I	—
	1.2	8	3	—
	L3	8	3	—
S Window	L1	4 × 100	99	92
	1.2	8 × 100	293	275
	L3	8 × 100	293	275
		Similarity Based		
Direct	SI	9	3	—
	S2	6	2	—
	S3	6	2	—
S. Window	SI	9 × 100	294	272
	S2	5 × 100	196	185
	$3	5 × 100	196	185

independent sensors that are positioned throughout the body. These nodes are located in the chest, the arms, and the legs. Three distinct types of sensors—an accelerometer, a gyroscope, and a magnetometer—are used in the implementation of the similarity-based technique. It is possible to extract all nine initial characteristics by using the direct technique; Table 10.1 demonstrates that each sensor has three axes corresponding to it. As an example, the second component of location-based approaches is responsible for the collection of data by merging the results from three different sensors. When there are windows, the number of features is directly proportional to the length of the window plus the number of features. This is the case when windows are present. By way of illustration, the production of 9,100 features is achieved by combining L2 with a location-based technique by itself.

Both AE and PCA are useful tools for efficiently using the various strategies for reducing the amount of data indicated in Table 10.1. Whether PCA or AE is used, the data reduction rates that are shown in Table 10.1 continue to be applicable. While using PCA, the degree of reduction is determined by the number of major components that are selected; while using AE, however, the degree of reduction is determined by the number of neurons in the bottleneck layer. When it comes to both the location-based and the similarity-based strategies, the task of reducing the amount of information that reaches each edge node falls within the purview of a single AE.

PCA may be independently carried out at each and every node in the network.

There are a total of 90 sliding window data reduction tests since there are three unique scenarios, three different window widths, five different reduction rates, and two different methodologies (AE and PCA). In addition, six tests involving direct reduction are carried out. These studies include a total of three unique scenarios and two alternate methods. At this point, there have been 96 studies that have had their data reductions completed.

10.4.2.2 Nonreversible

The only no reversible approach that is taken into consideration is the size of the vector that is being considered. As a direct result of this, the three-axis data that was collected from the measurements of the accelerometer, gyroscope, and magnetometer has been scaled down to only one dimension. In the same way that reversible procedures may be carried out, the reduction can be implemented either with or without the sliding window. There is a possibility that the number of features will decrease from 21 to 7 if the vector magnitude is applied to all of the data outside of the window.

There are currently just 175 and 700 features available for sliding windows 25, 50, and 100, respectively; this is a significant decrease from the previous numbers of 525, 1,050, and 2,100. There are now four separate experiments being conducted, and they are as follows: there are three for every size of the window, with the exception of rooms that do not have any sliding windows, which results in one less.

10.4.3 Cloud ML

Following the completion of the edge-trimming phase, the data are uploaded to the cloud in order to undergo the last stage of processing. The last part of the HAR job is called "categorization," and it entails determining the kind of activity that is being performed. In contrast to the cloud, where all of the data from the edge nodes is merged into a single model, each node on the edge has its own ML model that is responsible for processing the data that comes at that node. This is in contrast to the cloud, where all of the data from the edge nodes is processed by a single model.

10.4.3.1 ML with Reduced Data

For the purpose of classification, the data that was reduced from each edge node is used in its raw form. Because of its adaptability, this tactic may be used with either reversible or irreversible approaches to the resolution of a problem. A feed-forward neural network, commonly referred to as an FFNN, was used in order to complete the final categorization of the HAR task. However, when the reduction rate increases, there are fewer input nodes present, despite the fact that the FFNN contains a total of 12 output nodes. After the data have been compressed, the number of characteristics that are still accessible is shown by the output nodes. The overall number of input characteristics dictated the exact distribution of hidden layers and neurons, but the amount of those attributes was up for grabs. When there were more than 350 input features, the FFNN used all three secret layers, but when there were less than 350, it only utilized two of the hidden levels. There were 420-128-32-12 nodes discovered in the hidden layers when 420 input characteristics were used; however, this number was decreasing at an alarming rate. Despite the fact that the number of neurons used in the buried layer varied from one trial to the next, this approach demonstrated extraordinarily high levels of accuracy.

10.4.3.2 ML with Reproduced Data

The completion of this procedure is contingent upon the completion of these two phases. Following the completion of the reduction phase, it will be essential to classify the data that was provided beforehand. Obviously, this is only relevant in situations where there is the opportunity to alter the order in which the edge data reduction operations are carried out. Due to the fact that the number of features in this dataset is identical to the number of features in the first dataset, this method necessitates the use of more complex models and incurs higher processing costs than ML, which makes use of a smaller number of data points. Due to the fact that this was the primary motivation for their creation in the first place, the copies of the original material do, in fact, have the potential to be used in later initiatives. In order to finish the classification, the FFNN method is used, despite the fact that there is a much less amount of training data. In addition, the ML strategy is used here in order to choose the amount of layers and neurons that are included inside the hidden layers. Since the number of features increases as there are more duplicate versions of the data, the same procedure will create more layers and neurons than it would have if there had been fewer copies of the data to begin with. This is because the more copies of the data there are, the more features there are. This occurs as a result of the availability of more functionalities.

10.5 ANALYSIS AND INTERPRETATION

After presenting the results of the data reduction and network traffic analysis, we now go on to the next section, which examines the implications of those findings.

10.5.1 Data Reduction

Memory and precision are often evaluated throughout the test, in addition to the accuracy that is being evaluated. Possibly, this might be linked to the fact that they are used extensively in HAR research.

$$\text{Prescison} = \frac{TP}{TP + FP}$$

$$\text{Recall} = \frac{TP}{TP + FN}$$

On the other hand, the initials "TP" and "TN" stand for true positives and true negatives, respectively, while the acronyms "FP" and "FN" stand for both false positives and negatives. The classification accuracy for reversible techniques is then shown in Table 10.2, which makes use of a sliding window with 100 points and a data reduction of 66%. This was done in order to simplify the analysis that was being performed. When it comes to accuracy, it has been shown that the sliding window strategy is superior to approach methods that are direct. This operates in a manner that is similar to that of traditional ML. This is the case regardless of the approach (AE or PAC), both of which are instances of independent variables, as well as the configuration (all sensors, location-based, or similarity-based). Among the several types of location-based setups, similarity-based configurations are available. In addition to the differences between approaches that are reduced and those that are duplicated, the difference between AE and PCA is not very important. The accuracy was equivalent to that of normal cloud-based ML, despite the fact that the amount of data used was reduced by 66%. This was a very successful feat. Following further investigation, it was discovered that the accuracy patterns shown in Table 10.2 were comparable to the recall and precision patterns.

This table investigate the drop of 66%. Nevertheless, this chart takes into account nonreversible choices as well, in contrast to chart 3, which solely takes into account reversible treatments. Results obtained by the vector magnitude approach are much less accurate when compared to those obtained through methods that can be reversed. The reason for this is that the vector magnitude approach does not provide credence to the concept of reversibility. The examination of classification accuracy that is shown in Table 10.2 makes use of a data reduction factor of 66%, and the sliding window 100 is the sole feature that is taken into consideration. It is done in this manner so that we may focus only on determining whether or not the category is correct.

10.5.2 Network Traffic

At this stage of the inquiry, the possibility of reducing the amount of data that is accessible in terms of the number of features has been taken into consideration. However, once the system is completely operational, the network's extra overhead will prevent

TABLE 10.2
Using a 100-Point Sliding Window and Reversible Classification Techniques, We Were Able to Reduce the Amount of Data by 66%

	AE		PCA	
Scenarios	**Reduced (%)**	**Reproduce (%)**	**Reduced (%)**	**Reproduce (%)**
		All Sensors		
Direct	99.26	98.36	99	99.21
S. Window	100	100	100	100
		Location Based		
Direct	99.16	98.52	99.6	99.38
S. Window	98.89	99.95	99.89	99.89
		Similarity Based		
Direct	98.76	99.24	99.36	99.35
S. Window	99.91	99.93	99.89	99.86

the actual traffic levels from exactly matching the feature reduction rates. This will be the case even if the feature reduction rates remain the same. For the purpose of analyzing the flow of network traffic, a simulation of the edge-cloud architecture that was just described was carried out. Depending on the data presented in Section 10.4, both the location-based and the similarity-based scenarios need a total of three nodes, one of which should be assigned to each of the location similarity groups. On the other hand, the direct technique needs just one edge node to function properly. Each edge node is simulated by a single virtual machine, each of which has 2 gigabytes of memory and a single-core CPU. The so-called cloud was really a Windows server equipped with an octal-core central processing unit and six gigabytes of random access memory. It was determined how much bandwidth was required for communication to take place between the server and the edge nodes through sockets. Socket servers, which are able to handle multiple threads, make it possible for several edge nodes and the server to communicate with one another simultaneously. Encoder components of trained AEs are deployed on the server, while decoder components and classification models are hosted on edge nodes. The encoder components of the trained AEs have been installed on the server, which has now been deployed. Even if a change in the processing capability of the edge nodes had no impact whatsoever on the traffic on the network, it must still be sufficient to encrypt the data. The minimum amount of processing power that must be present at the network's edge is determined by the size of the encoder network, which is in turn determined by the size of the sliding window.

The network traffic for each of the different situations is analyzed and compared in Table 10.3. This includes both the cases in which there is and does not exist a feature reduction of 66%. Additionally, it provides percentages of traffic reduction to illustrate how much traffic was dropped in contrast to the same scenario that existed before a reduction was put into place. This comparison is made using the same conditions as before the reduction was implemented. The sliding window 100 traffic

TABLE 10.3
Network Traffic Doesn't Decrease, but 66% Less Data is Transferred

		Reduced		
Scenarios	**No Reduc.**	**All Sensors**	**Location Based**	**Similarity Based**
		Consumed Bandwidth MB		
Direct	85.31	36.63	31.15	33.96
S. Window 100	7135.01	3586.40	3658.89	3616.36
S. Window 50	3549.73	1775.32	1695.53	1639.25
S. Window 25	1832.30	868.88	846.27	841.79
		Traffic Reduction %		
Direct	—	60.37	59.74	59.99
S. Window 100	—	50.71	49.85	51.35
S. Window 50	—	53.97	53.37	54.64
S. Window 25	—	55.49	55.33	56.37

reduction reveals a decrease in size, going from 7135MB for no reduction to 3586MB for all sensors. This modification is shown by a drop in traffic that is 50.71% lower for sliding window 100. It is possible to demonstrate that the network traffic is consistent across all sensors, including those that are based on location and those that are based on similarities, for each and every one of the different scenarios. However, the quantity of network traffic that is required for scenarios that need sliding windows is much more than that which is required for direct solutions. This is the case regardless of whether the data has been decreased or not. This issue was caused by the sliding window having a step size of $k = 1$, which led to the readings being classified as belonging to distinct sliding windows. As a direct result of this, several repetitions of the same readings have been received. You may be able to avoid any delays that are brought on by the software's allowance for window length if you use the sliding step that is appropriate to the length of the sliding window.

10.6 RESULT AND DISCUSSION

The findings of the study indicate that using the approach that was suggested has the potential to reduce the quantity of data that is uploaded to the cloud by as much as 75% without having a major impact on the precision of the procedure. Even after applying reduction to data that has previously been subjected to sliding window preprocessing, the accuracy of the results is increased. This is the case both before and after the use of reduction. This is the case even if the reduction was done after preprocessing. Findings generated with window sizes of 25 and 50, respectively, are often less accurate than those generated with window widths of 100 and 50, which yield results that are equally accurate, taking into account the proximity of each sensor to the others in the group. Even if the sliding windows were shrunk down to a tenth of their current size, the precision would not be greatly improved. Even when the accuracy is reduced by as much as 90%, as seen in Figure 10.4, it remains relatively unchanged.

One of the disadvantages that are associated with sliding window circumstances is the collection of data on the edge. Even if a smaller amount of data is transported to the cloud with each time step, there will still be a large amount of network traffic since sensor readings will come from several windows. This is the reason why there

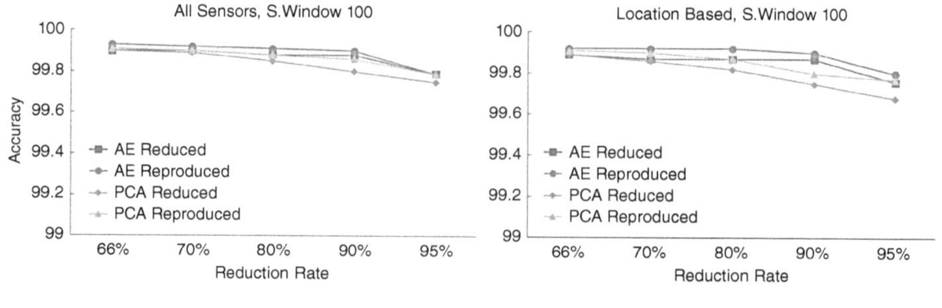

FIGURE 10.4 Window size of 100 maximizes accuracy of classification over a wide range of reduction rates.

will be a substantial amount of network traffic. It is necessary for the application scenario to make allowances for a delay in the length of the window. It is feasible to lessen the amount of traffic on the network by using a sliding step that is either the same size or larger than the size of the window. This eliminates the possibility that the readings were obtained from windows that were different sizes.

Classification performed slightly better when compared to limited data; the difference became more obvious when the windows were reduced in size (Figure 10.5). When the window size was increased to 50 and 100, the performance of AE and PCA were comparable; however, when the window size was reduced to 25, the performance of AE was superior to that of PCA for all reduction rates. It is possible that this is due to the fact that the nonlinear transformations utilized by the AE, in contrast to the linear transformations used by the PCA, were better at capturing the complexities of the relationships being studied.

The outputs of all of the sensors were approximately identical to those obtained by the location-based technique and the similarity-based method (see Figure 10.6), but the location-based approach had the benefit of permitting data reduction over a large number of nodes, which the similarity-based method did not. This was the case despite the fact that the location-based technique and those that were generated by the similarity-based method were essentially the same. In addition, the location-based strategy enables edge nodes to be positioned nearer to the data sources, which may be useful in situations in which the data sources are scattered over a vast geographical area.

In addition, research on network traffic has indicated that sliding windows that overlap should not be utilized since doing so increases network traffic. This suggests that using sliding windows that overlap is not recommended. Even though it's best to avoid employing overlapping windows in edge-cloud deployments, AE and classification FFNN networks may still be trained with their help. This is because windows that overlap each other provide more information about the data being seen. The strategy that has been suggested may be used for a broad variety of IoT tasks and data sets; the MHEALTH dataset was utilized to try it out for the HAR task. A good sensor reading correlation will result in significant savings in the amount of data that must be stored, which will be required to be preserved. In addition, the rates of reduction will be different for the various ML tasks and applications since they will be dependent on the usefulness of the various data components for each individual work or application. This is the case due to the fact that the value of the data will vary based on the task at hand and the program being used.

10.7 CONCLUSIONS

In the past, ML has profited from data collected from the IoT by storing and analyzing it on the cloud or another analogous centralized system. Because of the proliferation of networked devices, there will be longer delays and more strain placed on the various communication networks. This study studied the use of edge computing in conjunction with cloud computing in order to apply ML to data collected from IoT devices. The goal of this research was to reduce the amount of traffic on the network as well as the latencies. The researchers looked at three distinct scenarios: one based

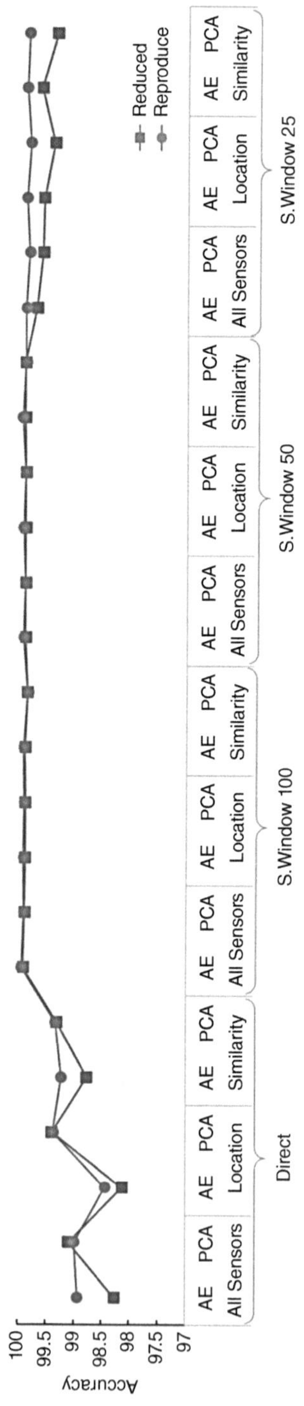

FIGURE 10.5 Rate of reduction is 66% for both the direct and sliding window methods of classification.

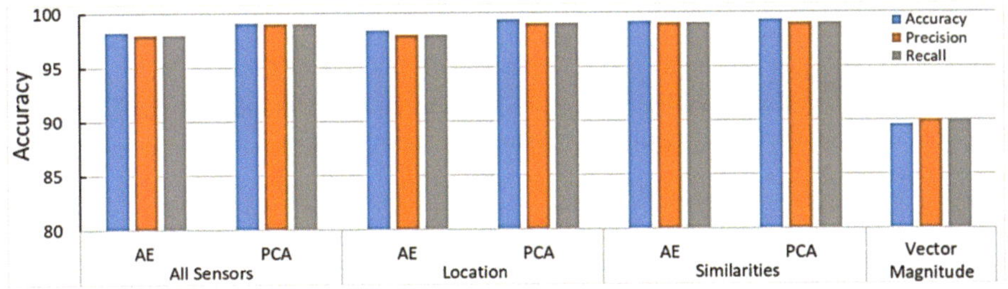

FIGURE 10.6 Direct (no window), reduced (66%), reversible, and nonreversible methods all achieve high levels of accuracy in classification.

on location, one based on similarity, and one that included all of the sensors. The data was grouped in the location-based scenario according to the locations of IoT devices; similarly, the data was grouped in the similarity-based scenario; and lastly, in the all-sensors scenario, data was integrated from all of the sensors at the same time. In order to fulfill the requirements of the HAR challenge, research was conducted and evaluations were performed on three nonreversible methods: AE, PCA, and vector magnitude. According to the results, data and the associated network traffic may be cut by up to around 80% without causing a discernible drop in the degree of accuracy achieved provided that a large sliding window is applied in the preprocessing. This can be accomplished without requiring any additional hardware or software. The fact that the findings demonstrated that a huge sliding window could be used made the realization of this possibility possible. The accuracy of strategies that were based on location and similarity was equivalent to that of strategies that were based on sensors, but these strategies could execute reduction on a wider variety of edge nodes. The edge-cloud methodology will undergo more investigation to see whether or not it is applicable to a wide variety of sensor kinds and uses.

REFERENCES

1. J. Pan and J. McElhannon, "Future Edge Cloud and Edge Computing for Internet of Things Applications," *IEEE Internet of Things Journal*, vol. 5, no. 1, pp. 439–449, February 2018.
2. L. Zhao, W. Sun, Y. Shi, and J. Liu, "Optimal Placement of Cloudlets for Access Delay Minimization in SDN-Based Internet of Things Networks," *IEEE Internet of Things Journal*, vol. 5, no. 2, pp. 1334–1344, April 2018.
3. C.E. Shannon, "A Mathematical Theory of Communication," *The Bell System Technical Journal*, vol. 27, no. 3, pp. 379–423, October 1948.
4. L. Chettri and R. Bera, "A Comprehensive Survey on Internet of Things (IoT) Toward 5G Wireless Systems," *IEEE Internet of Things Journal*, vol. 7, no. 1, pp. 16–32, January 2020.
5. M.Z. Chowdhury, M. Shahjalal, S. Ahmed, and Y.M. Jang, "6G Wireless Communication Systems: Applications, Requirements, Technologies, Challenges, and Research Directions," *IEEE Open Journal of the Communications Society*, vol. 1, pp. 957–975, 2020.

6. W. Jiang, B. Han, M.A. Habibi, and H.D. Schotten, "The Road Towards 6G: A Comprehensive Survey," *IEEE Open Journal of the Communications Society*, pp. 1–1, 2021. DOI: 10.1109/OJCOMS.2021.3057679
7. S. Deng, H. Zhao, W. Fang, J. Yin, S. Dustdar, and A.Y. Zomaya, "Edge Intelligence: The Confluence of Edge Computing and Artificial Intelligence," *IEEE Internet of Things Journal*, vol. 7, no. 8, pp. 7457–7469, August 2020.
8. U.M. Malik, M.A. Javed, S. Zeadally, and S.U. Islam, "Energy Efficient Fog Computing for 6G enabled Massive IoT: Recent Trends and Future Opportunities," *IEEE Internet of Things Journal*, vol. 9, pp. 1–1, 2021.
9. M. Di Renzo, A. Zappone, M. Debbah, M.-S. Alouini, C. Yuen, J. de Rosny, and S. Tretyakov, "Smart Radio Environments Empowered by Reconfigurable Intelligent Surfaces: How It Works, State of Research, and The Road Ahead," *IEEE Journal on Selected Areas in Communications*, vol. 38, no. 11, pp. 2450–2525, November 2020.
10. H. Habibzadeh, K. Dinesh, O.R. Shishvan, A. Boggio-Dandry, G. Sharma, and T. Soyata, "A Survey of Healthcare Internet of Things (HIoT): A Clinical Perspective," *IEEE Internet of Things Journal*, vol. 7, no. 1, pp. 53–71, January 2020.
11. S.S. Saheb, P.B.N. Kiran, B.U.Bhaskara Ganesh, N. Roopalatha, S.M. Syed and P. William, "Artificial Neural Networks Based Risk Management Analysis of Modern Commercial Banks Using Behavioral Finance Theory," *2023 4th International Conference on Computation, Automation and Knowledge Management (ICCAKM)*, Dubai, United Arab Emirates, 2023, pp. 1–6. DOI: 10.1109/ICCAKM58659.2023.10449627
12. P. William, A. Agrawal, N. Rawat, A. Shrivastava, A.P. Srivastava and Ashish, "Enterprise Human Resource Management Model By Artificial Intelligence Digital Technology," *2023 4th International Conference on Computation, Automation and Knowledge Management (ICCAKM)*, Dubai, United Arab Emirates, 2023, pp. 01–06. DOI: 10.1109/ICCAKM58659.2023.10449624
13. P. William, A. Panicker, A. Falah, A. Hussain, A. Shrivastava and A.K. Khan, "The Emergence of Artificial Intelligence and Machine Learning in Contemporary Business Management," *2023 4th International Conference on Computation, Automation and Knowledge Management (ICCAKM)*, Dubai, United Arab Emirates, 2023, pp. 1–6. DOI: 10.1109/ICCAKM58659.2023.10449493
14. P. William, G. Sharma, K. Kapil, P. Srivastava, A. Shrivastava and R. Kumar, "Automation Techniques Using AI Based Cloud Computing and Blockchain for Business Management," *2023 4th International Conference on Computation, Automation and Knowledge Management (ICCAKM)*, Dubai, United Arab Emirates, 2023, pp. 1–6. DOI: 10.1109/ICCAKM58659.2023.10449534
15. A.R. More, O.B. Shendkar, K.G. Pathak, P.D. Sanap, S.N. Pachore and P. William, "Survey on Framework for Governing Modern Cyber Attacks in Computer Network," *2023 4th International Conference on Computation, Automation and Knowledge Management (ICCAKM)*, Dubai, United Arab Emirates, 2023, pp. 01–06. DOI: 10.1109/ICCAKM58659.2023.10449582
16. C. Nayak, P. William, R. Kumar, A. Deepak, K. Yadav, A.L.N. Rao, A. Srivastava, & A. Shrivastava (2024). Edge Cloud Server Deployment with Machine Learning for 6G Internet of Things. *International Journal of Intelligent Systems and Applications in Engineering*, vol. 12, 328. https://ijisae.org/index.php/IJISAE/article/view/4826
17. S.K. Hegde, P. William, M.S. Basvant, A. Deepak, A. Badhoutiya, A.L.N. Rao, A. Srivastava, & A. Shrivastava (2024). Energy-Efficient Bio-Inspired Hybrid Deep Learning Model for Network Intrusion Detection Based on Intelligent Decision Making. *International Journal of Intelligent Systems and Applications in Engineering*, vol. 12, 306. https://ijisae.org/index.php/IJISAE/article/view/4823

18. R. Rawat, S. Telang, P. William, Upinder Kaur, and C.U.O. Kumar (Eds.). *Dark Web Pattern Recognition and Crime Analysis Using Machine Intelligence*. IGI Global, 2022.
19. N. Yogeesh, and P. William, Sensor-Enabled Biomedical Decision Support System Using Deep Learning and Fuzzy Logic. In *Advances in Ubiquitous Sensing Applications for Healthcare, Deep Learning Applications in Translational Bioinformatics* (Vol. 15, pp. 33–53). Academic Press, 2024. DOI: 10.1016/B978-0-443-22299-3.00003-7
20. P. William, M. Rageeb, M.R. Boina, T.R.V. Lakshmi, A. Sharma, and N.K. Marriwala (2024). Empirical Analysis of Machine Learning in Enhancing the E-Business Through Structural Equation Modeling. In N.K. Marriwala, S. Dhingra, S. Jain, and D. Kumar (Eds.), *Mobile Radio Communications and 5G Networks. MRCN 2023*. Lecture Notes in Networks and Systems (vol 915). Springer. DOI: 10.1007/978-981-97-0700-3_45
21. P. William, N. Chinthamu, A. Saxena, T.R.V. Lakshmi, and M. Tiwari (2024). Integration of Secure Data Communication with Wireless Sensor Network Using Cryptographic Techniquc. In N.K. Marriwala, S. Dhingra, S. Jain, and D. Kumar (Eds.), *Mobile Radio Communications and 5G Networks. MRCN 2023*. Lecture Notes in Networks and Systems (Vol. 915). Springer. DOI: 10.1007/978-981-97-0700-3_46
22. G.S. Chhabra, P. William, G.R. Lanke, K. Jain, T.R.V. Lakshmi, and N. Varshney (2024). Comparative Analysis of Data Mining Based Performance Evaluation Using Hybrid Deep Learning Approach. In N.K. Marriwala, S. Dhingra, S. Jain, and D. Kumar (Eds.), *Mobile Radio Communications and 5G Networks. MRCN 2023*. Lecture Notes in Networks and Systems (Vol. 915). Springer. DOI: 10.1007/978-981-97-0700-3_47
23. P.B. Khatkale, P. William, O.J. Oyebode, A. Sharma, V. Kumari, and V. Singh (2024). Probing of Instructional Data Mining Effectiveness in Decision-Making for Industrial and Educational Applications. In N.K. Marriwala, S. Dhingra, S. Jain, and D. Kumar (Eds.), *Mobile Radio Communications and 5G Networks. MRCN 2023*. Lecture Notes in Networks and Systems (Vol. 915). Springer. DOI: 10.1007/978-981-97-0700-3_48
24. P. William, N. Chinthamu, M. Chiranjivi, T.R.V. Lakshmi, R. Kumar, and N.K. Marriwala (2024). Assessment of Wireless Sensor Networks Integrated with Various Cluster-Based Routing Protocols. In N.K. Marriwala, S. Dhingra, S. Jain, and D. Kumar (Eds.), *Mobile Radio Communications and 5G Networks. MRCN 2023*. Lecture Notes in Networks and Systems (Vol. 915). Springer. DOI: 10.1007/978-981-97-0700-3_49

11 Algorithms for Machine Learning in Big Data Analytics

P. William, Shrikaant Kulkarni, Dharmendra Kumar Roy and N Yogeesh

11.1 INTRODUCTION

The exponential growth of data, which has become a distinctive characteristic in this era of digital transformation, is one of the characteristics that defines our interconnected global system. The Internet of Things (IoT), social media, and advanced sensing technologies have all contributed to the gathering of an unprecedented quantity of data in terms of volume, velocity, and variety. This growth has been brought about by the expansion of these technologies. It is common practice to refer to this phenomenon as "big data." This boom in the acquisition of data has faced organizations of all sizes with a number of challenges as well as opportunities, which has necessitated the creation of innovative methods in order to make use of the potential that it has. In this context, the synergy that exists between machine learning (ML) and big data analytics has emerged as a critical catalyst for the extraction of significant insights from the vast ocean of information. This is because Big Data Analytics is able to analyze large amounts of data. The discipline of artificial intelligence (AI) encompasses a subsection known as ML, which allows computer systems to learn from data patterns and make predictions or judgments without the need for explicit programming. ML is a subfield of AI. Big data analytics, on the other hand, refers to the process of analyzing and studying huge databases with the goal of revealing patterns, correlations, and trends that were previously hidden. It is feasible that a powerful paradigm may develop as a result of the combination of these two domains, which would make it possible for organizations to extract meaningful insights from massive datasets. The purpose of this article is to shed light on the uses of these algorithms, the challenges they encounter, and the changes that are required for their effective utilization in the area of big data analytics. This is accomplished by a study of the algorithms that constitute the foundation of this mutually beneficial link [1].

As we continue our inquiry, it is becoming more apparent that the traditional approaches and tools for processing data are often incapable of dealing with the sheer scale and complexity of big data. This is becoming more and more apparent as we go on. ML algorithms, which provide a potential solution to the issue, provide adaptive models that are able to develop and learn from the continuous input of data. When it

DOI: 10.1201/9781032703718-15

comes to the process of discovering pertinent insights that drive informed decision-making, ML algorithms are an element that plays a crucial role. Some examples of ML algorithms include predictive modeling, classification, clustering, and regression. Other examples include regression and clustering. The objective of this work is to offer an overview of a broad variety of ML algorithms. These algorithms may include, but are not limited to, supervised and unsupervised learning, deep learning, ensemble techniques, and reinforcement learning. An overview of these algorithms is the aim of this work. An investigation of the suitability and adaptability of each algorithm in the context of big data analytics will be carried out, with a particular focus on the need for solutions that are proficient in both scalability and efficiency. In addition, the discussion will broaden to include the optimization approaches and parallel computing paradigms that are necessary for resolving the computational challenges that are brought about by the massive datasets. We hope that by conducting this in-depth investigation, we will not only be able to provide a guide for academics and practitioners who are attempting to navigate the complex terrain of ML in big data analytics, but we will also be able to make a contribution to the conversation that is currently taking place on the combination of these two exciting and revolutionary domains. This is something that we hope to accomplish. We may be able to open up new avenues for innovation and pave the way for breakthroughs that make the most of the possibilities, given by the data-driven age by maximizing its potential if we are able to obtain an understanding of the intricacies of these algorithms and how they interact with enormous volumes of data [2].

The explosion of digital data has burst through the conventional boundaries of size and complexity, which have been imposed by the world of information technology, which is continuing to undergo rapid development. An unprecedented increase in the collection of data is one of the defining characteristics of the contemporary age. This surge in data collection is driven by a broad range of sources, such as interactions on social media platforms, sensor networks, and the ubiquitous integration of the Internet of Things (IoT). A phenomenon that is often referred to as "big data" has emerged as a consequence of this exponential expansion in the amount of data. The concept of big data is a dynamic and complex entity that presents challenges as well as opportunities across a wide range of industries. It is in the midst of this deluge of data that the combination of ML algorithms and big data analytics has arisen as a force that is disruptive. Using the huge and complicated numbers that make up our linked world, it has the potential to provide insights that have not been before available [3].

As we go through the next pages, we are going to embark on a comprehensive journey across the complex landscape of ML algorithms. In this investigation, we are going to look at their uses, the challenges that they provide, and the technological advancements that support their integration with big data analytics. Through the process of deciphering the complexity of this mutually beneficial connection, our objective is to make a contribution to the ongoing discourse that is taking place about the revolutionary potential of ML in the era of big data. This study is not only an academic exercise; rather, it is a road map for academics and practitioners who are going to be traversing the undiscovered frontiers of a future that will be driven by data [4].

11.2 REVIEW OF LITERATURE

Every single day, gigabytes of data are put into existence in the contemporary world. There is a possibility that some of this data might have characteristics such as high speed, huge volume, uncertainty, non-stationary data, real-time data, and a variety of other characteristics. The conventional methods of ML are not the most effective choices for the management of exceptionally large amounts of data due to the problems that have been outlined above. In addition, the conventional approaches to the processing and storage of information do not fulfill the criteria. The purpose of this post was to discuss a variety of potential problems that may arise when using standard Machine Learning Techniques (MLT) for Big Data Analytics, as well as some potential solutions to these problems. As a result of our study, we have arrived at the conclusion that graphics processing units (GPUs), deep learning, online learning, incremental learning, parallel processing, dimensionality reduction approaches, and map reduce tasks are some of the possible answers to the issues that are associated with big data analytics [5].

Machine learning, sometimes known as ML for short, is the scientific study of statistical models and methods that computer systems use to do particular tasks without the need for explicit programming. This field of study is known as ML technology. The field of study that we are referring to here is known as ML technology. When we speak about this issue, we are discussing the field of study that is known as ML technology. It is generally agreed upon by experts that further research on this subject is required. The ability to comprehend algorithms for a wide range of applications that are used in daily life. When it comes to doing internet searches, a search engine like Google is an excellent choice because of its effectiveness. This is due to the fact that its algorithm is always learning how to rank web pages. There are several reasons why search engines have become so popular on the internet, and this is one of the most important ones. Search engines are used by a large number of individuals on the internet, and this may assist in understanding why this is the case. When it comes to the sheer number of individuals who use search engines on the internet, this is a good place to begin. These approaches have been put to use in a variety of industries, including image processing, data mining, predictive analytics, and other specific areas of research, amongst others. Obtaining the data necessary to carry out input analysis is one of the numerous advantages of ML. Another advantage is that an algorithm may be able to function alone and independently of other algorithms. With the purpose of providing a concise review and point of view on the great variety of tasks that may be accomplished via the use of various ML algorithms, this article strives to deliver [6].

The usage of big data is a significant aspect that facilitates the transfer of information and knowledge from one kind of end user to another. This is an essential thing to keep in mind. As a result of the need for automation in the management of such a large amount of data, there has been a growth in the use of data processing and ML techniques. With the intention of assisting professionals in automatically managing and learning from their bodies of knowledge, these platforms and tools are now being created and made accessible in the sphere of information and communications technology, as well as in a wide variety of other commercial and analytical sectors.

The vast majority of these platforms originate from large corporations like Microsoft or Google, or from incubators that are managed by the Apache Foundation. This group of organizations is the one that is responsible for providing the vast majority of these platforms. The primary objective of this project is to investigate the ways in which ML techniques may be used for the analysis of enormous amounts of data. As a result of the ML process, we are compelled to make decisions in situations where there is no clearly defined "right path" to take with respect to a particular problem. This notion is founded on the conceptual foundation that is comprised of the significant lessons that we have learned up to this point. In addition to that, it provides a synopsis of some of the tools most often used for modeling and data analysis [7].

Over the course of the past decade, ML techniques have shown to be an efficient approach to resolving a considerable number of problems that have arisen as a consequence of the accumulation of enormous amounts of data. ML encompasses a wide variety of ML approaches that may be used in a variety of settings. These techniques can vary in their application. Variations that are semi-supervised, supervised, and unsupervised are all covered in this collection of training methodologies. Other variations include versions that are unsupervised. On the other hand, there are a variety of approaches that may be used to handle a broad range of problems, such as the imbalance of data, the translation of machine language, the advancement of robots, and other challenges. Not only do these techniques include decision trees, but they also include preprocessing, association rules, random forests, decision trees, support vector machines (SVMs), and other methods that are linked with decision trees. In order to solve many problems, such as prediction analysis, in a variety of applications, such as e-healthcare (big data: data generated from connected electronically smart devices) or other applications (agriculture, e-commerce, defense, etc.), we now need to know a few fundamental facts about ML techniques. This is necessary in order to solve many problems. As a result, this helps to explain why the majority of researchers have difficulty and hesitation when it comes to selecting the most appropriate method or measurement to utilize while doing research. Among all the many approaches, which one is the most appropriate for describing the ways in which data mining and ML are distinct from one another? Due to the fact that this is the case, this article examines a significant number of prior studies and publications in an effort to address all of the researchers who have conducted studies and published works that are analogous to the topics that are being discussed. This therapy has the potential to reduce anxiety associated with ML and data mining from the very beginning. Furthermore, it has the ability to considerably reduce anxiety about ML methods in general (as opposed to deep learning). The purpose of this research is to provide a broad range of data that may be used for ML and to look further into the challenges that come with having a huge quantity of data. In conclusion, the findings of the inquiry provide the reader with a substantial amount of information to absorb. After the presentation of the recommendations for the future, an investigation into evaluation metrics and other pertinent criteria was carried out, which led to the conclusion of this article. This investigation was carried out immediately after the presentation [8].

One of the most recent advancements in technology is known as big data analytics, which asserts that it may facilitate the extraction of more insightful information from massive volumes of data that are not visibly connected to one another. During the process of big data analytics, the selection of large data storage and the most appropriate computer architecture is made. Both of these components are subsequently improved by the development of scalable ML algorithms. On the other hand, there is still a dearth of a comprehensive literature review dedicated to parallel data-intensive ML approaches for enormous data sets. In spite of the fact that big data analytics and the advantages it offers have received a lot of attention, this is still the case. As part of the scope of the research, a comprehensive analysis of the various ML approaches that are used for big data analytics is presented. Through this study, we want to fill in some of the gaps that have been identified in the existing body of research about parallel scalable approaches for very small data sets. These efforts are being made with the intention of laying the groundwork for future study in this field that is of a better quality. In 2016, the copyright was officially transferred to John Wiley & Sons, Ltd., which was the official year of the transfer [9, 10].

When taking into consideration the present environment, which is characterized by the proliferation of many data sets distributed in enormous quantities on a worldwide scale, the objective of intelligent data analysis has become an endeavor that is becoming more difficult to accomplish. Taking this into consideration, it is of the utmost importance to have the appropriate algorithms in place, in addition to a distributed and parallel architecture that is capable of dealing with these very challenging situations. It seems possible that these ML approaches will be successful in this environment, given that they need relatively little input from humans. This is due to the fact that they need a reduced amount of support from other individuals. The purpose of this chapter is to present an overview of the many challenges that are connected with the management and storage of enormous quantities of data, as well as the tools, technologies, and algorithms that may be used to handle those challenges. In addition, a case study that provides information on an application that is a component of the department that is responsible for healthcare analytics is presented. This section will discuss a few distributed algorithms that are often used in the data mining business. All of these algorithms are distributed. Everyone has access to these algorithms in their entirety. All of these algorithms are accessible to anybody who wants to use them. In addition, the methods that were discussed before could be discovered in other information sources. You are cordially encouraged to read the comprehensive explanation of these algorithms that may be found on the page that follows. Within the last part, you will find a comprehensive analysis of several ML techniques and the possible applications of these techniques to big data analytics [11–14].

11.3 SEMI-SUPERVISED AND REINFORCEMENT LEARNING ALGORITHMS

Semi-supervised learning and reinforcement learning represent two distinct yet powerful paradigms within the realm of ML, each offering unique strategies for tackling complex learning tasks. Semi-supervised learning endeavors to capitalize on the abundance of unlabeled data that often accompanies labeled datasets, recognizing that in many real-world scenarios, annotating large amounts of data is costly and time-consuming. By harnessing both labeled and unlabeled data, semi-supervised learning algorithms aim to improve model generalization and performance by leveraging the inherent structure and patterns latent within the unlabeled data. This is achieved through a variety of techniques, such as self-training, co-training, and graph-based methods, which iteratively refine the model's understanding of the data by incorporating predictions on unlabeled instances into the training process. Such approaches allow semi-supervised learning algorithms to extract valuable information from vast pools of unlabeled data, effectively enhancing their ability to make accurate predictions on unseen examples while mitigating the need for extensive labeling efforts [15–17].

On the other hand, the paradigm of reinforcement learning was developed expressly for sequential decision-making in contexts that are unexpected. While supervised learning and unsupervised learning need labeled examples and explicit teaching, respectively, reinforcement learning agents learn how to traverse their environment by making mistakes and ultimately optimizing cumulative rewards. This is in contrast to supervised learning, which requires an explicit instruction approach. It is important to note that this stands in contrast to the methods of learning that are supervised and unsupervised. On the other hand, events that have been adequately marked are required for both supervised and unsupervised learning. This is accomplished by the use of a feedback loop that includes the process of learning the rules, regularly interacting with the environment, and expecting rewards or punishments related to the environment. Agents that are equipped with the ability to learn via reinforcement may investigate and exploit their environment in order to discover the most effective means of accomplishing their objectives, and then constantly improve their policies as a result of this process [18, 19].

The goals of the task are reflected in the reward functions, and the success of reinforcement learning approaches is contingent on the selection of suitable policy optimization procedures. Methods such as policy gradients, Q-learning, and deep reinforcement learning are examples of approaches that fall under this area. Through the use of deep neural networks and reinforcement learning strategies, researchers have achieved remarkable progress in a wide range of fields, including but not limited to natural language processing, autonomous driving, robotics, and gaming, among others. The exceptional results that these researchers have achieved are a direct result of their efforts to conquer difficult difficulties in a variety of fields. The procedures that are involved in identifying the input and output values, as well as the training of the mapping function based on ML, are shown in Figure 11.1. In order to choose the best mapping function f, ML algorithms make use of scientific mathematics at their disposal. This function is designed to ensure that, given an input (X) and an output (Y), Y is identical to f(X). This is the function's specific purpose. The specific

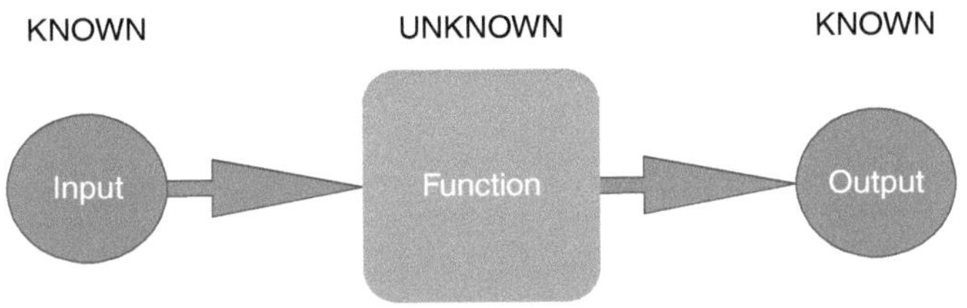

FIGURE 11.1 Supervised learning.

purpose of the function is to do this. Following a more in-depth investigation, it is possible to identify what seems to be an observer of the learning process for pupils.

When we take into account the fact that we are already familiar with the replies, algorithms make an attempt to translate the function in such a manner that the predicted solutions are almost similar to the ones that are really being used. With the use of a mapping function f that it has been given, the computer is now in a position to make predictions about the values Y' for each and every X. The learning process is said to have reached its conclusion when there is not enough of a difference between the two sets of data, Y' and Y, to meet a threshold that has been established in advance. Following the receipt of shape photographs as input, the ML model generates data that is annotated with the names of shapes [20, 22]. This procedure is shown in Figure 11.2, which serves as an example. Through the utilization of both the input and output data, the model is able to cultivate the capability of predicting the category of image data that has not yet been seen. It also gains the capacity to predict the following categories: hexagon, triangle, circle, and rectangle kinds. In addition to this, it acquires the power to anticipate hexagons [21, 22].

As shown in Figure 11.2, the X-axis represents the number of years of experience that the individual has. According to the Y-axis, a certain amount of rupees is given out on a monthly basis for each and every degree of talent that an individual has. Additionally, the X and Y coordinates are represented by the green dots that are present in both the input and output data. In order to solve the regression issue, you will need to locate a continuous mapping function that connects the variables that are being input and those that are being output. Agents may learn the best decision-making strategies using reinforcement learning, which is in contrast to semi-supervised learning, which employs both labeled and unlabeled data to increase model performance and generalizability. Reinforcement learning allows agents to learn the best decision-making strategies by interacting with developing environments and feedback systems. When brought together, these paradigms provide a powerful toolset for the field of ML. They are a significant contributor to the advancement of AI and provide adaptable solutions to a broad variety of problems that are encountered in the real world.

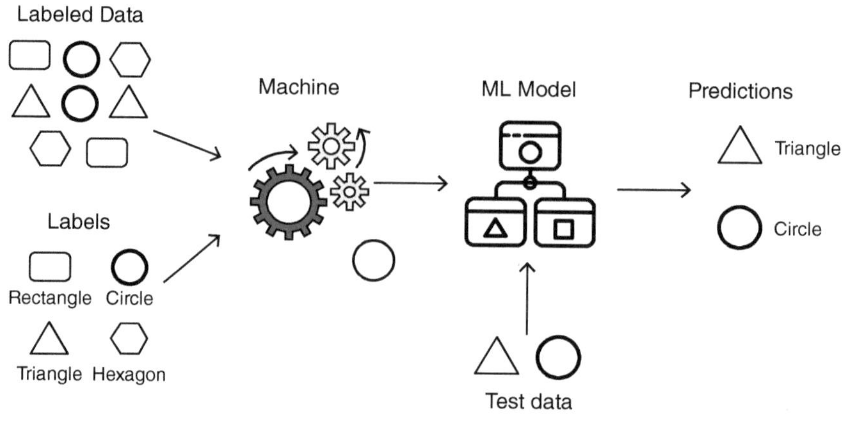

FIGURE 11.2 Supervised learning taking.

11.4 RESEARCH METHODOLOGY

In order to learn about the complexities that are involved in the mutually beneficial relationship that exists between ML algorithms and big data analytics, this research makes use of a strategy that integrates theoretical investigation, empirical analysis, and practical insights. A deliberate combination of algorithmic implementation, real-world case studies, and literature study is used in this method in order to give a comprehensive understanding of the relationship between ML and big data analytics.

11.4.1 Algorithmic Panorama

In dissecting the rich tapestry of ML algorithms in the context of big data analytics, our analysis unveils a diverse landscape. Supervised learning algorithms, including linear regression and SVMs, exhibit prowess in predictive modeling, while unsupervised counterparts like k-means clustering showcase their ability to discern patterns in unstructured data. Deep learning algorithms, such as convolutional neural networks (CNNs) and recurrent neural networks (RNNs), demonstrate unparalleled capabilities in handling complex, high-dimensional data. Ensemble methods, typified by random forests and gradient boosting, embody collaborative strength, enhancing predictive accuracy. Reinforcement learning algorithms showcase their potential in dynamic decision-making scenarios. This panoramic view sets the stage for a nuanced understanding of their applications in big data analytics.

11.4.2 Real-World Resonance

As we traverse the application landscape, our analysis emphasizes the tangible impact of ML algorithms in real-world scenarios. From healthcare to finance, manufacturing to marketing, these algorithms permeate diverse sectors, offering solutions to intricate problems. Case studies illuminate their role in predicting disease outbreaks, optimizing supply chain logistics, and personalizing customer experiences. The real-world resonance underscores the algorithms' adaptability and effectiveness in extracting actionable insights from large and complex datasets.

11.4.3 Algorithmic Scrutiny

Our exploration begins with an in-depth analysis of the diverse set of ML algorithms. This phase involves a systematic review of literature, scholarly articles, and authoritative publications, enabling the identification of key algorithms relevant to big data analytics. The emphasis is on understanding the underlying principles, mathematical formulations, and practical applications of each algorithm, spanning supervised and unsupervised learning, deep learning, ensemble methods, and reinforcement learning.

11.4.4 Application Landscape

Moving beyond theoretical foundations, our research methodology involves a meticulous examination of the practical applications of these algorithms within the landscape of big data analytics. Case studies, real-world implementations, and industry use-cases are considered to gauge the effectiveness of each algorithm in extracting meaningful insights from large datasets. This empirical lens allows us to draw connections between algorithmic prowess and real-world problem-solving.

11.4.5 Technological Advancements

To comprehend the evolving landscape, our research methodology includes an investigation into the latest technological advancements that augment the integration of ML algorithms and big data analytics. This involves a survey of parallel computing paradigms, optimization strategies, and advancements in hardware infrastructure that facilitate the seamless execution of algorithms on vast datasets.

The culmination of our research methodology involves synthesizing the findings from the algorithmic scrutiny, application landscape assessment, challenges and limitations exploration, technological advancements investigation, and comparative analysis. This synthesis provides a comprehensive understanding of the interplay between ML algorithms and big data analytics, offering insights into the overarching trends, potential breakthroughs, and avenues for future research and innovation. Through this methodological framework, our objective is not only to dissect the algorithms but to weave a narrative that transcends the theoretical realms, providing a practical guide for navigating the complexities of ML in the context of big data analytics.

11.5 RESULT AND DISCUSSION

The analysis of ML algorithms in the realm of big data analytics unveils a multifaceted landscape characterized by diversity and adaptability. Supervised learning algorithms, exemplified by linear regression and SVMs, demonstrate proficiency in predictive modeling. Unsupervised counterparts, including k-means clustering, showcase their ability to discern patterns in unstructured datasets. Deep learning algorithms, such as CNNs and RNNs, prove effective in handling complex, high-dimensional data. Ensemble methods, represented by random forests and gradient boosting, exhibit collaborative strength, enhancing predictive accuracy. Reinforcement learning algorithms emerge as potent tools for dynamic decision-making scenarios. Real-world applications underscore the tangible impact of these algorithms across diverse sectors. From healthcare and finance to manufacturing and marketing, ML algorithms play pivotal roles in predicting disease outbreaks, optimizing supply chain logistics, and personalizing customer experiences. However, the analysis also unveils intricacies inherent in the convergence of ML and big data. Scalability issues, algorithmic biases, ethical considerations, and the interpretability of complex models pose challenges that demand innovative solutions.

Technological advancements, including parallel computing paradigms like Apache Spark and Hadoop, optimization strategies like feature engineering, and advancements in hardware infrastructure such as GPUs contribute to a symphony of innovation. This technological progress not only addresses existing challenges but propels the fusion of ML and big data analytics into new frontiers. Through comparative analysis, the strengths and weaknesses of different algorithms become evident, providing a nuanced understanding that guides practitioners in selecting the most suitable tools for specific analytical objectives. The synthesis of findings culminates in a rich tapestry that encapsulates the essence of ML in big data analytics. The interplay between algorithms, their real-world applications, challenges, technological advancements, and comparative nuances converges to offer insights into overarching trends and future trajectories. This synthesis serves as a compass, guiding stakeholders toward informed decision-making and inspiring future explorations in the dynamic intersection of ML and big data analytics.

An approach for supervised ML known as the SVM is used most often for the purpose of addressing categorization problems. The flip side of the coin is that it could also solve problems associated with regression. The visualization of each data item is accomplished by the use of an n-dimensional space, where n represents the total number of characteristics. Both the coordinate value and the item value are, for all intents and purposes, completely interchangeable. Please take into mind the following example, which is included in this letter. For the sake of this conversation, let us make the assumption for the time being that a sample that is typical of the population is constituted of males and females in proportions that are equal to one another. It is necessary for us to develop a few criteria by conducting an analysis of the characteristics of this sample set in order to guarantee that the gender of a new individual can be accurately established by using this standard set of guidelines. In the sector, the SVM is a technology that is frequently used, and it has the potential to efficiently tackle situations of this kind. Height and length of the hair are the characteristics of the sample that are being examined in this particular case. Because of these two characteristics, the group was obviously split in half, as shown in Figure 11.3, which is an illustration of the first data plot that was constructed using these criteria.

The males in this specific painting are shown as squares, while the females are depicted as circles. There is the possibility of drawing conclusions about the two needs by using the data set that was shown earlier in this paragraph. The precise

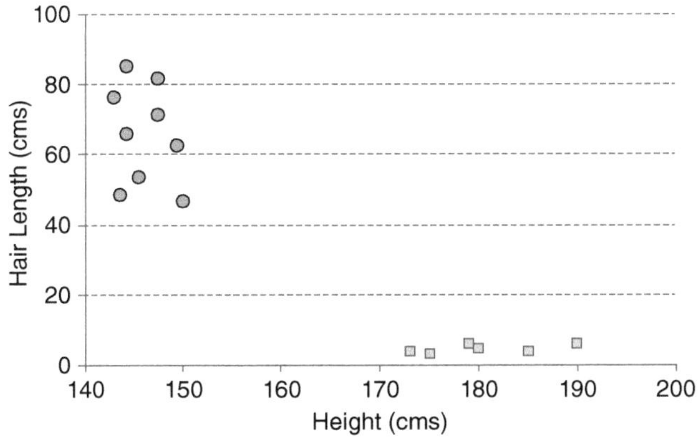

FIGURE 11.3 Hair length and height are mapped as features.

position that a single observation may be said to represent is referred to as the support vector. Regarding this particular illustration, the support vector (45, 150) represents a depiction of a feminine representation. Take advantage of an innovative method known as SVM in order to divide the two groups in the most effective manner feasible. It's possible that you'll discover that there are rival strategies that might assist you in selecting the most advantageous border. This is due to the fact that depending on the circumstances, alternative strategies could be more effective. By determining the shortest distance between a border and the support vector that is closest to it, we may be able to get a better understanding of the objective function of an SVM in the most basic manner feasible. It is possible for this particular support vector to provide support for any class. Once we have determined the distances to each of the support vectors, we will be able to choose the border that is the furthest away from the support vector that is closest to us. The statistical approach known as principal component analysis is shown using a methodological example for the purpose of illustrating Figure 11.4. This is accomplished by the use of an orthogonal transformation, which results in the generation of a new set of values for variables that are linearly isolated from one another. For this to be possible, one must begin with a collection of observations for variables that may be connected to one another. Within the context of this particular scenario, we are able to reduce the dimensionality of the data, which makes the calculations a great deal easier to understand. In order to offer a linear explanation for the variance-covariance structure of a collection of variables, this style of explanation involves doing the aforementioned kind of explanation. A method that is often used is known as the dimensionality-reduction strategy.

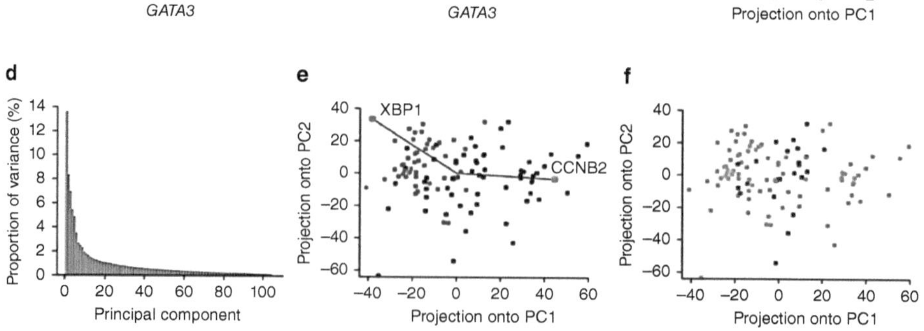

FIGURE 11.4 Principal component analysis.

11.6 DISCUSSION

An intricate and diverse landscape is shown in the essay by means of a thorough navigation of the delicate interaction between big data analytics and ML algorithms. Deep learning, which is used for managing high-dimensional data; supervised learning, which is used for predictive modeling; unsupervised learning, which is used for pattern recognition; ensemble learning, which is used to improve prediction accuracy; and reinforcement learning, which is used for dynamic decision-making are some of the ML approaches that are investigated in this article. A thorough examination is conducted on the applicability and adaptability of each approach within the framework of big data analytics, with a particular focus placed on the need for solutions that are both scalable and efficient.

In addition to this, the chapter discusses parallel computing paradigms and optimization approaches, both of which are vital for overcoming the computational challenges that are posed by massive datasets. The chapter examines practical applications in a wide range of sectors, demonstrating how ML algorithms may be used to forecast the occurrence of disease outbreaks, enhance the operations of supply chain management, and personalize the experiences of consumers. According to the findings of the research, however, there are also issues that call for innovative solutions. These issues include algorithmic biases, limits in scalability, ethical challenges, and the interpretability of intricate models.

11.7 CONCLUSIONS

A complete perspective on the benefits, challenges, and applications of combining ML algorithms with big data analytics is presented as the summary of the study's findings. By seeing the linkages that exist between these two revolutionary fields, practitioners and researchers have the potential to develop solutions that successfully bring the data-driven future to fruition. Combining big data analytics with ML has the potential to fundamentally disrupt a number of different industries by opening the door to insights and data-driven decision-making. This promise may be realized via more research and development.

REFERENCES

1. Assuncao, M., Calheiros, R., Bianchi, S., Netto, M. (2015). Big Data Computing and Clouds: Trends and Future. *Journal of Parallel and Distributed Computing*, 75, 3–15.
2. Tsai, C.W., Lai, C.F., Chao, H.C., Vasilakos, A.V. (2015). Big Data Analytics: A Survey. *Journal of Big Data*, 2, 21.
3. Qiu, J., Wu, Q., Ding, G., Xu, Y., Feng, S. (2016, December). A Survey of Machine Learning for Big Data Processing. *EURASIP Journal on Advances in Signal Processing*, 67. https://doi.org/10.1186/s13634-016-0355-x
4. Wang, L., Alexander, C.A. (2016). Machine Learning in Big Data. *International Journal of Mathematical, Engineering and Management Sciences*, 1(2), 52–61.
5. Najafabadi, M. M., Villanustre, F., Khoshgoftaar, T. M., Seliya, N., Wald, R., Muharemagic, E. (2015). Deep Learning Applications and Challenges in Big Data Analytics. *Journal of Big Data*, 2, 1–21.

6. Zhang, G., Ou, S.-X., Huang, Y.-H., Wang, C.-R. (2015, January 06). Semisupervised Learning Methods for Large Scale Healthcare Data Analysis. *International Journal of Computers in Healthcare*, 2, 98–110.
7. Kumar, A., Tyagi, A. K., Tyagi, S. K. (2014). Data Mining: Various Issues and Challenges for Future a Short Discussion on Data Mining Issues for Future Work. *International Journal of Emerging Technology and Advanced Engineering*, 4(1), 1–8.
8. Moniruzzaman, A.B.M. (2014). NewSQL: Towards Next Generation Scalable RDBMS for Online Transaction Processing (OLTP) for big data management. *International Journal of Database Theory & Application*, 7, 121–130.
9. Pal, A.K., Dey, N., Samanta, S., Das, A., Chaudhuri, S.S. (2013, December). A Hybrid Reversible Watermarking Technique for Color Biomedical Images. In *2013 IEEE International Conference on Computational Intelligence and Computing Research (ICCIC)* (pp. 1–6). IEEE.
10. Saheb, S.S., Kiran, P.B.N., Bhaskara Ganesh, B.U., Roopalatha, N., Syed, S.M., William, P. (2023). Artificial Neural Networks Based Risk Management Analysis of Modern Commercial Banks Using Behavioral Finance Theory. In *2023 4th International Conference on Computation, Automation and Knowledge Management (ICCAKM)*, Dubai, United Arab Emirates (pp. 1–6). https://doi.org/10.1109/ICCAKM58659.2023.10449627
11. William, P., Panicker, A., Falah, A., Hussain, A., Shrivastava, A., Khan, A.K. (2023). The Emergence of Artificial Intelligence and Machine Learning in Contemporary Business Management. In *2023 4th International Conference on Computation, Automation and Knowledge Management (ICCAKM)*, Dubai, United Arab Emirates (pp. 1–6). https://doi.org/10.1109/ICCAKM58659.2023.10449493
12. William, P., Sharma, G., Kapil, K., Srivastava, P., Shrivastava, A., Kumar, R. (2023). Automation Techniques Using AI Based Cloud Computing and Blockchain for Business Management. In *2023 4th International Conference on Computation, Automation and Knowledge Management (ICCAKM)*, Dubai, United Arab Emirates (pp. 1–6). https://doi.org/10.1109/ICCAKM58659.2023.10449534
13. More, A.R., Shendkar, O.B., Pathak, K.G., Sanap, P.D., Pachore, S.N., William, P. (2023). Survey on Framework for Governing Modern Cyber Attacks in Computer Network. In *2023 4th International Conference on Computation, Automation and Knowledge Management (ICCAKM)*, Dubai, United Arab Emirates (pp. 01–06). https://doi.org/10.1109/ICCAKM58659.2023.10449582
14. Nayak, C., William, P., Kumar, R., Deepak, A., Yadav, K., Rao, A.L.N., Srivastava, A., Shrivastava, A. (2024). Edge Cloud Server Deployment With Machine Learning for 6G Internet of Things. *International Journal of Intelligent Systems and Applications in Engineering*, 12(16s), 328. https://ijisae.org/index.php/IJISAE/article/view/4826
15. Hegde, S.K., William, P., Basvant, M.S., Deepak, A., Badhoutiya, A., Rao, A.L.N., Srivastava, A., Shrivastava, A. (2024). Energy-Efficient Bio-Inspired Hybrid Deep Learning Model for Network Intrusion Detection Based on Intelligent Decision Making. *International Journal of Intelligent Systems and Applications in Engineering*, 12(16s), 306. https://ijisae.org/index.php/IJISAE/article/view/4823
16. Rawat, R., Telang, S., P. William, Kaur, U., Om Kumar, C.U. (Eds.). (2022). *Dark Web Pattern Recognition and Crime Analysis Using Machine Intelligence*. IGI Global.
17. Yogeesh, N., William, P. (2024). Sensor-enabled biomedical decision support system using deep learning and fuzzy logic, In *Advances in Ubiquitous Sensing Applications for Healthcare, Deep Learning Applications in Translational Bioinformatics*, vol. 15, pp. 33–53. Academic Press. https://doi.org/10.1016/B978-0-443-22299-3.00003-7

18. William, P., Rageeb, M., Boina, M.R., Lakshmi, T.R.V., Sharma, A., Marriwala, N.K. (2024). Empirical Analysis of Machine Learning in Enhancing the E-Business Through Structural Equation Modeling. In: Marriwala, N.K., Dhingra, S., Jain, S., Kumar, D. (eds) *Mobile Radio Communications and 5G Networks. MRCN 2023*. Lecture Notes in Networks and Systems, vol 915. Springer. https://doi.org/10.1007/978-981-97-0700-3_45
19. William, P., Chinthamu, N., Saxena, A., Lakshmi, T.R.V., Tiwari, M. (2024). Integration of Secure Data Communication with Wireless Sensor Network Using Cryptographic Technique. In: Marriwala, N.K., Dhingra, S., Jain, S., Kumar, D. (eds) *Mobile Radio Communications and 5G Networks. MRCN 2023*. Lecture Notes in Networks and Systems, vol 915. Springer. https://doi.org/10.1007/978-981-97-0700-3_46
20. Chhabra, G.S., William, P., Lanke, G.R., Jain, K., Lakshmi, T.R.V., Varshney, N. (2024). Comparative Analysis of Data Mining Based Performance Evaluation Using Hybrid Deep Learning Approach. In: Marriwala, N.K., Dhingra, S., Jain, S., Kumar, D. (eds) *Mobile Radio Communications and 5G Networks. MRCN 2023*. Lecture Notes in Networks and Systems, vol 915. Springer. https://doi.org/10.1007/978-981-97-0700-3_47
21. Khatkale, P.B., William, P., Oyebode, O.J., Sharma, A., Kumari, V., Singh, V. (2024). Probing of Instructional Data Mining Effectiveness in Decision-Making for Industrial and Educational Applications. In: Marriwala, N.K., Dhingra, S., Jain, S., Kumar, D. (eds) *Mobile Radio Communications and 5G Networks. MRCN 2023*. Lecture Notes in Networks and Systems, vol 915. Springer. https://doi.org/10.1007/978-981-97-0700-3_48
22. William, P., Chinthamu, N., Chiranjivi, M., Vijaya Lakshmi, T.R., Kumar, R., Marriwala, N.K. (2024). Assessment of Wireless Sensor Networks Integrated with Various Cluster-Based Routing Protocols. In: Marriwala, N.K., Dhingra, S., Jain, S., Kumar, D. (eds) *Mobile Radio Communications and 5G Networks. MRCN 2023*. Lecture Notes in Networks and Systems, vol 915. Springer. https://doi.org/10.1007/978-981-97-0700-3_49

Part V

Case Studies and Applications of AI in Computing

12 Machine Learning Algorithms and Sustainable AI-Driven IoT Systems

Paving the Way toward Environmental Stewardship

Bharati Ainapure and Bhargav Appasani

12.1 BACKGROUND AND MOTIVATION

The rapid spread of IoT has fundamentally changed our interactions with the physical world. IoT represents a vast network of interconnected devices, sensors, and objects capable of collecting and sharing data over the internet. These devices are present in diverse domains, encompassing transportation, healthcare, smart cities, and agriculture [1]. As IoT continues to expand its reach, it brings forth significant opportunities for innovation, efficiency, and convenience. However, this exponential growth also raises profound concerns about its environmental impact.

IoT devices, particularly those designed without energy efficiency in mind, can contribute to substantial power consumption and electronic waste. Furthermore, the computational demands of processing the massive data streams generated by IoT often require resource-intensive Artificial Intelligence (AI) and Machine Learning (ML) algorithms. This reliance on energy-intensive computing resources in data centers further compounds environmental challenges [2]. To address these concerns and unlock the full potential of IoT and AI/ML, there is a growing imperative to explore sustainable practices at the convergence of these domains.

AI and ML have witnessed unprecedented advancements, reshaping industries and augmenting decision-making processes. ML algorithms have excelled in tasks like image classification, predictive analytics, and natural language processing. In the context of IoT, AI/ML technologies provide a transformative layer of intelligence, enabling devices to make autonomous decisions, recognize patterns, and optimize operations [3]. However, this amalgamation of IoT and AI/ML introduces an additional layer of environmental concern as the training and deployment of complex models demand substantial computational resources, notably energy.

DOI: 10.1201/9781032703718-17

The environmental challenges stemming from IoT and AI/ML cannot be underestimated. The United Nations Sustainable Development Goals (SDGs) underscore the pressing need to confront climate change and advocate for sustainable principles. [4]. IoT and AI, with their potential for energy efficiency and data-driven optimization, hold the promise of aligning with these global sustainability goals. This chapter seeks to investigate the confluence of ML algorithms and sustainable AI-driven IoT systems, highlighting their potential to mitigate environmental impacts while driving technological innovation and environmental stewardship.

The motivation behind this book chapter lies in the critical need to reconcile technological advancement with environmental responsibility. As IoT proliferates and AI/ML applications grow in complexity, it becomes increasingly vital to find sustainable solutions that mitigate the carbon footprint of these systems. By exploring the synergy between ML algorithms and sustainable AI-driven IoT, we aim to not only identify the challenges but also present practical strategies to harness these technologies for environmental stewardship. Our motivation is fueled by the understanding that the world is facing pressing environmental challenges, from climate change to resource depletion, and technology must play a pivotal role in mitigating these issues. Sustainable AI-driven IoT systems offer a promising avenue to leverage technological innovation in support of a more eco-conscious and sustainable future. Through this chapter, we aspire to inspire researchers, industry leaders, and policymakers to take proactive steps toward realizing this vision of environmental stewardship through technology.

12.2 OVERVIEW OF ML, IoT, AND SUSTAINABILITY

In the 21st century, the world has been facing a multitude of complex challenges, from climate change to resource depletion and social inequalities. To address these challenges, the convergence of ML, Internet of Things (IoT), and sustainability has emerged as a powerful paradigm. Here, we deeply explore each of these domains, highlighting their latest developments, and also explore how their convergence is reshaping industries and fostering a more sustainable future.

12.2.1 Machine Learning (ML)

ML constitutes a subset of AI, dedicated to creating algorithms and models that empower computer systems to learn from data and subsequently make predictions or decisions. Recent years have witnessed remarkable advancements in ML, driven by the proliferation of data, increased computational power, and innovative algorithmic approaches. Some key aspects of ML include the following:

Deep Learning: Convolutional Neural Networks (CNNs) have demonstrated exceptional performance in tasks related to image recognition, whereas Recurrent Neural Networks (RNNs) have made notable advancements in the domains of natural language processing and the analysis of sequential data.

Transfer Learning: Transfer learning enables models trained on one task to be adapted for related tasks, saving time and computational resources.

This approach has found applications in various domains, including healthcare, finance, and autonomous driving.

Explainable AI: Ensuring transparency and interpretability in ML models has become increasingly important. Explainable AI techniques aim to make the decision-making process of ML models more understandable, essential for critical applications like healthcare and finance.

AI Ethics: The ethical considerations surrounding AI and ML have gained prominence. Ensuring fairness, avoiding bias, and addressing ethical concerns in data collection and model development have become focal points.

Natural Language Processing (NLP): NLP has seen rapid progress, with models like GPT-3 enabling human-like text generation and understanding. Applications range from chatbots to content generation and translation.

12.3 INTERNET OF THINGS (IoT)

The Internet of Things refers to the vast network of interconnected devices, physical objects, and sensors that gather and share data over the internet. IoT has experienced explosive growth due to advancements in sensor technology, connectivity options, and edge computing. Key facets of IoT include:

Sensors and Devices: IoT encompasses a wide array of devices, from wearables to industrial sensors and smart thermostats and autonomous vehicles. These devices collect diverse types of data, from environmental conditions to user behavior.

Connectivity: IoT relies on various communication protocols, such as cellular networks, Bluetooth, Wi-Fi, and Low Power Wide Area Networks (LPWAN), to transmit data to central systems or other connected devices.

Edge Computing: Edge computing presents computational capabilities nearer to the data source, decreasing latency and enabling real-time decision-making. This is crucial for applications like autonomous vehicles and industrial automation.

Security: As the number of connected devices surges, IoT security becomes paramount. Protecting data integrity and ensuring secure communication are major challenges.

Applications: IoT applications span a wide spectrum, including agriculture, industrial automation, smart cities, healthcare, and environmental monitoring.

12.4 SUSTAINABILITY

Sustainability focuses on practices and initiatives aimed at minimizing the negative environmental, social, and economic impacts of human activities. In a world grappling with climate change, resource scarcity, and social disparities, sustainability initiatives have gained significant traction. Key dimensions of sustainability include the following:

Environmental Sustainability: This facet addresses environmental challenges, such as decreasing greenhouse gas secretions, preserving natural resources, and protecting ecosystems. Renewable energy adoption, circular economy practices, and waste reduction are essential components.

Social Sustainability: Social sustainability emphasizes fair labor practices, social equity, and community well-being. This involves promoting diversity, ensuring worker rights, and supporting local communities.

Economic Sustainability: Economic sustainability needs to balance economic growth with resource conservation and societal welfare. Circular economy principles, responsible business practices, and ethical investments align with this dimension.

Sustainable Development Goals (SDGs): The United Nations has outlined 17 Sustainable Development Goals as a global blueprint for a more sustainable future. These goals encompass various aspects of sustainability, including poverty reduction, clean energy, and gender equality.

Internet of Things (IoT): The term 'IoT' stands for the Internet of Things, which represents a vast network connecting physical objects, devices, and sensors designed to collect and exchange data over the internet. These devices encompass a wide range, spanning from intelligent thermostats and wearable fitness trackers to industrial sensors utilized in factory settings. IoT carries the potential to revolutionize our interactions with the world and our methods of gathering information.

The latest trends in IoT involve edge computing, where data processing occurs near the source (i.e., device) rather than depend solely on centralized cloud servers. This decreases latency and enhances real-time decision-making. Furthermore, the security of IoT has emerged as a critical concern in light of the widespread adoption of interconnected devices.

Sustainability: Sustainability encompasses practices and initiatives aimed at minimizing the negative environmental, economic, and social impact of human activities. With global challenges such as resource depletion, climate change, and social inequalities, sustainability has gained significant attention.

The latest developments in sustainability comprise the adoption of renewable energy sources like wind power and solar, the circular economy concept that promotes recycling and reducing waste, and the integration of sustainability into corporate strategies and supply chains through Environmental, Social, and Governance (ESG) frameworks.

12.5 CONVERGENCE OF ML, IoT, AND SUSTAINABILITY

The convergence of ML, IoT, and sustainability offers transformative opportunities:

Environmental Monitoring: IoT sensors can collect data from different sources like water quality, air quality, and wildlife tracking, while ML algorithms can analyze this data to detect pollution trends, support conservation efforts, and enhance disaster preparedness [5].

Energy Efficiency: ML algorithms can enhance energy efficiency in buildings and industrial operations by leveraging real-time data from IoT devices. This not only reduces carbon emissions but also cuts operational expenses [6], [7].

Predictive Maintenance: IoT-enabled machinery and infrastructure can be monitored for wear and tear. ML models can predict maintenance needs, reducing resource waste and minimizing downtime [8] [9].

Smart Agriculture: IoT sensors provide data on soil conditions, crop health, and weather. ML can offer insights into optimal planting, irrigation, and pest control strategies, promoting sustainable farming practices and food security [10].

Supply Chain Transparency: IoT can track products throughout the supply chain, while ML can analyze this data to ensure sustainable sourcing, ethical production, and fair labor practices [11].

Circular Economy: ML can identify opportunities for recycling and reusing materials within a circular economy, reducing waste and conserving resources [12].

Climate Prediction and Adaptation: ML models can analyze climate data from IoT sensors to improve climate change modeling and adaptation strategies, helping communities better prepare for extreme weather events [13].

In summary, the convergence of ML, IoT, and sustainability holds the potential to revolutionize industries and address pressing global challenges. It empowers us to make data-driven decisions that minimize environmental impact, optimize resource use, and create a more sustainable future [14]. Figure 12.1 illustrates the convergence of ML, IoT, and sustainability. At its core, the convergence point represents the synergy between these domains. ML encompasses deep learning (DL), transfer learning, and ethical AI, while IoT includes sensors, edge computing, and security.

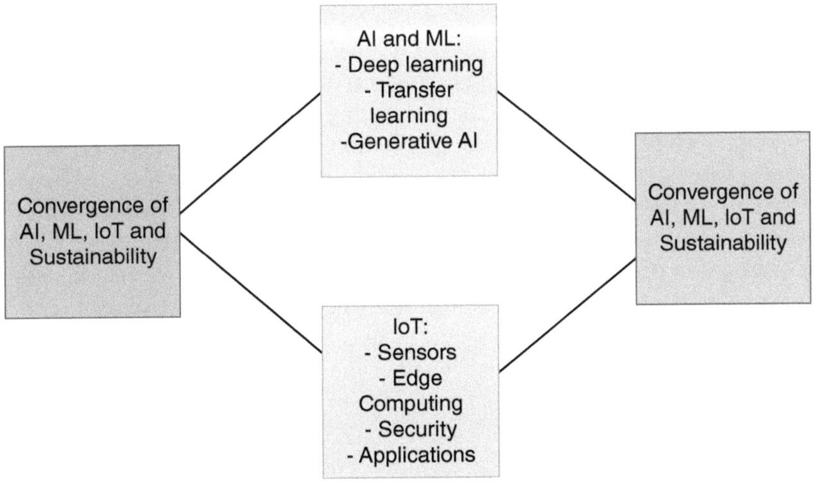

FIGURE 12.1 Convergence of ML, IoT, and sustainability.

Sustainability addresses environmental, social, and economic dimensions along with the United Nations' Sustainable Development Goals. Together, they form a dynamic ecosystem where data-driven insights and real-time monitoring lead to applications such as predictive maintenance, energy efficiency, smart agriculture, and supply chain transparency. This convergence fosters innovation and sustainability, making it a pivotal force in addressing complex global challenges [15].

12.6 FUNDAMENTALS OF MACHINE LEARNING IN AI-DRIVEN IoT SYSTEMS

ML holds significant prominence in the contemporary landscape, particularly within the domain of AI-driven IoT systems [16]. Since the inception of computers, there has been a longstanding curiosity about whether computers could autonomously acquire knowledge. The potential impact of this capability is profound, as it could enable computers to automatically enhance their performance through accumulated experience. Take, for instance, AI-powered personal assistant systems; they continuously learn user preferences to offer tailored services. Moreover, in the context of healthcare IoT, these systems can analyze medical records to provide personalized treatment recommendations for emerging diseases [17]. In essence, ML is a technique that integrates human-like learning abilities into information processing to augment future system performance. The primary emphasis in this field lies on self-directed learning methods, where algorithms autonomously acquire knowledge from past experiences. The essence of learning encompasses three critical elements: performance, tasks, and experience. The overarching goal is for learning to enhance system performance as it accumulates experience in handling specific tasks.

In ML, a learning model is constructed using a dataset, typically involving a two-stage process: training and testing. The division of the dataset into these two subsets, training and testing data, depends on the specific problem the ML model aims to address. This division is accomplished by selecting random samples from the overall dataset.

During the training phase, the model is trained to acquire knowledge from the training dataset. This entails exposing the model to the training data and letting it learn patterns, relationships, and associations within the data. The goal is for the model to understand and capture the underlying information in the training dataset, thereby improving its ability to make predictions or classifications.

Conversely, in the testing phase, the model's performance is assessed using a separate and previously unrevealed testing dataset. This dataset, distinct from the one used for training, serves as an objective evaluation ground. The model is presented with this unseen data to determine how well it generalizes its learned knowledge to make accurate predictions or classifications. The primary objective of this two-stage process is to assess the model's accuracy and efficiency. By testing it on new and unseen data, researchers can assess whether the model has effectively learned from the training data and can apply its knowledge to make reliable predictions or classifications on unfamiliar instances.

The journey begins with data collection, where relevant and representative data sources are identified and gathered [18]. This step is crucial as the quantity and

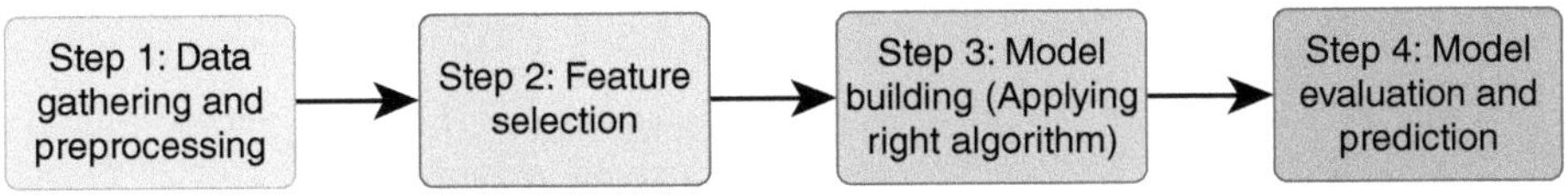

FIGURE 12.2 Steps of machine learning model.

quality of data significantly impact model performance. Advances in data collection methods, such as IoT sensors, enhance the availability of diverse data types. Diagramatically, this method is shown in Figure 12.2.

Raw data often requires preprocessing to clean, transform, and prepare it for modeling. Techniques like missing data imputation, feature scaling, and outlier detection ensure that data is suitable for analysis. Recent developments include automated data preprocessing tools that streamline this phase. Feature engineering encompasses the process of choosing, generating, or modifying pertinent features from the available data. Domain knowledge and creative feature engineering can significantly boost model performance. Automated feature engineering libraries have emerged to expedite this process [19].

Choosing an appropriate ML algorithm is essential. Recent advancements in reinforcement and learning DL have expanded the range of models available for various tasks. Model training is the process of teaching the algorithm to make predictions based on the data. It involves optimizing model parameters using optimization techniques like stochastic gradient descent and advanced training methods such as transfer learning.

Evaluating model performance ensures it meets the desired objectives. Metrics like accuracy, precision, recall, and F1-score are used to assess different aspects of model performance. Recent research has focused on interpretable evaluation metrics to enhance model explainability. Once a model is trained and evaluated, it can be deployed in real-world applications. Advances in containerization technologies like Docker [20] have simplified the deployment process, enabling seamless integration into various platforms.

12.7 TRADITIONAL APPROACH

ML algorithms can undergo training using various methods, each possessing its own distinct advantages and disadvantages. To comprehend these merits and drawbacks, it is essential to first understand the types of data employed in ML algorithms. There are two primary types of data utilized in training ML models: labeled data and unlabeled data [21]. Labeled data is structured in a machine-readable format, encompassing both input data in the form of features and output data presented as labels. In contrast, unlabeled data lacks output labels. Regardless of the data format employed in ML, algorithms can be generally classified into three major groups [18], as depicted in Figure 12.3.

- Supervised learning
- Unsupervised learning
- Reinforcement learning

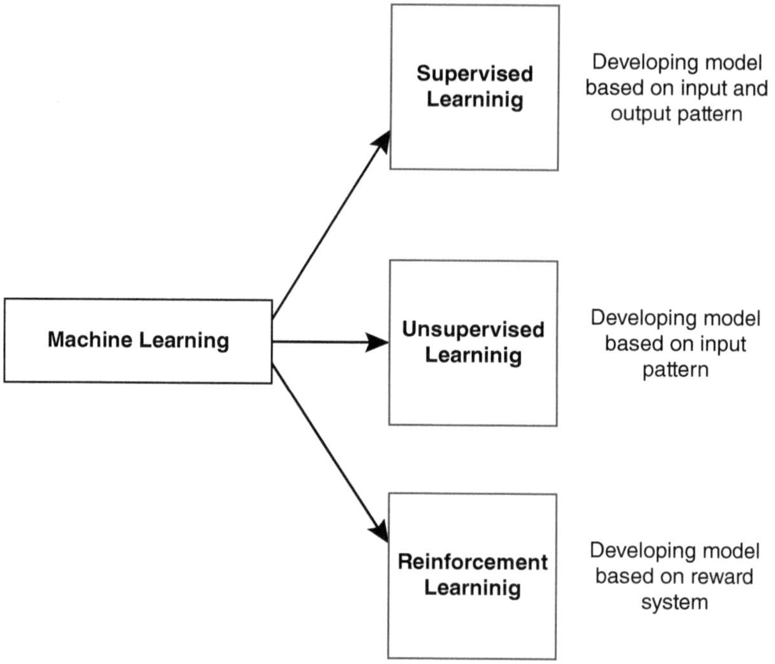

FIGURE 12.3 Types of machine learning.

Supervised learning plays a pivotal role in AI-driven IoT Systems by harnessing labeled data to enable intelligent decision-making and predictive capabilities. In the realm of IoT, where vast streams of sensor data flow continuously, supervised learning is a valuable tool for enhancing efficiency and reliability. Supervised learning algorithms include K-Nearest Neighbor (KNN), Support Vector Machine (SVM), Naive Bayes, Decision Tree, Logistic regression, Artificial Neural Network (ANN), etc.

One significant application of supervised learning in AI-driven IoT is predictive maintenance. By training models on historical data that includes both sensor readings and corresponding failure labels, IoT systems can predict equipment breakdowns before they occur. This active approach decreases maintenance costs and downtime.

In smart homes, supervised learning is employed for energy management. IoT devices learn from labeled data about user preferences and environmental conditions to improve heating, cooling, and lighting, resulting in energy savings [22]. Furthermore, in healthcare IoT, supervised learning aids in remote patient monitoring. By analyzing labeled patient data, predictive models can detect anomalies or deteriorating health conditions, enabling timely interventions and improving patient care [23].

Unsupervised learning plays a crucial role in AI-driven IoT systems by enabling them to uncover hidden patterns, relationships, and structures within vast and unstructured data streams from connected devices and sensors. With respect to IoT, where data can be highly heterogeneous and unlabeled, unsupervised learning techniques are instrumental in extracting valuable insights and enhancing system efficiency. Unsupervised learning in AI-driven IoT empowers systems to autonomously identify trends, group data, and uncover hidden insights, leading to more efficient resource allocation, improved decision-making, and enhanced operational effectiveness.

One prominent application of unsupervised learning in AI-driven IoT is data clustering [3]. By grouping similar sensor data patterns, IoT systems can identify commonalities, anomalies, or trends. For example, in a smart city, unsupervised learning can categorize traffic data to optimize traffic flow and reduce congestion. In industrial IoT, anomaly detection is paramount. Unsupervised learning models can detect irregularities in sensor data without the need for prior labeled data, contributing to predictive maintenance and ensuring equipment reliability.

Reinforcement learning (RL) is a dynamic and critical component of AI-driven IoT Systems, infusing them with adaptive and autonomous decision-making capabilities. In the context of IoT, where devices and sensors must respond to changing environments and make real-time decisions, RL is a powerful tool. RL empowers devices to learn from experiences, make adaptive decisions, and optimize operations in complex and dynamic environments. This technology paves the way for more efficient, responsive, and autonomous IoT systems, enhancing their capabilities across various domains [24].

One prominent application of RL in AI-driven IoT is autonomous navigation and control. IoT-enabled drones or autonomous vehicles can use RL to navigate complex environments, adapting their actions based on sensor inputs to maximize rewards, such as reaching a destination safely or avoiding obstacles [25]. Furthermore, energy management in smart buildings benefits from RL. IoT systems can learn to adjust heating, cooling, and lighting based on energy consumption patterns and user preferences, resulting in energy savings and reduced costs.

There are some drawbacks to traditional learning. For example, they require complex artificial feature engineering, are sensitive to data sets, and become less effective when the data set is sufficiently big. Despite these drawbacks, traditional ML is simpler to deploy than DL and RL and consumes less energy and computing capacity. Because of the distributed nature of edge computing, deployment of traditional ML algorithms on edge devices will be beneficial considering the resource and task requirements.

12.8 DEEP LEARNING (DL) APPROACH

DL architecture is the backbone of modern AI, enabling computers to mimic the complex information processing of the human brain. This architecture is a critical component in a wide range of applications, from image identification to natural language understanding and autonomous systems. Understanding its key components is essential for harnessing its power. The overall architecture design, including the number of layers, nodes, and connections [3], as shown in Figure 12.4. Deeper networks with more layers can capture more complex patterns but may require more data and computational resources. The architecture must be tailored to the specific problem and dataset.

At the core of DL architecture are neural networks, which are inspired by the structure and functioning of biological neurons. These networks consist of layers of

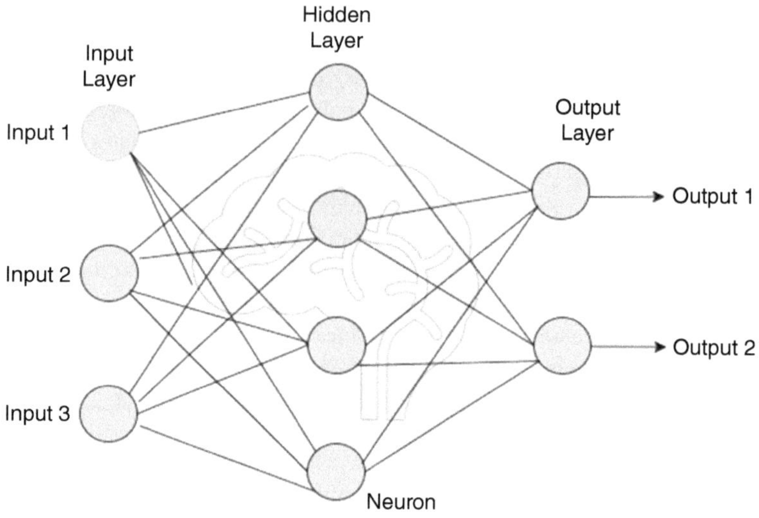

FIGURE 12.4 Deep learning.

interconnected nodes, or artificial neurons. Each neuron receives input signals, processes them, and produces an output signal. These layers include the input layer, hidden layers, and the output layer. The input layer receives raw data, and the hidden layers perform complex computations, while the output layer generates the final result or prediction.

The connections between neurons are governed by weights and biases. Weights determine the strength of connections, controlling how much influence one neuron's output has on another. Biases allow the network to model complex relationships by shifting activation functions. Activation functions introduce non-linearity into the architecture, making it capable of learning intricate patterns. Common activation functions include the Rectified Linear Unit (ReLU), sigmoid, and tanh. These functions decide whether a neuron should be activated based on the weighted sum of its inputs.

The training of DL models involves adjusting these weights and biases to minimize a loss function, also known as the cost or objective function. This function measures the error between the network's predictions and the actual target values. Optimization algorithms, such as stochastic gradient descent and Adam, iteratively update the weights and biases during training to minimize the loss function. They control the learning rate and the direction in which the parameters are adjusted.

To prevent overfitting, which occurs when the model performs well on training data but poorly on unseen data, DL architectures incorporate regularization techniques. These techniques, like dropout and L1/L2 regularization, reduce model complexity and encourage better generalization. Batch normalization is another vital component that normalizes inputs within a mini-batch during training, enhancing training stability and convergence speed.

DL architecture has revolutionized various fields, contributing to advancements in computer vision, natural language processing, and robotics. In computer vision, deep CNNs are adept at tasks like image classification and object detection. In natural language processing, RNNs and transformers are used for tasks such as text generation and sentiment analysis [26], [27]. In autonomous systems, deep RL is employed to make decisions in real-time, as seen in self-driving cars and robotics.

While DL has achieved remarkable success, it comes with challenges. Training deep models can be computationally intensive, requiring substantial hardware resources. Additionally, acquiring large, labeled datasets for training can be time-consuming and expensive. Model interpretability is another challenge, as deep networks can be considered "black boxes" that make it difficult to understand their decision-making processes.

12.9 EDGE INTELLIGENCE AND REAL-TIME DECISION-MAKING

Edge intelligence and real-time decision-making are two interconnected concepts that play a crucial role in modern computing and technology systems. These two concepts, when integrated effectively, can revolutionize the way we manage resources, reduce waste, and minimize environmental impact. In the context of sustainable IoT, they become essential components of a more efficient and environmentally responsible future.

Edge intelligence, also known as edge computing, addresses the need for local data processing and analytics in IoT systems. This approach reduces the reliance on centralized cloud servers, which can consume significant energy and network bandwidth. In sustainable IoT systems, edge intelligence plays a pivotal role by allowing devices at the edge of the network to process data locally as shown in Figure 12.5. For instance,

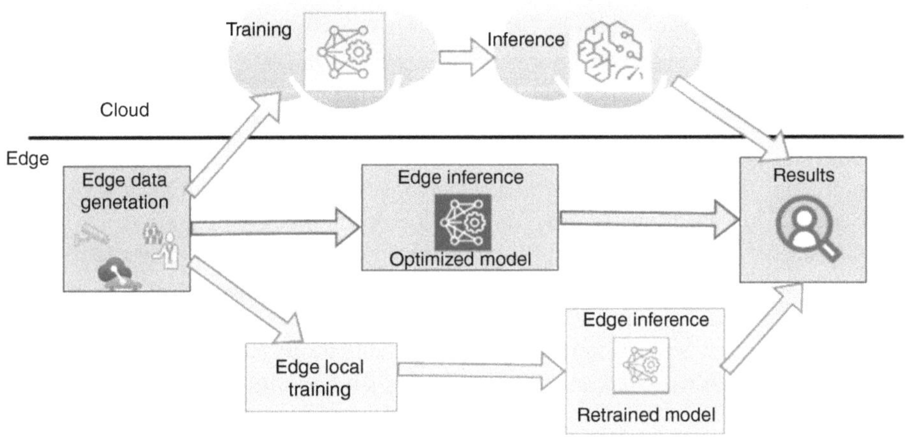

FIGURE 12.5 Flow of edge computing.

in smart buildings, edge devices equipped with sensors can monitor occupancy, temperature, and lighting conditions. Using edge intelligence, these devices can autonomously adjust heating, cooling, and lighting systems based on real-time data, optimizing energy usage and enhancing sustainability. By minimizing the need for continuous data transmission to the cloud, edge intelligence reduces energy consumption and greenhouse gas emissions associated with data processing [28].

In the realm of edge computing, AI models undergo initial training and validation in the cloud to address resource limitations on edge devices. Once these models pass the testing phase, they can be deployed on edge devices for real-time data predictions. Any updates resulting from these predictions are then transmitted back to cloud servers to maintain model currency. This approach eliminates the need for extensive data transfers between edge devices and the cloud, effectively tackling issues such as latency, scalability, and privacy often associated with traditional cloud computing.

Edge computing empowers localized computational capabilities, positioning them in close proximity to edge devices. For instance, an edge compute node could be strategically placed within a local network, near an IoT gateway, or adjacent to a cellular base station. This close proximity enhances the efficiency and responsiveness of AI processing, making it a valuable solution for scenarios where immediate data analysis and decision-making are crucial.

Real-time decision-making in sustainable IoT systems empowers devices to respond promptly to changing conditions. This capability is invaluable for resource management and conservation. For instance, in precision agriculture, AI algorithms process real-time data from soil sensors, weather stations, and crop health monitors at the edge [29]. When anomalies or adverse conditions are detected, these algorithms can trigger automated responses, such as adjusting irrigation levels or applying targeted fertilizers, thus reducing water and chemical usage.

In the context of renewable energy, real-time decision-making can optimize the operation of solar panels and wind turbines [30]. When AI systems analyze data from weather sensors and energy production sensors at the edge, they can adjust the orientation of solar panels or the pitch of wind turbine blades to maximize energy generation, ensuring that renewable energy sources are utilized efficiently.

The synergy between edge intelligence and real-time decision-making is where sustainable IoT truly shines. By processing data locally and making rapid decisions, IoT devices can achieve a level of efficiency and responsiveness that was previously unattainable. This synergy is particularly critical in scenarios with limited or unreliable network connectivity, such as remote agricultural fields or disaster-stricken areas.

Consider a smart grid system that integrates both edge intelligence and real-time decision-making. Local energy generation sources, like solar panels and wind turbines, continuously generate data at the edge. Edge devices process this data to assess energy supply and demand in real time. When fluctuations occur, AI algorithms make immediate decisions about energy distribution and storage, ensuring a stable and sustainable power grid.

Moreover, the combination of edge intelligence and real-time decision-making enhances system resilience. In the event of network disruptions or cyberattacks, edge devices can continue to operate autonomously, safeguarding critical infrastructure and services.

12.10 CASE STUDIES: SUSTAINABLE AI-DRIVEN IoT APPLICATIONS

Sustainable AI-driven IoT applications have the potential to address pressing environmental and resource challenges while improving efficiency and reducing waste. Here are two case studies that illustrate the real-world impact of these technologies.

12.10.1 Smart Agriculture for Precision Farming

Challenge: Agriculture is a resource-intensive industry that faces increasing pressure to produce more food with fewer resources while minimizing environmental impact.

Solution: Sustainable AI-driven IoT applications are transforming agriculture through precision farming. By combining edge intelligence and real-time decision-making, farmers can optimize resource usage, reduce waste, and improve crop yields.

Case Study: The "Hands-Free Hectare" project in the UK demonstrates the power of sustainable AI-driven IoT in agriculture. In this project, an entire hectare of land was farmed autonomously using AI and IoT technologies. Sensors and cameras installed on tractors and drones collected data on soil conditions, crop health, and weather. AI algorithms processed this data in real time, enabling the autonomous vehicles to make decisions about planting, fertilizing, and harvesting [31], [32].

Impact: The project resulted in a successful barley harvest without any human intervention. It showcased how sustainable AI-driven IoT can optimize crop management, reduce the need for chemical inputs, and improve resource efficiency. This technology has the potential to revolutionize agriculture by enabling more sustainable and efficient food production.

12.11 ENERGY MANAGEMENT IN SMART BUILDINGS

Challenge: Buildings account for a significant portion of global energy consumption. There is a pressing need to reduce energy usage, lower carbon emissions, and increase energy efficiency in buildings.

Solution: Sustainable AI-driven IoT applications are being used to create smart buildings that autonomously manage energy consumption and reduce environmental impact.

Case Study: The Edge, a smart building in Amsterdam, exemplifies the use of AI and IoT for sustainable energy management. It employs a network of sensors, including occupancy detectors, temperature sensors, and light sensors, distributed throughout the building. These sensors continuously collect data on occupancy patterns, temperature, and natural light levels. AI algorithms process this data in real time and make decisions to optimize heating, cooling, lighting, and ventilation systems [33], [34].

Impact: The Edge has achieved impressive results, reducing energy consumption by up to 70% compared to traditional buildings. It has also earned the highest sustainability rating from BREEAM (Building Research Establishment Environmental Assessment Method), showcasing how sustainable AI-driven IoT can drastically improve the energy efficiency and environmental performance of buildings.

These case studies demonstrate the transformative potential of sustainable AI-driven IoT applications in addressing complex environmental and resource challenges. Whether in agriculture or building management, the integration of edge intelligence, real-time decision-making, and IoT technologies enables more efficient resource utilization, reduced waste, and a significant reduction in environmental impact. These applications represent just a glimpse of the promising future where technology contributes to a more sustainable world.

12.12 SUSTAINABILITY METRICS AND PERFORMANCE EVALUATION

Sustainability metrics and performance evaluation are critical components in assessing and improving the environmental, social, and economic impact of sustainable AI-driven IoT (Internet of Things) systems. These systems have the potential to drive positive changes in various domains, but they must also be monitored and evaluated to ensure they meet sustainability goals. Figure 12.6 shows sustainability metrics and performance evaluation are applied in the context of sustainable AI-driven IoT systems [35].

12.12.1 Environmental Metrics

Energy Efficiency: IoT devices and AI algorithms can be evaluated for their energy efficiency. Metrics like energy consumption per data transaction or inference can provide insights into the environmental impact of AI-driven IoT systems. The goal is to minimize energy use while maintaining functionality.

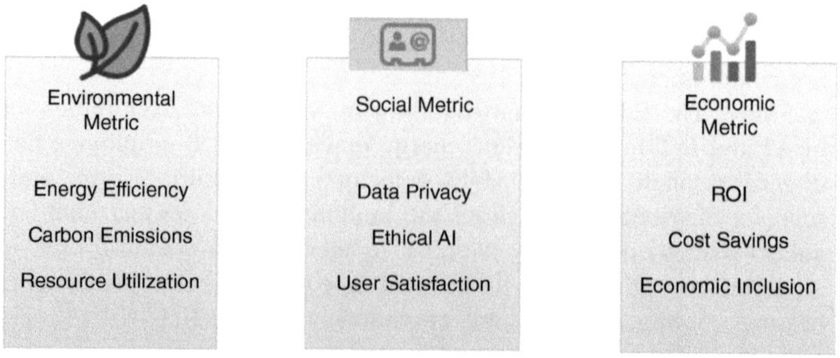

FIGURE 12.6 Sustainable metrics.

Carbon Emissions: Organizations can track and report the carbon emissions associated with AI-driven IoT operations, considering factors like data centers, device manufacturing, and network infrastructure. Reducing carbon emissions is essential for sustainable IoT.

Resource Utilization: Sustainability metrics can assess the efficient use of resources such as memory, storage, and processing power in AI-driven IoT devices. Maximizing resource utilization reduces waste and environmental impact.

12.12.2 Social Metrics

Data Privacy: Ensuring data privacy is a crucial social aspect of sustainable AI-driven IoT systems. Metrics can evaluate compliance with data protection regulations, the security of data storage and transmission, and the transparency of data collection practices.

Ethical AI: Performance evaluation should include ethical considerations, such as the fairness and bias of AI algorithms. Metrics like demographic parity and disparate impact can assess whether AI systems are treating different groups equitably.

User Satisfaction: User satisfaction metrics can gauge the social impact of IoT applications. High user satisfaction indicates that AI-driven IoT systems are meeting user needs effectively and responsibly.

12.12.3 Economic Metrics

Return on Investment (RoI): Organizations can assess the financial performance of their AI-driven IoT investments. RoI metrics help determine whether these systems are delivering economic value and supporting long-term sustainability goals.

Cost Savings: Sustainability metrics can evaluate cost savings achieved through energy efficiency improvements, predictive maintenance, and resource optimization facilitated by AI-driven IoT.

Economic Inclusion: Assessing economic inclusion metrics can help determine whether AI-driven IoT systems contribute to broader economic development and provide opportunities for underserved communities.

12.12.4 Performance Evaluation and Reporting

Data Collection: Organizations collect data from AI-driven IoT systems, including energy consumption, data transfer rates, user interactions, and system outputs.

Analysis: Sustainability analysts evaluate data to assess the system's impact on the environment, society, and economics. They may look for patterns, correlations, and anomalies in the data.

Benchmarking: Organizations compare their AI-driven IoT system's performance against industry benchmarks and sustainability standards to identify areas for improvement.

Reporting: Sustainability reports or disclosures are prepared to communicate findings to stakeholders, such as regulators, investors, customers, and the public. These reports may follow recognized frameworks like GRI or SASB.

Continuous Improvement: Insights gained from performance evaluation are used to refine AI-driven IoT systems continually. Organizations may adjust algorithms, hardware, or data management practices to align with sustainability goals.

12.12.5 Challenges and Future Directions

Challenges in sustainability metrics and performance evaluation for AI-driven IoT systems include the need for standardized metrics, the complexity of interrelated impacts, and the evolving nature of AI technologies. As these systems become more integral to various industries, stakeholders must collaborate to develop robust evaluation frameworks that consider the broader sustainability picture.

In conclusion, sustainability metrics and performance evaluation are essential for ensuring that AI-driven IoT systems contribute positively to environmental, social, and economic sustainability. These systems have the potential to drive efficiency, reduce waste, and improve resource utilization, but monitoring and evaluation are necessary to fulfill their sustainability promises and mitigate potential negative impacts.

12.13 CONCLUSION

In conclusion, this chapter has taken a deep dive into the transformative potential of ML algorithms within the context of sustainable AI-driven Internet of Things (IoT) systems. We have witnessed how this convergence of technologies is not just a harbinger of change but a powerful force for environmental stewardship and sustainability. ML algorithms serve as the intelligence behind sustainable AI-driven IoT systems, imbuing them with the capability to analyze vast datasets and make informed, real-time decisions. This profound synergy facilitates resource optimization, energy efficiency, and waste reduction across various domains, from smart cities to precision agriculture. The generation of comprehensive sustainability metrics is a game-changer, allowing organizations to quantitatively assess their environmental impact. From calculating carbon footprints to evaluating resource utilization efficiency, these metrics provide a roadmap for data-driven decision-making, promoting accountability and progress toward sustainability goals.

Nonetheless, the adoption of these technologies is not without its challenges. Ethical considerations, such as data privacy, fairness, and transparency, demand our unwavering attention. Striking the right balance between technological advancement and ethical responsibility is paramount. As we move forward, the promise of sustainable AI-driven IoT systems, guided by ML algorithms, shines brightly. They are not just tools for change but the architects of a more sustainable and interconnected future. With innovation, collaboration, and a commitment to ethical principles, we embark on a journey towards environmental stewardship, where the intelligence of AI-driven IoT systems paves the way for a brighter, more sustainable world.

REFERENCES

[1] L. Atzori, A. Iera, and G. Morabito, "The Internet of Things: A survey," *Comput. Networks*, vol. 54, no. 15, 2010.
[2] J. Gubbi, R. Buyya, S. Marusic, and M. Palaniswami, "Internet of Things (IoT): A vision, architectural elements, and future directions," *Futur. Gener. Comput. Syst.*, vol. 29, no. 7, 2013.
[3] Y. Lecun, Y. Bengio, and G. Hinton, "Deep learning," *Nature*, vol. 521, no. 7553, May 2015.
[4] "The Global Movement for Our Children's Future- World Top 20 Project." [Online]. https://worldtop20.org/global-movement/?gad=1 Accessed: 15 Sep. 2023.
[5] S. L. Ullo and G. R. Sinha, "Advances in smart environment monitoring systems using IoT and sensors," *Sensors (Switzerland)*, vol. 20, no. 11, 2020.
[6] Z. Xiang et al., "Energy-effective artificial internet-of-things application deployment in edge-cloud systems," *Peer-to-Peer Netw. Appl.*, vol. 15, no. 2, 2022.
[7] M. Zekić-Sušac, S. Mitrović, and A. Has, "Machine learning based system for managing energy efficiency of public sector as an approach towards smart cities," *Int. J. Inf. Manage.*, vol. 58, 2021.
[8] M. Sisode and M. Devare, "A review on machine learning techniques for predictive maintenance in Industry 4.0." In *Proceedings of the International Conference on Applications of Machine Intelligence and Data Analytics (ICAMIDA 2022)*, vol. 1, 2023.
[9] T. Zonta, C. A. da Costa, R. da Rosa Righi, M. J. de Lima, E. S. da Trindade, and G. P. Li, "Predictive maintenance in the Industry 4.0: A systematic literature review," *Comput. Ind. Eng.*, vol. 150, December 2020.
[10] V. Saiz-Rubio and F. Rovira-Más, "From smart farming towards agriculture 5.0: A review on crop data management," *Agronomy*, vol. 10, no. 2, 2020.
[11] G. George and S. J. D. Schillebeeckx, "Digital transformation, sustainability, and purpose in the multinational enterprise," *J. World Bus.*, vol. 57, no. 3, 2022.
[12] A. Ghaithan, M. Khan, A. Mohammed, and L. Hadidi, "Impact of industry 4.0 and lean manufacturing on the sustainability performance of plastic and petrochemical organizations in Saudi Arabia," *Sustain.*, vol. 13, no. 20, 2021.
[13] Y. K. Dwivedi et al., "Climate change and COP26: Are digital technologies and information management part of the problem or the solution? An editorial reflection and call to action," *Int. J. Inf. Manage.*, vol. 63, November 2021.
[14] S. E. Bibri, A. Alexandre, A. Sharifi, and J. Krogstie, "Environmentally sustainable smart cities and their converging AI, IoT, and big data technologies and solutions: An integrated approach to an extensive literature review," *Energy Informat.*, vol. 6, no. 1, 2023.
[15] S. Singh, P. K. Sharma, B. Yoon, M. Shojafar, G. H. Cho, and I. H. Ra, "Convergence of blockchain and artificial intelligence in IoT network for the sustainable smart city," *Sustain. Cities Soc.*, vol. 63, December 2020.
[16] M. W. B. Galiveeti Poornima, Sandeep Prabhu M, Mirzanur Rahman, Naresh Vurukonda, Adiseshaiah Sade, "View of Machine Learning For Iot Health Care Applications," *J. Posit. Sch. Psychol.*, vol. 6, no. 8, 2022.
[17] M. Soori, B. Arezoo, and R. Dastres, "Artificial intelligence, machine learning and deep learning in advanced robotics, a review," *Cogn. Robot.*, vol. 3, January 01, 2023.
[18] I. H. Sarker, "Machine learning: Algorithms, real-world applications and research directions," *SN Comput. Sci.*, vol. 2, no. 3, May 2021.
[19] M. M. Taye, "Understanding of machine learning with deep learning: Architectures, workflow, applications and future directions," *Comput. Secur.*, vol. 12, no. 5, April 25, 2023.

[20] J. Matelsky, G. Kiar, E. Johnson, C. Rivera, M. Toma, and W. Gray-Roncal, "Container-based clinical solutions for portable and reproducible image analysis," *J. Digit. Imaging*, vol. 31, no. 3, June 2018.
[21] S. Badillo et al., "An introduction to machine learning," *Clin. Pharmacol. Ther.*, vol. 107, no. 4, April 2020.
[22] A. A. Saleem, M. M. Hassan, and I. A. Ali, "Smart homes powered by machine learning: A review." In *Proceedings of the 2nd 2022 International Conference on Computer Science and Software Engineering, CSASE 2022*, pp. 355–361, 2022.
[23] S. S. Preethi Palanisamy, Amudhavalli Padmanabhan, Asokan Ramasamy, and Sakthivel Subramaniam, "Remote patient activity monitoring system by integrating IoT," *Sensors*, vol. 23, no. 5869, 2023.
[24] Y. Xu et al., "Artificial intelligence: A powerful paradigm for scientific research," *The Innovation*, vol. 2, no. 4, November 2021.
[25] F. Sana, N. L. Azad, and K. Raahemifar, "Autonomous vehicle decision-making and control in complex and unconventional scenarios—A review," *Machines*, vol. 11, no. 7, June 2023.
[26] B. S. Ainapure, M. Boopathi, C. Sekhar Kolli, and C. Jackulin, "Deep ensemble model for spam classification in Twitter via sentiment extraction: Bio-inspiration-based classification model," *Int. J. Image Graph.*, vol. 23, no. 4, July 2022. https://doi.org/10.1142/S0219467823500341
[27] B. S. Ainapure et al., "Sentiment analysis of COVID-19 Tweets using deep learning and lexicon-based approaches," *Sustainability*, vol. 15, no. 3, p. 2573, January 2023.
[28] S. Iftikhar et al., "AI-based fog and edge computing: A systematic review, taxonomy and future directions," *Internet of Things*, vol. 21, 2022.
[29] M. J. O'Grady, D. Langton, and G. M. P. O'Hare, "Edge computing: A tractable model for smart agriculture?," *Artif. Intell. Agric.*, vol. 3, September 2019.
[30] L. Abualigah et al., "Wind, solar, and photovoltaic renewable energy systems with and without energy storage optimization: A survey of advanced machine learning and deep learning techniques," *Energies*, vol. 15, no. 2, January 2022.
[31] G. Fastellini and C. Schillaci, "Precision farming and IoT case studies across the world," *Agric. Internet Things Decis. Support Precis. Smart Farming*, vol. 2020, January 2020.
[32] J. E. Relf-Eckstein, A. T. Ballantyne, and P. W. B. Phillips, "Farming reimagined: A case study of autonomous farm equipment and creating an innovation opportunity space for broadacre smart farming," *NJAS Wageningen J. Life Sci.*, vol. 90–91, December 2019.
[33] U. Mir, U. Abbasi, T. Mir, S. Kanwal, and S. Alamri, "Energy management in smart buildings and homes: Current approaches, a hypothetical solution, and open issues and challenges," *IEEE Access*, vol. 9, 2021.
[34] "Case study: Artificial intelligence for building energy management systems," p. 1, 2019. https://www.iea.org/articles/case-study-artificial-intelligence-for-building-energy-management-systems
[35] C. Farchi, B. Touzi, F. Farchi, and A. Mousrij, "Sustainable performance assessment: A systematic literature review," *J. Sustain. Dev. Transp. Logist.*, vol. 6, no. 2, 2021.

13 Elevating Education

Exploring Chatbots and Their Significance in the Academic Realm

Fatima Amer Jid Almahri, Zameer Gulzar, Motea Alsamawi, Muaadh Abdo Al Sabri, Ebrahim Mohammed Senan and Mowaffak Othman Ahmed Albaraq

13.1 INTRODUCTION

The integration of technology into education has been a steady progress. From the advent of electronic learning in the 1960s to the current proliferation of e-learning platforms, educators have been constantly looking for ways to effectively use technology in teaching and learning. A chatbot is referred to as a "chatterbot" [1], bots [2], an artificial conversational entity [1], or an interactive conversation agent [3]. A chatbot is a computer program that conducts a conversation with a user in a natural language, similar to human communication [4] using textual or auditory methods or both. However, a study by [5] states that the interaction between computers and humans can be achieved using text, speech, gesture, haptics, and other modes of communication. Chatbots can reply to users' questions, suggest topics to discuss, and provide comments, to name a few of their abilities. Chatbots are used in different applications, including but not limited to finances, customer services, entertainment, and education, to name a few [1].

According to [2], chatbots are algorithms designed to understand and reply to user inputs during the conversation. This is achieved as easily as having a rule-based system that follows a script or as complex as chatbots that learn and adapt from user interactions. To achieve this, Natural Language Processing (NLP) is used. NLP is a branch of AI that focuses on the interaction between computers and humans using natural language [2]. Chatbots are widely used in many sectors to solve a variety of problems: as personal assistants on mobile phones such as Siri, as health intervention tools and as technical support over the telephone [6], [7], and as private tutors in the educational domain [7]. The increasing availability of e-learning platforms and online educational materials has paved the way for the integration of chatbots into the learning process. Initially, their role was limited to handling simple queries and assisting with administrative tasks such as registration or scheduling.

DOI: 10.1201/9781032703718-18

Artificial Intelligence (AI) is a broad field of computer sciences that aims to create machines or systems that imitate human intelligence and are able to perform tasks that would be done only using human intelligence. Examples of these tasks include image recognition, natural language understanding, problem-solving, and decision-making. To achieve this, various algorithms and software have been created and adopted that respond to various situations [8]. Arthur Samuel constructs the concept of Machine Learning [9]. ML is defined as

> a process of building computer systems that automatically improve with experience, and implement a learning process. Machine Learning can still be defined as learning the theory automatically from the data, through a process of inference, model fitting, or learning from examples
>
> ([10], P.2)

ML is an important subfield of AI. ML focuses mainly on creating algorithms that allow machines to learn from data and gradually improve their accuracy and implement what they learn in different scenarios. ML can make predictions, recognize patterns, and learn through experiences without being explicitly programmed. ML algorithms are employed in serval applications, including image and speech recognition, and recommendation systems [11].

According to [8], AI has various techniques for imitating human intelligence such as ML. ML is a crucial technique of AI that is used to perform tasks that require learning from data. ML creates models that allow machines to do tasks that can be done only by humans such as analyzing data, predicting price or performance, or categorizing images. AI system uses ML to process data, extract information, learn from that, and use that knowledge to improve their performance. This study aims to examine the transformative role of persona-based chatbots in enhancing the educational landscape by offering personalized academic support, fostering interactive learning environments, and promoting self-directed study through a design science research (DSR) methodology. The rest of the chapter is structured as follows. Section 13.2 provides an overview of AI, ML, and NLP, and the relationship between these concepts. Section 13.3 covers chatbot interaction; it presents how AI and NLP run effectively to provide answers on contextual understanding, adjust learning paths based on their progress and performance, and provide real-time feedback, to name a few. Section 13.4 covers generic and customized chatbots in education. Also, it covers the challenges faced by generic chatbots. Section 13.5 covers chatbot design and development including the factors that influence chatbot design. Also, it covers the chatbot design techniques and approaches. Section 13.6 covers the DSR methodology used in this study to design, build, and evaluate the persona3D model, and it covers the technologies used in developing the chatbots. Section 13.7 summarizes the chapter.

13.2 LITERATURE REVIEW

Existing literature review studies summarized the current efforts in applying chatbots in educational settings. A study by [12] presents the advantages of using chatbots in educational settings for instructors and learners and how its benefits outweigh the limitations. Chatbots are powerful learning tools to build effective learning experiences. While a study by [13] presents the challenges of implementing chatbots in educational settings along with their benefits, a study by [7] focuses on how chatbots are used to improve learning outcomes and [14] discusses how chatbots are used to enhance students' learning experience. A study by [15] identifies the learning outcome that can be obtained from each type of chatbot.

Incorporating technology into education leads to a remarkable transformation. It brought many benefits, including personalized learning experiences, immediate feedback and assessment, administrative efficiency, and time saving. Modern pedagogy asserts the significance of personalized learning. It is known that students learn differently based on their style, prior knowledge, and pace. Chatbots provide customized learning pathways to each type of user. This can be achieved by analyzing performance metrics, past interactions, and even preferred study time. As a result, it increases student engagement and retention. Furthermore, chatbots that support personalized learning provide an optimal solution for students who are left behind in normal traditional settings. A study by [16] highlights the impact of educational chatbots on project-based learning; it asserts that these chatbots facilitate personalized learning experiences. They provide the target support and needs to each individual and enhance learning outcomes in a team-based design course.

Modern pedagogy asserts the significance of personalized learning. It is known that students learn differently based on their style, prior knowledge, and pace. Chatbots can be designed to support personalized learning by providing customized learning pathways to each type of user. This can be achieved by analyzing performance metrics, past interactions, and even preferred study time, thus increasing student's engagement and retention. Chatbots that provide personalized learning are an optimal solution for students who are left behind in normal traditional settings [3].

Feedback plays a significant role in the learning process. In the normal traditional setting, there might be difficulty in providing feedback to all students, especially in a large class setting. However, using chatbots in educational settings can provide immediate feedback to students on any type of assessment including quizzes, assignments, or any general queries. Students should get feedback about what is correct and what went wrong. Immediate feedback will enhance students' confidence and their understanding of the topics and thus improve students' satisfaction and learning outcomes. According to [17], AI chatbots provide immediate support by answering students' queries, further explanation of the topics, and extra resources so students can understand the concept [17].

In addition to the educational benefits of using chatbots in educational settings, chatbots also simplify administrative tasks. Chatbots can handle various administrative tasks efficiently, such as providing reminders about assignments, project deadlines, or midterm or final exam dates. Also, chatbots are considered a good tool for answering FAQs about the enrollment process, course content, etc. Thus, students will get accurate information on time, instructors will get relief from the burden of administrative tasks as they can save their time to focus more on actual teaching and enhance the overall teaching experience [18]. The integration of technology into education leads to a significant improvement in the learning process because of the continuous evolvement and development of fields such as AI and NLP.

The integration of technology into education has led to a significant improvement in the learning process. However, integration of chatbots into education is not only because chatbot technology is a new one that should be implemented but because of the continuous evolvement and development of fields such as AI and NLP.

Artificial Intelligence (AI) is the ability of computers to imitate human intelligence and do tasks that are usually done by humans. AI is a branch of computer sciences that focuses on creating systems/applications that usually require human intelligence. These tasks include decision-making, understanding language, pattern recognition, and problem-solving [19]. AI applications have grown dramatically during the past few decades, including sectors such as finance, healthcare, and education.

Natural Language Processing (NLP) is a branch of computer science and more specifically the branch of AI. It is concerned with giving computers the ability to understand the natural language whether it is text or spoken word in the same way as humans do [20]. However, according to [21], NLP is a branch of AI, linguistics, and computer science that focuses on the interaction between humans and computers using a natural language. Natural language refers to any human language that he/she earns from the environment and uses to communicate with other humans. Humans use language to express their emotions and knowledge or even reply to humans' queries.

13.3 CHATBOTS INTERACTION

AI and NLP enable chatbots to interact with students effectively by providing answers based on contextual understanding, adjusting learning paths based on their progress and performance, and providing real-time feedback, to name a few.

Contextual Understanding: Chatbots equipped with AI and NLP do not work only on predefined inputs. They go beyond that; they can understand the intent and meaning behind each student's interaction. So, whenever a student asks a question or has a conversation, it is very important for the chatbots to understand the context of that conversation or question, prior questions, and the topic discussed. Thus, chatbots are capable of providing more relevant answers or replies, which are also grammatically correct [22].

Adaptive Learning Path: Educational chatbots can adjust the learning path of a student who is struggling to understand a particular topic and introduce extra supporting materials or exercises to support their understanding of the topic. This can be achieved by analyzing student performance, checking their progress, and adjusting the delivery path accordingly [23].

Real-Time Feedback: As discussed above, immediate feedback improves students' satisfaction and enhances learning outcomes. NLP allows chatbots to process student input immediately. For example, in assessments such as quizzes, NLP allows chatbots to provide explanations and corrections of incorrect answers. Thus, the learning process becomes interactive and interesting.

Personalization: AI algorithms are capable of drawing a pattern and making predictions based on the obtained data. Chatbots are built upon AI and NLP; this allows chatbots to provide personalized learning to students based on their interactions with chatbots over time. Also, chatbots can provide some suggestions based on students' progress, ensuring that the learning process is engaging and relevant. A study by [24] explores the application of NLP to develop a personalized learning assistant tailored for school education.

Multimodal Interaction: This is based on the foundation of NLP. It is achieved by combining different modes of interactions, including text, speech, gesture, facial expression, and images, because humans do not communicate with each other using a single mode of interaction. Therefore, systems that rely on multimodal try to understand human queries that use a combination of this mode of interactions and provide the most suitable response [25]. As a result, the interactions between computers and humans become natural and flexible regardless of communication styles and preferences. Also, it becomes more convenient for students with disabilities and different learning preferences.

One of the top challenges that instructors face in the traditional and digital classroom is guaranteeing student engagement. Interactivity in learning environment improves students' retention and students' interest in the subject. Chatbots are one of the tools that promise to add interactivity to the learning environment and enhance students' engagement. Chatbots create a lively and interactive learning environment using different techniques as follows:

Instant Response Mechanism: Using chatbots, students are getting instantaneous responses to their queries. In contrast to forum and email-based query systems, where students have to wait for answers to their queries [7].

Personalized Interactions: Educational chatbots provide students with responses differently for each user type based on their learning history. This is similar to having a private one-to-one tutor who communicates with students, understands their level, and suggests the right materials for each one [23].

Gamification of Learning: In the educational context, this refers to including elements of game design and game mechanism in a non-game context such as education. The objective is to make the learning process more effective, motivating, and engaging. For example, gamification elements include a scoring system, challenges, and quizzes. A study by [26] incorporating gamification education setting influences student learning and behavior and enhances students' engagement.

Multimodal Learning Experiences: Chatbots enriched with AI and NLP can scientifically enhance the multimodal learning experience. Chatbots can provide different modes of interaction via text, speech, gestures, facial expressions, and images [27].

Providing Immediate Feedback: In the traditional model of learning, feedback is delayed due to human constraints; however, with chatbots that are built based on the NLP and AI techniques, timely and constructive feedback is given to students. This bolsters students' confidence, understanding, and their academic performance. Chatbots play a role in offering instant feedback on assignments and assessments, including automated evaluation, dynamic, and consistent feedback.

Instant Feedback: Automated Evaluation: Can be achieved using predefined algorithms, AI, and NLP integration into chatbots. A variety of assignment types starting from multiple-choice questions to more challenging ones will be included as assessment. Students' responses will be assessed against predefined criteria and appropriate feedback will be given to each student [7].

Dynamic Feedback: In contrast with a static assessment tool that provides general feedback, chatbots can provide feedback based on students' progress and performance. For example, chatbots can provide further explanations or additional resources related to the difficult part that students struggle [23].

Consistency: Chatbots ensure consistent feedback to all students, which creates a fair assessment environment, in contrast to human evaluator, who can affected by different factors such as subjectivity and fatigue [28].

Chatbots that provide timely feedback on students' assessments and assignments provide many benefits to student progress as follows:

Enhanced Retention: Providing instant feedback to students about their understanding of the topic will help students grasp the right information and correct misconceptions, thus leading to better understanding and retention [29].

Increase Motivation: Getting instant feedback about their understanding or performance whether it is constructive or positive will motivate students to stay engaged in their studies [30].

Iterative Learning: Immediate learning becomes iterative learning where students learn, assess their understanding, get feedback, reassess it, and thus lead to improvement in real time [31].

Personal Growth: With timely feedback, students are able to control their learning journey. Students will be able to develop their self-learning skills by regularly identifying their strengths and weaknesses in the learning process. Also, students will develop self-awareness and foster a growth mindset [32].

13.4 GENERIC AND CUSTOMIZED CHATBOTS IN EDUCATION

The deployment of chatbots in various domains has been used widely with tremendous growth. Even though chatbots are used in education to support the learning process from different perspectives, it is essentially to evaluate the effectiveness of using these generic chatbots in education that does not consider individual or group needs. These generic chatbots will lead to a series of challenges.

Using a generic chatbot approach in education leads to several limitations including but not limited to the following:

(1) **Lack of context awareness**: Generic chatbots lack context-specific awareness. To be most beneficial, they must understand the specific requirements of each student, their academic context, and their curriculum. Otherwise, the generated responses from chatbots will be irrelevant or unhelpful [7].
(2) **No personalization**: Generic chatbots are not capable of understanding individual unique learning paths, challenges, and preferences, which make the benefits of having generic chatbots limited [33].
(3) **Data Privacy concerns**: Generic chatbots probably are not designed with specific data protection requirements of educational institutions. This means sensitive information and students' data might be vulnerable to data breaches or not compatible with educational institution regulations [34].
(4) **Integration issues**: Generic chatbots may have compatibility issues in integration with educational institution software. According to [35], while the use of chatbots is increasing as educational tools, there are serious integration challenges including compatibility with existing educational institutions' platforms.

Customized chatbots in educational settings are needed for several reasons:

(1) **Tailored Content delivery**: Customized chatbots are relevant and beneficial for students' needs and align with certain curricula [36].
(2) **Adaptive Learning Support**: Customized chatbots support adaptive learning techniques; they provide responses to students based on their needs and individual student performance [37].
(3) **Improved engagement**: Customized chatbots provide the learners with the exact responses he/she is aiming for as the chatbots understand the needs of the educational context and each learner. Thus, interaction becomes more engaging and meaningful, and this enhances students' involvement and motivations [16].
(4) **Enhanced Data Security**: Customized chatbots designed for educational settings are designed with specific privacy and data protections for these educational institutions to guarantee a safer environment for student data [38].

13.5 CHATBOT DESIGN AND DEVELOPMENT

Regards designing chatbots, there is no standard approach in this regard and no consensus toward the chatbot designing process. This stands as an obstacle to chatbots' improvement, and it is solved by constructing a complete knowledge base [39]. The factors affecting chatbot design and a comparison with nine selected papers are shown in Table 13.1. However, the table misses some essential techniques, such as email services and personas. Main chatbot design techniques and approaches are highlighted by [40] as follows:

AIML: AIML does not require high skills in a specific programming language.
Pattern matching: Common techniques used by many chatbots. It is used specifically in a question-answer system that uses matching types such as natural language inquiries, simple statements, and semantic meaning of inquire.

TABLE 13.1
A Summary of Selected Factors Influencing Chatbot Design Adapted From [4]

	Factors Influencing Chatbot Design										
Study	Voice	Text	Creating New Chatbots	Using Available Chatbots	AIML Usage	Persona	Email Services	SQL Usage (Relational Database)	Matching Technique	Corpus (Knowledgebase)	Application
Pereira and Coheur [44]	√	√		√	√	—	—		Edger chatbot matching technique	Edgar chatbot	Chatbot design
(Rosmalen et al. [45]		√		√	√	—	—	√	QA matching form	AIML	Medical education
(Lokman and Zain [46]		√	√		√	—	—	√	QA matching form	VP bot	Health assistance
(Lokman and Zain [47]		√		√		—	—	√	Prerequisite Matching	ViDi chatbot	Health assistance
(Lokman and Zain [48]		√		√		—	—	√	One-Match All-Match Category (OMAMC)	ViDi chatbot	Health assistance
Mikic et al. [49]		√		√	√	—	—		AIML category pattern matching	AIML	Educational systems
Bhargava and Nikhil [50]	√		√		√	—	—		AIML category pattern matching	AIML	E-learning
Vrajitoru [51]		√	√			—	—		Genetic Algorithm (GA)	Manual pattern and data were chosen	Any
Vrajitoru and Ratkiewicz [52]		√	√			—	—		Genetic Algorithm (GA)	Manual pattern and data were chosen	Any

Parsing: This is a technique that uses computer language or natural language to analyze text.

Chatscript: This is used when there are no matches in the AIML technique. It focuses on providing the ultimate syntax for generating a reasonable default answer.

Relational databases (SQL): This technique is used in chatbot design to allow chatbots to remember previous conversations [41].

Markov Chain: This technique produces applicable and potential replies and, thus, is more accurate. It shows the probability of occurrence for every word or letter in a text [42].

Language tricks: These are phrases, sentences, or paragraphs available in chatbots to add variety and convincing knowledge bases. There are several types of language tricks, such as non sequitur, typing errors, canned responses, and models of personal history.

Ontologies: This is defined as "a set of concepts that are interconnected relationally and hierarchically" [43, P.74]. It is called semantic networks. Ontologies are used in chatbots to compute relationships between concepts, such as synonyms. The interconnection between concepts can be represented in a graph. It enables the computer to search using a particular rule of reasoning.

13.6 DESIGN SCIENCE RESEARCH (DSR) METHODOLOGY

DSR is a methodology in the field of Information Systems research that uses novel and innovative artifacts to solve organizational and societal problems. Design science is a field within Information Systems (IS) research that builds and evaluates IT artifacts to offer a solution to an organizational issue [42]. The building focuses on creating an artifact to do certain tasks and answering the query "does it work?," whereas evaluating an artifact specifies whether or not it performs any progress, answering the query "how well does it work?" A study by [43] proposed a research framework that consists of two dimensions: research activities and research outputs. The former consists of four elements: build, evaluate, theories, and justify. While the latter contains four product categories as follows (Table 13.2).

- Constructs or concepts used to explain the problems in a certain domain and the proposed solutions.

TABLE 13.2
A Research Framework [43]

	Build	Evaluate	Theorize	Justify
Constructs				
Model				
Method				
Instantiation				

- Models are a set of statements that explain the relationship between constructs.
- Methods are the procedures used to do a certain task based on models and constructs.

The DSR phases proceeded as follows:

Design: "design is essentially a research process to discover an effective solution to a problem" [42, P.88]. This research designed a solution to support the aim of the study. The research design covers two phases. In the first iteration, persona model is designed based on the literature review and based on Machine Learning Algorithms on students' data. In the second iteration, a range of chatbots was designed for different student groups.

13.6.1 Design Persona3D model

The persona concept was proposed by Cooper [53] as a design process methodology. Personas are imaginary archetypes of actual users [54]. Persona templates have been covered in many studies, and various types of personas exist in the literature such as student personas [55] and company personas. Persona template elements differ based on the reasons behind creating them. Persona templates usually include demographic data, such as name, age, gender, occupation, language, place of residence, and picture. Furthermore, they can include users' interests, activities, preferences, and attitudes [56]. Moreover, they can cover skills and experience, such as educational level and IT experience. The initial student Persona3D template proposed in this study consists of the following categories as shown in Figure 13.1: demographic data motivations and interests and skills and experience.

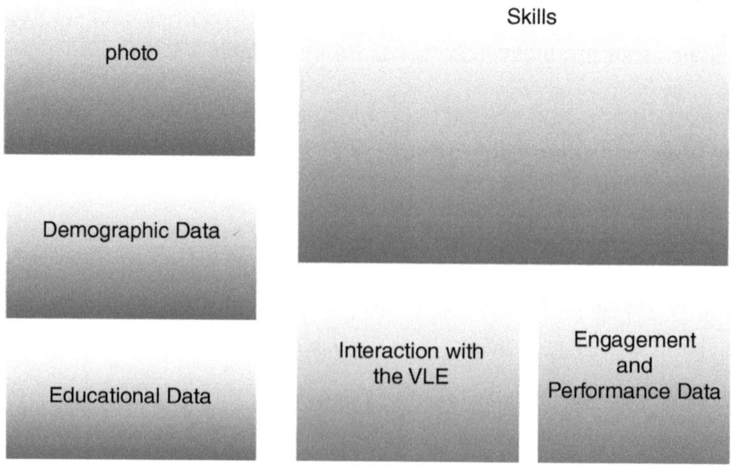

FIGURE 13.1 Persona3D template for university students. (Adapted from Ref. [57])

13.6.2 Build Persona 3D model

After identifying the Persona3D template, the next step was identifying a typical user and building the Persona3D model for each group to create a Persona3D model that represented a real person. Therefore, for each cluster, the average score is calculated. This iteration identified the groups and the attributes that distinguished them. The average score for each distinct criterion is computed, and a record for the student who had the score nearest to the average score of the cluster is chosen. The user was a typical user, and their data used to present the persona [58]. The student Persona3D in Figure 13.2 represents a persona3D model for top students, a high virtual and physical engagement and performance student persona. Physical engagement is represented by attendance, while virtual engagement is represented by interactions with VLEs [57].

This section evaluates the completeness of the Persona3D model. First, the completeness of the model is evaluated by comparing the elements of the Persona3D template extracted from a list of high-quality papers and comparing if the proposed Persona3D template contains these elements and others, as shown in Table 13.3.

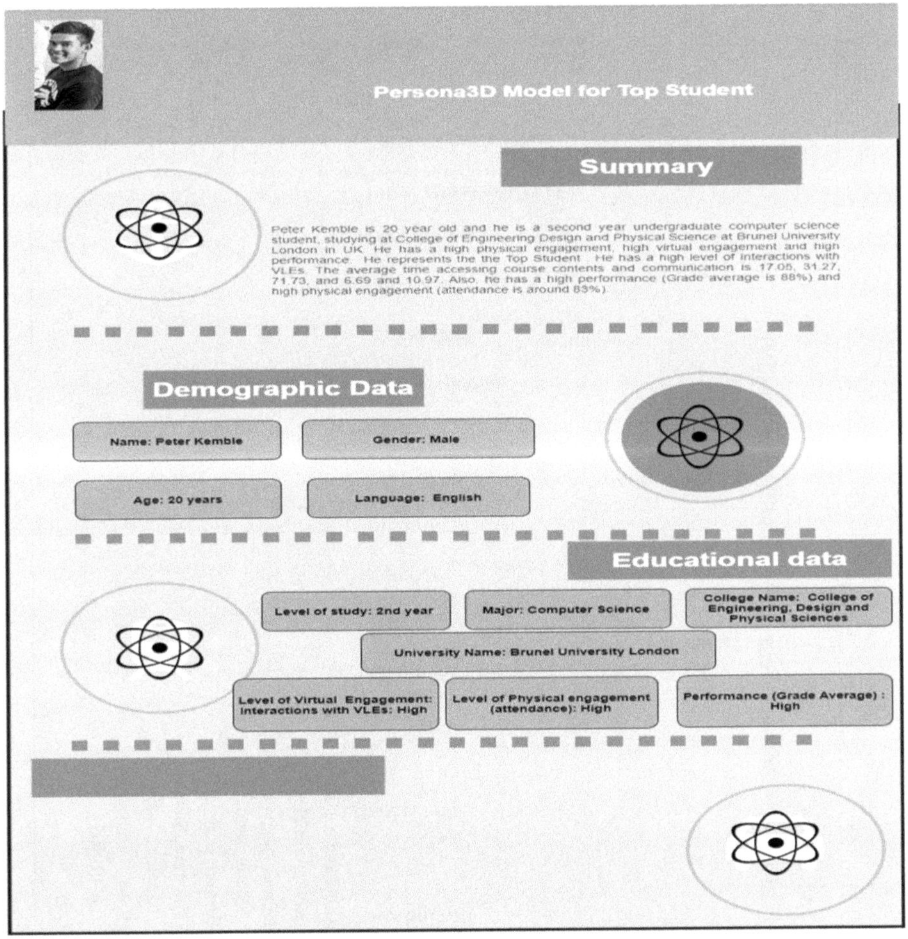

FIGURE 13.2 An example of a University Student Persona3D Model [59].

TABLE 13.3
Evaluating Completeness of Persona3D Model [59]

Authors	Name	Age	Gender	picture	Year of Study[i]	Major	College Name	University[ii]	Location[iii]	Persona Type	Interactions with VLEs	Physical engagement	Preference[iv]	Grade	Studying	Moving	Summary[v]	Technology used (or proposed)	Personality	General use of the computer and internet	Profession /job	Eating	Motivations for taking courses.	Residential status /relationship status
Shiga and Nishiuchi [60]	√	√	√	√	√									√										
Quintana et al. [61]	√	√	√	√													√	√					√	
Kimita, Nemoto and Shimomura, [62]	√	√	√	√	√	√		√			√													√
Ferreira et al. [63]	√	√	√	√	√															√			√	√
(Valentim, Silva and Conte, 2017) [64]	√	√		√					√												√			
(Polst, S. and Stüpfert, 2019) [65]	√	√		√							√						√		√		√			√
[56]	√	√	√	√	√	√	√	√	√	√	√	√	√	√	√	√	√	√	√	√	NA	NA	NA	NA

The table shows that the Persona3D template contains all the elements suitable for educational purposes; there are other elements not applicable to student personas. This confirms the completeness of the Persona3D model. Secondly, the efficiency of the Persona3D method is evaluated by comparing the proposed method (computational approach) with literature that uses workshops as a source to build personas.

The proposed approach mainly focuses on looking at the data and building the personas based on that, which is easier and takes less time and effort when compared to the traditional way of conducting the workshop to build personas. In summary, this evaluation confirms the completeness of the Persona3D model and the efficiency of the Persona3D method.

The practical effectiveness of the Persona3D model approach is assessed by building a range of chatbots. A range of chatbots will be developed in the Amazon Alexa platform, including the client (Alexa Skill Kit) and the server side (Amazon AWS developer). The architecture and snapshot of knowledge acquisition chatbot execution are shown in Figures 13.3 and 13.4, respectively.

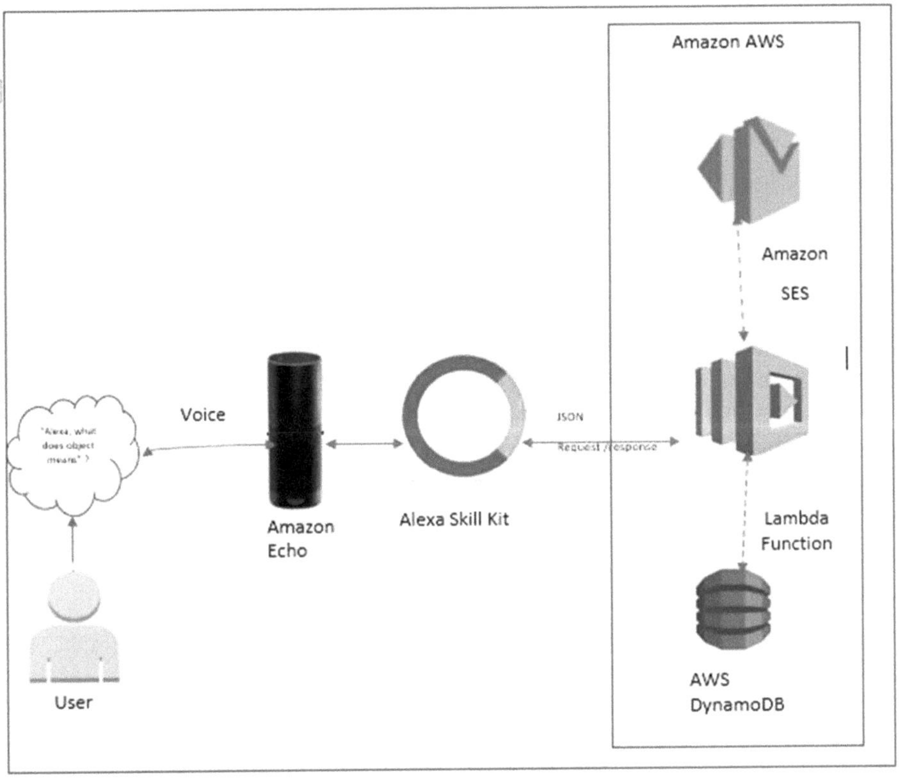

FIGURE 13.3 Knowledge acquisition chatbot architecture—Amazon Alexa platform [59].

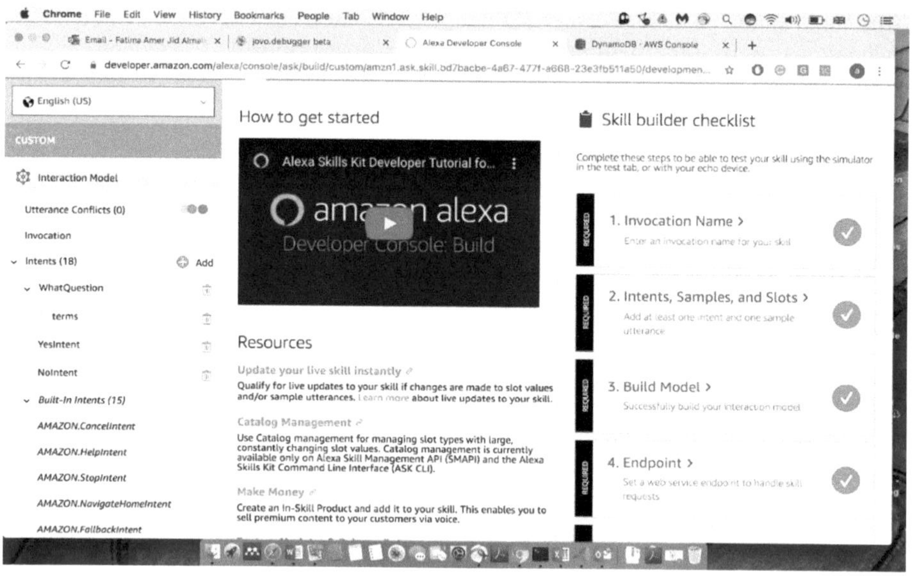

FIGURE 13.4 Knowledge acquisition chatbots—Execution [59].

13.7 CONCLUSION

In this chapter we have given an overview of how chatbots are used in different sectors including business, healthcare, customer services, finance, and education, to name a few. The integration of chatbots into education has been done easily due to the increasing use of online educational material and eLearning platforms. Persona-based chatbots have great potential in a number of areas, including resource guidance, academic counseling, and support for students' well-being. Their uses include helping students choose classes that match their goals, making recommendations for specific learning materials, encouraging independent study, and filling in knowledge gaps. Additionally, these chatbots give students a private area to talk about emotional difficulties while providing prompt assistance and insightful advice as needed. We also examine a DSR-based approach to persona- and context-driven chatbot development and evaluation. The use of DSR in Design Chatbots includes the practical methods necessary for a successful design, as well as the input and output artifacts. In the framework of DSR for chatbot development, we explore how to create a chatbot prototype with Amazon Alexa. We also discuss the theory and practical approaches for building instructional chatbots. We present the different artifacts, their classifications, and the evaluation procedure for each phase inside the DSR framework for chatbot analysis. First, we will conduct a long-term study to observe user satisfaction with using chatbots. Second, we will measure the effectiveness of using chatbots over time and how their learning progress is improved.

REFERENCES

1. H. Al-Zubaide and A. A. Issa, "Ontbot: Ontology based chatbot." In *International Symposium on Innovations in Information and Communications Technology*, Amman, Jordan, Nov. 2011, pp. 7–12.
2. D. Jurafsky and J. H. Martin, *Speech and Language Processing*, 3rd ed., Stanford University, 2019.
3. V. Hung, M. Elvir, A. J. Gonzalez, and R. F. DeMara, "Towards a method for evaluating naturalness in conversational dialog systems." In *Proceedings of the IEEE International Conference on Systems, Man, and Cybernetics (SMC)*, San Antonio, TX, USA, Oct. 2009. DOI: 10.1109/ICSMC.2009.5345904
4. S. A. Abdul-Kader and J. Woods, "Survey on chatbot design techniques in speech conversation systems." *International Journal of Advanced Computer Science and Applications*, vol. 6, no. 7, pp. 72–80, 2015. DOI: 10.14569/IJACSA.2015.060712
5. M. A. Kuhail, N. Alturki, S. Alramlawi, and K. Alhejori, "Interacting with educational chatbots: A systematic review." *Education and Information Technologies*, vol. 28, no. 1, pp. 973–1018, 2023.
6. I. V. Serban et al., "A deep reinforcement learning chatbot." arXiv preprint arXiv:1709.02349, 2017. DOI: 10.48550/arXiv.1709.02349
7. R. Winkler and M. Söllner, "Unleashing the potential of chatbots in education: A state-of-the-art analysis." In *Academy of Management Annual Meeting (AOM)*, 2018.
8. S. J. Russell and P. Norvig, *Artificial Intelligence: A Modern Approach*. Pearson Education Limited, 2020.
9. A. L. Samuel, "Some studies in machine learning." *IBM Journal of Research and Development*, vol. 44, no. 1.2, 1959.
10. T. Ayodele, "Machine learning overview." In Y. Zhang (Ed.), *New Advances in Machine Learning*. IntechOpen, 2010. DOI: 10.5772/9374
11. E. Alpaydin, *Introduction to Machine Learning*, 4th ed. MIT Press, 2020.
12. H. Thomas, "Critical literature review on chatbots in education." *International Journal of Trend in Scientific Research and Development (IJTSRD)*, vol. 4, no. 6, pp. 786–788, Oct. 2020. https://www.ijtsrd.com/engineering/electronics-and-communication-engineering/31845/critical-literature-review-on-chatbots-in-education/hephzibah-thomas&#8203
13. C. W. Okonkwo and A. Ade-Ibijola, "Python-Bot: A chatbot for teaching python programming." *Engineering Letters*, vol. 29, no. 1, 2020.
14. S. Cunningham-Nelson, W. Boles, L. Trouton, and E. Margerison, "A review of chatbots in education: practical steps forward." In *30th Annual Conference for the Australasian Association for Engineering Education (AAEE 2019): Educators Becoming Agents of Change: Innovate, Integrate, Motivate*, Brisbane, Australia, 2019, pp. 299–306.
15. J. Q. Pérez, T. Daradoumis, and J. M. M. Puig, "Rediscovering the use of chatbots in education: A systematic literature review." *Computer Applications in Engineering Education*, vol. 28, no. 6, pp. 1549–1565, Nov. 2020. DOI: 10.1002/cae.22326
16. Kumar, J.A. Educational chatbots for project-based learning: Investigating learning outcomes for a team-based design course. *Int J Educ Technol High Educ*, 18, 65 (2021). DOI: 10.1186/s41239-021-00302-w
17. L. Labadze, M. Grigolia, and L. Machaidze, "Role of AI chatbots in education: systematic literature review." *Int J Educ Technol High Educ*, vol. 20, no. 56, 2023. [Online]. DOI: 10.1186/s41239-023-00426-1s

18. L. Johnson, S. Adams, and M. Cummins, *The NMC Horizon Report: 2012 Higher Education Edition*, The New Media Consortium, 2012.
19. S. J. Russell and P. Norvig, *Artificial Intelligence: A Modern Approach*. Pearson Education Limited, 2016.
20. S. Bird, E. Klein, and E. Loper, *Natural Language Processing with Python: Analyzing Text with the Natural Language Toolkit*, 1st ed. O'Reilly Media, Inc., 2009.
21. D. Jurafsky and J. H. Martin, *Speech and Language Processing*, 3rd ed. Stanford University, 2019.
22. I. V. Serban, C. Sankar, M. Germain, S. Zhang, Z. Lin, S. Subramanian, T. Kim, M. Pieper, S. Chandar, N. R. Ke, A. de Brebisson, J. M. R. Sotelo, D. Suhubdy, V. Michalski, A. Nguyen, J. Pineau, and Y. Bengio, "A deep reinforcement learning chatbot." arXiv preprint arXiv:1709.02349, 2017.
23. D. A. Kane, "The role of chatbots in teaching and learning." *E-learning and the Academic Library: Essays on Innovative Initiatives*, vol. 131, pp. 131–147, 2016.
24. A. N. Mathew, V. Rohini, and J. Paulose, "NLP-based personal learning assistant for school education." *Int. J. Electr. Comput. Eng.*, vol. 11, no. 5, pp. 4522–4530, 2021.
25. T. Y. Chen, Y. C. Chiu, N. Bi, and R. T. H. Tsai, "Multi-modal chatbot in intelligent manufacturing." *IEEE Access*, vol. 9, pp. 82118–82129, 2021.
26. R. Smiderle, S. J. Rigo, L. B. Marques et al., "The impact of gamification on students' learning, engagement and behavior based on their personality traits." *Smart Learn. Environ.*, vol. 7, no. 3, 2020. [Online]. DOI: 10.1186/s40561-019-0098-x
27. M. McTear, Z. Callejas, and D. Griol, *The Conversational Interface: Talking to Smart Devices*. Springer, 2016.
28. S. D'Mello, A. Duckworth, and E. Dieterle, "Advanced, analytic, automated (AAA) measurement of engagement during learning." *Educational Psychologist*, vol. 52, no. 2, pp. 104–123, 2017.
29. V. J. Shute, "Focus on formative feedback." *Review of Educational Research*, vol. 78, no. 1, pp. 153–189, 2008.
30. J. Hattie and H. Timperley, "The power of feedback." *Review of Educational Research*, vol. 77, no. 1, pp. 81–112, 2007.
31. R. L. Bangert-Drowns, C. L. C. Kulik, J. A. Kulik, and M. Morgan, "The instructional effect of feedback in test-like events." *Review of Educational Research*, vol. 61, no. 2, pp. 213–238, 1991.
32. C. S. Dweck, *Mindset: The New Psychology of Success*. Random House Digital, Inc., 2006.
33. B. J. Zimmerman, "Becoming a self-regulated learner: An overview." *Theory into Practice*, vol. 41, no. 2, pp. 64–70, 2012.
34. P. M. Regan and J. Jesse, "Ethical challenges of edtech, big data and personalized learning: Twenty-first century student sorting and tracking." *Ethics and Information Technology*, vol. 21, no. 3, pp. 167–179, 2019.
35. D. Ramandanis and S. Xinogalos, "Investigating the support provided by chatbots to educational institutions and their students: A systematic literature review." *Multimodal Technol. Interact.*, vol. 7, no. 11, 103, 2023. DOI: 10.3390/mti7110103
36. P. Dillenbourg, "The evolution of research on digital education." *International Journal of Artificial Intelligence in Education*, vol. 26, no. 2, pp. 544–560, 2016. DOI: 10.1007/s40593-016-0106-z
37. S. Graf and Kinshuk, "Adaptivity and personalization in ubiquitous learning systems." In A. Holzinger, (Ed.), *HCI and Usability for Education and Work*. Springer, 2008, pp. 1–10, vol. 5298, Lecture Notes in Computer Science.
38. E. Zeide, "The structural consequences of big data-driven education." *Big Data*, vol. 5, no. 2, pp. 164–172, 2017.

39. N. A. Ahmad, M. H. Che, A. Zainal, M. F. Abd Rauf, and Z. Adnan, "Review of chatbots design techniques." *International Journal of Computer Applications*, vol. 181, no. 8, pp. 7–10, 2018.
40. S. A. Abdul-Kader and J. Woods, "Survey on chatbot design techniques in speech conversation systems." *International Journal of Advanced Computer Science and Applications*, vol. 6, no. 7, pp. 72–80, 2015. DOI: 10.14569/IJACSA.2015.060712
41. C. R. Anik, C. Jacob, and A. Mohanan, "A survey on web-based conversational bot design." *Journal of Emerging Technologies and Innovative Research (JETIR)*, vol. 3, no. 10, pp. 96–99, 2016.
42. A. R. Hevner et al., "Design science in information system research: an introduction to the special issue on design science research." *MIS Quarterly*, vol. 28, no. 1, pp. 725–730, 2004. DOI: 10.2307/25148869
43. S. T. March and G. F. Smith, "Design and natural science research on information technology." *Decision Support Systems*, vol. 15, no. 4, pp. 251–266, 1995.
44. M. J. Pereira and L. Coheur, "Just Chat – A platform for processing information to be used in chatbots." 2013, pp. 1–10.
45. P. van Rosmalen et al., "Towards a game-chatbot: Extending the interaction in serious games." Oct. 2012, pp. 4–5.
46. A. S. Lokman and J. M. Zain, "An architectural design of Virtual Dietitian (ViDi) for diabetic patients." 2009, pp. 408–411.
47. A. S. Lokman and J. M. Zain, "Extension and prerequisite: An algorithm to enable relations between responses in chatbot technology." *Journal of Computer Science*, vol. 6, no. 10, pp. 1212, 2010.
48. A. S. Lokman and J. M. Zain, "One-match and all-match categories for keywords matching in chatbot." *American Journal of Applied Sciences*, vol. 7, no. 10, pp. 1406, 2010.
49. F. A. Mikic, J. C. Burguillo, M. Llamas, D. A. Rodríguez, and E. Rodríguez, "CHARLIE: An AIML-based chatterbot which works as an interface among INES and humans." 2009, pp. 1–6.
50. V. Bhargava and M. Nikhil, "An intelligent speech recognition system for education system." 2009.
51. D. Vrajitoru, "Evolutionary sentence building for chatterbots." 2003, pp. 315–321.
52. D. Vrajitoru and J. Ratkiewicz, "Evolutionary sentence combination for chatterbots." In *The IASTED International Conference on Artificial Intelligence and Applications (AIA 2004)*, Feb. 2004, pp. 16–18.
53. A. Cooper, *The Inmates are Running the Asylum.* Sams Publishing, 1999. DOI: 10.1007/978-3-322-99786-9_1
54. E. Friess, "Personas and decision making in the design process: An ethnographic case study." In *Proceedings of the 2012 ACM Annual Conference on Human Factors in Computing Systems (CHI '12)*, 2012, pp. 1209–1218. DOI: 10.1145/2207676.2208572
55. M. Roussou et al., "A life of their own: Museum visitor personas penetrating the design lifecycle of a mobile experience." In *CHI 2013 Extended Abstracts*, Apr. 27–May 2, 2013, Paris, France. ACM, pp. 547–552. DOI: 10.1145/2468356.2468479
56. J. Nieters, S. Ivaturi, and I. Ahmed, "Making personas memorable." In *CHI '07 Extended Abstracts on Human Factors in Computing Systems*, Apr. 28–May 3, 2007, San Jose, CA, USA, ACM, pp. 1817–1824.
57. F. Almahri, D. Bell, and M. Arzoky, "Personas design for conversational systems in education." *Informatics*, vol. 6, no. 4, p. 46, Oct. 2019.
58. A. Shiga and N. Nishiuchi, "A support system for making persona using Bayesian network analysis." In *Proceedings of the 2013 International Conference on Biometrics and Kansei Engineering (ICBAKE 2013)*, pp. 281–284, 2013. DOI: 10.1109/ICBAKE.2013.55

59. F. A. Almahri, "Augmented educational interactions within a physical space." Ph.D. dissertation, Brunel University London, 2021.
60. A. Shiga and N. Nishiuchi, "A support system for making persona using Bayesian network analysis." In *Proceedings - 2013 International Conference on Biometrics and Kansei Engineering, ICBAKE 2013*, IEEE, 2013, pp. 281–284. DOI: 10.1109/ICBAKE.2013.55
61. R. M. Quintana et al., "The persona party: Using personas to design for learning at scale." In *Conference on Human Factors in Computing Systems - Proceedings*, Part F1276(1), 2017, pp. 933–941. DOI: 10.1145/3027063.3053355
62. K. Kimita, Y. Nemoto, and Y. Shimomura, "Application of a Requirement Analysis Template to Lectures in a Higher Education Institution." In *International Conference on Human Interface and the Management of Information*, Springer, 2014, pp. 594–601. DOI: 10.1007/978-3-319-07731-4_39
63. B. Ferreira et al., "Technique for representing requirements using personas: A controlled experiment." *IET Software*, vol. 12, no. 3, pp. 280–290, 2018. DOI: 10.1049/iet-sen.2017.0313
64. N. M. C. Valentim, W. Silva, and T. Conte, "The students' perspectives on applying design thinking for the design of mobile applications." In *Proceedings - 2017 IEEE/ACM 39th International Conference on Software Engineering: Software Engineering and Education Track, ICSE-SEET 2017*, 2017, pp. 77–86. DOI: 10.1109/ICSE-SEET.2017.10
65. S. Polst and P. Stüpfert, "A comprehensive persona template to understand citizens' mobility needs." In *International Conference on Human-Computer Interaction*, Springer, 2019, pp. 295–306. DOI: 10.1007/978-3-030-22666-4_31

14 Green Energy Management for Smart Homes that Leverages Big Data Analytics and IoT

D. B. Pardeshi, P. William, G Vijayakumar, Payal Rohidas Solase and Vaishali Bhanudas Ingle

14.1 INTRODUCTION

The proliferation of smart homes has ushered in an era of unprecedented connectivity and convenience, where everyday devices are seamlessly interwoven into an intelligent fabric. However, this surge in technological integration has also underscored the critical importance of efficient energy management within these smart ecosystems. As the number of interconnected devices continues to grow, so does the complexity of optimizing energy consumption, necessitating advanced solutions that harness the power of big data analytics and the Internet of Things (IoT). This chapter presents a cutting-edge energy-management solution designed specifically for smart homes, aiming to tackle the intricate challenge of balancing user comfort, operational efficiency, and environmental sustainability. By synergistically leveraging big data analytics and IoT technologies, our proposed system offers a comprehensive and adaptive approach to energy optimization [1].

At its core, the system integrates seamlessly with the diverse array of IoT-enabled devices prevalent in smart homes, including smart appliances, sensors, and energy meters. The real-time data generated by these devices becomes the lifeblood of our energy-management solution, flowing into a centralized analytics platform. This platform serves as the nerve center, where sophisticated algorithms and advanced analytics unravel the intricacies of energy consumption patterns, user behaviors, and external factors. The key innovation lies in the system's ability to transcend traditional energy-management paradigms through the application of machine learning algorithms and predictive modeling [2]. Rather than relying on static schedules or predefined rules, the proposed solution adapts dynamically to evolving user preferences, changing environmental conditions, and device-specific characteristics. This adaptability ensures that energy consumption is not only optimized but personalized to the unique needs and rhythms of each smart home's occupants.

As a result, the envisioned smart home environment becomes an oasis of energy efficiency, where wastage is minimized, costs are reduced, and sustainability is

DOI: 10.1201/9781032703718-19

prioritized. By harnessing the power of big data analytics and the IoT, our solution not only addresses the immediate challenges posed by the growing complexity of smart home ecosystems but also contributes to the broader goals of building a resilient, eco-friendly, and intelligent living space. This chapter delves into the intricacies of the proposed energy-management solution, exploring its architecture, functionality, and the tangible benefits it brings to the forefront of the smart home revolution. In the contemporary era, the proliferation of smart homes has revolutionized the way individuals interact with their living spaces. The integration of Internet of Things (IoT) technologies into everyday devices has paved the way for a new level of connectivity and automation, enhancing convenience and comfort. However, with the increasing complexity of these interconnected systems, there arises a pressing need for innovative energy-management solutions to ensure optimal resource utilization and sustainability.

We go into further detail about the technical features of our suggested energy-management strategy in the next parts of this study. We examine the centralized analytics platform's architecture, the predictive modeling techniques used by machine learning algorithms, and the real-world application of customized energy-management plans. We want to demonstrate via our investigation the revolutionary possibilities of using IoT and big data analytics to influence how energy management is done in smart homes going forward. Figure 14.1 illustrates a complex architecture for an

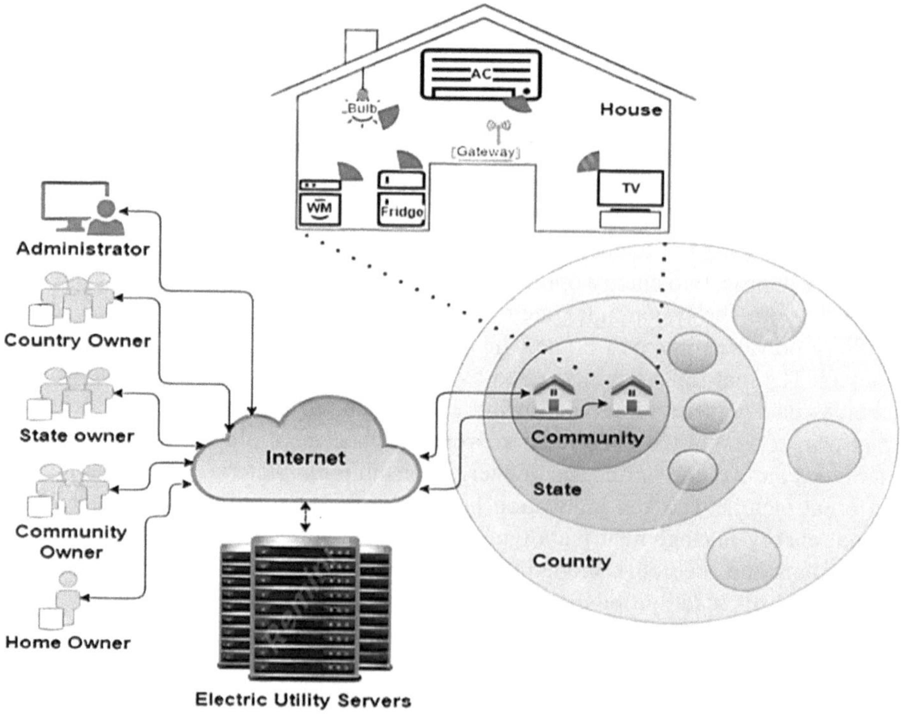

FIGURE 14.1 Energy-management ecosystem for smart homes using IoT and big data.

energy-management solution in smart homes, leveraging big data analytics and the Internet of Things (IoT) technologies [3]. This cutting-edge solution is designed to maximize energy use and boost effectiveness in homes. The smart home, which is outfitted with a variety of IoT devices including air conditioners (AC), TVs, washing machines (WM), and refrigerators (Fridge), is the central component of this system. These gadgets allow for easy data sharing and communication as they are linked to a central gateway within the house. The gateway is essential because it serves as a conduit for data between the home devices and the larger internet network, allowing data to be sent to and received from the Electric Utility Servers.

These servers are the nexus for big data analytics, processing vast amounts of data collected from individual homes. They analyze usage patterns, predict peak demand times, and can even adjust device settings in real time to enhance energy efficiency [4]. For instance, the system may learn the optimal times to run certain appliances or adjust temperature settings based on usage patterns and external weather conditions, leading to significant energy savings. The hierarchy of control and ownership in this model extends from individual homeowners to community, state, and country levels, signifying a scalable approach to energy management. Each level can monitor and manage energy consumption, contributing to broader initiatives like grid stability and reduced carbon footprints. The administrators at the top of this hierarchy oversee the entire operation, ensuring the system's integrity and effectiveness. By integrating IoT devices with big data analytics, this solution promises a transformative approach to energy management. It empowers homeowners with the ability to monitor and adjust their consumption, while utility providers can analyze big-picture trends and make data-driven decisions to optimize energy distribution and reduce waste. This advanced system is not only a step toward smarter energy use in homes but also a leap toward sustainable living and environmental [5].

14.2 REVIEW OF LITERATURE

Researchers are faced with new issues as a result of the huge volumes of data produced by European buildings from a variety of sources that are significant to energy saving. Examples of sources that fall under this category include sensors, smart meters, and other devices that are linked to the internet. The purpose of this research is to present an overview of a high-level data-driven architecture that was built for the purpose of performing activities related to building management, real-time processing, and data interchange [6]. This interdisciplinary big data ecosystem is founded on distributed ledger technology, which enables data from a wide variety of industries to be merged with artificial intelligence algorithms that have been created in recent years. Not only does it come with a wide range of features for visualization, querying, and exploration, but it also comes with a collection of analytical components that can be easily adapted to match the specific needs of any unique user. A wide variety of cutting-edge machine learning and deep learning techniques are carried out by these components, which are responsible for their execution. In addition to that, it incorporates an appropriate collection of application programming interfaces (APIs) that are designed to make the process of data transfer easier. Additionally included in this combo are a multitude of data repositories that are networked, multilingual, and semantically updated. These data archives provide representations that are exhaustive in scope. In this part, an overview and analysis of the results from the pilot deployment of the recommended framework are presented [7]. Through the use of a wide variety of data, the data-driven architecture encourages the creation and deployment of innovative services that highlight the need for energy conservation. As an additional benefit, it enhances the effectiveness and dependability of the policymaking process, which is an essential component in ensuring that structures continue to function without interruption.

Because of the ever-increasing demand for energy and the ever-increasing expense of energy, a lot of enterprises have been faced with the need to develop innovative systems for monitoring, managing, and conserving energy. Through the use of an efficient energy management system (EMS), it is possible to satisfactorily fulfill the present demand for energy while simultaneously lowering costs. Utilizing cutting-edge technologies like big data and the Internet of Things (IoT) in the commercial, industrial, and residential sectors has the potential to boost the efficacy of energy management and control. In order to communicate the findings of the inquiry, an EMS application that was developed specifically for intelligent homes is employed. With the help of this method, it is possible to connect any home appliance to a data-collecting module, which is a device that is a part of the Internet of Things and has its own distinctive Internet Protocol address. The culmination of this endeavor is the creation of a vast wireless mesh network that is comprised of a number of different devices. Every single gadget that is a part of a smart home is responsible for providing the data that is necessary for the System-on-Chip (SoC) modules to collect information on energy consumption measurements [8].

This information is then sent to a centralized server, where it is subjected to further processing and analysis. Massive amounts of data are generated from all of this information on residential areas, and these data are stored on the server of the power supplier. By merging business intelligence (BI) and big data analytics software technologies that are freely accessible to the public, the EMS that has been described has the ability to improve energy consumption control and meet the expectations of customers. For the purpose of carrying out a case study, heating, ventilation, and air conditioning (HVAC) systems were used in the research. Heat, ventilation, and air conditioning are the three components that make up HVAC. It is notably due to the fact that air conditioning accounts for 60 percent of the total electricity consumption in the countries that make up the Arab Gulf group. In order to simulate the HVAC system that would be present in a small living area, a prototype was built and put through its paces in a laboratory setting. As a result of the recent and significant increase in urbanization, there is an immediate need for solutions that are not only innovative but also cost-effective and long-lasting. The implementation of these solutions is necessary in a variety of domains, including the environment, transportation, government, and quality of life. With the advent of the Internet of Things, it is now feasible to deploy a broad variety of complex and all-encompassing applications. These apps have been developed with the express purpose of being suitable for smart cities. Because of the growing number of devices and the needs they have, applications for the Internet of Things are seeing an increase in the amount of energy they use. Intelligent cities are able to solve issues that are associated with energy efficiency, which is one of the most essential components of the solutions that they supply.

This is a consequence of the increasing significance of energy efficiency among many stakeholders. When installing advanced energy systems in smart cities, energy management is likely one of the most critical concerns that must be addressed. Smart cities are becoming more environmentally conscious. The purpose of this article is to offer a concise outline of the problems that are associated with energy management in smart cities, as well as some potential solutions to these problems. The subsequent items on the agenda include the optimization of energy efficiency as well as the development of a common framework for the scheduling schedule of a smart city that is based on the Internet of Things. In addition, we discuss the challenges that are connected with energy harvesting in smart cities, which is a possible method of extending the lifespan of low-power devices. Additionally, two case studies are analyzed in great detail and given on many occasions throughout the whole work [9]. When compared to the latter, the former is largely concerned with wireless power transmission for Internet of Things devices in smart cities, while the latter is mostly concerned with smart homes and energy-efficient scheduling. There exists a connection between the concept of smart cities and the two professions that are being discussed here. In the framework of the discussion on these two topics, the concept of "smart cities" is brought to the forefront. The results of the simulations, which were based on the case studies, demonstrate the extent to which aspects such as wireless power transfer and efficient energy-saving scheduling have an impact on the degree to which the Internet of Things performs effectively in smart cities. This project will implement its architecture, which will allow semantic integration of large-scale data sets. In the context of smart cities, the purpose of this concept is to encourage energy conservation. Using the technique that has been presented here, one can see the potential advantages that big data and ontologies may provide in order to assist smart cities in reducing their overall energy use. The anticipated benefits that these technologies may offer in the future make it possible to make use of these advantages.

The purpose of this article is to offer a comprehensive introduction to semantics in big data as well as a review of numerous research that study energy-saving approaches for smart cities and residences. In order to make it easier to accomplish this objective, we provide a helpful architecture that integrates big data, ontology, and multi-agent systems. This architecture may be accessed via the use of our services. Furthermore, the approach that has been provided provides an additional illustration of the capability of these technologies to reduce the amount of energy that smart cities use. In order to achieve the objective of enhancing the system's interoperability, the purpose of this research is to provide clarity on the roles that ontological paradigms and multi-agent systems play among the components of the system. In general, architecture that is supported by large amounts of dependable data is associated with a number of advantages. The purpose of this study is to demonstrate the possible advantages that might originate from the combination of these two components in order to provide a trustworthy solution for maximizing the efficiency with which energy is used in smart cities. There are a wide variety of applications that are presently accessible, and it is imperative that semantic technologies and massive data sets be used in a far more frequent manner. These applications include, but are not limited to, social networks, smart cities, healthcare, the Internet of Things, and a great number of other applications that are relevant to each of these industries. The findings provide a more nuanced view on the topic of saving energy and protecting the environment while also ensuring that the inhabitants experience the best degree of comfort that is possible in spite of the circumstances that have been presented [10–12]. Due to the fact that it provides more comprehensive ways for connecting big data platforms with ontologies, the work that is discussed in this article is an important contribution to the discipline. A successful long-term energy strategy has been implemented in an intelligent and sustainable environment, and all of the data that is presently available has been utilized to reduce the amount of energy that is used, encourage changes in behavior, and ensure that the appropriate level of comfort is maintained [13–14].

14.3 FOUNDATIONS OF ENERGY MANAGEMENT IN SMART HOMES

Energy management is an essential component that promotes cost-effectiveness, efficiency, and sustainability in the present era of smart homes, which is characterized by the pervasive presence of computer technology in everyday life. As part of this inquiry, the basic concepts that underpin energy management in smart homes are investigated. The findings shed light on the ways in which cutting-edge technologies and data-driven tactics are transforming the way in which individuals use, monitor, and optimize their energy use in their homes. The core of smart home energy management is the integration of automation systems, intelligent devices, and sensors that enable real-time monitoring and control of energy use. This combination is what makes smart home energy management possible. These devices, which include home appliances, lighting controls, smart thermostats, and home energy monitors, provide a networked environment that allows homeowners to manage their energy use in accordance with their preferences, routines, and the external environment [14–16].

In smart homes, one of the most important aspects of energy management is the collection of data and the performance of analysis on patterns of energy use. Having smart meters installed in homes allows for the collection of comprehensive data on the amount of gas, electricity, and water that is used. With the use of this information, homeowners are able to recognize trends and irregularities and make decisions that will reduce the amount of trash they produce and save money on their energy bills. This potential is further increased by the tools and algorithms that are used for data analytics. These tools and algorithms give practical insights and ideas for maximum energy utilization [17]. When it comes to energy management, automation plays a crucial role since it enables smart home devices to autonomously adjust their settings and behaviors in order to reduce the amount of energy they use. Smart lighting systems, for example, have the ability to adjust the level of brightness based on occupancy sensors and natural light conditions. Smart thermostats, on the other hand, may learn user preferences and occupancy patterns in order to optimize heating and cooling schedules.

When renewable energy sources such as solar and wind turbines are included in smart homes, the management of energy in these houses becomes much more challenging. It is possible for intelligent EMSs to autonomously coordinate the production, storage, and consumption of renewable energy sources [18–20]. This would allow such systems to optimize self-consumption while simultaneously reducing dependence on the grid. The resilience and flexibility of battery storage systems are further strengthened by their ability to store excess energy for utilization during times of high demand or grid outages. When it comes to energy management, however, privacy and cybersecurity become increasingly critical considerations to take into account as smart homes become more reliant on digital connectivity. To prevent unauthorized access to smart home devices and to ensure the safety of private information, it is essential to implement stringent data protection rules and security procedures [21–23].

The purpose of this inquiry is to establish the framework for a more in-depth assessment of the fundamental principles, technologies, and industry best practices that influence the management of energy in smart homes. As we go further into specific applications, challenges, and emerging trends, it becomes abundantly evident that energy management is about more than just making the most effective use of resources; it is also about allowing families to live lifestyles that are more sustainable and efficient in a world that is growing more interconnected. As seen in Figure 14.2, the manner in which big data analytics and the Internet of Things (IoT) are incorporated into smart home EMSs represents a significant step forward in the

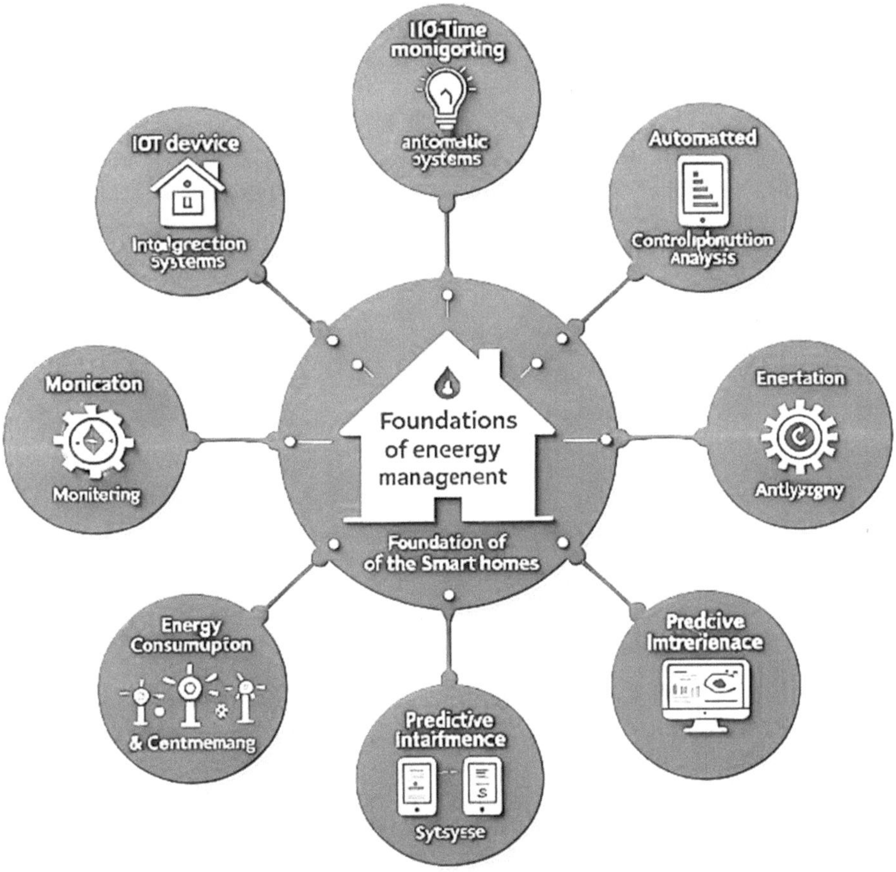

FIGURE 14.2 Smart home energy optimization framework.

manner in which we create and implement solutions for residential energy needs. In order to achieve this integration, it is necessary to create an environment that is highly sensitive, efficient, and self-regulating. This environment should not only maximize the efficiency with which energy is used, but it should also enhance the quality of life. The foundation of this system is comprised of a network of interconnected Internet of Things (IoT) devices. These devices include sophisticated HVAC systems, energy-efficient appliances, smart lighting, and thermostats. Integrated sensors are included in every electronic device, and their purpose is to continuously collect data on use patterns, environmental conditions, and operational status.

In order to effectively manage this massive volume of data, big data analytics is absolutely necessary. Through the use of intricate algorithms and other machine learning techniques, it is able to identify trends and irregularities, anticipate future energy needs, and provide suggestions for changes. This strategy, which is driven by data, enhances cost-effectiveness and avoids waste by ensuring that energy use closely matches the actual habits and preferences of the people who live there. Real-time monitoring is one of the most important aspects of this system. It gives homeowners the ability to witness the direct impacts of their energy use and to adjust their behavior accordingly. One of the most important aspects of this real-time feedback loop is the promotion of energy use awareness, which, over time, may lead to behaviors that are more environmentally friendly. When it comes to energy savings, automated control systems eliminate uncertainty by altering the settings of both the system and the devices in response to predictive analytics. A smart thermostat, for instance, may regulate the temperature in advance of a warm day, or a solar energy system can store excess energy during peak production hours for use during times of greater demand. Both of these examples are examples of how energy can be stored.

The component of the system that is responsible for energy production analysis examines the many techniques that are used to generate energy. These methods include traditional grid supplies as well as renewable sources such as solar or wind turbines that are integrated into smart houses. The system is able to identify the optimal periods to use, store, or sell back energy by analyzing the data that is generated. This allows the system to maximize the energy cycle and maybe generate a profit. One of the most significant aspects that has become obvious is predictive maintenance, which makes use of the information that has been obtained in order to anticipate any issues or inefficiencies in the energy systems of the home before anything happens. This ensures that everything continues to work properly, reduces the risk of damage and disruption, and extends the lifespan of both infrastructure and appliances. Not only do the energy management and consumption nodes work together to ensure that energy is utilized effectively, but they also make it simple to integrate energy into the routines of the family. Dimming the lights, shutting down certain devices that aren't absolutely necessary, and decreasing the temperature at which water is heated during off-peak hours are all examples of strategies that might be used. As a last point of emphasis, communication monitoring highlights the need for a robust and secure exchange of information between the devices and the central management system. It provides homeowners with the assurance that they can rely on the system to function as intended, therefore maintaining a comfortable and energy-efficient environment inside their home.

14.4 RESEARCH METHODOLOGY

As part of the research methodology for an energy-management solution for smart homes that leverages big data analytics and Internet of Things, a structured approach to the creation and evaluation of energy-management solutions in smart home settings is included. The first step in the research process is to conduct a comprehensive analysis of the existing body of literature in order to get an understanding of the current state of the art in energy management, big data analytics, and Internet of Things technologies inside smart homes. The subsequent phase is to develop and implement a prototype of an EMS that is capable of monitoring and optimizing energy consumption patterns via the integration of big data analytics and sensors connected to the Internet of Things. For the purpose of determining how effectively the system operates in terms of customer satisfaction, cost savings, and energy efficiency, real-world data from smart home installations is collected and analyzed. In addition, surveys and feedback from users are used in order to ascertain the degree to which the EMS is well received and how simple it is to operate. Putting energy-management ideas into practice in a way that is both practical and efficient may be accomplished via the use of big data analytics and Internet of Things (IoT) technologies in smart home environments. The study method is what comes into play at this point.

14.4.1 Mapping the Terrain: Contextualizing the Research Landscape

In establishing a robust research methodology for our energy-management solution in smart homes, it is imperative to commence with a comprehensive mapping of the contextual landscape. This involves a thorough review of existing literature, technological advancements, and industry practices related to energy management, big data analytics, and the Internet of Things (IoT). By immersing ourselves in the existing knowledge base, we aim to identify gaps, challenges, and opportunities that will inform the development of our innovative solution. This foundational step ensures that our research is positioned at the forefront of current knowledge and is poised to contribute meaningfully to the field.

14.4.2 Architectural Framework and System Integration

Central to our research methodology is the design and development of the architectural framework for the energy-management solution. This stage involves conceptualizing and detailing the integration of big data analytics and IoT technologies into a cohesive and scalable system. Our approach prioritizes the creation of a centralized analytics platform capable of seamlessly collecting, processing, and analyzing real-time data from IoT-enabled devices. The architectural blueprint encompasses considerations such as data flow, communication protocols, and interoperability to ensure the system's efficiency and adaptability within the dynamic environment of smart homes.

14.4.3 Machine Learning Algorithms and Predictive Modeling

A pivotal aspect of our research methodology revolves around the implementation of intelligent algorithms for data analysis and predictive modeling. Machine learning algorithms play a crucial role in deciphering patterns, forecasting energy demands, and creating adaptive strategies. This stage involves selecting and fine-tuning algorithms that align with the objectives of personalized energy management. Through iterative development and testing, we aim to optimize the algorithms for accuracy, responsiveness, and scalability. The implementation of these algorithms is not a static process; rather, it involves continuous refinement to enhance the system's learning capabilities and adaptability to evolving user behavior.

14.4.4 Real-Time Data Fusion and Integration

An integral component of our research methodology is the seamless fusion and integration of real-time data from diverse IoT devices. This process involves developing protocols for data aggregation, cleansing, and synchronization within the centralized analytics platform. The goal is to establish a cohesive and synchronized data ecosystem that provides a holistic view of the smart home's energy landscape. By connecting the dots between different devices, our solution aims to create a comprehensive understanding of energy consumption patterns, user behaviors, and external factors in real time, enabling the system to make informed decisions promptly.

14.4.5 Navigating Personalization

The research methodology places a significant emphasis on navigating the realm of personalization in energy management. User behavior analysis and feedback loops are integral components in tailoring the energy-management solution to individual preferences and requirements. Through the continuous analysis of user interactions, preferences, and feedback, the system adapts and refines its strategies to align with the unique characteristics of each household. This iterative process ensures that the energy-management solution becomes an intuitive and integral part of the smart home experience, enhancing user satisfaction and fostering sustained energy efficiency.

14.4.6 Field Testing: Validation in Real-World Smart Home Environments

Validation of the proposed energy-management solution is a critical stage in our research methodology. Field testing involves deploying the system in real-world smart home environments to assess its performance, usability, and effectiveness. This phase provides valuable insights into the practical challenges and opportunities associated with the implementation of the solution. Through collaboration with homeowners, data collection, and continuous monitoring, we gather empirical evidence to validate the efficacy of the energy-management solution, ensuring its viability and relevance in diverse residential settings.

14.4.7 Iterative Refinement and Continuous Improvement

The research methodology concludes with a commitment to iterative refinement and continuous improvement. By analyzing the findings from field testing, gathering user feedback, and monitoring system performance, we embark on a cycle of refinement to enhance the solution's robustness and adaptability. This iterative approach ensures that the energy-management solution remains at the forefront of technological advancements and user expectations, contributing to the evolution of smart home energy management. In the subsequent sections, we delve into the practical implementation of our research methodology, detailing the technical specifications, challenges encountered, and lessons learned throughout the development and testing phases.

14.5 RESULT AND DISCUSSION

It has been put into reality that our energy-management system for smart homes, which integrates the Internet of Things (IoT) with big data analytics, has been implemented, and the results are positive in a number of different ways. The seamless integration of real-time data from a large number of smart devices into a centralized analytics platform has made it feasible to get an understanding of the patterns of energy use that occur in smart homes. An integrated and synchronized energy environment has been made feasible as a result of the intricate interplay between the Internet of Things (IoT) and big data analytics. This environment allows the system to make decisions that are both timely and well-informed. Utilizing machine learning algorithms for predictive modeling is one way that the solution has shown its adaptability that has been demonstrated. These algorithms are able to predict energy demands and proactively improve methods by learning from prior data, user behavior, and real-time inputs. Through the process of integrating, cleansing, and synchronizing data from Internet of Things devices, the approach of real-time data fusion has made it possible to create an EMS that is both dynamic and responsive. This feature assures that the system can swiftly respond to changes in user behavior and outside environmental circumstances, which leads to greater efficiency. Research on user behavior has led to the development of methods that are tailored to meet the requirements and preferences of each individual. These methods have been produced as a result of the focus on personalized energy management. Not only does this individualized touch make the client more satisfied, but it also demonstrates how versatile and adaptable the solution is in terms of satisfying the diverse requirements of different places of residence.

The usability and practical performance of the EMS have been uncovered via real-world smart home field testing, which has produced several invaluable insights. The validation procedure, which takes into account user feedback and system performance indicators, has provided more evidence that the system is effective in a wide range of home settings. The analysis of data from field testing has made it possible to get a more nuanced understanding of the possibilities and challenges associated with the deployment of the solution. This research has also shed light on the relevance of user involvement, privacy concerns, and the scalability of the system. Through an iterative refinement process that is informed by insights from field testing and reflects a commitment to continuing development, the energy-management system will continue to be at the forefront of technological advancements and customer expectations. This is because the method indicates a commitment to continuous improvement.

When everything is taken into consideration, the results shed light on how big data analytics and Internet of Things (IoT) technologies have the potential to transform energy management in smart homes by promoting sustainability, efficiency, and a personalized user experience. The throughput performance, measured in kilobits per second (kbps), seems to be shown in Figure 14.3 for two unique Quality of Service (QoS) levels, namely 0 and 1, over a variety of client numbers. It is likely that these customers are connected to a network of Internet of Things devices, which is a component of EMSs for smart homes. The Y-axis shows the network throughput in kbps, while the X-axis logarithmically displays the number of customers, demonstrating an exponential increase in the number of clients who are connected to the network. A statistic that reflects how well a communications service functions overall from the perspective of the user is referred to as Quality of Service (QoS) in the field of networking. Providing assurance of service delivery parameters such as packet loss, delay, and jitter is what is meant by the term "quality of service" (QoS) level. In the context of MQTT, which is a protocol that is often used in Internet of Things applications for the purpose of message transmission, the term "at most once" delivery is referred to as "QoS zero." Messages are sent in this situation depending on the best efforts of the operating environment; nevertheless, there is no promise that message delivery will occur. In a case where Quality of Service 1 assures "at least once" delivery, it is possible for duplicates to occur, despite the fact that messages are guaranteed to arrive.

As can be seen in Figure 14.3, the throughput of the network initially remains the same for both quality-of-service levels, but it eventually starts to rise as the number of clients grows. It would seem from this that the system is able to successfully grow and accommodate an increasing number of consumers. However, there is a point at which the throughput generated by QoS 0 surpasses that generated by QoS 1. This might be due to the fact that Quality of Service 0 has a lower protocol overhead compared to Quality of Service 1, which means that the acknowledgment process is not required for message delivery. This could potentially cause communication to slow down when there are a large number of customers. For the purpose of assessing the

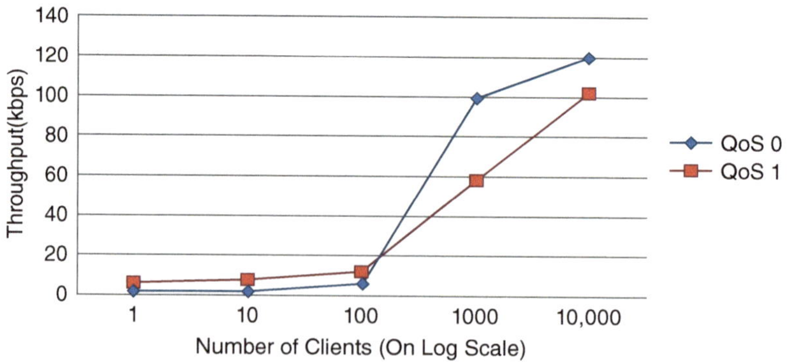

FIGURE 14.3 Throughput performance analysis of IoT network clients at varying QoS levels.

scalability and reliability of the system in an energy-management solution that makes use of big data analytics and the Internet of Things, this sort of research is very necessary. In order to effectively handle the data on energy usage that is collected in real time from a wide range of sensors and devices that are included inside a smart home network, the data throughput must be adequate. The quality of service (QoS) level that is chosen may have a significant influence on the performance of the system. At the same time, it can also have an effect on the speed and reliability with which data is transported. The analytics and decision-making algorithms of the EMS may therefore be affected by these elements, which may subsequently have an influence on the solution. The latency that is experienced in an Internet of Things (IoT) network is shown in Figure 14.4 as a function of the number of customers. This visualization is presented on a logarithmic scale. The two lines indicate how latency increases as the number of consumers in the network increases. They also represent QoS (Quality of Service) levels 0 and 1, respectively. The concept of quality of service is an essential component of network management. It describes the extent to which a telecommunications service performs in general from the point of view of the user. There is a correlation between the different quality of service levels and the reliability and prioritization of data transfer. For Internet of Things (IoT) applications, quality of service (QoS) is essential because it ensures that data is sent between devices and management systems in a manner that is both accurate and fast. This is especially important in smart homes that make use of big data analytics.

It is presumed that Quality of Service 0 represents a "best effort" service that does not guarantee the delivery of messages in Figure 14.4. On the other hand, Quality of Service 1 would imply that the message is transmitted at least once, with acknowledgments being required along the way. Both quality of service levels begin with similar low latencies, as seen in Figure 14.4, when the number of customers is minimal. When the number of clients increases, on the other hand, the latency of Quality of Service 1 increases more quickly than the latency of Quality of Service 0. This may be due to the fact that a bigger number of clients competing for network resources results in a higher overhead cost associated with sustaining message

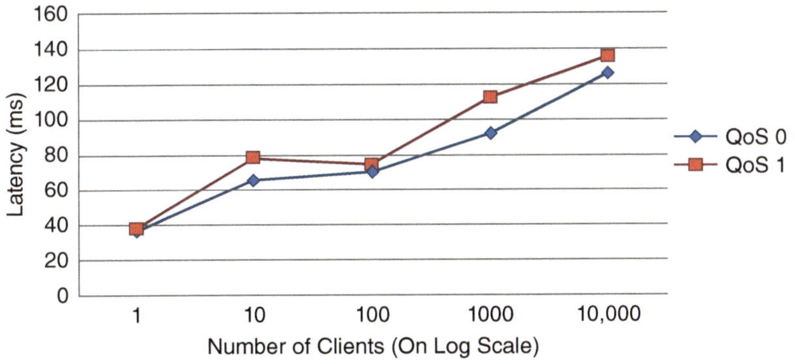

FIGURE 14.4 IoT network latency analysis under different quality of service (QoS) conditions.

delivery at better quality of service levels. When it comes to smart homes, an excessive amount of latency might cause essential activities to be delayed, which in turn reduces the efficiency of the system. For energy management and other automated operations, having data in real time from a number of different sensors and devices is required. When determining the appropriate quality of service (QoS) level for a variety of applications in a smart home environment, it is essential to take into consideration the needs for low latency and reliability. Figure 14.4 may be used to illustrate this point. When it comes to big data settings, where decisions and analytics are performed in real time or very real time, it is essential to have a solid understanding of the latency repercussions that stem from the increasing number of Internet of Things devices. This understanding contributes to the construction of systems that are able to scale effectively while maintaining performance. This helps ensure that the smart home will continue to be responsive and effective even as it grows with more devices and more complex data processing requirements.

14.6 DISCUSSION

This article addresses in great depth the incorporation of big data analytics and the Internet of Things (IoT) into smart homes for the purpose of efficient energy management. Integration allows for the optimization of energy use and the improvement of living quality, resulting in the creation of an ecosystem that is both responsive and self-regulating. The core of the system is comprised of Internet of Things devices that are wirelessly connected to one another and are fitted with sensors that collect data. Big data analytics makes use of intricate algorithms in order to examine data, identify trends, and make use of energy consumption to its fullest potential. Real-time monitoring and automated control systems are vital tools for modifying the settings of devices and fostering habits that are more environmentally friendly. There are further functions of the system, such as energy production analysis, secure communication monitoring, and predictive maintenance. Concerns about user involvement, privacy, scalability, and the trade-off between latency and dependability in Internet of Things networks are also discussed. Internet of Things networks are a topic of debate.

14.7 CONCLUSION

The proposed energy-management system for smart homes represents a significant step forward in terms of optimizing energy use since it integrates Internet of Things (IoT) with big data analytics. Additionally, the system demonstrates its adaptability by successfully reacting to changes in the environment and the behavior of users, so ensuring that it is both cost-effective and energy-efficient. The results of field testing have shown that it is both adaptable and practicable in a variety of home contexts. In addition to demonstrating how to make efficient use of technology in smart homes, the solution also demonstrates how to create living spaces that are more intelligent and environmentally friendly. The future implications include resolving difficulties pertaining to privacy and scalability, enhancing user involvement, and constantly enhancing the system in order to allow more efficient energy management in smart homes.

REFERENCES

1. Serra, J., Pubill, D., Antonopoulos, A., Verikoukis, C. (2014). Smart HVAC Control in IoT: Energy Consumption Minimization With User Comfort Constraints. *The Scientific World Journal*, Vol. 2014, pp 1–11.
2. Abbes, H., Gargouri, F. (2018). MongoDB-Based Modular Ontology Building for Big Data Integration. *Journal on Data Semantics*, Vol. 7, No. 1, pp. 1–27.
3. Bokolo, A. J., Petersen, S. A., Ahlers, D., Krogstie, J. (2019). API Deployment for Big Data Management Towards Sustainable Energy Prosumption in Smart Cities – A Layered Architecture Perspective. *International Journal of Sustainable Energy*, Vol. 39, No. 3, pp. 263–289.
4. Jawhar, I., Mohamed, N., Al-Jaroodi, J. (2018). Networking Architectures and Protocols for Smart City Systems. *Journal of Internet Services and Applications*, Vol. 9, No. 1, p. 26.
5. Mehta, M. Y., Buch, S. (2015). Big Data Mining and Semantic Technologies: Challenges and Opportunities. *International Journal on Recent and Innovation Trends in Computing and SASBE Communication (IJRITCC)*, Vol. 3, No. 7, pp. 4907–4913.
6. Merizig, A., Kazar, O. and Sanchez, M.L. (2019). A Multi-agent System Approach for Service Deployment in the Cloud. *International Journal of Communication Networks and Distributed Systems*, Vol. 1No. 23, pp. 69–92.
7. Yang, C., Huang, Q., Li, Z., Liu, K., Hu, F. (2017). Big Data and Cloud Computing: Innovation Opportunities and Challenges. *International Journal of Digital Earth*, Vol. 10, No. 1, pp. 13–53.
8. William, P., Agrawal, A., Rawat, N., Shrivastava, A., Srivastava, A. P., Ashish (2023). Enterprise Human Resource Management Model By Artificial Intelligence Digital Technology. *2023 4th International Conference on Computation, Automation and Knowledge Management (ICCAKM)*, Dubai, United Arab Emirates, pp. 01–06. DOI: 10.1109/ICCAKM58659.2023.10449624
9. William, P., Panicker, A., Falah, A., Hussain, A., Shrivastava, A., Khan, A. K. (2023). The Emergence of Artificial Intelligence and Machine Learning in Contemporary Business Management. *2023 4th International Conference on Computation, Automation and Knowledge Management (ICCAKM)*, Dubai, United Arab Emirates, pp. 1–6. DOI: 10.1109/ICCAKM58659.2023.10449493
10. William, P., Sharma, G., Kapil, K., Srivastava, P., Shrivastava, A., Kumar, R. (2023). Automation Techniques Using AI Based Cloud Computing and Blockchain for Business Management. *2023 4th International Conference on Computation, Automation and Knowledge Management (ICCAKM)*, Dubai, United Arab Emirates, pp. 1–6. DOI: 10.1109/ICCAKM58659.2023.10449534
11. More, A. R., Shendkar, O. B., Pathak, K. G., Sanap, P. D., Pachore, S. N., William, P. (2023). Survey on Framework for Governing Modern Cyber Attacks in Computer Network. *2023 4th International Conference on Computation, Automation and Knowledge Management (ICCAKM)*, Dubai, United Arab Emirates, pp. 01–06. DOI: 10.1109/ICCAKM58659.2023.10449582
12. Nayak, C., William, P., Kumar, R., Deepak, A., Yadav, K., Rao, A. L. N., Srivastava, A., Shrivastava, A. (2024). Edge Cloud Server Deployment with Machine Learning for 6G Internet of Things. *International Journal of Intelligent Systems and Applications in Engineering*, Vol. 12, No. 16s, p. 328. https://ijisae.org/index.php/IJISAE/article/view/4826
13. Hegde, S. K., William, P., Basvant, M. S., Deepak, A., Badhoutiya, A., Rao, A. L. N., Srivastava, A., Shrivastava, A. (2024). Energy-Efficient Bio-Inspired Hybrid Deep Learning Model for Network Intrusion Detection Based on Intelligent Decision Making. *International Journal of Intelligent Systems and Applications in Engineering*, Vol. 12, No. 16s, p. 306. https://ijisae.org/index.php/IJISAE/article/view/4823

14. Rawat, Romil, Telang, Shrikant, William, P., Kaur, Upinder, and Cu, Om Kumar (Eds.). (2022). *Dark Web Pattern Recognition and Crime Analysis Using Machine Intelligence.* IGI Global.
15. Yogeesh, N., William, P. (2024). Sensor-enabled biomedical decision support system using deep learning and fuzzy logic, In *Advances in Ubiquitous Sensing Applications for Healthcare, Deep Learning Applications in Translational Bioinformatics* (Vol. 15, pp. 33–53). Academic Press. https://doi.org/10.1016/B978-0-443-22299-3.00003-7
16. William, P., Rageeb, M., Boina, M.R., Lakshmi, T.R.V., Sharma, A., Marriwala, N.K. (2024). Empirical Analysis of Machine Learning in Enhancing the E-Business Through Structural Equation Modeling. In: Marriwala, N.K., Dhingra, S., Jain, S., Kumar, D. (Eds.), *Mobile Radio Communications and 5G Networks.* MRCN 2023. Lecture Notes in Networks and Systems, Vol. 915. Springer. https://doi.org/10.1007/978-981-97-0700-3_45
17. William, P., Chinthamu, N., Saxena, A., Lakshmi, T.R.V., Tiwari, M. (2024). Integration of Secure Data Communication with Wireless Sensor Network Using Cryptographic Technique. In: Marriwala, N.K., Dhingra, S., Jain, S., Kumar, D. (Eds.), *Mobile Radio Communications and 5G Networks.* MRCN 2023. Lecture Notes in Networks and Systems, Vol. 915. Springer. https://doi.org/10.1007/978-981-97-0700-3_46
18. Chhabra, G.S., William, P., Lanke, G.R., Jain, K., Lakshmi, T.R.V., Varshney, N. (2024). Comparative Analysis of Data Mining Based Performance Evaluation Using Hybrid Deep Learning Approach. In: Marriwala, N.K., Dhingra, S., Jain, S., Kumar, D. (Eds.), *Mobile Radio Communications and 5G Networks.* MRCN 2023. Lecture Notes in Networks and Systems, Vol. 915. Springer. https://doi.org/10.1007/978-981-97-0700-3_47
19. Khatkale, P.B., William, P., Oyebode, O.J., Sharma, A., Kumari, V., Singh, V. (2024). Probing of Instructional Data Mining Effectiveness in Decision-Making for Industrial and Educational Applications. In: Marriwala, N.K., Dhingra, S., Jain, S., Kumar, D. (Eds.), *Mobile Radio Communications and 5G Networks.* MRCN 2023. Lecture Notes in Networks and Systems, Vol. 915. Springer. https://doi.org/10.1007/978-981-97-0700-3_48
20. William, P., Chinthamu, N., Chiranjivi, M., Vijaya Lakshmi, T.R., Kumar, R., Marriwala, N.K. (2024). Assessment of Wireless Sensor Networks Integrated with Various Cluster-Based Routing Protocols. In: N. K. Marriwala, S. Dhingra, S. Jain, D. Kumar (Eds.), *Mobile Radio Communications and 5G Networks.* MRCN 2023. Lecture Notes in Networks and Systems, Vol. 915. Springer. https://doi.org/10.1007/978-981-97-0700-3_49
21. Aicha, N., Englebienne, G., Krse, B. (2014). Modeling visit behaviour in smart homes using unsupervised learning. *Proceedings of the 2014 ACM International Joint Conference on Pervasive and Ubiquitous Computing: Adjunct Publication, ser. UbiComp '14 Adjunct*, New York, NY, USA, 13–17 September 2014, pp. 1193–1200.
22. Mingming, G., Liangshan, S., Xiaowei, H., Qingwei, S. (2010). The System of Wireless Smart House Based on GSM and ZigBee. *2010 International Conference on Intelligent Computation Technology and Automation*, Changsha, pp. 1017–1020.
23. Dittawit, K., Aagesen, F. A. (2014). Home energy management system for electricity cost savings and comfort preservation. *2014 IEEE Fourth International Conference on Consumer Electronics Berlin (ICCEBerlin)*, Berlin, pp. 309–313.

15 Collaborative Computing of Big Data and Internet of Things Applications in Smart Environments

G Vijayakumar, D B Pardeshi, P. William, Abhishek Shankar Ippar and Dnyaneshwar Tulshiram Sangale

15.1 INTRODUCTION

The convergence of Big Data (BD) and the Internet of Things (IoT) has emerged as a revolutionary agent in the present era of unprecedented technological advancement. This convergence is revolutionizing the landscape of intelligent settings across a variety of industries. This comprehensive study investigates the intricate relationships that exist between IoT applications and BD, illuminating the mutually beneficial potential of these two types of applications as well as the major ramifications that they have for intelligent ecosystems [1]. At a time when our world is becoming increasingly linked, the seamless integration of these technologies presents an opportunity for a paradigm change. It paves the way for new opportunities for enhanced connection, decision-making that is driven by data, and the optimization of a wide range of sectors, including healthcare, energy, transportation, and urban planning. The capacity to manage and analyse massive volumes of data in order to get insights that were previously unachievable yet beneficial is the essence of what is known as "Big Data." This synergy ushers in a new era of efficiency, creativity, and sustainability for smart settings when it is paired with the ubiquitous connectivity that the IoTs provides. BD analytics provides stakeholders with access to real-time information that enables them to foresee trends, make decisions that are well-informed, and take proactive actions to address problems. The data collected from IoT devices is the lifeblood of Big Data analytics.

As an example, the transformation of patient care and administration in the healthcare business has been brought about by the combination of IoT applications with BD. Wearable technology, remote monitoring systems, and health sensors all contribute to the generation of a substantial amount of data pertaining to many aspects of

DOI: 10.1201/9781032703718-20

health. This information is used in the development of customized treatment regimens, the early diagnosis of illnesses, and the improvement of overall health. Similarly, the incorporation of these technologies into transportation opens the way for the development of autonomous systems, intelligent traffic management, and predictive vehicle maintenance, so ushering in a new era of mobility that is both safer and more efficient. There are, however, a number of challenges associated with this synergy. Concerns about data security, privacy, scalability, and interoperability pose a substantial barrier to the integration of IoT networks and BD in intelligent environments. In addition to illuminating the transformative potential of these technologies, our objective is to address the complexities and subtleties that are associated with the implementation of these technologies as we go further into this thorough study.

The purpose of this research is to provide academics, professionals, and policymakers with a road map by analysing new trends, creative methodologies, and best practices for harnessing the potential of Big Data and the Internet of Things. Therefore, this study gives a road map. By digging into the complexity of smart environments, we want to make a contribution to a deeper understanding of the shifting terrain. This will allow us to open the door to a future that is more intelligent, sustainable, and connected [2]. The investigation of this dynamic interface between IoT and Big Data applications in smart environments has the potential to totally revolutionize how we perceive our surroundings, how we interact with them, and how we optimize them. BD and the IoT are expected to have a significant impact on a number of different sectors, including urban planning, energy, transportation, and healthcare, among others. By way of illustration, the coupling of BD analytics with IoT devices, such as wearable health monitors, makes it feasible for the healthcare sector to do real-time patient monitoring, customized treatment regimens, and predictive healthcare interventions. In a similar vein, the integration of BD with the IoTs makes it possible to develop autonomous transportation systems, predictive maintenance for automobiles, and intelligent traffic management in the realm of transportation.

It may be challenging for computational intelligence systems to manage the enormous volumes of data that they are required to gather, store, and analyse, despite the fact that smart environmental applications have reaped significant benefits from the IoTs. Real-time or almost real-time analysis of high-speed data streams is a need for applications designed for smart environments. This is necessary in order to accomplish the results that are desired [3]. It is as a result of this that it is very necessary to carry out a comprehensive and efficient data flow analysis. Users are confronted with a job that is exceedingly difficult as it pertains to the evaluation, exchange, and extraction of information from huge amounts of data. The fast growth in the amount as well as the variety of innovative sensors that are being introduced to the market may be responsible for this change. The application centerfielder smart settings that are based on Big Data and the IoTs are now the focus of study, which brings significant opportunities as well as exciting challenges. Our team is presently analysing the findings of this investigation. In the future, there is a possibility that technologies related to the IoTs may be included in already existing applications, which will open up new possibilities for the development of applications. Creating a structural framework of ubiquitous networks that includes intelligent gadgets, networked sensors, and a large number of data sources was the objective that led to the creation of the IoT. The integration of a wide variety of tools and applications is another factor that has contributed to the expansion of communication that has been made possible by Web 2.0. A wide variety of data-gathering sources, powerful data analysis capabilities, and the current environment are all factors that may be used in combination with visualization tools. For the creation of applications for smart environments, it is really fascinating to investigate the possibilities that this brings about. We came to the conclusion that Big Data technology may be used for transmission, processing, storage, and analysis throughout the full ecosystem of applications that are associated with smart environments after conducting an examination of the current state of the art in research pertaining to massive amounts of data and the IoT [4]. The primary instruments that were used in the process of reducing the size of this region are shown in Figure 15.1.

As we delve deeper into this study, we will navigate the challenges and opportunities inherent in the marriage of BD and IoT. Issues of data security, scalability, and interoperability loom large, demanding innovative solutions to ensure the seamless integration and utilization of these technologies. Moreover, the study will explore the implications of this integration on privacy concerns and ethical considerations, shedding light on the responsible deployment of these technologies in smart environments. Furthermore, the research will uncover emerging trends and best practices that showcase the transformative capabilities of BD and IoT. From advanced data analytics techniques to edge computing solutions, the study aims to provide a nuanced understanding of the evolving landscape and to serve as a valuable resource for researchers, practitioners, and policymakers navigating the complex terrain of smart environments. As we embark on this journey, the profound implications of the integration of BD and IoT in smart environments come into sharper focus, promising a future where data-driven insights reshape the very fabric of our interconnected world.

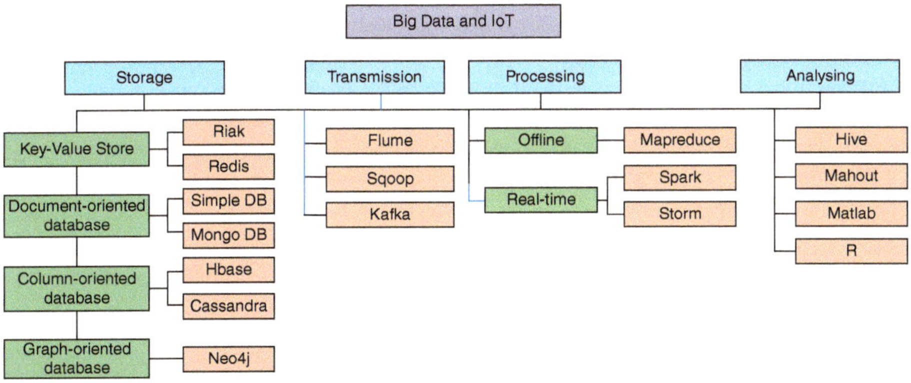

FIGURE 15.1 Main tools used in IoT and Big Data.

15.1.1 Objectives of the Study

The primary objectives of this study are threefold: firstly, to conduct a comprehensive review of the existing literature on the applications of BD and IoT in smart environments; secondly, to analyse the impact of these technologies on specific domains, identifying challenges and opportunities; and, thirdly, to provide valuable insights into emerging trends, best practices, and novel approaches that can guide future research and implementation efforts in the field. By addressing these objectives, we aim to contribute to the scholarly discourse surrounding the integration of BD and IoT in the dynamic landscape of smart environments [5].

15.2 REVIEW OF LITERATURE

After the study's results are presented, it is evident that there seems to be a correlation between the world's growing population and consumers' growing demand for goods and services. To meet this need, strategies that optimize the use of already available materials and natural resources must be developed. One area where the most recent advancements in information and communication technology have negatively impacted people's lives is the environment. Along with the environment, another sector that has suffered is the public health system. These technological advancements have had a detrimental effect on the environment. Because of this, human civilization is generally utilizing less energy and nonrenewable resources and is heading towards a future [6] where there will be less of an impact on the environment due to a general decrease in the quantity of energy and raw materials needed. As a result, this often results in a decrease in the amount of pollutants generated. The green IoTs, or G-IoT, is a crucial part of building an environmentally friendly house since information technology is quickly becoming identified as a means of addressing environmental issues. A thorough data analysis is necessary to provide a pertinent overview of the enormous and varied amount of data generated by the IoT. The information gathered will be helpful for doing various tasks related to creating smart urban services in addition to being helpful for forecasting and decision-making. After all is said and done, this will help with the process of continuing to develop technologies related to the IoT. IoT technology and the knowledge gained from research will eventually lead to cities becoming smarter, safer, and more environmentally friendly. The outcome of these two things together will be this. To make matters worse, this is true even in the very unlikely event that intelligent and sustainable cities are constructed. The main goal of this study is to create cities that optimize available resources, reduce pollution, and enhance the overall well-being of the populace. The city will combine the development of cutting-edge technology with the concentration of its resources in order to achieve this goal. Giving the most correct description of the data being utilized for analysis is always crucial when it comes to the practice of BD research. Statistical distributions are used in the applied sciences to describe data, as shown by a wealth of current research. Our goal is to create a distinct family of statistical models that, in our view, would provide the most realistic depiction of a wireless sensor network's data life cycle in existence. We can achieve this aim with the efforts we are now making. This work employs the previously described methodologies to do a thorough analysis of a new submodel known as the new exponent power-Weibull distribution. It is feasible to show that the model being offered is of a reasonable quality by looking at the wireless sensor network's data life cycle [7].

The idea of the Energy Internet (EI) was developed lately with the goal of making the process of building smart grids easier. This is achieved by combining several energy sources into a system that operates with a high level of flexibility and efficiency. In the process of conducting our inquiry, we have thoroughly examined IoT applications that might support smart environments and smart grids [8]. Smart metres, energy management systems, smart houses, and smart cities are a few instances of applications that fit under this category. Determining whether or if it is feasible to create IoT applications that are based on EI is one of our main research goals. These applications provide some intriguing new potential for the idea of electric intelligence, given that it is often considered to be one of the key causes leading to its proliferation. In addition, a number of important research topics were covered, such as the difficulties, unresolved problems, and potential future developments regarding the idea of environment intelligence, which is based on networks of IoT devices.

To accomplish the goals of this study, BD and IoT applications are examined in what are referred to as "smart settings." By conducting this research, we want to achieve our goal, which is to identify the data structures, typical patterns, application domains, and recurring issues related to this industry. The aim of this research is to accomplish this goal by using scholarly publications that were published in peer-reviewed journals between 2011 and 2019. Such an extensive investigation has never been conducted before in any kind of study. The selection process consists of four steps: identification, screening, eligibility, and inclusion. The thorough assessment of every single article that was looked at led to the discussion and resolution of six important research challenges [8–10]. It is clear from the results of combining BD and IoT technologies that there are numerous opportunities for creating smart environment applications that can monitor, protect, and enhance natural resources. Examples of technology developments in these fields include smart metering, smart farming and agriculture, smart environment monitoring, and smart disaster warning. For instance, Wacom gave its clients a summary of the most well-known strategies related to BD and the IoTs. Our analysis's findings have led us to the conclusion that further study is necessary [11–12].

The events that transpire in our immediate surroundings have a significant influence on the daily activities that we participate in. Some of these changes have an effect on the basic materials required for life. Examples of these changes are the filthy air and water that are commonplace across the world [13–14]. An environment that has been equipped with technology to offer a variety of services and solutions to address various environmental application issues is referred to as a "smart environment." Water quality and health, air pollution, weather, radiation monitoring, waste management, natural disasters, and a host of other environmental indicators are among the many environmental issues that have an environmental component. There is an environmental component to each of these environmental issues. The integration of sensors intended for smart environments with "Internet of Things" technology could lead to the creation of a new method for tracking, detecting, and monitoring environmental objects. It is possible that they will produce advantages that aid in the creation of a sustainable and ecologically conscious living environment. The IoT theory proposes that environmental sensors will be able to establish connections with other electronic devices, such as smartphones, via the use of Bluetooth or Wi-Fi. It would be possible for the sensors to transmit a substantial amount of data to the network as a consequence of this. Under these circumstances, the transmission and collection of data from environmental sensors would be made possible. It's likely that this will assist us in gaining a deeper understanding of our surroundings and coming up with solutions that are practical to the environmental problems that the contemporary world is now experiencing. This review article will provide a concise explanation of the environmental research disciplines that are based on the IoT, as well as the specific uses of these disciplines in the field of environmental studies [15–17]. In addition, we will investigate a variety of technologies that are based on the IoT in order to conduct research on the environment.

15.3 INTERNET OF THINGS (IoT) ARCHITECTURE FOR SMART ENVIRONMENTS

In the era of pervasive connectivity, the IoT has emerged as a transformative force, promising to infuse intelligence into our environments and redefine the way we interact with the world around us. At the heart of this paradigm shift lies the architecture designed to underpin smart environments, where interconnected devices seamlessly collaborate to enhance efficiency, convenience, and sustainability. This introduction explores the fundamental principles of IoT architecture for smart environments, illuminating the intricate web of connections that weave together to create intelligent and responsive ecosystems. The essence of IoT architecture lies in its ability to orchestrate a symphony of diverse devices, sensors, and actuators within smart environments. These environments, whether homes, cities, or industrial settings, are characterized by an intricate interplay of devices designed to collect, communicate, and act upon data. The architecture is the blueprint that orchestrates this intricate dance, ensuring that devices work in harmony to deliver meaningful and context-aware experiences [18–20].

Central to IoT architecture is the concept of edge computing, where data processing occurs closer to the source of data generation rather than relying solely on centralized cloud servers. This decentralized approach minimizes latency, optimizes bandwidth usage, and enhances the overall responsiveness of IoT applications. Edge computing within the architecture enables real-time decision-making, a critical factor in applications ranging from smart homes to industrial automation. Moreover, the architecture encompasses connectivity protocols that facilitate seamless communication between devices. Whether it's through traditional Wi-Fi, low-power protocols like Zigbee, or cellular networks, the choice of communication protocols plays a pivotal role in determining the efficiency and reliability of the IoT ecosystem. Security protocols are equally crucial, safeguarding data integrity and user privacy in an environment where diverse devices constantly exchange information.

As we get further into the levels of the IoT architecture, the importance of interoperability becomes more apparent. The standardization of communication protocols and data formats ensures that devices manufactured by different manufacturers are able to communicate and collaborate effectively with one another. The capacity to communicate with one another is the cornerstone upon which a unified and scalable smart environment may be constructed. A comprehensive analysis of IoT architecture for intelligent settings is now possible as a result of this. We set out to investigate the difficulties and opportunities hidden in the architecture that influence the creation of intelligent and flexible living environments [21–23]. This was accomplished by obtaining an understanding of the underlying ideas that guide the coordination of hardware, data, and communication. The complicated architecture of the IoT as it relates to smart environments is shown in Figure 15.2, which is a vivid mind map that may be used as a tool for teaching purposes. The mind map, in its most basic form, provides an overview of the intricate architecture of IoT technologies, which are the basis for smart environments. The primary node, which is clearly titled "IoT Architecture for Smart Environments," branches out into six vital components, each of which is represented by a different hue. This is done to promote both visual distinction and cognitive comprehension. The first node, which is denoted by the colour blue and is referred to as "Sensors and Actuators," is a representation of the many devices

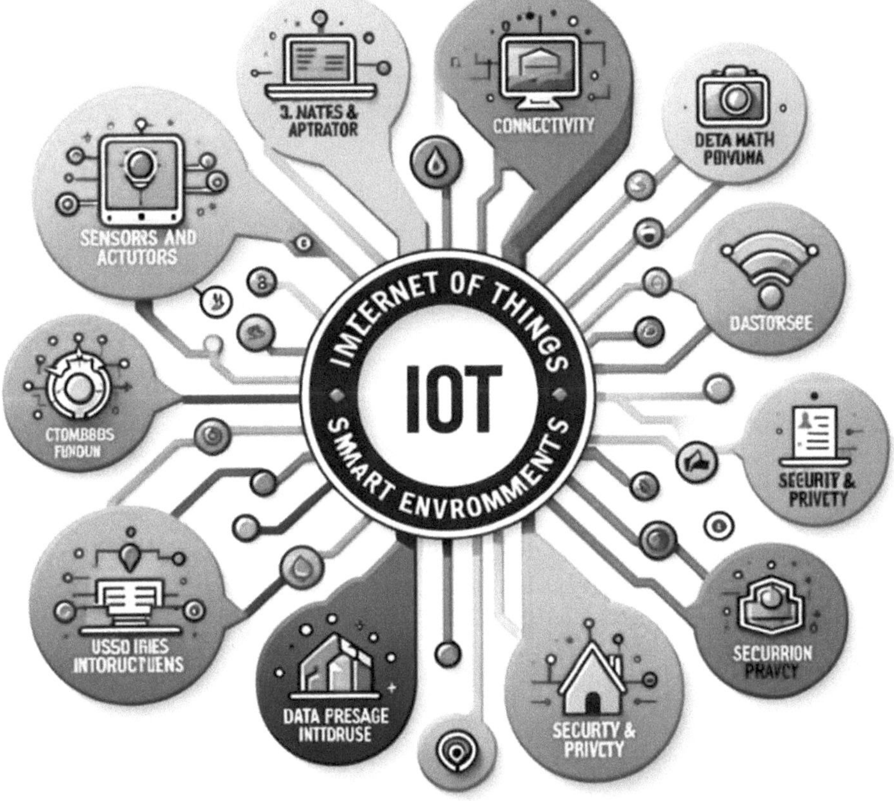

FIGURE 15.2 Multidimensional mind map of IoT architecture components.

that are able to perceive their environment (sensors) and those that are able to react to it (actuators). These are the endpoints of the IoTs; they serve as the actual physical interfaces between the virtual world and the real world. The "connection" node, which is shown in a fiery red colour, is the foundation of the connection of the IoTs. It is comprised of a number of protocols and network technologies that provide the seamless movement of data across various sites. All of these protocols, ranging from the more traditional Ethernet and Wi-Fi to particular IoT protocols that prioritize energy efficiency and long-range communication, are included in this category [24].

The Data Processing node, depicted in green, symbolizes the analytical engines and computing platforms that process and interpret the vast streams of data generated by sensors. This is where raw data is transformed into meaningful insights, driving automated responses and informed decision-making. Encased in orange, the Data Storage node refers to the databases and storage systems that securely house the collected information, ensuring it is retained for real-time and historical analysis. The "User Interface" node, shaded in purple, represents the point of human interaction with the IoT system. This is where users can configure, manage, and extract value from the IoT ecosystem, typically through dashboards, mobile applications, or other control systems. Lastly, the Security and Privacy node, coloured in yellow, underscores the paramount importance of securing the IoT infrastructure against unauthorized access and ensuring that data privacy is upheld. This encompasses the strategies, technologies, and policies that protect IoT devices and data from cyber threats. Collectively, this mind map not only serves as an introduction but also encapsulates the intricate interplay of technology and strategy that underpins IoT systems in smart environments. It showcases the convergence of various technological domains and highlights the importance of a holistic approach to designing IoT ecosystems that are robust, user-friendly, and secure.

15.4 RESEARCH METHODOLOGY

The Preferred Reporting Items for Systematic Reviews and Meta-Analysis (PRISMA) approach was used in order to carry out a systematic review (SR) for the aim of this investigation. It is possible to develop and organize SRs, which are a sort of meta-analysis, by using the PRISMA framework, which is a core set of evidence-based principles that serves as the foundation for the design and structuring of various types of meta-analyses. The design of the inclusion and exclusion criteria, the conduct of the search, and the identification of the research questions are the three phases of the review process that we have used in our study. These steps made up the review technique. In the following sections, we will delve further into these methodologies and discuss the ways in which they might be applied to the topic of our inquiry in a more general sense.

15.4.1 Definition of Research Questions

This SR has been organized in such a way that it incorporates the evaluation and categorization of relevant literature in order to include the whole spectrum of research

TABLE 15.1
IoT Smart ENV Configuration Registry

Research Question	Motivation
What is the breakdown of the number of articles that have been published on the IoT and BD in environmental applications, broken down by year, authors, country, context, and publishing venues?	In the event that the answer to this question is discovered, it will be feasible to ascertain the who, what, and when of the research initiatives that have been carried out.
What are the reasons for the use of massive amounts of data and the IoTs in the context of environmental applications?	This answer explains why BD and the IoTs will be crucial components of future applications for smart environments by providing an explanation of why these components will be vital.
When it comes to environmental applications, the IoT and BD pose the issue of what the most important obstacles are.	The answer to this question not only serves to evaluate the primary issues that are associated with the use of BD and the IoTs, but it also highlights the advantages and disadvantages of the solutions that are now available.
What are the most important technologies and approaches that are associated with the IoT and BD when it comes to applications that are connected to the environment?	It would be really helpful to know the answer to this question in order to determine which pieces of equipment and methods are now being used in applications.
Which of the most significant findings and inferences that have been drawn from the use of BD and the IoTs in the field of environmental science are the most significant?	The answer to this inquiry provides an overview of the primary inferences that may be drawn from the works that are the subject of the research.
The IoT and BD applied to environmental applications in the future are the subject of the sixth research topic, which inquires about the open views and research avenues for these technologies.	Finding relevant research subjects that have not yet been researched is made easier by the answer to this inquiry.

that was investigated. In order to determine the extent to which past papers have been covered, it is important to first determine the research problems that now need attention. By assessing research that is comparable to one another, we have the opportunity to deliver a variety of insights. There is a possibility that these findings will assist academics in developing new theoretical frameworks. Each of the study topics that were employed in our SR is outlined in Table 15.1, which can be found in this paragraph.

15.4.2 Conduction of SR

For the purpose of this research, the PRISMA flow diagram was used to choose articles that were relevant. Figure 15.3 illustrates the following essential procedures: inclusion, eligibility review, screening, and identification of the individuals interested in participating. A comprehensive procedure that must be carried out in order to choose a search strategy is shown in Figure 15.3, which can be found here. We were

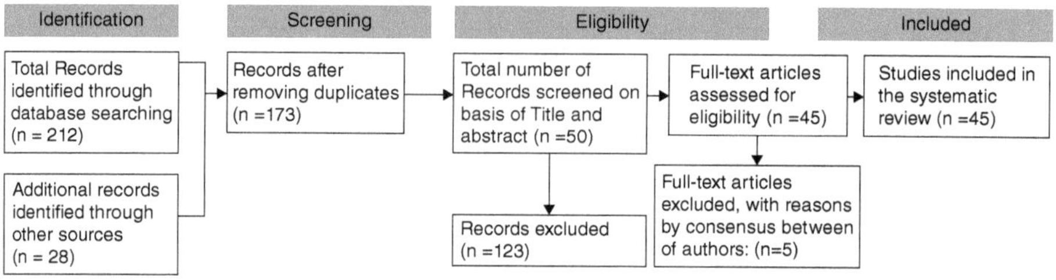

FIGURE 15.3 The systematic review process.

able to locate 212 of the 240 objects that were included in our original inventory by conducting searches utilizing electronic databases and search engines. The other 28 items were discovered via the utilization of additional sources. After eliminating all of the duplicates, the total number of results was ultimately brought down to 173. After applying the qualifying criteria that were based on the abstract and title to these 173, we were able to get 50 results, which was an increase from the volume of 173 that we had previously obtained. In spite of this, we were finally successful in acquiring 45 results by applying additional qualifying criteria that were based on the whole text. It is necessary to do a comprehensive study of these 45 research in order to arrive at the findings that will be detailed in the next section.

15.4.3 Quantitative Insights into Case Studies

The analysis of quantitative data extracted from real-world case studies offers a quantitative understanding of the outcomes achieved through the integration of BD and IoT technologies. Key performance indicators, such as efficiency gains, cost reductions, and improved decision-making, are quantified to demonstrate the tangible benefits observed in specific smart environment implementations.

15.4.4 Thematic Analysis of Interviews and Focus Groups

Thematic analysis is applied to the qualitative data gathered through interviews and focus groups. Open coding, axial coding, and selective coding techniques are utilized to identify recurring themes, patterns, and emergent concepts. The qualitative analysis uncovers nuanced perspectives, challenges faced by stakeholders, and innovative solutions employed in the integration of BD and IoT in smart environments.

15.4.5 Cross-Sectoral Comparative Analysis

The cross-sectoral comparative analysis involves examining similarities and differences in the impact of BD and IoT applications across diverse smart environment domains. Patterns of success and challenges common to multiple sectors are identified, providing a holistic view of the implications of these technologies on a broader scale.

15.5 RESULT AND DISCUSSION

An in-depth investigation of the uses of the IoT and BD in smart environments uncovers a revolutionary narrative of the integration of technology. According to the findings of the research, BD and the IoTs are both extensively employed and complement one another to produce intelligent ecosystems. When paired with the pervasive connectivity of IoT devices, BD analytics will become a driver for quick reactions and well-informed decision-making in smart environments. According to the findings of this study, the seamless integration of these technologies leads to improvements in resource management, energy efficiency, and sustainability in general across a variety of smart applications. The research forecasts that in the future, the world will become more data-driven and networked. BD and the IoTs will continue to be the driving forces behind innovations that will influence the development of smart environments in the direction of enhanced efficiency, responsiveness, and capacity for flexibility. Figure 15.4 presents a hypothetical estimate of the global share of IoT projects in the year 2023, split down by various IoT applications. The "Smart City" efforts are expected to continue to dominate the urban environment, as shown by this prognosis. This is most likely the result of the incorporation of IoT technology into urban management systems, which include controls for traffic, public safety, administration of utilities, and other relevant systems. This trend is a reflection of

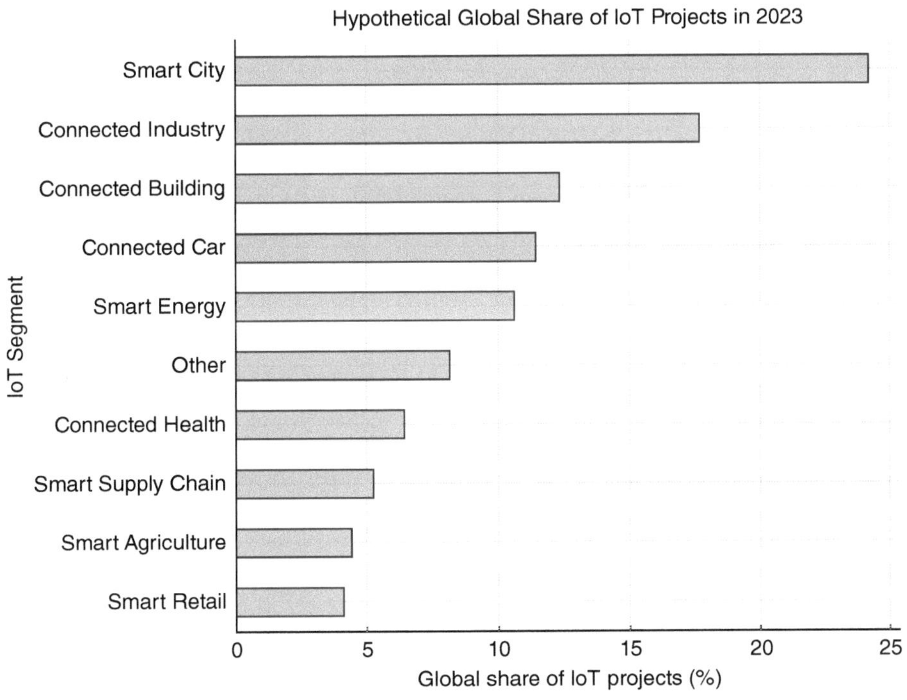

FIGURE 15.4 Projected distribution of IoT project segments in 2023.

the rising need for cities all around the globe to become smarter and more efficient. Following on from the "Smart City" category, the "Connected Industry" part suggests making a significant investment in Industrial Internet of Things (IIoT), which represents the ongoing digital transformation in the manufacturing and production sectors. Specifically, this entails combining machine-to-machine communication and sensors in order to simplify procedures, increase security, and save costs.

The sections under "Connected Building" and "Connected Car" demonstrate how the IoT is being used to make residential and commercial buildings safer, more energy-efficient, and more responsive to the needs of their occupants. Additionally, these sections demonstrate how automotive technology is expanding to produce more connected and autonomous vehicles. The phrase "smart energy" refers to the growing number of programmes that are aimed at modernizing energy grids and integrating renewable energy sources. This indicates that there is a greater focus on energy efficiency and sustainability. As a reflection of the diverse and ever-changing nature of IoT technology use cases, the "Other" category includes a wide variety of IoT applications that are still in their infancy and are highly specialized. The phrase "connected health" refers to the investments that the healthcare sector has made in the IoT for the purpose of providing patient care, remote monitoring, and service streamlining. All of these areas are very important in a world where healthcare costs are increasing, and the population is becoming older. There has been significant advancement in IoT-enabled logistics, supply chain management, and agricultural efficiency optimization in the "Smart Supply Chain" and "Smart Agriculture" categories, despite the fact that these sectors are smaller. The implementation of these enhancements is essential in order to guarantee food security and effectively manage the complexities of the supply chain. Additionally, "Smart Retail" exemplifies how the retail sector is promoting the use of the IoT to manage inventory, customize shopping experiences, and combine online and offline channels, all of which are essential in today's market that is driven by consumers. Table 15.2 provides a comparison of a number of wireless communication protocols that are fundamental to the infrastructure of IoT applications and BD applications in smart environments. Bluetooth, ZigBee, LoRaWAN, and SigFox are the four unique technologies that are broken down into their respective characteristics. It contains information on the range of each

TABLE 15.2
Comparative Analysis of Wireless Communication Standards for IoT in Smart Environments

Wireless Standards	Data Rates (kbps)	Network Topology	Frequency Band (MHz)	Range Capability (LoS) (m)
Bluetooth	750	P2P and Star	2500	10
ZigBee	20, 60, 280	Star, Tree, mesh	888, 915, 2400	100
LoRaWAN	70	Star	858, 919	10,000
SigFox	1	Star	888, 802	40,000

one, the frequency bands that are operational, the data transmission speeds, and the topologies of networking networks. Bluetooth is an industry-standard technology that is mostly used in consumer devices and is generally acknowledged for use in short-range communication. It operates on the frequency spectrum of 2.5 GHz, has a data throughput of 750 kbps, and is ideally suited for communication over short distances and with minimal power consumption (often within a range of 10 metres). Through its support for both star and point-to-point (P2P) configurations, its network architecture makes it possible to establish flexible network connections between devices.

ZigBee is another standard that has a larger range than Bluetooth, despite the fact that these two technologies may provide lower data speeds. In addition to being able to operate on a number of different frequency bands, it can be employed in star, tree, and mesh network topologies. As a result of its versatility, ZigBee may be used to establish networks that have a range of one hundred metres and are relatively long-range. Examples of such networks include those found in industrial controls and home automation systems. LoRaWAN is a technology that stands out and is an essential technology for wide-area IoT applications. It has a range of 10 kilometres. Because of its lower data rate of 70 kbps and its ability to connect devices over long distances without consuming much power, LoRaWAN is ideal for applications such as smart city applications, agricultural sensors, and any other application in which devices need to communicate over long distances without the need for frequent battery changes. Although it has a relatively low data rate of 1 kbps, the ultra-narrowband technology developed by SigFox has the largest range, which can reach up to 40 km. The fact that it is able to transmit small amounts of data over long distances makes it an excellent choice for applications such as utility metres or sensors that are located at a considerable distance.

BD is generated in IoT ecosystems from a variety of sources, and the development of each of these standards is vital to the growth of these ecosystems. Which wireless standard is the most suitable for a certain application is determined by the specific requirements of that application, taking into account the trade-offs between data rate, range, power consumption, and network complexity. These wireless technologies enable the collection of data simple and efficient, which in turn improves the intelligence and functionality of the environment in intelligent settings where real-time analytics and decision-making are of critical importance. Figure 15.5 presents a complete organization of the technologies and frameworks that are used to enable applications that include BD and the IoT in artificial intelligence contexts. It comprises the depth and breadth of platforms, methodologies, and technologies that are crucial to the process of collecting, processing, storing, and analysing the huge amounts of data that are created by networked sensors and devices. One of the most important aspects of this design is the Hadoop Ecosystem, which provides a variety of tools for distributed programming (including MapReduce, Spark, and Storm), data ingestion (including Apache Flume, Sqoop, and Kafka), and a distributed file system (HDFS) that is necessary for the management of enormous amounts of data. The usage of data analysis technologies such as Elasticsearch, Pig, and Apache Hive allows for the transformation and interpretation of enormous amounts of data into insights that may be of considerable utility. Because they are not constrained by the limits of traditional relational databases, NoSQL databases, which include Apache Redis (Key-Value

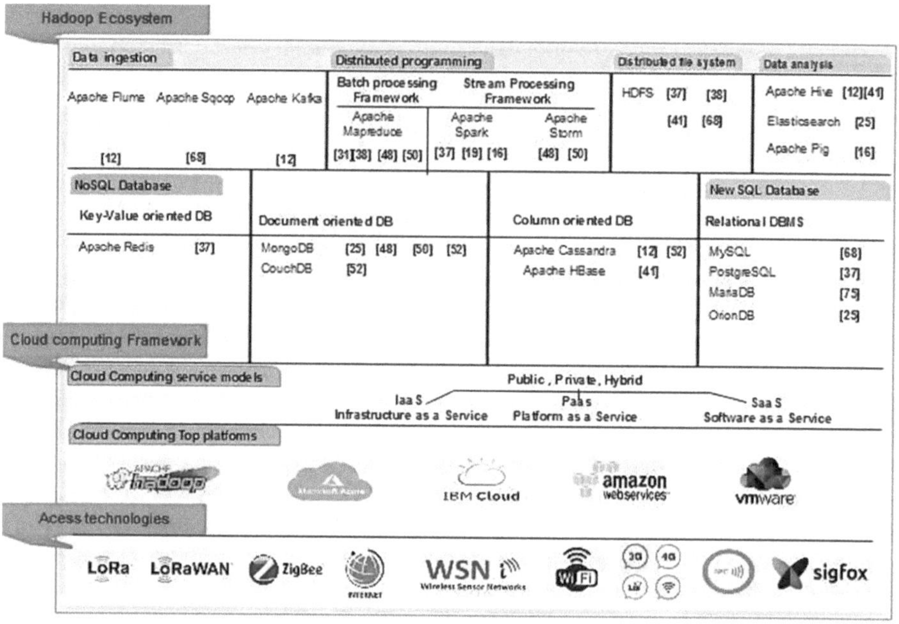

FIGURE 15.5 Infrastructure and technologies for IoT and BD in smart ecosystems.

oriented), MongoDB and CouchDB (Document oriented), and Apache Cassandra and HBase (Column oriented), are essential for managing the diverse, unstructured, and semi-structured data. This is due to the scalability and versatility of these databases, which allow them to handle the dynamic nature of massive amounts of data.

New SQL databases such as MariaDB, OrionDB, PostgreSQL, and MySQL are examples of the technological advancements that have been made in relational database systems. These databases maintain the ACID (Atomicity, Consistency, Isolation, and Durability) characteristics while expanding to meet the requirements of massive amounts of data and providing data management that is trustworthy and not susceptible to interference. There are many different service models that are described by the Cloud Computing Framework. Some of these models include Infrastructure as a Service (IaaS), Platform as a Service (PaaS), and Software as a Service (SaaS). Examples of prominent platforms that are included in the framework are Apache Hadoop, Microsoft Azure, IBM Cloud, Amazon Web Services, and VMware. The development environments, storage, and processing power that are required to design, deploy, and manage applications for the IoTs are offered by these services and platforms. Lastly, the Access Technologies section provides a description of the various connectivity options available for IoT devices. The following are some examples of these possibilities: Wi-Fi for local networking, ZigBee for mesh networks, LoRa and LoRaWAN for long-range connection, and SigFox for low-power wide-area network capabilities. These technologies make it possible for IoT devices to communicate and transmit data in an efficient manner, which is a crucial component for the functioning of environmentally intelligent settings. When it comes to the creation of smart environments, such as smart cities and smart healthcare, this network of networked technology demonstrates how BD and the IoTs are vital components. Additionally, it highlights the need for a multi-layered approach to the infrastructure of the IoT owing to the necessary technological diversity and specialization in order to manage the challenges that are provided by a range of applications.

15.5.1 Discussion

In the context of smart environments, the convergence of IoT and BD provides a spectrum of obstacles in addition to a kingdom of possibilities. As a reflection of the widespread interest and possible effect, the study highlights the growing body of academic work that is devoted to this convergence. Specifically, it focuses on the creation of smart cities, healthcare systems, and energy systems as the particular goals of deploying IoTs and BD in a variety of industries. Furthermore, the research sheds light on the major technical tools that are used to support these applications, while simultaneously conducting an in-depth analysis of the issues that are encountered, such as the protection of data privacy and the incorporation of heterogeneous systems. Additionally, the discussion offers insights into the outcomes that have been accomplished by the apps that are now being used for the IoTs and BD. These applications bring about benefits in terms of both efficiency and decision-making in smart settings.

15.6 CONCLUSIONS

Based on the findings of this comprehensive study, it is evident that the integration of IoT and BD is propelling smart environments to new levels of functionality and intelligence. Through the convergence of various technologies, development is being accelerated in a variety of domains, living standards are being raised, and sustainability is being promoted. Nevertheless, the paper makes notice of the fact that in order to fully fulfil this potential, it is required to navigate the issues around integration, privacy, and security with competence. The conclusion of the paper emphasizes the necessity of ongoing innovation and strategy development to address these issues. Additionally, it highlights the identification of attractive avenues for future research to ensure that the benefits of BD and the IoTs continue to materialize in the dynamic field of smart environments.

REFERENCES

1. Shafik, W., Matinkhah, S. M., Etemadinejad, P., and Sanda, M. N. (2020). Reinforcement learning rebirth, techniques, challenges, and resolutions. *JOIV: International Journal on Informatics Visualization*, 4(3), 127–135.
2. Shafik, W., Matinkhah, S. M., Sanda, M. N., and Afolabi, S. S. (2020). A 3-dimensional fast machine learning algorithm for mobile unmanned aerial vehicle base stations. *International Journal of Advances in Applied Sciences*, 10(1), 28–38.
3. Liu, X., Liu, A., Wang, T. et al. (2020). Adaptive data and verified message disjoint security routing for gathering big data in energy harvesting networks. *Journal of Parallel and Distributed Computing*, 13(5), 140–155.

4. Ghasemaghaei, M. and Calic, G. (2020). Assessing the impact of big data on firm innovation performance: big data is not always better data. *Journal of Business Research*, 10(8), 147–162.
5. Wu, Y., Huang, H., Wu, N., Wang, Y., and Wang, M. Z. (2020). An incentive-based protection and recovery strategy for secure big data in social networks. *Information Sciences*, 50(8), 79–91.
6. Qi, C.-C. (2020). Big data management in the mining industry. *International Journal of Minerals, Metallurgy and Materials*, 27(2), 131–139.
7. Maksimovic, M. (2017). The role of green internet of things (G-IoT) and big data in making cities smarter, safer and more sustainable. *International Journal of Computing and Digital Systems*, 6(4), 175–184.
8. Nandyala, C. S., and Kim, H.-K. (2016). Green IoT agriculture and healthcare application (GAHA). *International Journal of Smart Home*, 10(4), 289–300.
9. Gomez, C. (2019). Internet of Things for enabling smart environments: A technology centric perspective. *Journal of Ambient Intelligence and Smart Environments*, 11(1), 23–43.
10. Lazarescu, M. T. (2013). Design of a WSN platform for long-term environmental monitoring for IoT applications. *Proceedings of the IEEE Journal on Emerging and Selected Topics in Circuits and Systems*, 3(1), 45–54.
11. Saheb, S. S., Kiran, P. B. N., Bhaskara Ganesh, B. U., Roopalatha, N., Syed, S. M., and William, P. (2023). Artificial neural networks based risk management analysis of modern commercial banks using behavioral finance theory. In *2023 4th International Conference on Computation, Automation and Knowledge Management (ICCAKM)*, Dubai, United Arab Emirates (pp. 1–6). DOI: 10.1109/ICCAKM58659.2023.10449627
12. William, P., Agrawal, A., Rawat, N., Shrivastava, A., Srivastava, A. P., and Ashish (2023). Enterprise human resource management model by artificial intelligence digital technology. In *2023 4th International Conference on Computation, Automation and Knowledge Management (ICCAKM)*, Dubai, United Arab Emirates (pp. 01–06). DOI: 10.1109/ICCAKM58659.2023.10449624
13. William, P., Panicker, A., Falah, A., Hussain, A., Shrivastava, A., and Khan, A. K. (2023). The emergence of artificial intelligence and machine learning in contemporary business management. In *2023 4th International Conference on Computation, Automation and Knowledge Management (ICCAKM)*, Dubai, United Arab Emirates (pp. 1–6). DOI: 10.1109/ICCAKM58659.2023.10449493
14. William, P., Sharma, G., Kapil, K., Srivastava, P., Shrivastava, A., and Kumar, R. (2023). Automation techniques using AI based cloud computing and blockchain for business management. In *2023 4th International Conference on Computation, Automation and Knowledge Management (ICCAKM)*, Dubai, United Arab Emirates (pp. 1–6). DOI: 10.1109/ICCAKM58659.2023.10449534
15. More, A. R., Shendkar, O. B., Pathak, K. G., Sanap, P. D., Pachore, S. N., and William, P. (2023). Survey on framework for governing modern cyber attacks in computer network. In *2023 4th International Conference on Computation, Automation and Knowledge Management (ICCAKM)*, Dubai, United Arab Emirates (pp. 01–06). DOI: 10.1109/ICCAKM58659.2023.10449582
16. Nayak, C., William, P., Kumar, R., Deepak, A., Yadav, K., Rao, A. L. N., Srivastava, A., and Shrivastava, A. (2024). Edge cloud server deployment with machine learning for 6G Internet of Things. *International Journal of Intelligent Systems and Applications in Engineering*, 12(16s), 328. https://ijisae.org/index.php/IJISAE/article/view/4826

17. Hegde, S. K., William, P., Basvant, M. S., Deepak, A., Badhoutiya, A., Rao, A. L. N., Srivastava, A., and Shrivastava, A. (2024). Energy-efficient bio-inspired hybrid deep learning model for network intrusion detection based on intelligent decision making. *International Journal of Intelligent Systems and Applications in Engineering*, 12(16s), 306. https://ijisae.org/index.php/IJISAE/article/view/4823
18. Rawat, R., Telang, S., William, P., Kaur, U., and Cu, O. K. (Eds.). (2022). *Dark Web Pattern Recognition and Crime Analysis Using Machine Intelligence*. IGI Global.
19. Yogeesh, N., and William, P. (2024). Sensor-enabled biomedical decision support system using deep learning and fuzzy logic. In *Advances in Ubiquitous Sensing Applications for Healthcare, Deep Learning Applications in Translational Bioinformatics* (Vol. 15, 33–53). Academic Press. DOI: 10.1016/B978-0-443-22299-3.00003-7
20. William, P., Rageeb, M., Boina, M. R., Lakshmi, T. R. V., Sharma, A., and Marriwala, N. K. (2024). Empirical analysis of machine learning in enhancing the E-business through structural equation modeling. In N. K. Marriwala, S. Dhingra, S. Jain, and D. Kumar (Eds.), *Mobile Radio Communications and 5G Networks*. MRCN 2023. Lecture Notes in Networks and Systems (Vol. 915). Springer. DOI: 10.1007/978-981-97-0700-3_45
21. William, P., Chinthamu, N., Saxena, A., Lakshmi, T.R.V., and Tiwari, M. (2024). Integration of Secure Data Communication with Wireless Sensor Network Using Cryptographic Technique. In N. K. Marriwala, S. Dhingra, S. Jain, and D. Kumar (Eds.), *Mobile Radio Communications and 5G Networks*. MRCN 2023. Lecture Notes in Networks and Systems (Vol. 915). Springer. DOI: 10.1007/978-981-97-0700-3_46
22. Chhabra, G. S., William, P., Lanke, G. R., Jain, K., Lakshmi, T. R. V., and Varshney, N. (2024). Comparative Analysis of Data Mining Based Performance Evaluation Using Hybrid Deep Learning Approach. In N. K. Marriwala, S. Dhingra, S. Jain, and D. Kumar (Eds.), *Mobile Radio Communications and 5G Networks*. MRCN 2023. Lecture Notes in Networks and Systems (Vol. 915). Springer. DOI: 10.1007/978-981-97-0700-3_47
23. Khatkale, P. B., William, P., Oyebode, O. J., Sharma, A., Kumari, V., and Singh, V. (2024). Probing of Instructional Data Mining Effectiveness in Decision-Making for Industrial and Educational Applications. In N. K. Marriwala, S. Dhingra, S. Jain, and D. Kumar (Eds.), *Mobile Radio Communications and 5G Networks*. MRCN 2023. Lecture Notes in Networks and Systems (Vol. 915). Springer. DOI: 10.1007/978-981-97-0700-3_48
24. William, P., Chinthamu, N., Chiranjivi, M., Vijaya Lakshmi, T. R., Kumar, R., and Marriwala, N. K. (2024). Assessment of Wireless Sensor Networks Integrated with Various Cluster-Based Routing Protocols. In N. K. Marriwala, S. Dhingra, S. Jain, and D. Kumar (Eds.), *Mobile Radio Communications and 5G Networks*. MRCN 2023. Lecture Notes in Networks and Systems (Vol. 915). Springer. DOI: 10.1007/978-981-97-0700-3_49

16 A Systematic and Analytical Review on Drowsiness Detection System-based Real-Time Application

Anshu Kumar Dwivedi, Vishwanath Bijalwan, Rupesh Kumar Mishra and Ratnesh Ranjan

16.1 INTRODUCTION

The growth in population and car use has raised the severe ramifications of traffic accidents, crashes, loss of valuable life, economic difficulties, and lifelong physical and psychological illnesses. In 2020, the National Crime Records Bureau (NCRB) submitted a paper on the statistical data of highway accidents [1]. According to the paper, over 6 lakh road accidents are registered in a year, with 69 per cent resulting in substantial destruction to property and life. The study then explores further the factors that lead to road accidents. Lethargy and the motorist's psychological condition are vital in car accidents and careless driving. Sleep deprivation causes the body to react inefficiently, decreasing response time and alertness [2]. Drowsiness in the driver might be caused by restless driving, weariness, or drug usage, while the driver's psychological condition could be intense fury, frustration, or even extreme happiness. According to the study report, driving activity is a crucial cause of road accidents, which motivates many researchers to track and identify drivers' drowsiness mechanisms. Even though the frequency of traffic accidents and the death of valuable lives is rising, specific preliminary study results have been employed in real time to eliminate road accidents [3]. It also causes low alertness and loss of concentration, which limits the capacity to execute activities requiring care, such as driving a car. In-car safety technology, such as driver sleepiness detection, is critical for preventing traffic accidents.

In today's world, automobiles play a crucial role in daily commutes, providing enhanced living standards, comfort, and helping individuals meet time constraints. This widespread reliance on vehicles has led to significant traffic congestion in cities and on roads, resulting in an increased number of traffic accidents due to various factors. One primary cause of these accidents is driver fatigue. To mitigate this issue, an

DOI: 10.1201/9781032703718-21

efficient way to prevent driver sleepiness is to detect it early and sound an alarm. The National Highway Traffic Safety Administration (NHTSA) reports that driver drowsiness is a major factor in traffic incidents, accounting for approximately 73,000 accidents, 820 fatalities, and 45,000 injuries annually in the United States. Additionally, in India, over 147,000 people lost their lives in traffic accidents in 2017. Annually, over a million people are killed in road accidents, and more than four times that number are wounded. In India, an average of 1,36,118 individuals perished in road accidents during the previous decade. Sixty per cent of people killed in car accidents in 2016 were between the ages of 18 and 35 [4–6]. In India, over 500 people have died due to accidents on the Yamuna expressway since 2012, while over 100 have been killed due to car wrecks on the Agra-Lucknow expressway. According to law enforcement personnel and patrol squads on such significant highways, most road crashes happen around 2:30 and 5:30 a.m. due to sleepy driving.

Lack of sleep is a significant cause of accidents, making the technology for detecting driver sleepiness crucial for preventing road mishaps. Various signs of driver fatigue, such as difficulty keeping eyes open, frequent yawning, and leaning forward, can be observed while driving. To analyse the extent of driver sleepiness, several methods are employed, which can be categorized into physiological assessments, behavioural measures, and vehicle-based metrics. Among these, behavioural metrics, which focus on the driver's actions rather than the vehicle's movements, are highly effective. In this context, a digital webcam is often used to collect data on the driver.

Our proposed approach for detecting driver fatigue employs behavioural observations. Photos of someone's face and tracking of visual facts and eye movement patterns are used to identify weariness. Face image analysis is a major academic topic, with applications ranging from face recognition to virtual tools to biometric technology safety systems. This research investigates eye clustering, which requires inspecting the entire picture of the person's face and determining the location of the eyes using a well-proposed imaging visualization approach. After selecting the location of the eyes, the system is supposed to detect exhaustion and decide whether the eyes have been opened or shut. This article proposes a machine learning-based system to detect driver fatigue, utilizing Computer Vision with OpenCV for imaging visualization. The system integrates a web camera with OpenCV and employs Haar classifiers for feature-based face detection and eyelid classification. The developed attentiveness system monitors eyelid status to alert the driver if drowsiness is detected. Additionally, physiological tests such as electrocardiography (ECG), EEG, and electrooculography are used to analyse the driver's condition [7, 8]. EEG technology records neural electrical impulses using scalp electrodes. After artifact removal from the original EEG data, the rhythmic activity is divided into several frequency bands: Delta (0.5–5 Hz), Theta (4–9 Hz), Alpha (8–14 Hz), Beta (13–31 Hz), and Gamma (more than 31 Hz), as listed in [9]. The human eye is an electric dipole between the retina and the cornea—the energy gap between the retina and the cornea changes depending on the eyeball's location. An electrooculogram, or EOG, is the resultant signal. The EOG signal is valuable in measuring and studying eye movements and can thus be used in a variety of medical applications [10]. Online courses are the most popular way to learn since they are inexpensive, flexible, have diverse sessions, provide a pleasant atmosphere, and allow anybody to attend classes offered by world-class faculty from leading colleges. eLearning, on the other hand, is less communicative than in-person classes. When a teacher notices that a student is inattentive due to tiredness, they might reawaken the student's interest by asking them topic-related questions. In virtual classrooms, there is no possibility for multiple communication between the professor and the participant. Put another way, no one is watching the students' behaviour while the course is being given. A student's Eye Aspect Ratio (EAR) and Mouth Aspect Ratio (MAR) were calculated to determine their level of sleepiness [11]. This process involved identifying and extracting the necessary facial action units. A snapshot of the instance was taken to ensure accurate computation of the EAR and MAR. The captured image was then used as an assessment for pre-trained Convolutional Neural Network model [12]. Among the various pre-trained models we tested, ResNet50 significantly outperformed others, such as MobileNet and GoogleNet. ResNet50, a 50-layer CNN trained on over a million images from the ImageNet dataset [13, 14], originally classified images into 1,000 different classes. We customized the network to classify the images into the relevant groups for our application. When the student is recognized as sleepy, the question discussion problem module is triggered. Based on the content of the video up to that point, this module creates check questionnaires. Because one question may not be enough to pique the user's interest, the GUI allows them to answer any questions they desire [15].

Drowsiness has been detected using a variety of methodologies developed by researchers. The researchers suggested quasi-methods based on electrooculography [16, 17]. This method collects electric pulses from the tissues around the eyes and analyses data from eye movement. Similarly, the author in [18–20] suggested that by adding sensors to the muscles near the eyes, electromyography and electroencephalograms may be used to analyse electrical impulses around the eyes. These approaches that don't rely on images enable for quicker data collection. However, challenges arise when the sensor detects sounds created by the user's movements, leading to lower accuracy. Additionally, attaching a sensor to a user for sleep detection can be cumbersome.

16.2 LITERATURE REVIEW

After reviewing several papers, the following methodologies and techniques are identified, and their behavioural parameters are as follows.

16.2.1 Facial Expression

In the laboratory, the researchers employ Finite Element Analysis, a complicated method that uses a dataset of facial expressions as a prototype and diagnoses sleepiness based on database findings. Infrared light is used in the hardware system because it offers several benefits, such as simplicity of use and independence from external illumination conditions. [21]. The system initially detects the face area from the input images using a background subtraction approach. Horizontal projection and pattern matching are then employed to generate facial emotions. In the tracking phase, previously detected components are monitored using pattern matching, and the occurrence of drowsiness is assessed by analysing changes in facial modules. Changes in three primary aspects—eyebrow-raising, yawning, and eye-closing—over a specified period are considered early signs of tiredness, prompting the system to create an alarm.

16.2.2 Yawning

Yawning is characterized as an involuntary broad opening of the mouth with maximum jaw expansion, followed by a lengthy and deep inhale via the mouth and nose, followed by a leisurely expiration, all accompanied by a sensation of comfort [21]. A typical yawn lasts 5 seconds. Furthermore, in humans, yawning is typically followed by limb stretching. Yawning has long after yawning (P = 0.002) and 15 been regarded as a symptom of weariness, and it is frequently taken as rude when done in the company of others. It's also contagious because yawning may be induced by seeing, hearing, reading, or simply thinking about it. Several studies have discovered that yawning increases arousal, as demonstrated by a considerable shift in numerous physiological indicators. A survey of 48 students reported a substantial increase in heart rate during the peak of yawning, 10 seconds after yawning, and 15 seconds after yawning when compared to baseline values. This rise in heart rate was also reported to continue for at least 5 seconds, as there was no significant change in heart rates at the peak of yawning and 5 seconds after yawning. Additionally, skin conductance significantly increased at the height of yawning and at 6-second intervals after yawning [22].

The driver's driving photos utilized in this investigation were contributed by Biteda, an information technology business. This learning found the tentative results and split the dataset in a 3:7 ratio. Numerous data sets were divided into four classes, some as follows. Eyes (2,111 images; the images of open mouth (1996) snaps; 1,397 training and 599 test samples) (2,005 images; 1,404 training and 602 test samples), closed eyes (1,774 images; 1,242 training and 532 test samples), and closed mouth (1997) images; 1,398 training and 600 test samples) (2005 images; 1,404 training and 602 test samples) are all mentioned [23]. A few examples from the training set are shown in Figure 16.1. The training and test sets are same, but the drivers are not.

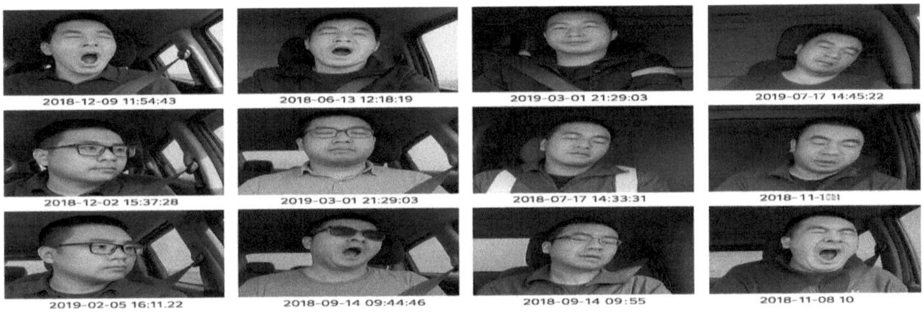

FIGURE 16.1 Example of training data (yawning).

Four classes of datasets were identified: open mouth (1,996 images; 1,397 training and 599 test samples), closed mouth (1,997 images; 1,398 training and 600 test samples), open eyes (2,226 images; 1,558 training and 668 test samples), and closed eyes (1,774 images; 1,242 training and 532 test samples) [23]. Figure 16.1 illustrates some training set samples. The assessment sets correspond to the drill sets but feature unlike drivers.

16.2.3 Eye Closure

Quantifying the change in the eye's condition after blinking is challenging, so the eye state is determined by computing eye closure using device detection. In Figure 16.2, this method's flowchart is displayed. After deciding on the area of interest (ROI), the binary picture is smoothed using dilation and erosion methods in order to describe the state of the eyes. A black area can be used to represent the binocular image region, and both the total number of pixels in the ROI and the number of black pixels are tallied [23]. Figure 16.2(a)(b) shows the completed images of the eyes and lips.

The batch size is set to 33 during training, and the improved approach uses a 0.0001 learning rate. All training sets are processed once, and the batch is processed 100 times per epoch. Python 3.5.2 and Keras 2.2.4 are used for training and testing MTCNN and EM-CNN, with Tensor Flow 1.12.0 as the backend. Because drivers show significant variations in mouth conditions and less in eye conditions when tired, the proposed EM-CNN is more specialized and focused on the mouth's condition than the eyes. Table 16.1 presents the classification results based on the receiver operating characteristic (ROC) curve, indicating that a higher area under the curve value corresponds to a healthier organization effect [24]. According to the testing

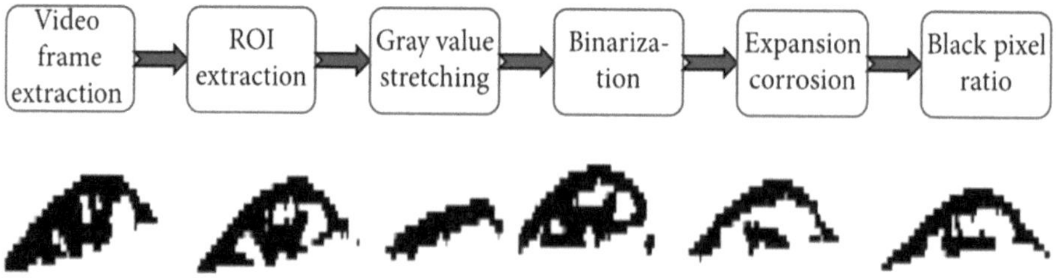

FIGURE 16.2 (a). Various states of eye. (b). Various states of mouth.

TABLE 16.1
Numerous Eye State

State	AUC (%)
Closed eye	97.913
Opened eye	99.1
Closed mouth	99.854
Opened mouth	99.918

FIGURE 16.3 Machine vision-based eye closure calculations.

consequences, the proposed EM-CNN has a stronger classification effect on the mouth condition compared to the eyes.

When combined with the time-based correlation of eye state changes based on blink rate, drowsy driving can be identified by monitoring the condition of the eyes in the video frame sequence. An open eye is denoted as "1," and a closed eye is denoted as "0." In the video frame sequence, the blink process so appears as a series of "0" and "1." In a similar vein, by documenting the state of the lips during the video frame sequence, the frequency of yawning is utilized to evaluate driver weariness. An open mouth is represented as "1" and a closed mouth as "0," with the yawning process reflected as a succession of "0" and "1" [24].

Existing results cannot be applied directly since thresholds vary due to different methodologies in various studies. Figure 16.3 illustrates the PERCLOS (Percentage of Eyelid Closure) and POM (Percentage of Mouth Opening) thresholds, which require experimental validation. The fatigue threshold helps determine whether a driver is drowsy. The test findings indicate that when PERCLOS reaches 0.25, the driver remains in a closed-eye condition for a significant duration [19, 24]. Similarly, when POM approaches 0.5, the driver stays in the open-mouth position for an extended period. It's important to note that as these indicators increase, so does the level of exhaustion [26].

16.2.4 Head Posture

Teyeb proposed employing eye closure and head postures to identify sleepy drivers. They begin by taking a video using a camera, and each video frame is subjected to the following operations [27]. ROI is identified using the Viola-Jones approach for detecting faces and eyes. When a closed eye is detected in the frames, the duration of the closure is measured; if this duration exceeds a predetermined threshold, a sleepiness condition is identified. The established method then calculates the head's inclination (left, right, forward, backward) and rotation (left or right). The video is divided into frames, and images of the head are retrieved to calculate image coordinates [29]. Finally, the system calculates sleepiness by integrating the eye closure time with the head position calculation. Many studies are conducted on 10 volunteers in various scenarios to evaluate the system. The findings suggest that the systems are approximately 80% accurate. The resulting difference is compared against a threshold to distinguish objects from non-objects based on learned data.

A Haar-like feature provides a significant advantage over most other features in terms of computation speed. The three most essential components of how Haar-like features work are the integral image, classifier training, and cascading. An integral image can be created by summing the pixel values above and to the left of the initial pixel, facilitating the construction of a rectangle used for comparison purposes. There are 18 distinct types of features available. In these features, one half of the rectangle is black, while the other half is white. First, the totals of the black and white regions are added together. Then, the total of the white regions is subtracted from the total of the black regions. The classifier training involves selecting features through the AdaBoost algorithm.

16.3 DRIVER FATIGUE DETECTION BASED ON EEG

Human organs cease functioning due to tiredness, and the mind progressively loses awareness. Before micro-sleep episodes occur, several physiological activities begin. Fatigue can influence heart rate, core body temperature, brain activity, and pupillary light reflex time. Measuring these physiological responses is considered the most dependable and adaptable method for monitoring and assessing fatigue. Fatigue detection systems use various technologies, with one of the most effective methods being ASTiD (Automated Steering Input Device). ASTiD counts steering errors during peak circadian cycle phases when the likelihood of fatigue is higher, typically from 3 p.m. to 5 p.m. and 2 a.m. to 6 a.m. This study evaluates fatigue levels by analysing physiological changes in the brain. Table 16.2 shows how EEG rhythms reflect a person's mental state. A high meditation state follows gradual relaxation in the early stages of tiredness. EEG rhythms were used to calculate a tiredness index for a person at three distinct periods and states in this investigation.

The literature has various research and journal papers on EEG-based driver tiredness detection. Accurately recognizing weariness via EEG data is one of the most difficult difficulties in EEG signal processing. A new EEG signal processing approach is provided to overcome this issue. This method uses multilayer feature extraction and a unique hybrid feature selection method (RFINCA) to construct EEG signal classification for tiredness diagnosis. The primary goal of the given multi-layered feature extraction technique is to eliminate low, medium, and high-level characteristics. For this, we employed both percussive and scientific characteristics in tandem. The four-level 1D-DWT with 4 Symlets filter, shown in Figure 16.4, is utilized for feature extraction and multilayer pre-processing since 1D-DWT is commonly used for noise reduction and signal dissection. RFINCA is frequently used to identify significant features, which are then categorized with superficial classifiers.

TABLE 16.2
Associations Between EEG Rhythm Bands and Mental Activities

Brainwave Band	Frequency Range (Hz)	Associated Mental State
Alpha	8–13	Relaxation
Beta	14–26	Thinking and attention
Theta	4–7.5	Unconscious or deep meditation
Delta	0.5–4	Deep sleep
Gamma	30–45	Movement of fingers, toes, and tongue

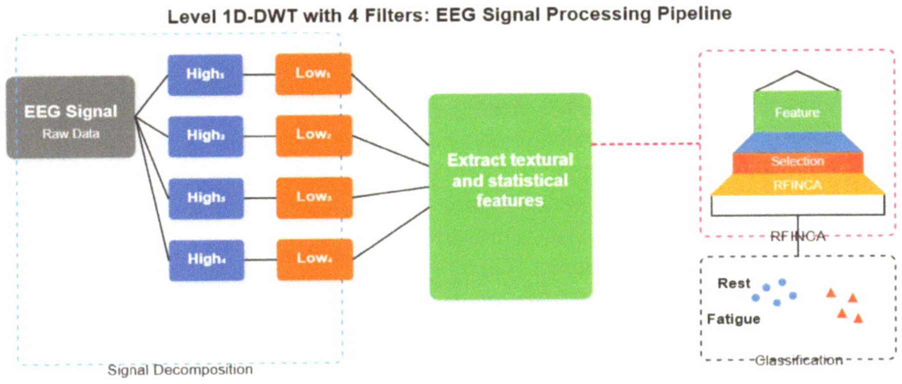

FIGURE 16.4 Level 1D-DWT with four filters.

16.3.1 Driver Fatigue Detection Based on Heartbeat

Under optimal conditions, facial image analysis can effectively detect fatigue, but the detection rate decreases when critical facial areas, such as the eyes, are obscured (e.g., by sunglasses). Combining image processing with heart rate analysis can enhance detection accuracy. However, existing ECG or heart rate monitoring devices often fail to synchronize in real time with their servers or backup systems. Consequently, they can only be used for probabilistic analysis of accident causes rather than for real-time prevention by alerting the driver [33].

The pulse rate is defined as the number of times all arteries (blood vessels) expand and contract in response to the heartbeat within one minute. Pulse width is used to determine the heart rate, as cardiac contractions elevate heart rate and blood pressure in the arteries. Essentially, pulse and heart rate are synonymous. The sinoatrial node is the origin of cardiac depolarization, so the pulse rate in a healthy heart corresponds to the rate of depolarization.

Like blood pressure and breathing rate, heart rate varies with age. For adults, a normal pulse ranges from 60 to 100 beats per minute (bpm). In contrast, children typically have a faster heartbeat. Bradycardia, characterized by a pulse rate of fewer than 60 bpm in adults, and tachycardia, characterized by a pulse rate exceeding 100 bpm in adults, are both considered abnormal heart rhythms. When the atria and ventricles are not synchronized, the pulse rate can be derived separately for each. For instance, in ventricular fibrillation, the ventricular rate can range from 300 to 600 bpm, while the atrial rate might remain within the normal range (60–100 bpm) or be slightly elevated (100–150 bpm) [32].

Meanwhile, someone's heart rate drops by about eight beats per minute as they reach the relaxation phase. Miriam R. Waldeck (2003) determined this by recording the difference between each subject's average and lowest heart rates at night [46]. A reduction in blood pressure happens due to this, which happens during falling asleep. During sleep, blood moves from the brain, relaxing the arteries and expanding bodily tissues. The heart's parasympathetic nerves, which activate when a person becomes fatigued, can also induce a drop in pulse rate. These nerves govern the autonomic functions of the heart, operating without conscious control. There are two types of autonomic nerves in the heart: sympathetic and parasympathetic nerves [32]. The sympathetic nerves enhance heart cell function during periods of activity, while the parasympathetic nerves reduce heart cell function when the body is at rest. Consequently, the parasympathetic nerves actively limit cardiac cell activity during sleep, allowing the body to rest.

In a sleepiness detection system, pulse rate sensors collect data from the driver's pulse through the skin. This data is transmitted to a computer for processing. Since the signal produced by the sensor is analog in nature, it must be converted to digital form using the Arduino Nano's Analog to Digital Converter.

To begin the computation, the system will evaluate the PPG data obtained from the detector to guess how much the BPM is necessary. This system will calculate the worth of the IBI; after the IBI has been received, it may be searched to determine how much BPM that individual has. The system and detectors will then adjust by computing the mean heart rate in the first 5 seconds after the user puts his finger on the sensor, and after the mean heart rate in 5 seconds is attained, the buzzer will light up. Also displayed on the monitor will be the mean pulse, suggesting that the measurement was completed. Next, the system will begin and continuously monitor the pulse. Figure 16.5 shows the flowchart of heartbeat monitoring. After establishing an average, the detector will analyse the pulse and measure it to the lower limit of the user's pre-specified pulse. Lower limits are found by multiplying the average pulse by eight. The algorithm determines the item is asleep if the pulse is eight beats slower than the preceding average. A warning displays on the screen to advise the user that they are tired if the item is tired, that is, eight beats below the mean or the pulse is not readable for even more than 2 seconds [32].

16.3.2 Driver Fatigue Detection Based on EOG

Among the most significant options for raising traffic safety and lowering accident rates is developing a monitoring system to evaluate sleepy driving accurately. The electro-cablegram signal (EOG) has several benefits over other research methods [34]. Many fatigue-driving tracking systems based on various characteristics have been created recently. In previous systems, many indications produced by the driver are considered to be useful fatigue-tracking features. Unlike other neural impulse signals, EOG-based systems have seen rapid growth in recent years in the drowsy driving detection systems due to their substantial potential for applicability and cost.

Theoretical foundations for a sleepy driving system based on EOGs using existing tools and software are given. Figure 16.6 depicts the structure of the propound outline. Biological signal recognition technology is one of the objective detection technologies most commonly used to assess whether a driver is tired by examining the change rule of the driver's biological signal. Physiological signs like eye activity, facial gestures, head movements, sagging body position, physiological electrical impulses, and so on can be used to evaluate the driver's physiological condition. Electrooculography (EOG) provides extensive information about eyelid movement and other eye movement characteristics as it captures physiological and electrical signals from the human body. Rapid Eye Movement (REM) [35], Slow Eye Movement (SEM) [36], and Eyelid Movement [37] are only a few of the aspects of

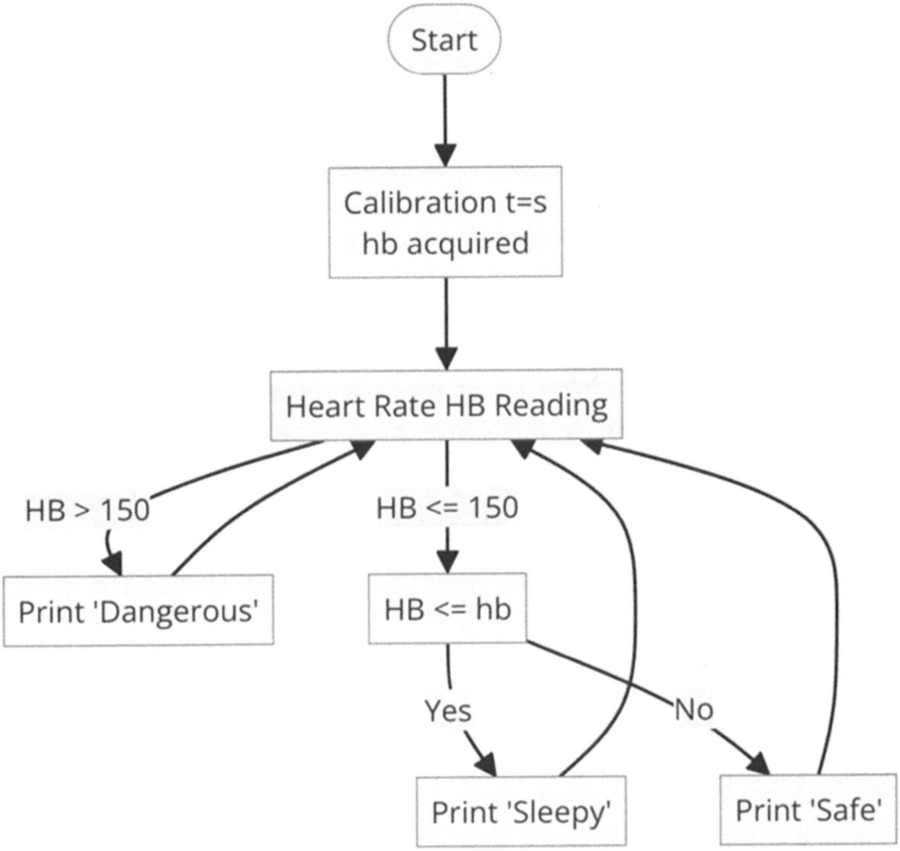

FIGURE 16.5 Flowchart of heartbeat monitoring.

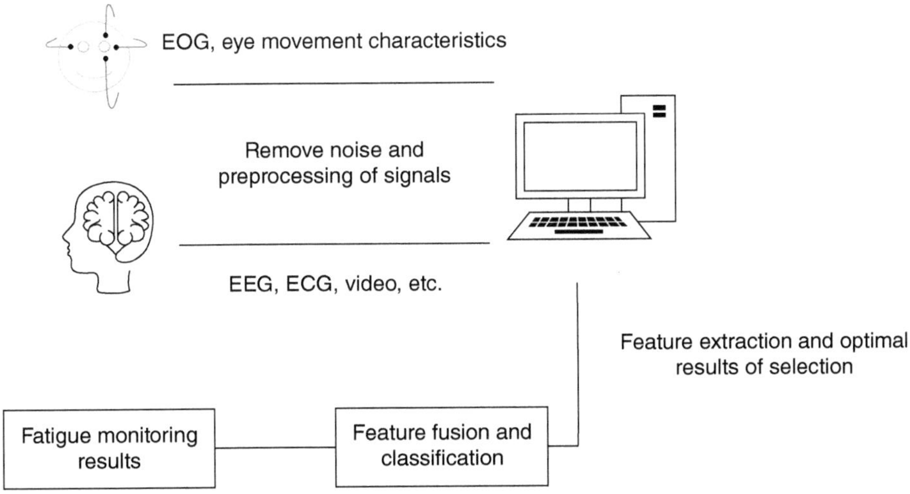

FIGURE 16.6 Structure of the feature extraction.

eye movement that may be identified with EOGs. In order to create a horizontal electrooculogram (HEO) and a vertical electrooculogram (VEO) from forehead electro-oculograms, one research used a unique electrode positioning on the forehead [38]. In order to provide new quantitative methods for evaluating mental exhaustion, EOGs are frequently coupled with other signals [39, 40]. A 5 per cent false alarm rate fatigue diagnosis approach was developed by using brain and ocular activity [41]. This method assessed drivers' mental tiredness levels using multimodal EEG, ECG, EOG, and interpretative near-infrared spectroscopy (INIRS) data.

16.3.3 Application in Detection of Drowsiness in Online Class

C++ based OpenCV is used to build the application that connects to the computer's camera in actual time. In this scenario, frames are taken from video, and cvHaar Detect Objects is utilized to recognize faces within every frame. The built-in torrents of face and eye, namely "haar cascade frontal face alt.xml" and "haar cascade eye tree eyeglasses.xml," are used to detect them. After successfully detecting a face and an eye, we must crop an eye from the detected image in order to perform eye state classification. To crop an image, OpenCV provides a method called Mat::crop(), which we may use to crop eyes. The crop function syntax is as follows: frame, Rect (r→x, r→y, r→width, r→height)) are as follows:

a) Frame: We want to crop this photograph or recording frame.
b) Rect: This determines which image section will be cropped.

Four distinct eye locations are employed for K-means classification: straight ahead, left, upward, and right. The label "looking downward" is omitted in this case since human eyes naturally seem closed when gazing downward, therefore they are identified as closed eyes. Segmentation is not used in this case since identifying eyes close together would cause the video to halt. The properties of the cropped open eye images are retrieved by computing the percent of darker versus brighter pixels in each cell of a 3 × 3 matrix of the eye. The pixel of an input dataset is expressed in three-dimensional (RGB) colour space to extract these characteristics, and the K-means grouping algorithm with K = 3 is used to split the data input image into set distinct hues [43]. This section describes the operation of the K–means algorithm in depth [44]. The K-mean method categorizes items into K groups based on qualities or traits. K is an integer that is more than or equal to one. Grouping is performed by minimizing the sum of squares of the distance between the data and the corresponding group midpoint.

The following is the definition of the K-means function [45]. Given a sample of data ($X_1, X_2, \ldots, X_n$), each of which is a d-dimensional mathematical technique, K-means grouping seeks to divide the n data into k (n) groups S = S1, S2,..., Sk to minimize within sum of squares (WCSS). In other terms, it tries to know

$$\arg_{smin} \sum_{i=1}^{k} x \in si \left\| X - \mu i \right\|^2$$

As a result, K-means clustering's purpose is to categorize the data. The user provides the number of groups wanted, and K-means rapidly identifies an acceptable place for those cluster centres, with "good" indicating that the cluster centres are in the core of natural data clusters. Given the anatomy of the eye, these three separate colours roughly depict the iris, skin around the eye, and sclera in descending order of darkness to lightness. The second cluster is ignored to remove the skin from consideration. Each filtered pixel is then repositioned within the image in its original location. After partitioning the image into 3 × 3 grids, the percentages of cluster 1 out of cluster 1 and 3 pixels are determined in each region to generate the set of features. K-means clustering is depicted in Figure 16.7. The pixels that represent the iris are highlighted in red here. The image's centre is found using filtered pixels, and then red pixels are computed.

The computation of both (centre and red pixel) identifies the direction the person is looking, and if the eye states are not accurate (i.e., eyes are closed or the person is staring beyond the glass window), the video is immediately paused. This work is spread across 80 videos. Faces may be found in practically all of the photographs. Figure 16.8 depicts the results of real face and eye detection. Faces with spectacles or small eyes are not well identified, or only one eye is detected. Eyes are also not detected adequately if there is insufficient brightness. Figure 16.9 depicts a partially true detection of a face and an eye in which the face is detected properly but only one eye is detected or no eye is detected. Face and two eyes are successfully detected in 80 per cent of the frames, that is, 56 frames. For 53 frames, eye state classification is done flawlessly. So, the overall result for eye tracking and classification of eye states

FIGURE 16.7 K-means clustering for four distinct iris directions.

FIGURE 16.8 Results of real face and eye detection.

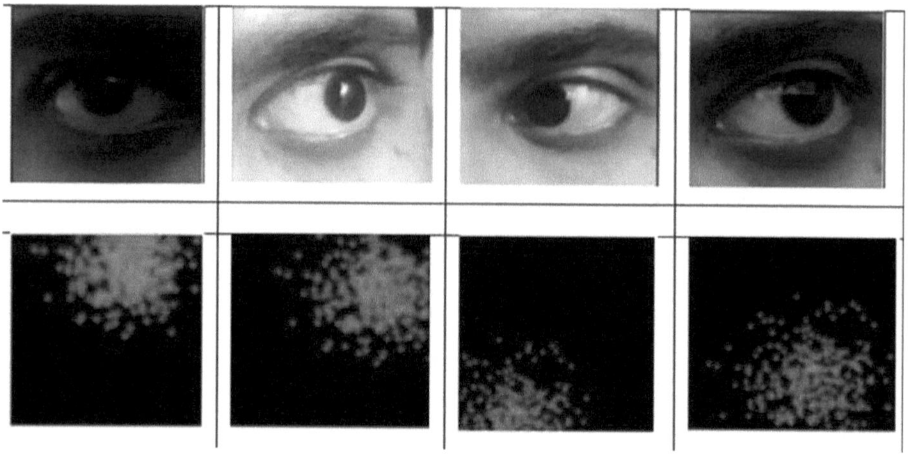

FIGURE 16.9 Partially detection of a face and an eye.

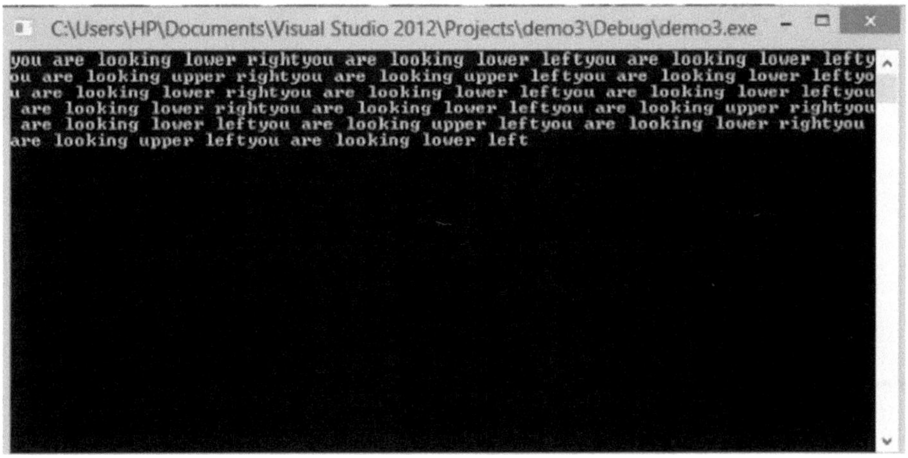

FIGURE 16.10 GUI Representation of eye state classification.

is 75.71 per cent. Accuracy can be improved if eye recognition and tracking are done more precisely, because following eye tracking, eye state categorization delivers the correct result in virtually all circumstances.

Figure 16.10 depicts the output of our GUI programme, which shows the direction the user is looking. For each frame of input video, the message linked to iris position is presented. The individual sitting in front of the webcam changes his or her iris position by staring in different directions, and the message displayed on the screen changes accordingly. If the iris position is incorrect, the video will be immediately halted.

16.4 CONCLUSION

The current system is made up of several techniques, such as image processing, EEG, vehicular, and voice metrics, among others. Any of these ways will not produce perfect outcomes. EEG-based techniques produce the best results, but they are obtrusive. Other procedures, however, have limits that prevent them from creating a faultless output. Thus, based on our study, combining two or more ways can help us lessen the limits of other approaches and, therefore, provide the best outcome. This can lead to the development of a nonintrusive and highly effective driver sleepiness detection system. Some image processing algorithms can be combined with vehicular and physiological metrics. Heart rate and breathing rates are two physiological measurements that are clear signs of tiredness. To eliminate the invasive character of physiological measurements, wireless sensors that can be efficiently integrated into seat belts, seat coverings, and so on can be used.

REFERENCES

1. NCRB Report. (2020). https://ncrb.gov.in/en/accidental-deaths-suicides-inindia?page=82
2. Bener, A., Yildirim, E., Ozkan, T., & Lajunen, T. (2017). Driver sleepiness, fatigue, careless behavior and risk of motor vehicle crash and injury: Population based case and control study. *Journal of Traffic and Transportation Engineering*, 4(5), 496–502.
3. Schwarz, C., Gaspar, J., Miller, T., & Yousefian, R. (2019). The detection of drowsiness using a driver monitoring system. *Traffic Injury Prevention*, 20(sup1), S157–S161.
4. Amodio, A., Ermidoro, M., Maggi, D., Formentin, S., & Savaresi, S. M. (2018). Automatic detection of driver impairment based on pupillary light reflex. *IEEE Transactions on Intelligent Transportation Systems*, 20(8), 3038–3048.
5. Yang, J. H., Mao, Z. H., Tijerina, L., Pilutti, T., Coughlin, J. F., & Feron, E. (2009). Detection of driver fatigue caused by sleep deprivation. *IEEE Transactions on systems, man, and cybernetics-part A: Systems and humans*, 39(4), 694–705.
6. Hu, S., & Zheng, G. (2009). Driver drowsiness detection with eyelid related parameters by support vector machine. *Expert Systems with Applications*, 36(4), 7651–7658.
7. Noori, S. M. R., & Mikaeili, M. (2016). Driving drowsiness detection using fusion of electroencephalography, electrooculography, and driving quality signals. *Journal of Medical Signals and Sensors*, 6(1), 39.
8. Dang, K., & Sharma, S. (2017, January). Review and comparison of face detection algorithms. In *2017 7th International Conference on Cloud Computing, Data Science & Engineering-Confluence* (pp. 629–633). IEEE.
9. Papadelis, C., Chen, Z., Kourtidou-Papadeli, C., Bamidis, P. D., Chouvarda, I., Bekiaris, E., & Maglaveras, N. (2007). Monitoring sleepiness with on-board electrophysiological recordings for preventing sleep-deprived traffic accidents. *Clinical Neurophysiology*, 118(9), 1906–1922.
10. Jambhekar, P. U., & Ram, S. P. (2017). EOG based study of eye movements and its applications in drowsiness detection. *International Journal of Advanced Research in Electrical, Electronics and Instrumentation Engineering*, 6(3), 1811–1818.
11. Sazon, J. L., Magano, M. S., Salting, K. I., Co, M. P., Sapang, O. D., & Roque, M. A. C. (2019). Driver's attention monitoring system with low light capability. *International Journal of Advanced Trends in Computer Science and Engineering*, 8(4), 1153.
12. Alom, M. Z., et al. (2018). The history began from AlexNet: A comprehensive survey on deep learning approaches. arXiv preprint arXiv:1803.01164
13. Russakovsky, O., & Deng, J., Su, H., Krause, J., Satheesh, S., Ma, S., Huang, Z., Karpathy, A., Khosla, A., Bernstein, M., Berg, A., & Fei-Fei, L. (2014). ImageNet Large Scale Visual Recognition Challenge. *International Journal of Computer Vision*. 115. 10.1007/s11263-015-0816-y
14. Deng, J. et al. (2009). Imagenet: A large-scale, hierarchical, image, database. In *IEEE, Conference, on Computer, Vision, and Pattern, Recognition (CVPR)* (pp. 248–255).
15. Lahoti, U., Joshi, R., Vyas, N., Deshpande, K., & Jain, S. (2020). Drowsiness detection system for online courses. *International Journal of Advanced Trends in Computer Science and Engineering*, 9(2), 1930–1934.
16. Hsieh, C. S., & Tai, C. C. (2013). An improved and portable eye-blink duration detection system to warn of driver fatigue. *Instrumentation Science & Technology*, 41(5), 429–444.
17. Bulling, A., Ward, J. A., Gellersen, H., & Tröster, G. (2010). Eye movement analysis for activity recognition using electrooculography. *IEEE Transactions on Pattern Analysis and Machine Intelligence*, 33(4), 741–753.

18. Chittaro, L., & Sioni, R. (2013, September). Exploring eye-blink startle response as a physiological measure for affective computing. In *2013 Humaine Association Conference on Affective Computing and Intelligent Interaction* (pp. 227–232). IEEE.
19. Champaty, B., Pal, K., & Dash, A. (2013, June). Functional electrical stimulation using voluntary eyeblink for foot drop correction. In *2013 Annual International Conference on Emerging Research Areas and 2013 International Conference on Microelectronics, Communications and Renewable Energy* (pp. 1–4). IEEE.
20. Chang, W. D., Lim, J. H., & Im, C. H. (2016). An unsupervised eye blink artifact detection method for real-time electroencephalogram processing. *Physiological Measurement*, 37(3), 401.
21. Ramzan, M., Khan, H. U., Awan, S. M., Ismail, A., Ilyas, M., & Mahmood, A. (2019). A survey on state-of-the-art drowsiness detection techniques. *IEEE Access*, 7, 61904–61919.
22. Gupta, S., & Mittal, S. (2013). Yawning and its physiological significance. *International Journal of Applied and Basic Medical Research*, 3(1), 11.
23. Zhao, Z., Zhou, N., Zhang, L., Yan, H., Xu, Y., & Zhang, Z. (2020). Driver fatigue detection based on convolutional neural networks using EM-CNN. *Computational Intelligence and Neuroscience*, 2020, 1–11.
24. Parra Alonso, I., Izquierdo Gonzalo, R, Alonso, J., Garcia Morcillo, A., Fernandez Llorca, D., & Sotelo, M. A. (2017). The experience of drivertive-driverless cooperative vehicle team in the 2016 gcdc. *IEEE Transactions on Intelligent Transportation Systems*, 19(4), 1322–1334.
26. Ahmad, X. Q., et al. July (2016). Driving fatigue detection with fusion of EEG and forehead EOG. In *Proceedings of the International Joint Conference on Neural Networks* (pp. 897–904), Vancouver, Canada.
27. Rohit, F., Kulathumani, V., Kavi, R., Elwarfalli, I., Kecojevic, V., & Nimbarte, A. (2017). Real-time drowsiness detection using wearable, lightweight brain sensing headbands. *IET Intelligent Transport Systems*, 11(5), 255–263.
29. Santoshi, M. G. (2020). *Automated driver drowsiness detection for non 2 wheelers* (Doctoral dissertation, Andhra University).
32. Purnamasari, P. D., & Hazmi, A. Z. (2018, September). Heart beat based drowsiness detection system for driver. In *2018 International Seminar on Application for Technology of Information and Communication* (pp. 585–590). IEEE.
33. Gromer, M., Salb, D., Walzer, T., Madrid, N. M., & Seepold, R. (2019). ECG sensor for detection of driver's drowsiness. *Procedia Computer Science*, 159, 1938–1946.
34. Tian, Y., & Cao, J. (2021). Fatigue driving detection based on electrooculography: a review. *EURASIP Journal on Image and Video Processing*, 2021(1), 1–17.
35. Schleicher, R., Galley, N., Briest, S., & Galley, L. (2008). Blinks and saccades as indicators of fatigue in sleepiness warnings: looking tired? *Ergonomics*, 51(7), 982–1010.
36. Cona, F., Pizza, F., Provini, F., & Magosso, E. (2014). An improved algorithm for the automatic detection and characterisation of slow eye movements. *Medical Engineering & Physics*, 36(7), 954–961.
37. Kim, Y. S., Baek, H. J., Kim, J. S., Lee, H. B., Choi, J. M., & Park, K. S. (2009). Helmetbased physiological signal monitoring system. *European Journal of Applied Physiology*, 105(3), 365–372.
38. Zhang, Y. F., Gao, X. Y., Zhu, J. Y., Zheng, W. L., & Lu, B. L. (2015, April). A novel approach to driving fatigue detection using forehead EOG. In *2015 7th International IEEE/EMBS Conference on Neural Engineering (NER)* (pp. 707–710). IEEE.
39. Nazari, S. S. H., Moradi, A., & Rahmani, K. (2017). A systematic review of the effect of various interventions on reducing fatigue and sleepiness while driving. *Chinese journal of traumatology*, 20(5), 249–258.

40. Wang, H., Wu, C., Li, T., He, Y., Chen, P., & Bezerianos, A. (2019). Driving fatigue classification based on fusion entropy analysis combining EOG and EEG. *IEEE Access*, 7, 61975–61986.
41. Picot, A., Charbonnier, S., & Caplier, A. (2011). Online detection of drowsiness using brain and visual information. *IEEE Transactions on systems, man, and cybernetics-part A: systems and humans*, 42(3), 764–775.
43. Joshi, K. V., Kangda, A., & Patel, S. (2016). Real time system for student fatigue detection during online learning. *International Journal of Hybrid Information Technology*, 9(3), 341–346.
44. Bhatia, M. P. S., & Khurana, D. (2013). Experimental study of Data clustering using k-Means and modified algorithms. *International Journal of Data Mining & Knowledge Management Process*, 3(3), 17.
45. Panjeta, A., & Kumar, A. (2014). Comparative performance to changeability of measuring software components. *International Journal of Advanced Research in Computer Science and Software Engineering*, 4(8).
46. Waldeck, M. R., Lambert, M. I. Heart rate during sleep: implications for monitoring training status. *Journal of Science and Medicine* 2003. December 1, 2(4):133–138. PMID: 24688273; PMCID: PMC3963245.

Index

Pages in *italics* refer to figures and pages in **bold** refer to tables.

H

I

J

K

L

M

N

O

P

R

S